W9-CLD-987

Toward Global Equilibrium: Collected Papers

Toward Global Equilibrium: Collected Papers

Edited by
Dennis L. Meadows and
Donella H. Meadows

WRIGHT-ALLEN PRESS, INC.
238 Main Street
Cambridge, Massachusetts   02142

Preface

This book presents a series of papers written by members of the System Dynamics Group in the Alfred P. Sloan School of Management at the Massachusetts Institute of Technology to explore the nature and implications of physical growth on a finite planet. Using systems analysis tools developed under Professor Jay W. Forrester at M.I.T., it has been our objective to identify the various feasible modes of long-term social evolution and to determine how society might best move from its current dependence on growth toward a stable accommodation within the finite resources and environment of the earth. Obviously, no one group and no single methodology can fully satisfy that objective. Our work is reported here not as a final answer but as a contribution to better understanding and a foundation upon which the work of others may be based.

Over the past two years our research at M.I.T. has been sponsored by The Club of Rome and the Volkswagen Foundation. The Club of Rome is comprised of about seventy individuals from twenty-six countries who are united by a deep concern for the future of the world. Their objective is to sponsor research that will address global problems from an interdisciplinary, transnational, and long-term perspective. The Club of Rome was attracted to system dynamics and the research team developed under Professor Jay W. Forrester. Using system dynamics, Professor Forrester had constructed a model of global population growth and economic development.[1] Because the model provided a tentative explanation for many relevant problems, the Club decided in July 1970 to sponsor a project at M.I.T. to test and extend the model to provide more detailed analyses of the technological and economic forces that are leading to social stresses. I assembled a group of scientists and students in the System Dynamics Laboratory for that purpose and directed them in an eighteen-month study. The results of our work are summarized in three volumes.

---

[1] Professor Forrester's preliminary model, World2, is described in Jay W. Forrester, *World Dynamics* (Cambridge, Mass.: Wright-Allen Press, 1971).

The first volume, *The Limits to Growth*,[2] is a general, nontechnical report of our research, written to apprise policy makers and the public of the project's general objectives and conclusions. That report was released through Universe Books and Potomac Associates in early March 1972.

This book is the second volume of the project report. It incorporates thirteen of the papers written by the research team to introduce or enlarge upon various detailed aspects of the world modeling project.

In Part One of this volume, two introductory papers describe the general approach of system dynamics and the objectives of The Club of Rome's program. Seven detailed reports on the project's technical substudies are presented in Part Two. Each of these reports describes a complete simulation model constructed to determine the dynamic characteristics and implications of important relationships within one or more of the five global model subsectors: population, pollution, agriculture, nonrenewable resources, and capital equipment. Part Three contains four papers that were written to examine the economic, political, and ethical implications of the project findings.

Each paper in this volume deals with causes or consequences of growth in the globe's population or material output. Each of the thirteen papers was originally prepared and disseminated as an individual statement. They are published here to provide in one place a collection of the more important, shorter documents from the project. The papers retain essentially the form in which they first appeared. Only a few sections in several of the interpretive papers have been removed to decrease redundancy. Each paper is accompanied by a brief summary of the circumstances that led to its preparation and by a description of its contribution to the total program of research.

The third volume to be released in conjunction with the M.I.T. effort is a technical presentation of World3, the refined global simulation model constructed by the project team. That book, *The Dynamics of Growth in a Finite World,* will describe the revised global model, equation by equation, present and discuss the data underlying each assumption, indicate the relative strengths and weaknesses of various sectors in the model, and point to important future extensions of the work.

With the release of the third volume, the research at M.I.T. will no longer be supported by The Club of Rome. However, members of the M.I.T. system dynamics team will continue to study issues raised by the initial research and to cooperate with university groups interested in the transition to global equilibrium. Groups in at least five countries have already begun to carry the goals and methods of our work into studies of long-term problems related to population and material growth in their own countries.

While the proliferation of this research is encouraging, the effort directed toward issues posed by a transition to global equilibrium must clearly be enlarged

[2] Donella H. Meadows, Dennis L. Meadows, Jørgen Randers, and William W. Behrens III, *The Limits to Growth* (New York: Universe Books, for Potomac Associates, 1972).

much beyond its current scope if any significant change is to be brought about in short-term policy making.

None of the papers included in this volume maps the path toward material and population equilibrium in detail. However, we believe that each sheds a little light on the general direction that must be followed, the questions that must be raised and answered, and the long-term, holistic philosophy that must be the basis of the many decisions along the way. We earnestly hope that the issues raised by our own preliminary efforts will stimulate the formation of other groups with a long time perspective, a global horizon, and the resources to begin interdisciplinary inquiry into the prospect and promise of global equilibrium.

Dennis L. Meadows
Donella H. Meadows

Dartmouth College
Hanover, New Hampshire
November 1972

Contents

Part One
Introductory Papers

An important part of the work at the M.I.T. System Dynamics Laboratory has been the dissemination of information on the methodology and the research results of the various projects undertaken in the System Dynamics Laboratory. The following two papers were written to apprise those outside M.I.T. of the progress of work on the Club of Rome project. They describe the history of the field, the components of the computer-based approach, and indicate the nature of the research undertaken.

1
Counterintuitive Behavior of Social Systems

Jay W. Forrester

On October 7, 1970, Professor Forrester was asked to testify before the Subcommittee on Urban Growth of the Committee on Banking and Currency, U.S. House of Representatives. He prepared for his presentation the following description of the need for quantitative models of social systems and a brief summary of the conclusions that had emerged from the work in his Urban Dynamics *and* World Dynamics *books.* *

This paper provides a particularly cogent summary of the rationale for the application of formal models to the study of social systems. The use of such models to analyze alternative policies is compared with the more customary use of mental models. The details of the world model described here have been changed as a result of a year's further research. However, the general conclusions about the behavioral tendencies of the world system have not been significantly altered by the subsequent studies reported in this volume and in The Limits to Growth.*

This chapter is drawn from the author's book World Dynamics *and first appeared in the* Technology Review, *vol. 73, no. 3 (January 1971).*

---

*Cited in "Related Books" at the end of this volume.

1
Counterintuitive Behavior
of Social Systems

4

This paper addresses several issues of broad concern in the United States: population trends; the quality of urban life; national policy for urban growth; and the unexpected, ineffective, or detrimental results often generated by government programs in these areas.

The nation exhibits a growing sense of futility as it repeatedly attacks deficiencies in our social system while the symptoms continue to worsen. Legislation is debated and passed with great promise and hope. But many programs prove to be ineffective. Results often seem unrelated to those expected when the programs were planned. At times programs cause exactly the reverse of desired results.

It is now possible to explain how such contrary results can happen. There are fundamental reasons why people misjudge the behavior of social systems. Orderly processes are at work in the creation of human judgment and intuition, which frequently lead people to wrong decisions when faced with complex and highly interacting systems. Until we come to a much better understanding of social systems, we should expect that attempts to develop corrective programs will continue to disappoint us.

The purpose of this paper is to leave with its readers a sense of caution about continuing to depend on the same past approaches that have led to our present feeling of frustration and to suggest an approach that can eventually lead to a better understanding of our social systems and thereby to more effective policies for guiding the future.

A New Approach to Social Systems

It is my basic theme that the human mind is not adapted to interpreting how social systems behave. Our social systems belong to the class called multiple-loop nonlinear feedback systems. In the long history of human evolution it has not been necessary for man to understand these systems until very recent historical times. Evolutionary processes have not given us the mental skill needed to interpret properly the dynamic behavior of the systems of which we have now become a part.

In addition, the social sciences have fallen into some mistaken "scientific" practices that compound man's natural shortcomings. Computers are often used for what the computer does poorly and the human mind does well. At the same time the human mind is used for what the human mind does poorly and the computer does well. Even worse, impossible tasks are attempted while achievable and important goals are ignored.

Until recently, there has been no way to estimate the behavior of social systems except by contemplation, discussion, argument, and guesswork. To point a way out of our present dilemma about social systems, I shall sketch an approach that combines the strength of the human mind and the strength of today's computers. The approach is an outgrowth of developments over the last forty years, in which much of the research has been at the Massachusetts Institute of Technology. The concepts of feedback system behavior apply sweepingly from physical systems through social systems. The ideas were first developed and applied to engineering systems. They have now reached practical usefulness in major aspects of our social systems.

I am speaking of what was earlier called "industrial dynamics." The name was a misnomer because the methods apply to complex systems regardless of the field in which they are located. A more appropriate name is system dynamics. In our own work, applications have been made to corporate policy, to the dynamics of diabetes as a medical system, to the growth and stagnation of an urban area, and most recently to world dynamics representing the interactions of population, pollution, industrialization, natural resources, and food. System dynamics, as an extension of the earlier design of physical systems, has been under development at M.I.T. since 1956. The approach is easy to understand but difficult to practice. Few people have the required high level of skill, but preliminary work is developing all over the world. Some European countries and especially Japan have begun centers of education and research.

Computer Models of Social Systems

People would never attempt to send a space ship to the moon without first testing the equipment by constructing prototype models and by computer simulation of the anticipated space trajectories. No company would put a new kind of household appliance or electronic computer into production without first making laboratory tests. Such models and laboratory tests do not guarantee against failure, but they do identify many weakness that can then be corrected before they cause full-scale disasters.

Our social systems are far more complex and harder to understand than our technological systems. Why, then, do we not use the same approach of making models of social systems and conducting laboratory experiments on those models before we try new laws and government programs in real life? The stated answer is often that our knowledge of social systems is insufficient for constructing useful models. But what justification can there be for the apparent assumption that we do not know enough to construct models but believe we do know enough to design new social systems directly by passing laws and starting new social programs? I am suggesting that we now do know enough to make useful models of social systems. Conversely, we do not know enough to design the most effective social systems directly without first going through a model-building experimental phase. But I am confident, and substantial supporting evidence is beginning to accumulate, that the proper use of models of social systems can lead to far better systems, laws, and programs.

It is now possible to construct realistic models of social systems in the laboratory. Such models are simplifications of the actual social system but can be far more comprehensive than the mental models that we otherwise use as the basis for debating governmental action.

Before going further, I should emphasize that there is nothing new in the use of models to represent social systems. Each of us uses models constantly. Every person in his private life and in his business life instinctively uses models for decision making. The mental image of the world around us that we carry in our heads is a model. One does not have a city or a government or a country in his head. He has only selected concepts and relationships, which he uses to represent the real system. A mental image is a model. All our decisions are taken on the basis of models. All our laws are passed on the basis of models. All executive actions are taken on the basis of models. The question is not to use or ignore models. The question is only a choice among alternative models.

The mental model is fuzzy. It is incomplete. It is imprecisely stated. Furthermore, within one individual a mental model changes with time and even during the flow of a single conversation. The human mind assembles a few relationships to fit the context of a discussion. As the subject shifts, so does the model. When only a single topic is being discussed, each participant in a conversation employs a different mental model to interpret the subject. Fundamental assumptions differ but are never brought into the open. Goals are different and are left unstated. It is little wonder that compromise takes so long. And it is not surprising that consensus leads to laws and programs that fail in their objectives or produce new difficulties greater than those that have been relieved.

For these reasons we stress the importance of being explicit about assumptions and interrelating them in a computer model. Any concept or assumption that can be clearly described in words can be incorporated in a computer model. When expressed in a form appropriate for computer analysis, the ideas become clear. Assumptions are exposed so that they may be understood and debated.

But the most important difference between the properly conceived computer model and the mental model is in the ability to determine the dynamic consequences when the assumptions within the model interact with one another. The human mind is not adapted to sensing correctly the consequences of a mental model. The mental model may be correct in structure and assumptions but, even so, the human mind—either individually or as a group consensus—is most apt to draw the wrong conclusions. There is no doubt about the digital computer routinely and accurately tracing through the sequences of actions that result from following the statements of behavior for individual points in the model system. This inability of the human mind to use its own mental models is clearly shown when a computer model is constructed to reproduce the assumptions held by a single person. In other words, the model is refined until it is fully agreeable in all its assumptions to the perceptions and ideas of a particular person. Then it usually happens that the system that has been described does not act the way the person anticipated. Usually there is an internal contradiction in mental models between the assumed structure and the assumed future consequences. Ordinarily the assumptions about structure and internal motivations are more nearly correct than are the assumptions about the implied behavior.

The system dynamics computer models that I am discussing are strikingly similar to mental models. They are derived from the same sources. They may be discussed in the same terms. But computer models differ from mental models in important ways. The computer models are stated explicitly. The "mathematical" notation used for describing the model is unambiguous. It is a language that is clearer, simpler, and more precise than such spoken languages as English or French. Its advantage is in the clarity of meaning and the simplicity of the language syntax. The language of a computer model can be understood by almost anyone, regardless of educational background. Furthermore, any concept and relationship that can be clearly stated in ordinary language can be translated into computer model language.

There are many approaches to computer models. Some are naïve. Some are conceptually and structurally inconsistent with the nature of actual systems. Some are based on methodologies for obtaining input data that commit the models to omitting major concepts and relationships in the psychological and human reaction areas that we all know to be crucial. With so much activity in computer models and with the same terminology having different meanings in the different approaches, the situation must be confusing to the casual observer. The key to success is not in having a computer; the important thing is how the computer is used. With respect to models, the key is not to computerize a model but to have a model structure and relationships that properly represent the system that is being considered.

I am speaking here of a kind of computer model that is very different from the models that are now most common in the social sciences. Such a computer model is not derived statistically from time-series data. Instead, the kind of computer model I am discussing is a statement of system structure. It contains the assumptions being made about the system. The model is only as good as the expertise that lies behind its formulation. Great and correct theories in physics or in economics are few and far between. A great computer model is distinguished from a poor one by the degree to which it captures more of the essence of the social system that it presumes to represent. Many mathematical models are limited because they are formulated by techniques and according to a conceptual structure that will not accept the multiple-feedback-loop and nonlinear nature of real systems. Other models are defective because of lack of knowledge or deficiencies of perception on the part of the persons who have formulated them.

But a recently developed kind of computer modeling is now beginning to show the characteristics of behavior of actual systems. These models explain why we are having the present difficulties with our actual social systems, and furthermore explain why so many efforts to improve social systems have failed. In spite of their shortcomings, models can now be constructed that are far superior to the intuitive models in our heads on which we are now basing national social programs.

The system dynamics approach to social systems differs in two important ways from common practice in the social sciences and government. There seems to be a common attitude that the major difficulty is the shortage of information and data. Once data are collected, people feel confident in interpreting the implications. I differ with both these attitudes. The problem is not the shortage of data but rather our inability to perceive the consequences of the information we already possess. The system dynamics approach starts with the concepts and information on which people are already acting. These are usually sufficient. The available perceptions are then assembled in a computer model that can show the consequences of the well-known and properly perceived parts of the system. Generally, the consequences are unexpected.

Counterintuitive Nature of Social Systems

Our first insights into complex social systems came from our corporate work. Time after time we have gone into a corporation that is having severe and well-known difficulties. The difficulties can be major and obvious, such as a falling market share, low profitability, or instability of employment. Such difficulties are known throughout the company and by anyone outside who reads the management press. One can enter such a company and discuss with people in key decision points what they are doing to solve the problem. Generally speaking we find that people perceive correctly their immediate environment. They know what they are trying to accomplish. They know the crises that will force certain actions. They are sensitive to the power structure of the organization, to traditions, and to their own personal goals and welfare. In general, when circumstances are conducive to frank disclosure, people can state what they are doing and can give rational reasons for their actions. In a troubled company, people are usually trying in good conscience and to the best of their abilities to solve the major difficulties. Policies are being followed at various points in the organization on the presumption that they will alleviate the difficulties. One can combine these policies into a computer model to show the consequences of how the policies interact with one another. In many instances it then emerges that the known policies describe a system that actually causes the troubles. In other words, the known and intended practices of the organization are fully sufficient to create the difficulty, regardless of what happens outside the company or in the marketplace. In fact, a downward spiral develops in which the presumed solution makes the difficulty worse and thereby causes redoubling of the presumed solution.

The same downward spiral frequently develops in government. Judgment and debate lead to a program that appears to be sound. Commitment increases to the apparent solution. If the presumed solution actually makes matters worse, the process by which this happens is not evident. So, when the troubles increase, the efforts that are actually worsening the problem are intensified.

Dynamics of Urban Systems

Our first major excursion outside of corporate policy began in February, 1968, when John F. Collins, former mayor of Boston, became Professor of Urban Affairs at M.I.T. He and I discussed my work in industrial dynamics[1] and his experience with urban difficulties. A close collaboration led to applying to the dynamics of the city the same methods that had been created for understanding

---

[1] Jay W. Forrester, *Industrial Dynamics* (Cambridge, Mass.: The M.I.T. Press, 1961).

the social and policy structure of the corporation. A model structure was developed to represent the fundamental urban processes. The proposed structure shows how industry, housing, and people interact with each other as a city grows and decays. The results are described in my book *Urban Dynamics.*[2]

I had not previously been involved with urban behavior or urban policies. But the emerging story was strikingly similar to what we had seen in the corporation. Actions taken to alleviate the difficulties of a city can actually make matters worse. We examined four common programs for improving the depressed nature of the central city. One was making jobs available, for example, by busing the unemployed to the suburbs or through governmental jobs as an employer of last resort. The second was a training program to increase the skills of the lowest income group. The third was financial aid to the depressed city as by federal subsidy. The fourth was the construction of low-cost housing. All are shown to lie between neutral and detrimental, almost irrespective of the criteria used for judgment. They range from ineffective to harmful judged either by their effect on the economic health of the city or by their long-range effect on the low-income population of the city.

The results both confirm and explain much of what has been happening over the last several decades in our cities.

In fact, it emerges that the fundamental cause of depressed areas in the cities comes from *excess* housing in the low-income category rather than from the commonly presumed housing shortage. The legal and tax structures have combined to give incentives for keeping old buildings in place. As industrial buildings age, the employment opportunities decline. As residential buildings age, they are used by lower-income groups who are forced to use them at a higher population density. Therefore, jobs decline and population rises while buildings age. Housing, at the higher population densities, accommodates more low-income urban population than can find jobs. A social trap is created where excess low-cost housing beckons low-income people inward because of the available housing. They continue coming to the city until their numbers so far exceed the available income opportunities that the standard of living declines far enough to stop further inflow. Income to the area is then too low to maintain all the housing. Excess housing falls into disrepair and is abandoned. One can simultaneously have extreme crowding in those buildings that are occupied, while other buildings become excess and are abandoned because the economy of the area cannot support all the residential structures. But the excess residential buildings threaten the area in two ways—they occupy the land so that it cannot be used for job-creating buildings, and they stand ready to accept a rise in population if the area should start to improve economically.

Any change that would otherwise raise the standard of living only takes off the economic pressure momentarily and causes the population to rise enough so that the standard of living again falls to the barely tolerable level. A self-regulating

---

[2] Jay W. Forrester, *Urban Dynamics* (Cambridge, Mass.: The M.I.T. Press, 1969).

system is thereby at work, which drives the condition of the depressed area down far enough to stop the increase in people.

At any time, a near-equilibrium exists affecting population mobility between the different areas of the country. To the extent that there is disequilibrium, it means that some area is slightly more attractive than others and population begins to move in the direction of the more attractive area. This movement continues until the rising population drives the more attractive area down in attractiveness so that the area is again in equilibrium with its surroundings. Other things being equal, an increase in the population of a city crowds housing, overloads job opportunities, causes congestion, increases pollution, encourages crime, and reduces almost every component of the quality of life.

This powerful dynamic force to reestablish an equilibrium in total attractiveness means that any social program must take into account the eventual shifts that will occur in the many components of *attractiveness*. As used here, attractiveness is the composite effect of all factors that cause population movement toward or away from an area. Most areas in a country have nearly equal attractiveness most of the time, with only sufficient disequilibrium in attractiveness to account for the shifts in population. But areas can have the same composite attractiveness with different mixes in the components of attractiveness. In one area component A could be high and B low, while the reverse could be true in another area that nevertheless had the same total composite attractiveness. If a program makes some aspect of an area more attractive than its neighbor's, and thereby makes total attractiveness higher momentarily, the population of that area rises until other components of attractiveness are driven down far enough to again establish an equilibrium. This means that efforts to improve the condition of our cities will result primarily in increasing the population of the cities and causing the population of the country to concentrate in the cities. The overall condition of urban life for any particular economic class of population cannot be appreciably better or worse than that of the remainder of the country to and from which people may come. Programs aimed at improving the city can succeed only if they result in eventually raising the average quality of life for the country as a whole.

On Raising the Quality of Life

But there is substantial doubt that our urban programs have been contributing to the national quality of life. By concentrating total population, and especially low-income population, in urban locations, undermining the strength and cohesiveness of the community, and making government and bureaucracy so big that the individual feels powerless to influence the system within which he is increasingly constrained, the quality of life is being reduced. In fact, if they have any effect, our efforts to improve our urban areas will in the long run tend to delay the concern about rising total population and thereby contribute directly to the eventual overcrowding of the country and the world.

Any proposed program must deal with both the quality of life and the factors affecting population. Raising the quality of life means releasing stress and pressures, reducing crowding, reducing pollution, alleviating hunger, and treating ill health. But these pressures are exactly the sources of concern and action that will lead to controlling total population to keep it within the bounds of the fixed world within which we live. If the pressures are relaxed, so is the concern about how we impinge on the environment. Population will then rise further until the pressures reappear with an intensity that can no longer be relieved. To try to raise the quality of life without intentionally creating compensating pressures to prevent a rise in population density will be self-defeating.

Consider the meaning of these interacting attractiveness components as they affect a depressed ghetto area of a city. First we must be clear about the way population density is in fact now being controlled. There is some set of forces determining that the density is not far higher or lower than it is. But there are many possible combinations of forces that an urban area can exert. The particular combination will determine the population mix of the area and the economic health of the city. I suggest that the depressed areas of most American cities are created by a combination of forces in which there is a job shortage and a housing excess. The availability of housing draws the lowest-income group until they so far exceed the opportunities of the area that the low standard of living, the frustration, and the crime rate counterbalance the housing availability. Until the pool of excess housing is reduced, little can be done to improve the economic condition of the city. A low-cost housing program alone moves exactly in the wrong direction. It draws more low-income people. It makes the area differentially more attractive to the poor who need jobs and less attractive to those who create jobs. In the new population equilibrium that develops, some characteristic of the social system must compensate for the additional attractiveness created by the low-cost housing. The counterbalance is a further decline of the economic condition for the area. But as the area becomes more destitute, pressures rise for more low-cost housing. The consequence is a downward spiral that draws in the low-income population, depresses their condition, prevents escape, and reduces hope. All of this is done with the best of intentions.

My book *Urban Dynamics*[3] suggests a reversal of present practice in order to simultaneously reduce the aging housing in our cities and allocate land to income-earning opportunities. The land shifted to industry permits the "balance of trade" of the area to be corrected by allowing labor to create and export a product to generate an income stream with which to buy the necessities of modern life from the outside. But the concurrent reduction of excess housing is absolutely essential. It supplies the land for new jobs. Equally important, the resulting housing shortage creates the population-stabilizing pressure that allows economic revival to proceed without being inundated by rising population. This can all be done without driving the present low-income residents out of the area. It can create *upward economic mobility* to convert the low-income population to a self-supporting basis.

[3] Ibid.

The first reaction of many people to these ideas is to believe that they will never be accepted by elected officials or by residents of depressed urban areas. But some of our strongest support and encouragement is coming from those very groups who are closest to the problems, who see the symptoms firsthand, who have lived through the failures of the past, and who must live with the present conditions until enduring solutions are found.

Over the past several decades the country has slipped into a set of attitudes about our cities that are leading to actions that have become an integral part of the system that is generating greater troubles. If we were malicious and wanted to create urban slums, trap low-income people in ghetto areas, and increase the number of people on welfare, we could do little better than follow the present policies. The trend toward stressing income and sales taxes and away from the real estate tax encourages old buildings to remain in place and block self-renewal. The concessions in the income tax laws to encourage low-income housing will in the long run actually increase the total low-income population of the country. Highway expenditures and government loans for suburban housing have made it easier for higher-income groups to abandon urban areas than to revive them. The pressures to expand the areas incorporated by urban government, in an effort to expand the revenue base, have been more than offset by lowered administrative efficiency, more citizen frustration, and the accelerated decline that is triggered in the annexed areas. The belief that more money will solve urban problems has taken attention away from correcting the underlying causes and has instead allowed the problems to grow to the limit of the available money, whatever that amount might be.[4]

Characteristics of Social Systems
I turn now to some characteristics of social systems that mislead people. These have been identified in our work with corporate and urban systems and in more recent work that I shall describe, which concerns the worldwide pressures that are now enveloping our planet.

First, social systems are inherently insensitive to most policy changes that people select in an effort to alter the behavior of the system. In fact, a social system tends to draw our attention to the very points at which an attempt to intervene will fail. Our experience, which has been developed from contact with simple systems, leads us to look near the symptoms of trouble for a cause. When we look, we discover that the social system presents us with an apparent cause that is plausible according to what we have learned from simple systems. But this apparent cause is usually a coincident occurrence that, like the trouble symptom itself, is being produced by the feedback-loop dynamics of a larger system. For example, as already discussed, we see human suffering in the cities; we observe that it is accompanied (some think caused) by inadequate housing. We increase

[4] Our continuing examination of urban behavior was made possible through a grant to M.I.T. from the Independence Foundation of Philadelphia.

the housing, and the population rises to compensate for the effort. More people are drawn into and trapped in the depressed social system. As another example, the symptoms of excess population are beginning to overshadow the country. These symptoms appear as urban crowding and social pressure. Rather than face the population problem squarely, we try to relieve the immediate pressure by planning industry in rural areas and by discussing new towns. If additional urban area is provided it will temporarily reduce the pressures and defer the need to face the underlying population question. The consequence, as it will be seen 25 years hence, will have been to contribute to increasing the population so much that even today's quality of life will be impossible.

A second characteristic of social systems is that all of them seem to have a few sensitive influence points through which the behavior of the system can be changed. These influence points are not in the locations most people expect. Furthermore, if one identifies in a model of a social system a sensitive point where influence can be exerted, the chances are high that a person guided by intuition and judgment will alter the system in the wrong direction. For example, in the urban system, housing is a sensitive control point. However, if one wishes to revive the economy of a city and make it a better place for low-income as well as other people, it appears that the amount of low-income housing must be reduced rather than increased. Another example is the worldwide problem of rising population and the disparity between the standards of living in the developed and the underdeveloped countries, an issue in the world system that will be discussed in the following paragraphs. But it is beginning to appear that a sensitive control point is the rate of generation of capital investment.

And how should one change the rate of capital accumulation? The common answer has been to increase industrialization, but recent examination suggests that hope lies only in reducing the rate of industrialization. This may actually help raise the quality of life and contribute to stabilizing population.

As a third characteristic of social systems, there is usually a fundamental conflict between the short-term and long-term consequences of a policy change. A policy that produces improvement in the short run, within five to ten years, is usually one that degrades the system in the long run, beyond ten years. Likewise, policies and programs that produce long-run improvement may initially depress the behavior of the system. This is especially treacherous. The short run is more visible and more compelling. It speaks loudly for immediate attention. But a series of actions all aimed at short-run improvement can eventually burden a system with long-run depressants so severe that even heroic short-run measures no longer suffice. Many of the problems we face today are the eventual result of short-run measures taken as long as two or three decades ago.

A Global Perspective

I have mentioned social organizations at the corporate level and then touched on work done on the dynamics of the city. More recently we began to examine issues of even broader scope.

In July 1970 we held a two-week international conference on world dynamics to examine the same problems of population, resources, industrialization, pollution, and worldwide disparities in standard of living on which many groups now focus. The meeting included the general theory and behavior of complex systems and talks on the behavior of specific social systems, ranging from corporations through commodity markets to biological systems, drug addiction in the community, and growth and decline of a city. Especially prepared for this conference was a dynamic model of the interactions between world population, industrialization, depletion of natural resources, agriculture, and pollution. A detailed discussion of this world system appear in my book *World Dynamics*.[5]

The simple model of world interactions as presented here shows several alternative futures depending on whether population growth is eventually suppressed by a shortage of natural resources, by pollution, by crowding and consequent social strife, or by insufficient food. Malthus dealt only with the latter, but it is possible for civilization to encounter other controlling pressures before a food shortage occurs.

It is certain that resource shortage, pollution, crowding, food failure, or some other equally powerful force will limit population and industrialization if persuasion and psychological factors do not. Exponential growth cannot continue forever. Our greatest immediate challenge is how we guide the transition from growth to equilibrium. There are many possible mechanisms of growth suppression. That some one or combination will occur is inevitable. Unless we come to understand and to choose, the natural system by its internal processes will choose for us. The natural mechanisms for terminating exponential growth appear to be the least desirable. Unless we understand and begin to act soon, we may be overwhelmed by a social and economic system we have created but can't control.

Figure 1-1 shows the system structure that has been assumed. It interrelates the mutual effects of population, capital investment, natural resources, pollution, and the fraction of capital devoted to agriculture. These five system "levels" are shown in the rectangles. Each level is caused to change by the rates of flow in and out, such as the birth rate and death rate that increase and decrease population. As shown by the dotted lines, the five system levels, through intermediate concepts shown at the circles, control the rates of flow. As an example, the death rate at Symbol 10 depends on population P and the "normal" lifetime as stated by death rate normal DRN. But the death rate also depends on conditions in other parts of the system. From Circle 12 comes the influence of pollution, which here assumes that the death rate will double if pollution becomes 20 times as severe as in 1970; and, progressively, that the death rate will increase by a factor of 10 if pollution becomes 60 times as much as in 1970. Likewise, from Circle 13 the effect of food per capita is to increase the death rate as food becomes less available. The detailed definition of the model states how each rate of flow is

[5] Jay W. Forrester, *World Dynamics* (Cambridge, Mass.: Wright-Allen Press, 1971).

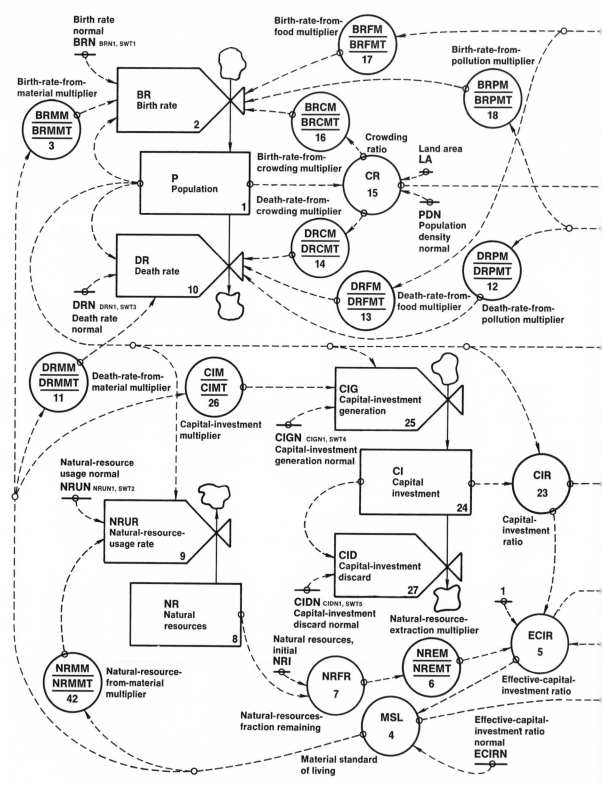

Figure 1-1 Upon this world model are based the author's analyses of the effects of changing population and economic growth factors in the next 50 years. It shows the inter-

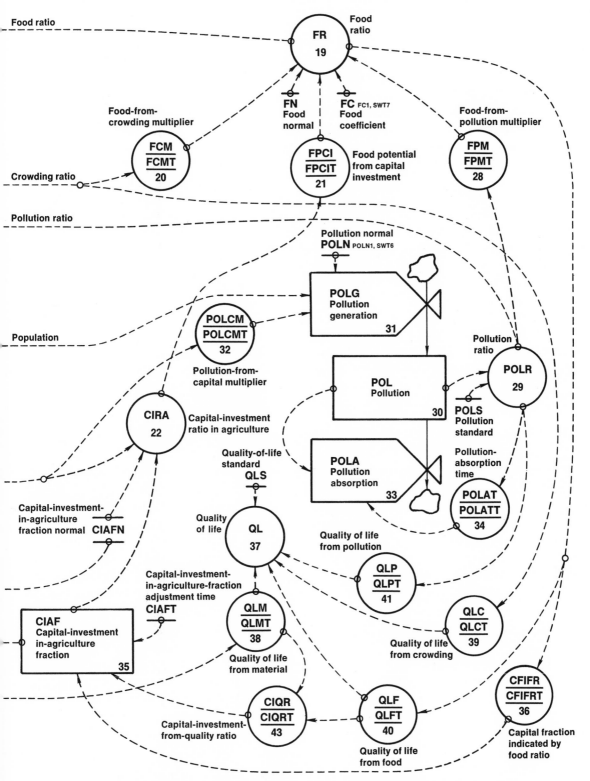

relation of population, capital investment, natural resources, pollution, and the fraction of capital devoted to agriculture on which is based the following discussion.

assumed to depend on the levels of population, natural resources, capital investment, capital devoted to food, and pollution.

Individually, the assumptions in the model are plausible, create little disagreement, and reflect common discussions and assertions about the individual
responses within the world system. But each is explicit and can be subjected to
scrutiny. From one viewpoint, the system of Figure 1-1 is very simplified. It
focuses on a few major factors and omits most of the substructure of world social
and economic activity. But from another viewpoint, Figure 1-1 is comprehensive
and complex. The system is far more complete and the theory described by the
accompanying computer model is much more explicit than the mental models
that are now being used as a basis for world and governmental planning. It
incorporates dozens of nonlinear relationships. The world system shown here
exhibits provocative and even frightening possibilities.

Transition from Growth to Equilibrium

With the model specified, a computer can be used to show how the system
would behave. Given a set of beginning conditions, the computer can calculate
and plot the results that unfold through time.

The world today seems to be entering a condition in which pressures are rising
simultaneously from every one of the influences that can suppress growth—
depleted resources, pollution, crowding, and insufficient food. It is still unclear
which will dominate if mankind continues along the present path. Figure 1-2
shows the mode of behavior of this world system, given the assumption that
population reaches a peak and then declines because industrialization is suppressed by falling natural resources. The model system starts with estimates of
conditions in 1900. Adjustments have been made so that the generated paths pass
through the conditions of 1970.

In Figure 1-2 the quality of life peaks in the 1950s and by 2020 has fallen far
enough to halt further rise in population. Declining resources and the consequent
fall in capital investment then exert further pressure to gradually reduce world
population.

But we may not be fortunate enough to run gradually out of natural resources. Science and technology may very well find ways to use the more plentiful metals and atomic energy so that resource depletion does not intervene. If so,
the way then remains open for some other pressure to arise within the system.
Figure 1-3 shows what happens within this system if the resource shortage is
foreseen and avoided. Here the only change from Figure 1-2 is in the usage rate of
natural resources after the year 1970. In Figure 1-3, resources are used after 1970
at a rate 75 percent less than assumed in Figure 1-2. In other words, the standard
of living is sustained with a lower drain on the expendable and irreplaceable
resources. But the picture is even less attractive. By not running out of resources,
population and capital investment are allowed to rise until a pollution crisis is
created. Pollution then acts directly to reduce the birth rate, increase the death
rate, and depress food production. Population, which according to this simple

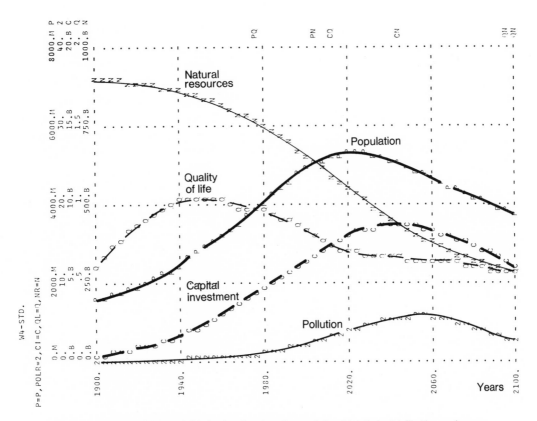

Figure 1-2   Basic world model behavior showing the mode in which industrialization and popu-
lation are suppressed by falling natural resources
Figures 1-2 through 1-8 courtesy of Technology Review *edited at the Massachusetts
Institute of Technology.*

model peaks at the year 2030, has fallen to one-sixth of the peak population
within an interval of 20 years—a worldwide catastrophe of a magnitude never
before experienced. Should it occur, one can speculate on which sectors of the
world population will suffer most. It is quite possible that the more industrialized
countries (which are the ones that have caused the disaster) would be the least
able to survive such a disruption of the environment and food supply. They might
be the ones to take the brunt of the collapse. The steep rise in the quality of life,
after the population decline, occurs because the simplified model assumes that the
remaining population has access to and full use of the best agricultural lands and
the still available capital plant. Because population, land, capital, and educational
know-how probably would not coincide, such a rise in the quality of life is not
probable.

Figure 1-3 shows how a technological success (reducing our dependence on
natural resources) can merely save us from one fate only to fall victim to something worse (a pollution catastrophe). There is now developing throughout the
world a strong undercurrent of doubt about technology as the savior of mankind.

There is a basis for such doubt. Of course, the source of the trouble is not technology as such but is instead the management of the entire technological-human-political-economic-natural complex.

Figure 1-3 is a dramatic example of the general process discussed earlier, wherein a program aimed at one trouble symptom results in creating a new set of troubles in some other part of the system. Here the success in alleviating a natural resource shortage throws the system over into the pollution-limited mode that is generated because the freedom from a resource restraint allows industrialization and population to grow until a new limit is reached. This process of a solution creating a new problem has defeated many of our past governmental programs and will continue to do so unless we devote more effort to understanding the dynamic behavior of our social systems.

Alternatives to Decline or Catastrophe

Suppose in the basic world system of Figures 1-1 and 1-2 we ask how to sustain the quality of life that is beginning to decline after 1950. One way to

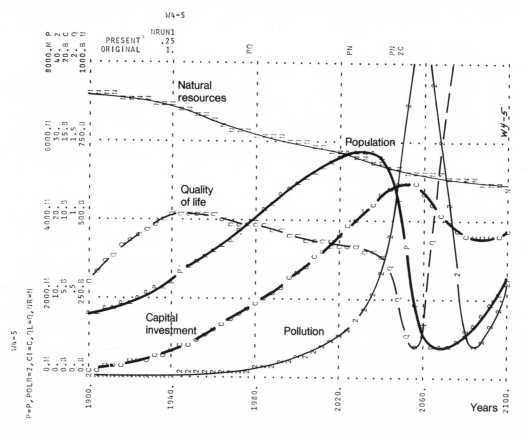

Figure 1-3 Pollution crisis precipitated by lower usage rate of natural resources. In 1970, natural resource usage is reduced 75 percent by more effective technology without affecting material standard of living.

attempt this, and it is the way the world is now choosing, might be to increase the rate of industrialization by raising the rate of capital investment. Models of the kind we are here using make such hypothetical questions answerable in a few minutes and at negligible cost. Figure 1-4 shows what happens if the "normal" rate of capital accumulation is increased by 20 percent in 1970. The pollution crisis reappears. This time the cause is not the more efficient use of natural resources but the upsurge of industrialization, which overtaxes the environment before resource depletion has a chance to depress industrialization. Again, an "obvious" desirable change in policy has caused troubles worse than the ones that were originally being corrected.

This result is important not only for its own message but because it demonstrates how an apparently desirable change in a social system can have unexpected and even disastrous results.

Figure 1-4 should make us cautious about rushing into programs on the basis of short-term humanitarian impulses. The eventual result can be antihumanitarian. Emotionally inspired efforts often fall into one of three traps set for us by the

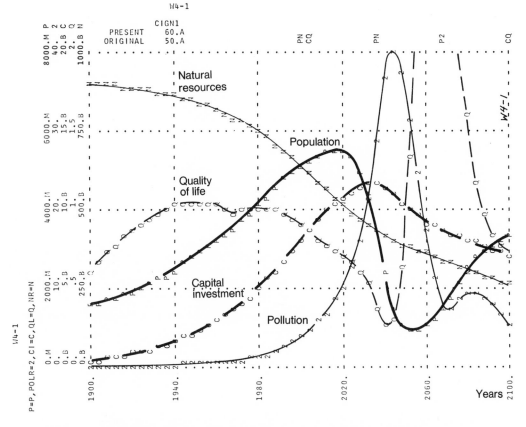

Figure 1-4 In 1970 the rate of capital accumulation is increased 20 percent in an effort to reverse the beginning decline in the quality of life. The pollution crisis occurs before natural resources are depleted.

nature of social systems. The programs are apt to address symptoms rather than causes and attempt to operate through points in the system that have little leverage for change; the characteristic of systems whereby a policy change has the opposite effect in the short run from the effect in the long run can eventually cause deepening difficulties after a sequence of short-term actions; and the effect of a program can be along an entirely different direction than was originally expected, so that suppressing one symptom only causes trouble to burst forth at another point.

Figure 1-5 retains the 20 percent additional capital investment rate after 1970 from Figure 1-4 but in addition explores birth reduction as a way of avoiding crisis. Here the "normal" birth rate has been cut in half in 1970. (Changes in normal rates refer to coefficients having the specified effect if all other things remain the same. But other things in the system change and also exert their effect on the actual system rates.) The result shows interesting behavior. The quality of life surges upward for thirty years for the reasons that are customarily asserted.

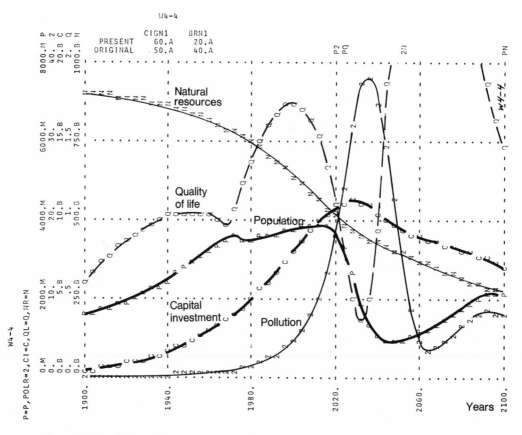

Figure 1-5 In 1970 the 20 percent increase in capital accumulation of Figure 1-4 is retained and "normal" birth rate is reduced 50 percent. Capital investment continues to grow until the pollution crisis develops. After an initial decline, population is again pushed up by the rapid rise in the quality of life that precedes the collapse.

Food per capita grows, the material standard of living rises, and crowding does not become as great. But the more affluent world population continues to use natural resources and to accumulate capital plant at about the same rate as in Figure 1-4. The load on the environment is more closely related to industrialization than to population, and the pollution crisis occurs at about the same point in time as in Figure 1-4.

Figure 1-5 shows that the 50 per cent reduction in the normal birth rate in 1970 was sufficient to start a decline in total population. But the rising quality of life and the reduction of pressures act to start the population curve upward again. This is especially evident in other computer runs where the reduction in the normal birth rate is not so drastic. This investigation raises serious questions about the effectiveness of birth control *alone* as a means of controlling population. The secondary consequence of starting a birth control program will be to increase the influences that the raise birth rate and reduce the apparent pressures that require population control. A birth control program that would be effective, all other things being equal, may largely fail because other things will not remain equal. Its very incipient success can set in motion forces to defeat the program.

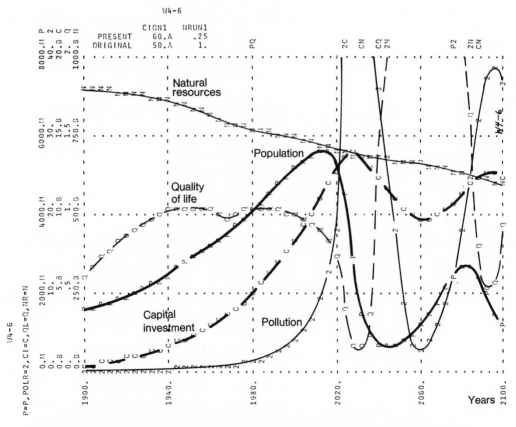

Figure 1-6 The 20 percent increase in capital investment from Figure 1-4 and the 75 percent reduction of natural resource usage from Figure 1-3 are combined.

Figure 1-6 combines the reduced resource usage rate and the increased capital investment rate of Figures 1-3 and 1-4. The result is to make the population collapse occur slightly sooner and more severely. Based on the modified system of Figure 1-6, Figure 1-7, then examines the result if technology finds ways to reduce the pollution generated by a given degree of industrialization. Here in Figure 1-7 the pollution rate, other things being the same, is reduced by 50 percent from that in Figure 1-6. The result is to postpone the day of reckoning by twenty years and to allow the world population to grow 25 percent before the population collapse occurs. The "solution" of reduced pollution has in effect caused more people to suffer the eventual consequences. Again we see the dangers of partial solutions. Actions that attempt to relieve one kind of distress at one point in a system produce an unexpected result in some other part of the system. If the interactions are not sufficiently understood, the consequences can be as bad as or worse than those that led to the initial action.

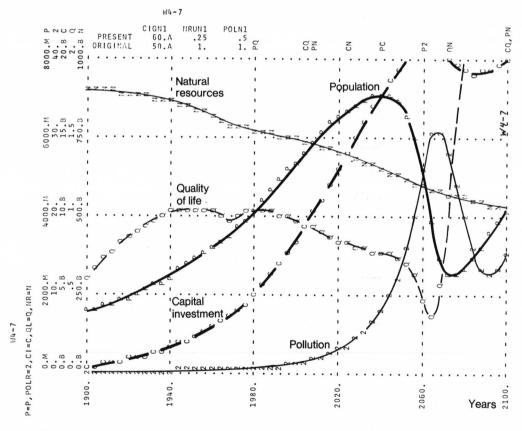

Figure 1-7   Increased capital investment rate and reduced natural resource usage from Figure 1-6 are retained. In addition, in 1970 the "normal" rate of pollution generation is reduced 50 percent. The effect of pollution control is to allow population to grow 25 percent further and to delay the pollution crisis by 20 years.

There are no utopias in our social systems. There appear to be no sustainable modes of behavior that are free of pressures and stresses. But there are many possible modes, and some are more desirable than others. Usually, the more attractive kinds of behavior in our social systems seem to be possible only if we have a good understanding of the system dynamics and are willing to endure the self-discipline and pressures that must accompany the desirable mode. The world system of Figure 1-1 can exhibit modes that are more hopeful than the crises of Figures 1-2 through 1-7. But to develop the more promising modes will require restraint and dedication to a long-range future that man may not be capable of sustaining.

Figure 1-8 shows the world system if several policy changes are adopted together in the year 1970. Population is stabilized. The quality of life rises about 50 percent. Pollution remains at about the 1970 level. Would such a world be accepted? It implies an end to population and economic growth.

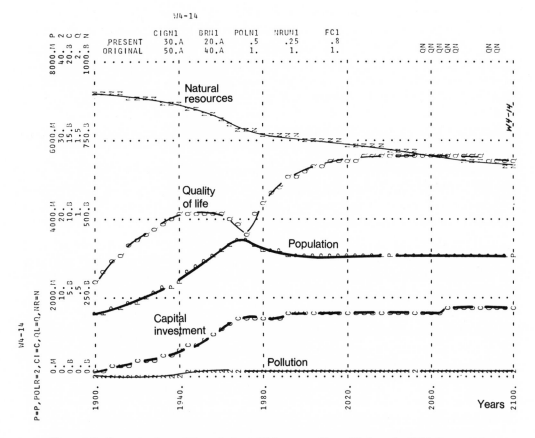

Figure 1-8 One set of conditions that establishes a world equilibrium. In 1970 the capital investment rate is reduced 40 percent, the birth rate is reduced 50 percent, pollution generation is reduced 50 percent, natural resource usage rate is reduced 75 percent, and food production is reduced 20 percent.

In Figure 1-8 the normal rate of capital accumulation is *reduced* 40 percent from its previous value. The normal birth rate is reduced 50 percent from its earlier value. The "normal" pollution generation is reduced 50 percent from the value before 1970. The normal rate of food production is *reduced* 20 percent from its previous value. (These changes in normal values are the changes for a specific set of system conditions. Actual system rates continue to be affected by the varying conditions of the system.) But a reduction in the investment rate and a reduction in agricultural emphasis are counterintuitive and not likely to be discovered or accepted without extensive system studies and years of argument—perhaps more years than are available. The changes in pollution generation and natural resource usage may be easier to understand and to achieve. The severe reduction in the worldwide birth rate is the most doubtful. Even if technical and biological methods existed, the improved condition of the world might remove the incentive for sustaining the birth reduction emphasis and discipline.

Future Policy Issues

The dynamics of world behavior bear directly on the future of the United States. American urbanization and industrialization are a major part of the world scene. The United States is setting a pattern that other parts of the world are trying to follow. That pattern is not sustainable. Our foreign policy and our overseas commercial activity seem to be running contrary to overwhelming forces that are developing in the world system. The following issues are raised by the preliminary investigations to date. They must, of course, be examined more deeply and confirmed by more thorough research into the assumptions about the structure and detail of the world system.

1. Industrialization may be a more fundamental disturbing force in world ecology than is population. In fact, the population explosion is perhaps best viewed as a result of technology and industrialization. I include medicine and public health as a part of industrialization.

2. Within the next century, man may be facing choices from a four-pronged dilemma—suppression of modern industrial society by a natural resource shortage, collapse of world population from changes wrought by pollution, population limitation by food shortage, or population control by war, disease, and social stresses caused by physical and psychological crowding.

3. We may now be living in a "golden age" when in spite of the worldwide feeling of malaise, the quality of life is, on the average, higher than ever before in history and higher now than the future offers.

4. Efforts for direct population control may be inherently self-defeating. If population control begins to result, as hoped, in a higher per capita food supply and material standard of living, these very improvements can generate forces to trigger a resurgence of population growth.

5. The high standard of living of modern industrial societies seems to result from a production of food and material goods that has been able to outrun the

rising population. But, as agriculture reaches a space limit, as industrialization reaches a natural resource limit, and as both reach a pollution limit, population tends to catch up. Population then grows until the quality of life falls far enough to generate sufficiently large pressures to stabilize population.

6. There may be no realistic hope for the present underdeveloped countries to reach the standard of living demonstrated by the present industrialized nations. The pollution and natural resource load placed on the world environmental system by each person in an advanced country is probably 10 to 20 times greater than the load now generated by a person in an underdeveloped country. With four times as much population in underdeveloped countries as in the present developed countries, their rising to the economic level of the United States could mean an increase of 10 times in the natural resource and pollution load on the world environment. Noting the destruction that has already occurred on land, in the air, and especially in the oceans, no capability appears to exist for handling such a rise in the standard of living for the present total population of the world.

7. A society with a high level of industrialization may be nonsustainable. It may be self-extinguishing if it exhausts the natural resources on which it depends. Or, if unending substitution for declining natural resources is possible, the international strife over "pollution and environmental rights" may pull the average world-wide standard of living back to the level of a century ago.

8. From the long view of a hundred years hence, the present efforts of underdeveloped countries to industrialize along Western patterns may be unwise. They may now be closer to the ultimate equilibrium with the environment than are the industrialized nations. The present underdeveloped countries may be in a better condition for surviving the forthcoming world-wide environmental and economic pressures than are the advanced countries. When one of the several forces materializes that is strong enough to cause a collapse in world population, the advanced countries may suffer far more than their share of the decline.

A New Frontier

It is now possible to take hypotheses about the separate parts of a social system, to combine them in a computer model, and to learn the consequences. The hypotheses may at first be no more correct than the ones we are using in our intuitive thinking. But the process of computer modeling and model testing requires that these hypotheses be stated more explicitly. The model comes out of the hazy realm of the mental model into an unambiguous model or statement to which all have access. Assumptions can then be checked against all available information and can be rapidly improved. The great uncertainty with mental models is the inability to anticipate the consequences of interactions between the parts of a system. This uncertainty is totally eliminated in computer models. Given a stated set of assumptions, the computer traces the resulting consequences without doubt or error. This is a powerful procedure for clarifying issues. It is not easy. Results will not be immediate.

We are on the threshold of a great new era in human pioneering. In the past there have been periods characterized by geographic exploration. Other periods have dealt with the formation of national governments. At other times the focus was on the creation of great literature. Most recently we have been through the pioneering frontier of science and technology. But science and technology are now a routine part of our life. Science is no longer a frontier. The process of scientific discovery is orderly and organized.

I suggest that the next frontier for human endeavor is to pioneer a better understanding of the nature of our social systems. The means are visible. The task will be no easier than the development of science and technology. For the next thirty years we can expect a rapid advance in understanding the complex dynamics of our social systems. To do so will require research, the development of teaching methods and materials, and the creation of appropriate educational programs. The research results of today will in one or two decades find their way into the secondary schools just as concepts of basic physics have moved from research to general education over the past three decades.

What we do today fundamentally affects our future two or three decades hence. If we follow intuition, the trends of the past will continue into deepening difficulty. If we set up research and educational programs, which are now possible but which have not yet been developed, we can expect to achieve a far sounder basis for action.

The Nation's Real Alternatives

The record to date implies that our people accept the future growth of population in the United States as preordained, beyond the purview and influence of legislative control, and as a ground rule that determines the nation's task as finding cities in which the future population can live. But I have been describing the circular processes of our social systems in which there is no unidirectional cause and effect but, instead, a ring of actions and consequences that close back on themselves. One could say, incompletely, that the population will grow and that cities, space, and food must be provided. But one can likewise say, also incompletely, that the provision of cities, space, and food will cause the population to grow. Population generates pressure for urban growth, but urban pressures help to limit population.

Population grows until stresses rise far enough, which is to say that the quality of life falls far enough, to stop further increase. Everything we do to reduce those pressures causes the population to rise further and faster and hastens the day when expediencies will no longer suffice. The United States is in the position of a wild animal running from its pursuers. We still have some space, natural resources, and agricultural land left. We can avoid the question of rising population as long as we can flee into this bountiful reservoir that nature provided. But it is obvious that the reservoirs are limited. The wild animal usually flees until he is cornered, until he has no more space. Then he turns to fight, but he no longer has room to maneuver. He is less able to forestall disaster than if he had fought in the open while there was still room to yield and to dodge. The United States is running away from its long-term threats by trying to relieve social pressures as they arise. But if we persist in treating only the symptoms and not the causes, the result will be to increase the magnitude of the ultimate threat and reduce our capability to respond when we no longer have space to flee.

What does this mean? Instead of automatically accepting the need for new towns and the desirability of locating industry in rural areas, we should consider confining our cities. If it were possible to prohibit the encroachment by housing and industry onto even a single additional acre of farm and forest, the resulting social pressures would hasten the day when we stabilize population. Some European countries are closer to realizing the necessity of curtailing urban growth than are we. For example, farmland surrounding Copenhagen cannot be used for either residence or industry until the severest pressures force the government to rezone small additional parcels. When land is rezoned, the corresponding rise in land price is heavily taxed to remove the incentive for land speculation. The waiting time for an empty apartment in Copenhagen may be years. Such pressures certainly cause the Danes to face the population problem more squarely than do we.

Our greatest challenge now is how to handle the transition from growth to equilibrium. Our society has behind it a thousand years of tradition that has encouraged and rewarded growth. The folklore and the success stories praise growth and expansion. But that is not the path of the future. Many of the present stresses in our society arise from the pressures that always accompany the conversion from growth to equilibrium.

In our studies of social systems, we have made a number of investigations of life cycles that start with growth and merge into equilibrium. There are always severe stresses in the transition. Pressures must rise far enough to suppress the forces that produced growth. Not only do we face the pressures that will stop the population growth; we also will encounter pressures that will stop the rise of industrialization and standard of living. The social stresses will rise. The economic forces will be ones for which we have no precedent. The psychological forces will be beyond those for which we are prepared. Our studies of urban systems demonstrated how the pressures from shortage of land and rising unemployment accompany the usual transition from urban growth to equilibrium. But the pressures we have seen in our cities are minor compared with those the nation is approaching. The population pressures and the economic forces in a city that was reaching equilibrium have in the past been able to escape to new land areas.

But that escape is becoming less possible. Until now we have had, in effect, an inexhaustible supply of farmland and food-growing potential. But now we are reaching the critical point where, all at the same time, population is overrunning productive land, agricultural land is almost fully employed for the first time, the rise in population is putting more demand on food supplies, and urbanization is pushing agriculture out of the fertile areas into marginal lands. For the first time, demand is reaching a condition in which supply will begin to fall while need increases. The crossover from plenty to shortage can occur abruptly.

The fiscal and monetary system of the country is a complex social-economic-financial system of the kind we have been discussing. It is clear the country is not agreed on the behavior of the interactions between government policy, growth, unemployment, and inflation. An article by a writer for *Finance* magazine in July 1970 suggests that the approach I have been discussing be applied in fiscal and monetary policy and their relationships to the economy. I estimate that such a task would be only a few times more difficult than was the investigation of urban growth and stagnation. The need to accomplish it becomes more urgent as the economy begins to move for the first time from a history of growth into the turbulent pressures that will accompany the transition from growth to one of the many possible kinds of equilibrium. We need to choose the kind of equilibrium before we arrive.

In a hierarchy of systems, a conflict usually exists between the goals of a subsystem and the welfare of the broader system. We see this in the urban system. The goal of the city is to expand and to raise its quality of life. But this increases population, industrialization, pollution, and demands on the food supply. The broader social system of the country and the world requires that the goals of the urban areas be curtailed and that the pressures of such curtailment become high enough to keep the urban areas and population within bounds that are satisfactory to the larger system of which the city is a part. If this nation chooses to continue to work for some of the traditional urban goals, and if it succeeds, as it may well do, the result will be to deepen the distress of the country as a whole and eventually to deepen the crisis in the cities themselves. We may be at the point where higher pressures in the present are necessary if insurmountable pressures are to be avoided in the future.

I have tried to give you a glimpse of the nature of multiloop feedback systems, the class of systems to which our social systems belong. I have attempted to indicate how these systems mislead us because our intuition and judgment have been formed to expect behavior different from that actually possessed by such systems. I believe that we are still pursuing national programs that will be at least as frustrating and futile as many of the past. But there is hope. We can now begin to understand the dynamic behavior of our social systems. Progress will be slow. There are many crosscurrents in the social sciences that will cause confusion and delay. The approach that I have been describing is very different from the emphasis on data gathering and statistical analysis that occupies much of the time of social research. But there have been breakthroughs in several areas. If we proceed expeditiously but thoughtfully, there is a basis for optimism.

2
Introduction to the Project

Dennis L. Meadows

There was considerable public interest in Professor Forrester's article on the counterintuitive nature of social systems (Chapter 1) and his book World Dynamics. *Many letters and telephone calls conveyed requests for additional information on the project. To answer those requests, Professor Meadows prepared a brief description of the project, its objectives, and the system dynamics methodology that was being employed to represent and analyze basic global relationships. The revised paper contains material on the World3 model, a brief summary of the project conclusions, and a description of the hierarchy of research being undertaken to determine short-term policy implications of the global model.*

2
Introduction to the Project

Background of the Project

For thousands of years the condition of the human race was characterized by very gradual growth and change. In the past one hundred years, that growth has accelerated. Technological development has mushroomed. Virgin natural resource stocks are being diminished by exponential growth in industrial production. The environment is being polluted at an ever-increasing rate. World population has more than doubled in the past hundred years, and it may double again within the next thirty years.

Material growth cannot continue indefinitely on a finite planet. Current rates of material growth probably cannot be sustained even for another century. Mankind is faced with an inevitable transition at some time in the future from worldwide growth to global equilibrium. Because of the time delays inherent in social system change, decisions made today are already influencing the nature of that future equilibrium. Will it be a state in which food shortages, the deterioration of the environment, and the depletion of important resources have risen to stifle growth? Or will man anticipate his material limits and move into a deliberate balance with them? The shift from growth to global equilibrium may be initiated by catastrophes such as wars, starvation, or epidemics. Alternatively, the transition could result from an enlightened, concerted, international effort to adopt new values, define new goals, and implement new institutions no longer dependent on growth in population and material output.

Individuals do perceive the isolated symptoms and components of profound social problems caused by rapid growth, but society has been stymied in its efforts to comprehend the total situation and to develop global solutions. While a few individuals have begun to recognize the inevitability and the potential dangers of an unplanned transition to equilibrium, thinking and action have been confined to short-term and narrowly defined problem areas. Demographers press for effective birth control measures. Ecologists seek a taxation on polluters of the natural environment. Agricultural experts search for more efficient food production. All would admit that there are important interactions among their various approaches, but the conceptual framework, the analytic methodologies, and the vocabulary to unite the different fields have been lacking.

Methodology of Phase One

The technique of system dynamics has been developed at the Massachusetts Institute of Technology during more than thirty years of continuous effort directed toward the analysis and control of complex system behavior. From its birth in the study of relatively simple mechanical systems, it has grown to provide a single framework for understanding the behavior of electronic, chemical, biological, and social systems whose elements interact through time to produce system changes.

As an important advantage, system dynamics represents real-world relationships pictorially and mathematically in terms quickly understood by everyone.

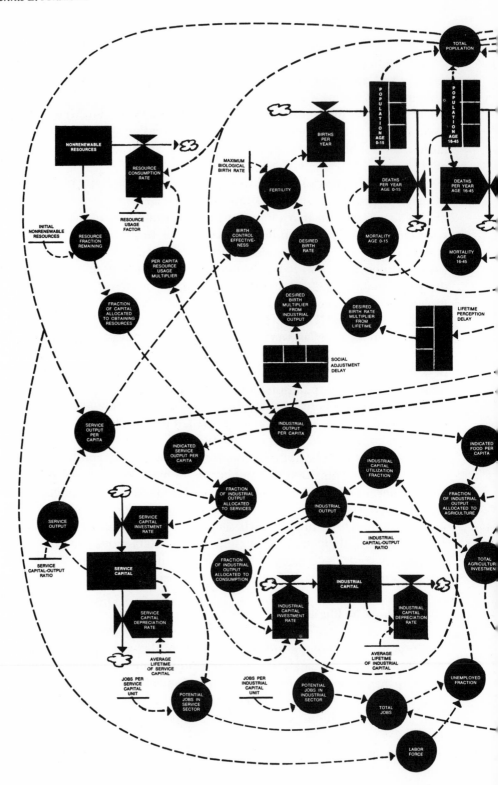

Figure 2-1 World3 DYNAMO flow diagram of the global model assumptions

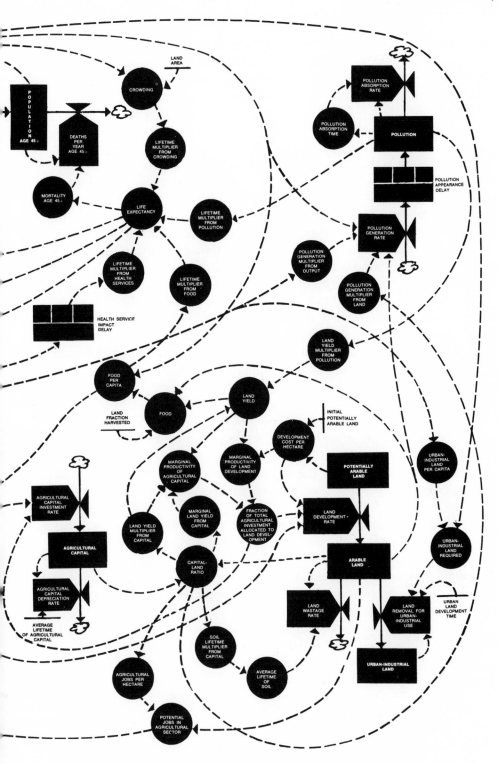

Figures 2-1,6 and 7 reprinted from Meadows et al., Limits to Growth, *(New York: Universe Books, 1972).*

Although the creation of useful models is difficult, specialized mathematical ability is not a prerequisite for understanding and using the results of a system dynamics study. Thus, governmental leaders and professionals in many different fields will be able to interpret the results from the perspective of their own areas of expertise.

A detailed description of the system dynamics approach is available in *Principles of Systems.*[1] The main features of the global model are briefly described here. The description will illustrate the use of system dynamics in understanding the causes and possible implications of current growth in global population and material output. Figure 2-1 is a flow diagram or pictorial representation of the assumptions in the revised model called World3. The assumptions deal explicitly with the interrelations among the processes of population growth, economic development, natural resource depletion, pollution generation, and food production. A detailed description of the data incorporated in the model will be published in the technical report, *The Dynamics of Growth in a Finite World.* While the specific variable names and many of the detailed relationships portrayed in the diagram of World3 differ from those in World2 devised by Jay W. Forrester (Figure 1-1), World3 retains many important features of the model from which it was derived.

Using the computer to conduct studies of model behavior requires that each assumption be expressed very precisely. According to the theory underlying system dynamics, only two types of variables, "levels" and "rates," are necessary to express any relationship in a system. Levels are the state variables or stocks of quantities that characterize the system at any point in time. Population, pollution, natural resources, industrial capital, and arable land are five of the levels in this version of the global model. All levels are represented by rectangles. Model behavior depends on the variation in the quantity in each level over time. Levels that are dynamically unimportant (usually sources or sinks) are represented by clouds.

Rates are the system's action or policy variables that effect changes in the levels. Birth rate, death rate, pollution generation rate, industrial capital investment rate and resource usage rate are among the rates important in understanding the global system. Rates are represented as valves. In this model, rates control flows of people, pollutants, capital equipment, land, and nonrenewable resources. These flows are represented by solid lines.

Since the rates acting on a level summarize all the biological, political, social, economic, and other factors that act to change that level, they are generally complex expressions. Often one or more components of a rate are sufficiently important to warrant individual attention. Called auxiliaries, these components are separated algebraically from the rate equations, assigned separate names, and represented pictorially as circles. One such auxiliary is the lifetime multiplier from health services, which represents the influence of health facilities on the average life expectancy of the population.

[1] Jay W. Forrester, *Principles of Systems* (Cambridge, Mass.: Wright-Allen Press, 1968).

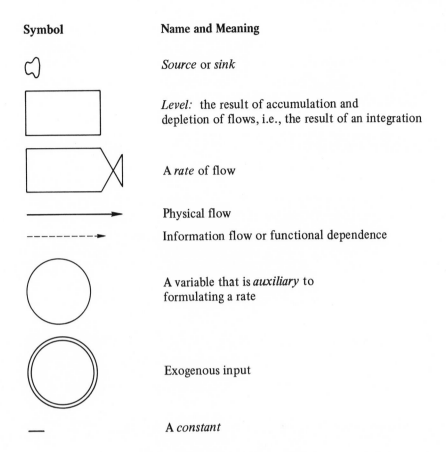

Symbol   **Name and Meaning**

Source or *sink*

Level: the result of accumulation and
depletion of flows, i.e., the result of an integration

A *rate* of flow

Physical flow

Information flow or functional dependence

A variable that is *auxiliary* to
formulating a rate

Exogenous input

A *constant*

Figure 2-2   DYNAMO symbols glossary

System dynamics flow diagram symbols are summarized in Figure 2-2. The dotted lines in the flow diagram indicate causal influence in the direction shown by the arrows. For example, health services, pollution, and food all influence the life expectancy. In the flow diagram, these dotted lines indicate only that a causal link connects two elements; they do not indicate the exact quantitative nature of the link.

Whenever a sequence of influences leads back to its own starting point and thus forms a closed circuit, it constitutes a feedback loop. One important feedback loop is that relating health services and population. The components of that loop are shown in Figure 2-3.

The sequence of influences in Figure 2-3 is a negative feedback loop. In any negative loop a change in one element sets in motion a chain of events around the loop that eventually produces a *counteracting* influence on that element. For example, an *increase* in services per capita increases the average health of the population after some delay. Better health services decrease the death rate and thereby increase the population growth rate. A larger population has the effect,

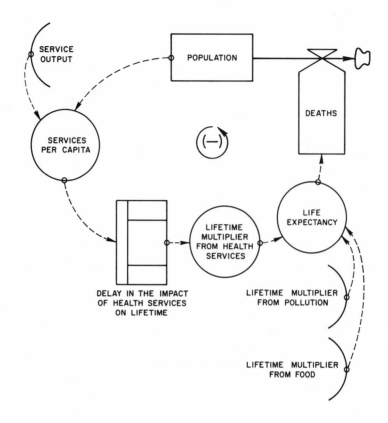

Figure 2-3 Elements of the feedback loop relating health services and population

all else being equal, of *decreasing* the health services per capita. Of course, other factors will in general be acting simultaneously on each factor in this loop. They, too, can be represented as a set of interconnected rates and levels.

Feedback loops may also be positive. In that case, a change in one element is propagated about the loop to result ultimately in a *reinforcing* change in the same element. Usually, each element in a system will be influenced by several positive and negative loops simultaneously. For example, population is also involved in a positive feedback relationship with the birth rate (Figure 2-4). If population were suddenly *increased,* the number of babies born per year would increase and thereby *raise* the population even more.

Feedback loops differ not only in their polarity, positive and negative, but also in the delay with which responses are propagated around the loop. The delays inherent in the positive loop shown in Figure 2-4 are about fifteen to twenty years, which is the time necessary for a newborn child to mature and have babies of its own. Delays in the former loop, involving health and population, may be thirty years or more. Thus it is in general very difficult to determine intuitively the direction, timing, and magnitude of the influence on one system element resulting from a change in some element elsewhere in the system. An initial

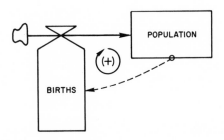

Figure 2-4 Population-birth rate feedback loop

decrease in population might ultimately lead in the model in Figure 2-4 to either more or less population than if the decrease had not occurred. The final direction of the response would depend on the strength and the delay of relationships inherent in each loop in which population is an element.

The human mind is poorly suited for tracing the behavior of a complex system. However, after human minds compile a consistent set of causal relationships about such a system, it becomes possible to use a computer to calculate their simultaneous interaction over time. In supplementing his intuition through the use of computers as bookkeeping devices, man may now consider many more factors in identifying better solutions to a problem.

One dimension of mankind's current dilemma is that actions made to alleviate one problem often aggravate others. Intensive use of fertilizers, for example, does increase land productivity, but it also exacerbates water pollution. Accelerated economic development raises material standards of living but increases pollution and the depletion of nonrenewable resources. Many alternative policies for improving mankind's condition have been proposed. Birth control, development of more efficient crops, increased recycling of natural resources, and changes in the societal values that govern investment in capital are a few examples. Some combination of these policies can be effective in improving the system behavior, but alternatives must be evaluated in the context of their total impact on all elements of the global society in both the short term and the long term. It is for this purpose that the World3 version of a world model was constructed.

Basic Structure of the Global Model

Figure 2-1 is a detailed elaboration of several cardinal assumptions about the relationships among important elements of the global system. The interrelationships among nineteen of the most important elements of the world model are illustrated in Figure 2-5. The lines and elements graphically represent the following assumptions. A given amount of industrial capital can produce a certain industrial output each year. Some of that output is investment in the form of factories and machines that increase the level of capital the next year. As a greater fraction of industrial output is diverted from investment, the growth rate of capital decreases. Output may be diverted to consumption and services, to agriculture,

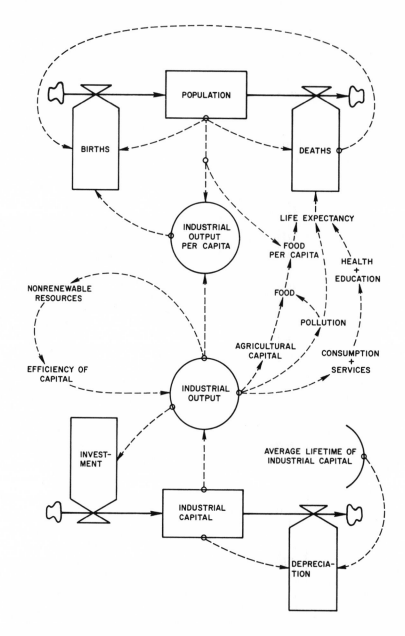

Figure 2-5 Basic interactions between population growth and capital accumulation

and to military expenditures. As consumption and services increase, health and education improve, average life expectancy becomes greater, deaths decrease, and population grows. This rise in population is ameliorated somewhat by the secondary influence of average life expectancy on the birth rate. A large fraction of mankind must rely on its own children for support in old age and for other important social and religious functions. As the probability of survival is raised through increases in the average life expectancy, the desired number of children decreases and the crude birth rate declines.

As output is diverted to form agricultural capital, greater food production becomes possible, which can lead to a higher average life expectancy. The primary determinant of the fraction of output invested in agriculture or reinvested in industry is the output per capita. If production per capita is low, most of the output must be diverted to consumption, services, and food. Therefore, less investment is possible to build a larger industrial capital base. At the same time, the high birth rate associated with low levels of industrialization stimulates the growth of population. For these reasons, population tends to increase much more easily than capital in traditional societies, especially if medical aid from outside has lowered the death rate without affecting the birth rate.

Industrial production also leads to the depletion of natural resources. As the stock of natural resources declines, the efficiency of capital decreases because relatively more capital must be devoted to mining and transporting poorer grades of ore. All else being equal, this would tend to decrease the industrial output available from a given stock of capital.

An increase in output has one additional effect: agricultural and industrial production generate pollution. Pollution has potentially negative effects on food production and on the average life expectancy of the population.

Although the preceding statements are a great simplification of the global model, most global problems have important roots in this simple set of interactions. Consider, for example, the long-term implications of the Green Revolution, the combination of new seed varieties with intensive use of agricultural chemicals that has boosted land productivity. Supporters of the program assume that an increase in food production in the less industrialized countries would permit less industrial output to be diverted to agriculture and thus permit more output to be reinvested in capital, moving the process of capital investment into the phase of self-sustaining growth.

Those who criticize the Green Revolution feel another conclusion might be justified. The increased food from the Green Revolution might as easily increase the food per capita, decrease the death rate, and cause the population to grow very rapidly. Should this happen, the increase in population might be very much greater than the increase in capital. Output per capita could remain the same or even decline, thereby maintaining a stagnant economy.

The Green Revolution has been widely implemented only recently. Thus, the resolution of this issue is still many years away. However, it is ironic that, while millions of dollars were spent in massive modeling efforts to think through every future step of a program to land three men on the moon, no similar effort was made to understand beforehand the possible implications of the Green Revolution for our ability to maintain three and one-half billion people on the globe. The global model is intended to be a further step in the development of the tools necessary for such analyses.

Preliminary Conclusions from the Global Model

The current version of the World3 model is based on the data found and summarized through eighteen months of effort. An enormous amount of research remains to be done. New relationships will be added to the model, and the data will be refined. However, all the revisions introduced into the model to date have not altered the following basic conclusions:

1. Exponential growth in population and material output is the dominant force in socioeconomic change in most contemporary societies.
2. Current growth rates of population and material output cannot be sustained indefinitely. Present growth trends would almost certainly overreach important physical limits if continued for another 50 to 100 years.
3. Growth may come to an end either through an orderly accommodation to global limits (a deliberate transition to equilibrium) or through an overshoot of those limits followed by uncontrolled decline.
4. Because of the delays in each of the feedback loops governing growth in material output and population, the most probable result of current global growth trends is overshoot of the ultimate limits to growth. An example of this behavior is illustrated in Figure 2-6. The overshoot behavior mode is the

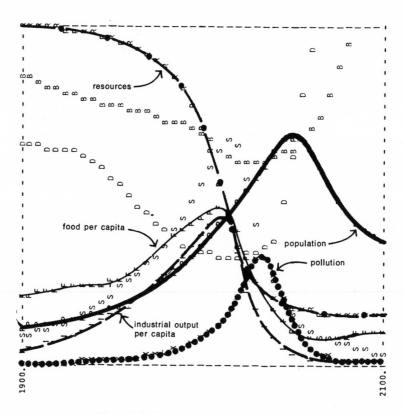

Figure 2-6   Resource depletion halts growth

dominant mode of the world system as long as the implicit value system continues to promote physical growth.

5. Technological solutions designed to release some pressure caused by growth (for example, hunger or escalating resource costs) can serve only to postpone the decline, if they are not accompanied by changes that decrease the social, economic, and political factors causing growth.

6. It seems possible to identify alternative states of material equilibrium on a global scale in which population and material output are essentially constant and in balance with the finite resources of the environment. These states could be defined in ways that would satisfy man's most fundamental needs, permit cultural progress, and sustain his society indefinitely. A model run illustrating one such equilibrium is shown in Figure 2-7. This particular computer output represents the results of a strenuous program, begun in 1970, to eliminate the biological, social, economic, and political stimulants of growth in population and material output.

7. There is no unique, optimal long-term population level. Rather, there is an entire set of trade-offs among personal freedom, material and social standard of living, and the population level. Given the finite and diminishing stock of

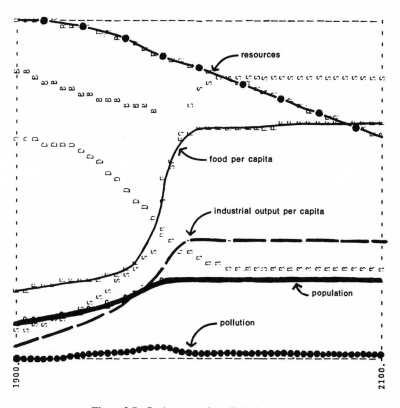

Figure 2-7   Socioeconomic policies halt growth

virgin resources on this globe, we are inevitably faced with the necessity of recognizing that a larger population implies a lower material standard of living over the long term.

8. Since the delays involved in negotiating an orderly transition to any state of equilibrium are very long, 50 to 150 years or more, it is essential that society begins soon to stop the implicit promotion of population and material growth. Each year of delay decreases the long-term options of society and lowers the probability of attaining a desirable equilibrium state.

Extensions of the Global Model

It has become clear that a global model based on data already available can provide insights into the general nature of the factors limiting growth and an overall context for discussions and investigations about specific aspects of global problems. Such a model can point very clearly to the necessary interface conditions that must be met by policies addressed to the problems in any particular problem sector and can aid in identifying the critical areas of effort. A global model, with the degree of aggregation it entails, is not, however, sufficient for the detailed formulation of improved national or regional policies.

To test the conclusions of World3 and to evaluate specific policy alternatives, it has been necessary to examine in detail each of the five sectors: capital, food

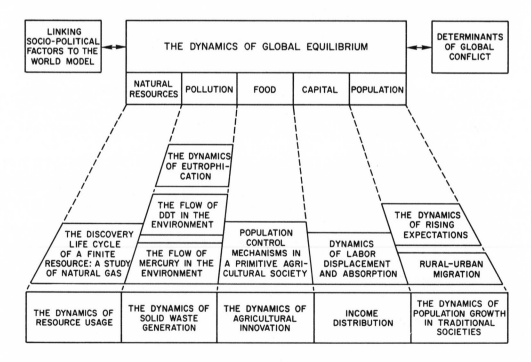

Figure 2-8 The hierarchy of research

production, pollution, population, and resources. Analyses of the global model pointed in each of the five sectors to critical problems that became the bases of separate modeling efforts. In these substudies we modeled certain social and political phenomena not specifically addressed by the global model. The results help to assess the effectiveness of specific policies, point to further problems that may be studied at an even more disaggregated level, and provide insights into important factors that should be included in revisions of the global model. The hierarchy of research portrayed graphically in Figure 2-8 was that actually undertaken. The final reports on seven of the studies make up the second part of this book.

Part Two
Simulation Substudy Reports

No formal model can possibly incorporate all the interrelationships in a complex system. The assumptions in any given model must be carefully chosen in reference to the specific set of related dynamic phenomena that are to be studied. This restriction leads directly to the concept of a model hierarchy. A superordinate model, World3, for example, may include the major, highly aggregated relationships that cause some long-term problem. This model can be used to determine limits and boundary conditions for the operation of the total system. Sensitivity analyses of the superordinate model will point to aspects of the system structure that must be understood in greater detail. Subordinate models focusing on one or more subsectors of World3 may then be employed to test the assumptions made in the more aggregated model and to provide the shorter-term perspectives needed for policy formulation. The following seven simulation studies were undertaken to clarify or confirm some aspect of the global model. They by no means exhaust the World3 relationships requiring more intensive research. They do, however, indicate the appropriate scope for such models and illustrate the processes of empirical validation that are appropriate at this increased level of detail.

3
DDT Movement in the Global Environment

Jørgen Randers

Several fundamental assumptions determine the behavior of the World3 pollution sector. One particularly important factor is the delay between the time a material is released into the environment and the time it is perceived or has its first impact on components of the global ecosystem. The precise magnitude and source of the delay will vary from one material to another. In World3 we assume that for most global pollutants the delay is long enough to have profound implications for the policies that may be implemented to control pollution. It is important to test this aspect of the global model by analyzing the time behavior of specific pollutants in the environment.

Since World3 is too aggregated to represent specific pollutants, several detailed substudies were undertaken. In the following paper, Jørgen Randers surveys the empirical literature on DDT, a pollutant of extreme persistence, and incorporates the available information into a model that traces DDT flows from the time the pesticide is first applied on land to its ultimate appearance in marine fish. The paper supports the concept of a pollution transmission delay and provides insights into the nature of the DDT problem. At the same time, it illustrates the processes through which incomplete empirical data may be incorporated into formal system models for sensitivity analysis and evaluation of policy alternatives.

As an illustration of the relative ease with which system dynamics assumptions can be understood and analyzed, this paper may usefully be compared with two other published models of DDT flows; H. L. Harrison et al., "Systems Studies of DDT Transport," Science, vol. 170 (1970), p. 503, and G. M. Woodwell et al., "DDT in the Biosphere: Where Does It Go?" Science, vol. 174 (1971), p. 1101.

3
DDT Movement
in the Global Environment

Introduction

The science of ecology has only recently been brought into the arena of political debate. As a result, most ecologists are confronted with an embarrassing quandary. As scientists they realize the imperfections in their knowledge of ecological systems, and they are understandably reluctant to make pronouncements about environmental policy until complete experimental evidence is available. However, as citizens they perceive man's increasing influence on ecological systems, and they realize that the lack of a formal environmental policy may in effect be a policy of uncontrolled destruction. They feel a pressure, most uncomfortable for any ethical scientist, to make decisions on the basis of incomplete data.

Managers of businesses and of governments, on the other hand, are accustomed to the necessity for making decisions within time deadlines. They have developed numerous management tools that help bring together the diverse pieces of information already available about a problem, assist in evaluating the relative importance of the pieces, and provide a coherent picture of the problem even when some pieces of information are missing.

This paper illustrates how system dynamics can be used to illuminate an ecological problem with immediate policy implications—the distribution of the insecticide DDT in the global environment. System dynamics models do not, of course, permit one to predict the future. Rather, the objective is experimental. It is to assemble the diverse bits of quantitative and qualitative information already available and evaluate which data are most important in understanding the system as a whole. The primary use of system dynamics is thus in making the best possible estimate of the impact of a given policy, using only the information currently available about the system.

System dynamics has another use as well. Much environmental research today is directed toward refining the estimates of factors that are already known well enough to permit improved policy. One should instead strive to focus the limited research resources on those areas of ignorance that are still great enough to make it impossible to identify the better of two alternative policies. System dynamics techniques are extremely useful for identifying more efficiently those parameters and structural relationships whose precise values are of critical importance to decision makers. To illustrate the application of system dynamics to these two aspects of environmental analysis, we chose to simulate the dynamics of DDT movements through the environment.

For that purpose we surveyed the literature on the individual physical aspects of the movement of DDT through the ecosystem. The picture is incomplete and in places contradictory. Our purpose was not to evaluate the reliability of others' experiments but to illustrate how the results of many individual studies may be assembled into a useful policy tool. There may be errors in the studies we review here, but the sensitivity analyses cited later suggest that their impact on our basic conclusions is small. Our understanding of the real system will never be perfect, though it will improve. We shall eventually be able to make better predictions than those possible today. Nevertheless, decisions to increase or decrease the use of DDT are being formulated now on the basis of implicit, mental models of the behavior of DDT in the environment. If current decisions are to benefit from the research already done, a process of synthesis and analysis similar to that described here is essential. With such a process, ecologists may be able to resolve the conflict between scientific ethics and personal concern.

Relevant Aspects of the DDT Issue.   When the insecticidal value of DDT was first discovered and the chemical was put to use in the 1940s, it was believed that the ultimate weapon in man's continuing struggle against pests and insect-borne diseases had finally been found. Indeed, the effects of this synthetic substance were spectacular. For example, DDT permitted a rapid reduction of malaria and an astonishing increase in agricultural productivity in many regions of the world. The discoverer, Paul Müller of Switzerland, won the Nobel Prize in 1948.

Today, however, after the appearance of strains of insects that are resistant to DDT and after the discovery of DDT residues in human and animal fat tissue literally all over the world (for instance, in Eskimos and in Antarctic penguins), doubt has entered the arena. The doubt is strongly enhanced by the known toxicity of DDT and by concern about possible long-run effects of its storage in animals, especially man. Thus only twenty-five years after the introduction of the wonder chemical, many people are advocating total prohibition of the use of DDT. One of the first objectors was Rachel Carson, who in 1962 made the general public aware of the possible side effects of DDT in her widely circulated book *Silent Spring.*[1] But even today, one decade later, the world is far from a general consensus on the question of whether DDT use should be continued.

Much of the controversy over the use of DDT has been attributed to lack of any real information about the effect of the chemical on the ecosystem. Although hundreds of scientific papers have been written about specific measurements of DDT passage to or through specific organisms, current understanding of the total picture is still incomplete. Thus, while a few scientists argue vociferously for a ban on the use of DDT, most are simply striving for more knowledge about the subject. In the meantime 150,000 metric tons of DDT per year are being released into the biosphere.[2]

The ultimate decision on mankind's use of DDT must rest on the answers to the following basic questions:

1. What are the actual benefits in health, comfort, and agricultural productivity gained by a given level of DDT usage?
2. What are the total costs, in human health and in disturbance of natural ecological balances, incurred as a result of a given level of DDT usage?

---

[1] Rachel Carson, *Silent Spring* (Greenwich, Conn.: Faucett Publications, 1962).
[2] Study of Critical Environmental Problems, *Man's Impact on the Global Environment* (Cambridge, Mass.: The M.I.T. Press, 1970), p. 131; hereafter cited as SCEP, *Man's Impact.*

3. How are the benefits and costs of a given pattern of DDT usage distributed over space and time?

4. How do possible alternative measures of insect control compare with DDT in terms of costs and benefits distributed over space and time?

Although all these questions are important to the policy maker, the third question is of particular interest on the international level, since it is possible that the costs of using DDT may be paid by a different group from that which reaps the immediate benefits. The question concerning the distribution of DDT's costs through time as a function of different application rates is of interest because analysis may reveal that policies that seem to be beneficial in view of their short-term effects may no longer seem so when the long-term consequences of the actions are realized and taken into account. In this paper we apply system dynamics analysis to the time aspect of the third question. The first two questions are already the basis for an extensive research effort around the world. The model presented here draws heavily on that research for many of its assumptions. The following analysis (but not the exact numerical results) also appears to be applicable to many other long-lived pollutants that are concentrated biologically. Mercury, lead, cadmium, other insecticides, and the polychlorobiphenyls (PCBs) are possible examples.

Dichlorodiphenyltrichloroethane (DDT) is an organic chemical compound that is biologically toxic to many kinds of organisms, and thus it is sprayed as an insecticide onto forests and cropland. DDT kills some of the insects living on the crop but not the crop itself; hence it tends to reduce the loss of crops to insects. DDT is also sprayed onto interior surfaces of buildings to kill malaria-carrying mosquitoes. The DDT molecule is extremely stable, and a single application remains toxic to insects for long periods of time. These two properties—persistence and toxicity—have made DDT a very successful pesticide, constituting a large fraction of the total amount of synthetic pesticide used in the world.

The DDT molecule is ultimately broken down into biologically innocuous compounds. (The molecule is broken down through the intermediate compounds DDD or DDE. These two organic substances are also biologically active and stable; thus when we write "DDT residues" we usually mean DDT plus DDD and DDE.) The breakdown of DDT occurs through biodegradation, either by microorganisms in soil and water or by the metabolic processes of larger organisms. However, since these processes may take years to decompose a given amount of DDT completely, the pesticide molecules can travel large distances and accumulate at high concentrations before degradation.

Where does DDT move during its lifetime? This question is important because DDT not only kills insects but also adversely affects higher animals such as birds and fish. DDT has caused total reproductive failure in trout at concentrations of 3 parts per million (ppm) by weight in body tissue.[3] It has also inhibited the

---

[3] G. E. Burdick et al., "The Accumulation of DDT in Lake Trout and the Effect on Reproduction," *Transactions of the American Fisheries Society*, vol. 93 (1964), p. 127.

reproduction of birds such as the peregrine falcon, brown pelican, osprey, and bald eagle (by reducing the eggshell thickness to the point where the egg breaks under the weight of the brooding bird).[4]

The concentration of DDT residues in the body fat of the average American is about 12 parts per million; in New Delhi the average is 26 ppm.[5] To determine how this substance has been able to accumulate in higher animals, including man, it seems worthwhile to trace the movement over time of the DDT currently being released into the environment. The next section gives a brief general description of the path of DDT flow in the environment. Then each separate step in the path is documented with a review of current knowledge about that step.

General Outline of the Flow of DDT in the Environment.   The principal flows of DDT in the environment are those shown in the diagram in Figure 3-1.

When DDT is sprayed onto a crop or in a home, only part of it reaches the target. The rest remains suspended in the atmosphere. Much of the DDT reaching the target also eventually finds its way into the atmosphere by evaporation from the soil. Once in the air, the pesticide can be carried long distances before it finally falls back on soil or into the ocean. Some DDT is also washed downstream in watersheds.

Some of the DDT in the ocean will be taken up by plankton and other organisms; as the plankton are eaten by fish, the DDT enters higher animals. Ultimately, fish-eating birds and man can absorb DDT by eating the DDT-containing fish—this is the food chain effect. The concentrations of DDT usually become higher as it progresses up the food chain, an effect commonly called biological concentration. Some DDT also returns to the ocean through excretion from fish, or simply when the fish dies. DDT residues survive this long journey because of their great stability. DDT is removed from the environment at each stage through degradation in soil, in water, and in living organisms.

Notice that we chose *not* to include in the model an explicit representation of the higher levels of the food chain—for example, fish-eating birds and human beings. This exclusion does not invalidate the accounting of DDT flows because the amounts of DDT that actually enter terrestrial organisms are very small relative to the flows included in the model. (The excluded small flows are important to ecosystem stability, however, because they are relatively concentrated.)

There is reasonable consensus that Figure 3-1 does in fact represent the flow of DDT in the environment. Some disagreement may exist about the relative importance of DDT transportation in rivers, of the sedimentation of DDT in oceans, of the uptake of DDT in plants, and of local or regional differences in DDT concentration, but by and large the heated discussions on DDT do not

[4] D. A. Ratcliffe, "Decrease in Eggshell Weight in Certain Birds of Prey," *Nature,* vol. 215 (1967), p. 208, and D. B. Peakall, "Pesticides and the Reproduction of Birds," *Scientific American,* April 1970, p. 72.
[5] W. J. Hayes, Jr., "Monitoring Food and People for Pesticide Content," in National Academy of Sciences, National Research Council, *Scientific Aspects of Pest Control,* Publication no. 1402 (Washington, D.C., 1966); hereafter cited as NAS-NRC, *Scientific Aspects.*

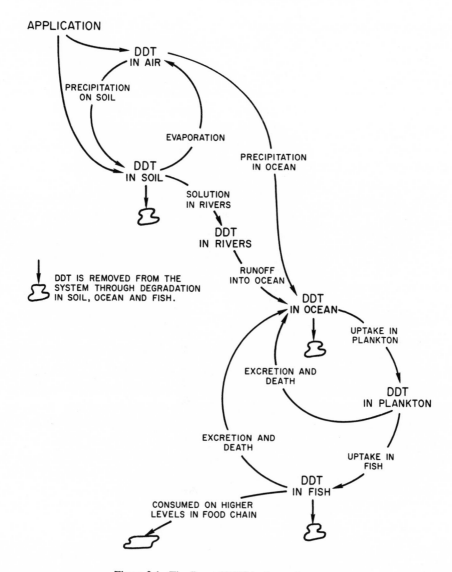

APPLICATION

DDT
IN AIR

PRECIPITATION
ON SOIL

EVAPORATION

DDT
IN SOIL

PRECIPITATION
IN OCEAN

SOLUTION
IN RIVERS

DDT
IN RIVERS

DDT IS REMOVED FROM THE
SYSTEM THROUGH DEGRADATION
IN SOIL, OCEAN AND FISH.

RUNOFF
INTO OCEAN

DDT
IN OCEAN

UPTAKE IN
PLANKTON

EXCRETION AND
DEATH

DDT
IN PLANKTON

EXCRETION AND
DEATH

UPTAKE IN
FISH

DDT
IN FISH

CONSUMED ON HIGHER
LEVELS IN FOOD CHAIN

Figure 3-1   The flow of DDT in the environment

question the structure outlined here. The disagreement occurs over the precise numerical values involved in the processes illustrated in Figure 3-1. For instance, how fast does DDT break down? How much of it sediments? At what rate does it evaporate? By what factor does it concentrate in fish?

In the following section, we describe the derivation of the structure shown in Figure 3-1 and indicate the choice of parameter values that we consider most reasonable. Since so little agreement exists concerning the actual numerical values, we later employ simulation analyses of the model to test the sensitivity of our conclusions to much higher and lower assumed values for each parameter in the model.

A Formalized Model of the DDT Flow

As we proceed in our verbal discussion of the different segments of the DDT flow, we shall accompany each section with a formalized flow diagram as a graphic restatement of the verbal assumptions discussed in the corresponding section. The flow diagram format used is one that corresponds precisely to the mathematical equations used for expressing our assumptions.[6]

The Application of DDT. After the factory production of DDT, the chemical is transported to the application area, where it is diluted and then used.

The application rate AR[7] equals the number of metric tons of DDT used per year.[8] For this inflow rate, we use historical data for the period 1940-1970, as shown in Figure 3-2. Indicative of the lack of physical knowledge about DDT is the fact that not even the global production of DDT is known precisely. The figures used here were obtained by taking the U.S. production of DDT and multiplying it by two. This approximation, suggested by the Study of Critical Environment Problems (SCEP), gives a rough upper limit of the total world production.[9]

According to the World Health Organization, 35,000 tons[10]—roughly 20 percent of the estimated total annual production of 150,000 tons[11] of DDT—is used for malaria control. In this use, the DDT is sprayed directly onto the inside walls of housing. These applications probably involve small *direct* losses to the atmosphere because the amount sprayed presumably settles immediately on the interior surfaces of the sprayed dwelling. The losses are considerably larger, however, for the remaining DDT, which is applied to cropland and forests through spraying (typically a pound of DDT per acre per year). G. M. Woodwell found in tests in New England forests that even in still weather and in the open as much as 50 percent of the amount sprayed never reached the ground but was dispersed in the air as very fine particles.[12] The amount of DDT that actually reaches the target depends on the wind and other meteorological conditions, the particle size, and the type of wake created around the airplane. It seems safe to assume that the fraction of DDT that remains in the atmosphere for extended periods is between 0.1 and 0.9, with 0.4 as a best estimate of the global average. Thus in Figure 3-3 we indicate the airborne fraction ABF of 0.4 as the determinant of the relative rates of application to air and soil. (We chose the airborne fraction ABF lower

---

[6] The system dynamics flow diagram notations are described in Chapter 2 and summarized in Figure 2-2.

[7] The capitalized abbreviations are the shorthand notations used in the computer program equations. A complete listing of the program is given in the appendix to this chapter.

[8] Note that DDT is measured in metric tons. All rates in this chapter are measured in tons per year; all levels (that is, storages) are measured in tons.

[9] SCEP, *Man's Impact*, p. 259.

[10] U.S. Department of Health, Education, and Welfare (HEW), *The Continuing Need for DDT in Anti-Malaria Programs* (Atlanta, Ga., 1971); hereafter cited as HEW, *Continuing Need for DDT*.

[11] SCEP, *Man's Impact*, p. 131.

[12] G. M. Woodwell, "Toxic Substances and Ecological Cycles," *Scientific American*, March 1967, p. 216.

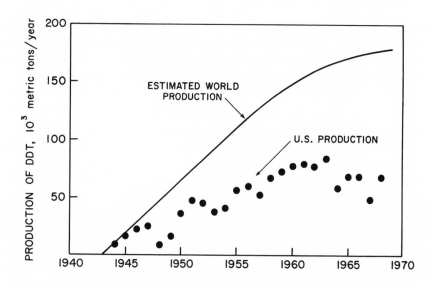

Figure 3-2   The historical production of DDT
Adapted from Study of Critical Environmental Problems,
Man's Impact on the Global Environment (*Cambridge,*
Mass.: The M.I.T. Press, 1970), *p. 259.*

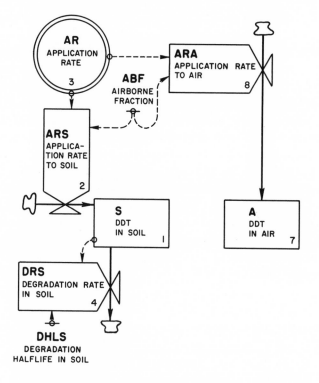

Figure 3-3   Application of DDT

than 0.5 because of the smaller losses involved in malaria eradication programs.) The upper and lower limits given for the parameter estimate are those actually employed in the simulation analyses to test the model's sensitivity to errors,[13] as are all other upper and lower bounds indicated throughout this paper.

DDT in Soil.   The amount of sprayed DDT that reaches its target thus settles on walls, on plants, or on the soil.

The DDT can be removed from walls only through evaporation, physical washing of the small DDT crystals to the soil, or on-the-spot degradation of the DDT into harmless substances. The same holds true for the DDT that settles on plants. In this case, however, there is an additional effect operating: some DDT falls onto the soil with the leaves at the end of the growing season.

That negligible amounts of DDT are removed from the sprayed area through the harvesting of crops can be inferred from the fact that the U.S. average total dietary intake of chlorinated hydrocarbons per person in 1968 was 0.072 mg per day.[14] If we make the assumption that all of this is DDT, that all of it comes from the consumption of crops, and finally that the total world population has the same uptake as U.S. citizens, the upper limit for the total human consumption of DDT from crops is about 100 tons per year. This is of course negligible compared with the 150,000 tons per year of DDT used.

The degradation of DDT into harmless material (through chemical decomposition, photodecomposition, and biological metabolism) is a very slow process under most conditions. Nash and Woolson mixed DDT uniformly into testbeds of soil and measured the decrease of DDT concentration in the soils, which were left undisturbed to minimize the evaporation over a sixteen-year period.[15] They found that the halflife—that is, the time for half of the original amount of DDT to disappear—varied with the soil type and the application density from 2.5 years to 35 years, with a best average estimate of 10.5 years. Because of the low evaporation and because no crops were removed from the soils, we took 10.5 years as an approximation for the degradation halflife of DDT in soil.

Neglecting evaporation for the moment, DDT does not seem to move after it has come in contact with soil particles except when the soil particles themselves move. Harris let water percolate through a column of soil, the top layers of which were mixed with DDT.[16] Measurements before and after the water treatment showed that the DDT had not moved in the column during the experiment. The reason is probably that DDT is bound very strongly to the soil particles and is only slightly soluble in water.

[13] See p. 79.

[14] U.S. Department of Health, Education, and Welfare (HEW), *Pesticides and Their Relationship to Environmental Health,* Report of the Secretary's Commission, pts. 1 and 2 (Washington, D.C., 1969), p. 135; hereafter cited as HEW, *Pesticides and Their Relationship.*

[15] R. G. Nash and E. A. Woolson, "Persistence of Chlorinated Hydrocarbon Insecticides in Soils," *Science,* vol. 157 (1967), p. 924.

[16] G. I. Harris, "Movement of Pesticides in Soil," *Journal of Agricultural and Food Chemistry,* vol. 17 (1969), p. 81.

The DDT can be carried away, however, when soil particles or pesticide crystallites themselves move because of wind or water erosion. That the washing effect of water is effective in removing pesticide particles from plant surfaces was shown by Mann and Chopra, who demonstrated that a washing of cabbage reduced the amount of residues on the plant by 94-97 percent.[17]

These conclusions, that DDT degrades slowly and is easily washed *onto* the soil but not further, indicate that most of the DDT that remains on land will be found on and in the soil throughout most of its long life. This assumption is strengthened by the fact that leaves fall to the ground every year, carrying with them any DDT on their surfaces.

Because of the relative immobility of DDT particles, we treated the DDT on walls, on plants, and on soil as one entity (DDT in soil S) with a common degradation halflife (degradation halflife in soil DHLS) equal to 10 years (bounded by 3 and 30 years) when there is no erosion, no removal through harvesting, and minimal evaporation.

Figure 3-3 shows the flow diagram segment incorporating the preceding relationships. The amount of DDT in soil S is reduced by the degradation rate in soil DRS, which is proportional to the amount of DDT actually stored in the soil. The relationship is of the type that displays exponential decay, namely,

$$\text{Rate} = (\text{amount stored}) / (1.5 \times \text{halflife}).$$

(The numerical factor 1.5 is inserted to achieve an approximate conversion of the "50 percent reduction" halflife to the "1/e reduction" halflife implicit in the mathematical relationship.)

Removal of DDT Through Rivers. Because of the tight binding of pesticide residues to soil particles, it has been suggested that the general pollution of water by pesticides occurs through the transport of soil particles to which the residues are attached.[18] However, there is reason to believe that the amount of DDT transported to the ocean via rivers is small. By assuming that all the river runoff from all the continents of the world contains the maximum concentration of DDT residue ever observed in rivers (0.1 ppb), SCEP estimates that not more than 100 tons per year—one thousandth of the annual production of DDT—reaches the ocean by surface runoff.[19]

Thus the solution halflife SHL of DDT, that is, the time to remove 50 percent of the DDT in soil S *only* by suspension of particles in rivers, is of the order of 500 years. This value is of course only a very rough estimate. However, all we need to know is that this process is very slow indeed compared to evaporation and degradation and that solution in rivers is therefore not an important mechanism for removing DDT from soil.

[17] G. S. Mann and S. L. Chopra, "Residues of Carbaryl on Crops," *Pesticides Monitoring Journal,* vol. 2 (1969), p. 163.
[18] E. P. Lichtenstein et al., "Toxicity and Fate of Insecticide Residues in Water," *Archives of Environmental Health,* vol. 12 (1966), p. 199.
[19] SCEP, *Man's Impact,* p. 132.

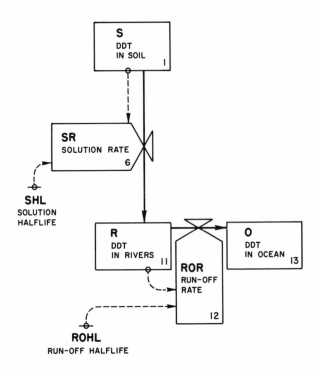

Figure 3-4   The movement of DDT from soil to
the ocean via rivers

Once suspended in river water, the DDT in rivers R is rapidly transferred to the ocean. The average turnover periods for the world's terrestrial water in rivers and soil moisture are, respectively, 2 weeks and 2-50 weeks.[20] We assumed a runoff halflife ROHL of 0.1 years. Because of its short stay in river water, we disregarded the degradation of DDT occurring in this medium. These assumptions are represented graphically in Figure 3-4.

Evaporation of DDT from Soil.   In malaria eradication programs it is found necessary to apply DDT to interior surfaces of houses every six months to obtain continuous protection for the inhabitants.[21]

Similarly, a large-scale monitoring program by the U.S. Department of Agriculture (USDA), especially in the cotton-growing areas of the Mississippi Delta, reports that DDT does not appear to build up in the topsoil.[22] In other words, these field experiments indicate that DDT used in agriculture disappears from the topsoil and plants before the next growing (and spraying) season starts, that is, within a year.

[20] K. Szesztay, "The Hydrosphere and the Human Environment," (Wellington, New Zealand, 1970).

[21] HEW, *Continuing Need for DDT.*

[22] J. W. Gentry, "Monitoring the Agricultural Use of Pesticides," in NAS-NRC, *Scientific Aspects,* p. 303.

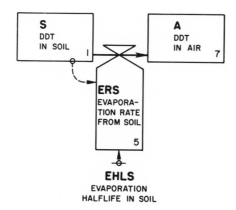

Figure 3-5 The evaporation of DDT

It should be noted that the field conditions under which the USDA monitoring was performed were different from those in the degradation experiments by Nash and Woolson cited earler.[23] Under field conditions the evaporation was large because the DDT was not mixed *into* the soil but was simply sprayed onto it.

Thus practical experience with DDT indicates that large fractions of the pesticide disappear in a time period of 1-2 years; that is, the actual halflife of DDT in soil is much shorter than that which can be explained from degradation and washing into rivers alone. This discrepancy suggests that there must be an additional mechanism that removes significant amounts of DDT from a sprayed area.

It seems reasonable to assume that this mechanism is the evaporation of DDT from the sprayed surfaces, a hypothesis substantiated by two additional pieces of information. First, it is an experimental fact that substantial amounts of DDT do occur in the atmosphere. Risebrough observed pesticides in the air over Barbados, an area remote from the agricultural use of DDT.[24] Of course, all this DDT may be due to actual losses during aerial spraying.

Second, Lloyd-Jones measured the evaporation of radioactive DDT solutions from glass plates and found an evaporation rate suggesting field-scale evaporation rates on the order of pounds per acre per year.[25] Although evaporation from glass is quite different from evaporation from soil, plants, and walls, Lloyd-Jones's observations seem to indicate that evaporation actually does occur, and possibly even rapidly enough to explain the disappearance of DDT from fields between two growing seasons and from the interior surfaces of houses in an equally short period of time.

As for the actual rate at which the evaporation from soil takes place, we could do nothing but rely on these rough indications in estimating the evaporation

[23] Nash and Woolson, "Persistence."
[24] R. W. Risebrough et al., "Pesticides: Transatlantic Movements in the Northeast Trades," *Science,* vol. 159 (1968), p. 1233.
[25] C. P. Lloyd-Jones, "Evaporation of DDT," *Nature,* vol. 229 (1971), p. 65.

halflife of DDT in soil EHLS. We assumed that the evaporation halflife is 2 years. Simulation was used to test the implications of values as low as 0.5 year and as high as 10 years.

Figure 3-5 shows the assumed evaporation mechanism (the evaporation rate ERS is assumed to be proportional to the amount of DDT actually stored in the soil S). Later we show that the model's behavior is not highly sensitive to changes in the evaporation halflife in soil EHLS over the interval tested; that is, the results were roughly the same for any value selected from this interval of uncertainty in the evaporation halflife in soil EHLS.

But as noted, the evaporation mechanism is purely hypothetical. We found no reference to direct measurements to prove that evaporation actually does occur at high rates from soil.[26]

The Precipitation of DDT from the Atmosphere.   From the discussion of losses both during application and through the evaporation mechanism, it follows that a large fraction of the sprayed DDT finally enters the atmosphere. Once there, the DDT molecules become highly mobile and can move great distances before they fall to the ground—as shown by the measurement of pesticide residues in the air at Barbados by Risebrough[27] and by the evidence of DDT in fish, animals, and humans in the Arctic and Antarctic.[28]

Experience with radioactive debris injected into the troposphere by nuclear explosions has established that the mean halflife of residence in the atmosphere for small particles ranges from a few days to about a month. Following Woodwell,[29] we assumed that these data also apply to pesticide crystallites and pesticides adsorbed to dust particles. We thus concluded that, once injected, DDT particles remain in the lower atmosphere for a period—the precipitation halflife PHL—varying between a few days and a month. In that time they can easily move around the globe.

The amount of pesticide degraded in the air by sunlight and reactive compounds is unknown.[30] However, given the short residence time (2 weeks) compared with the degradation halflife in soil (10 years), it seems safe to assume that the amount of DDT degraded in the atmosphere is small; hence it was neglected.

The ultimate fate of the pesticide particles is thus to settle back to earth, either in rain or through gravitation. The precipitation rate is governed by the

---

[26] The following experiment would give a good, direct estimate of the actual evaporation halflife in soil: A tract of land, preferably secluded from other areas where DDT is used, could be covered with some impermeable membrane (for example, plastic or concrete) and several inches of sterile soil spread out on top of it and kept inactive there for the duration of the experiment. If the soil is then sprayed with radioactively marked DDT, one can measure the activity as a function of time, and then easily infer the evaporation halflife of DDT from soil. This is so because all the DDT that has disappeared must have done so through evaporation. The impermeable membrane prohibits any leaking of DDT downward, and—although degradation will be low because of the lack of microorganisms in the sterilized soil—the breakdown that does occur does not disturb the measurement result because the radioactive breakdown products will remain in the soil.

[27] Risebrough, "Pesticides."

[28] T. J. Peterle, "DDT in Antarctic Snow," *Nature,* vol. 224 (1969), p. 620.

[29] Woodwell, "Toxic Substances."

[30] HEW, *Pesticides and Their Relationship.*

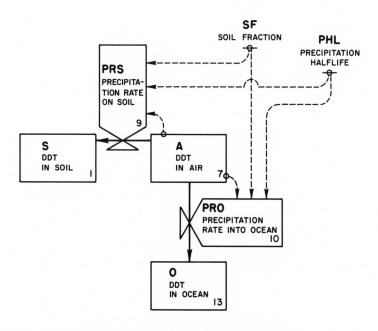

Figure 3-6 Precipitation of DDT from the air

precipitation halflife PHL which we chose to equal 0.05 years. Values from 0.01 to 0.2 years were used in the sensitivity analyses.

A certain fraction of the DDT precipitates on land. This fraction—the soil fraction SF—was assumed to be 30 percent, since that percentage of the globe is covered by land, and we assumed that the downpour of DDT is uniformly distributed. The rest, 70 percent, was assumed to fall into the sea. It is, of course, not true that DDT precipitates uniformly all over the globe; the downpour is certainly heavier close to the user area, that is, over land. However, this distinction can be simulated by changing the value of the soil fraction SF in the computer simulation, and an actual change of the soil fraction SF (to 0.8) had only a small effect on the results. The DDT that falls on land once more enters the processes of degradation, evaporation, and solution in rivers already described. The part that falls into the ocean, however, enters a different segment of the chain.

Figure 3-6 represents the assumptions about DDT in the atmosphere. The evaporation rate ERS was assumed to be proportional to the amount of DDT actually stored in the soil S; similarly the precipitation rates on soil PRS and into the ocean PRO were assumed to be proportional to the amount of DDT in the air A.

DDT in the Ocean.[31] When the DDT reaches the ocean, most of it is assumed to dissolve rather than to sediment out on the bottom. Solution still takes place

---

[31] Large freshwater bodies are assumed to be a part of the "ocean" in this discussion; smaller freshwater bodies belong to the "river" category. The determining property is the turnover rate of the water in the body: lakes with fast turnover are "rivers," and lakes with slow turnover belong to the "ocean."

because the surface layers of the ocean are not yet saturated with DDT. It has been estimated that the mixed layer of the ocean (the part of the ocean that is mixed by currents within a time period of roughly one year, that is, the upper 300 feet) is capable of accommodating ten times the total amount of DDT produced to date.[32] This is true in spite of the extremely low solubility of DDT in sea water (about 1 part per billion by weight).

Although sedimentation of DDT in time periods as short as one month has been observed experimentally in freshwater ponds by W. R. Bridges and by Cope,[33] we assumed that this is irrelevant to the solution of DDT in the ocean because of differences in concentration. The present concentration of DDT in the mixed layer of the ocean is estimated by SCEP to be 0.005 parts per billion,[34] whereas the freshwater pond experiments were done with DDT concentrations of 20 and 20,000 parts per billion, respectively.

It is probably not correct to assume that DDT becomes uniformly distributed in the mixed layer. DDT is highly soluble in hydrocarbons, and since a thin layer of oil can often be found on top of the ocean, it may be expected that much DDT will be found in oil layers. We chose to ignore this effect, however, and assumed that the dissolved DDT is uniformly distributed in the mixed layer. (The importance of variations in the mixing volume can be investigated through simulation analyses by varying the mass of the mixed layer MML, which is roughly equal to 3×10^{16} tons.)[35]

As mentioned, the average concentration of DDT in the ocean CO is very low (around 10^{-12} by weight). Therefore, the evaporation of DDT from the ocean is probably negligible in spite of the enormous area covered by the sea, and we chose to neglect this evaporation. If a significant amount of evaporation does occur, the DDT will simply cycle again through the atmosphere and settle back on land or water.

When one disregards evaporation and sedimentation, the only way in which significant amounts of DDT are removed from the ocean is through degradation. The process is slow, however, since DDT seems to be even more stable in seawater than in soil. Again, direct experiments have not been performed, but experts estimate the degradation halflife of DDT in ocean DHLO to be long, "certainly of the order of years, perhaps even decades."[36] The degradation halflife is probably longer in cold and nutrient-poor waters than in warm, rich waters. Biological degradation is also slower in deep waters, as was demonstrated clearly when a research submarine was rescued after ten months at a depth of 5,000 feet. Food

[32] SCEP, *Man's Impact*, p. 113.

[33] See W. R. Bridges et al., "Persistence of DDT and Its Metabolites in a Farm Pond," *Transactions of the American Fisheries Society,* vol. 93 (1964), p. 127, and O. B. Cope, "Agricultural Chemicals and Fresh-water Ecological Systems," in *Research in Pesticides,* ed. C. O. Chichester (New York: Academic Press, 1965), p. 115.

[34] SCEP, *Man's Impact*, p. 135.

[35] Ibid., p. 134.

[36] United Nations, Food and Agriculture Organization (FAO), *Seminar on Methods of Detection, Measurement and Monitoring of Pollutants in the Marine Environment* (Rome, 1970).

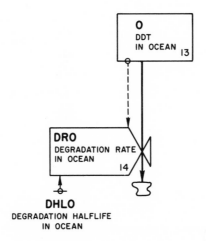

Figure 3-7   Degradation of DDT in the
ocean

found aboard the ship was completely unspoiled, and researchers concluded that the rate of biological degradation processes is an average of ten to one hundred times slower in the deep sea than it is on land.[37]

On the basis of the preceding information and the discussion on the degradation halflife of DDT in soil, we chose a degradation halflife in ocean DHLO of 15 years (varied between 8 years and 80 years in the sensitivity simulations). Thus the steady downpour of DDT from the atmosphere and the continued runoff from land slowly increase the DDT concentration in the upper layers of the ocean, while the only significant process removing the DDT is degradation. The degradation rate of DDT in the ocean DRO was assumed to be proportional to the amount of DDT in the ocean O. Figure 3-7 shows the corresponding flow diagram.

DDT in Plankton.   There is now a considerable body of evidence to suggest that some form of equilibrium exists between the concentration of DDT in water and in marine animals. This seems to be especially true for the smallest organisms in the food chain, the plankton. The concentration of DDT in plankton comes into equilibrium with respect to the concentration of DDT in the surrounding water within a matter of seconds.[38] The equilibrium concentration in plankton CP is typically some 2,000 times larger than the concentration in the surrounding ocean CO, since the typical concentration of DDT in plankton CP is 10 parts per billion and the typical concentration of DDT in the ocean is 0.005 parts per billion.[39] An

[37] H. W. Jannasch et al., "Microbial Degradation of Organic Matter in the Deep Sea," *Science,* vol. 171 (1971), p. 672.
[38] A. Sodergren, "Uptake and Accumulation of C-14 DDT by Chlorella Sp. (Chlorophyceae)," *Oikos,* vol. 19 (1968), p. 126.
[39] SCEP, *Man's Impact,* p. 134.

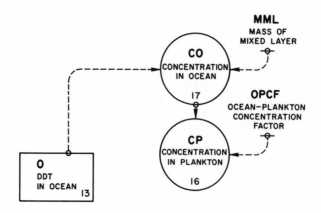

Figure 3-8   The concentration of DDT in plankton

ocean-plankton concentration factor OPCF of the order of 1,000 can be inferred from measurements by Woodwell.[40] In a U.S. East Coast estuary the DDT concentration was estimated to be 0.05 parts per billion in the water and measured to be 40 parts per billion in plankton.

Other sources give somewhat different values, but it seemed safe to assume that the ocean plankton concentration factor OPCF lies between 1,000 and 10,000 with a best estimate of 2,000. Figure 3-8 shows the relevant flow diagram.

DDT Uptake in Fish.   Fish absorb some DDT directly from the water in which they swim, but their major exposure to DDT is through their food. This was established for brook trout by Macek and Korn, who observed the increase in DDT concentration in trout (a) when kept in "clean" water and fed DDT-contaminated food, and (b) when kept in DDT-contaminated water and fed "clean" food. It was found that the trout absorbed 10-100 times more DDT in case (a) than in case (b).[41] Most of the world's fish live in the mixed layer of the ocean in areas where there are only a few trophic levels in the food chain.[42] Thus it was acceptable for purposes of this model to view the marine ecosystem as a two-level food chain in which the animals on the top level (fish) eat the organisms on the lower level (plankton).

The DDT uptake rate in fish URF, which is the rate at which DDT enters fish, is determined by the DDT concentration in plankton and the amount of plankton eaten by the total population of fish each year. A typical feeding rate is 1.5 percent of body weight per day, or 10 times a fish's body weight per year. Since

[40] G. M. Woodwell, "DDT Residues in an East Coast Estuary: A Case of Biological Concentration of a Persistent Insecticide," *Science,* vol. 157 (1967), p. 821.
[41] K. S. Macek and S. Korn, "Significance of the Food Chain in DDT Accumulation by Fish," *Journal of the Fisheries Research Board of Canada,* vol. 27/28 (1970), p. 1496.
[42] J. H. Ryther, "Photosynthesis and Fish Production in the Sea," *Science,* vol. 166 (1969), p. 72.

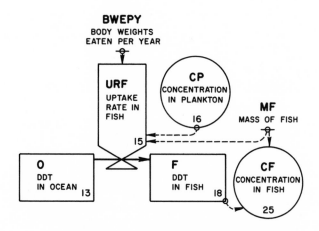

Figure 3-9   Consumption of DDT by fish

the total mass of fish MF is about 6×10^8 tons,[43] it may be assumed that 6×10^9 tons of plankton are eaten by fish annually. Multiplying that amount by the concentration of DDT in plankton CP gives the yearly uptake of DDT. Figure 3-9 expresses these assumptions.

DDT Elimination from Fish.   Having entered the fish through food or from the water, DDT can be removed from the living animal in two forms. First, it may simply be excreted, that is, returned to the ocean still in the form of DDT. Second, it may be degraded in the fish and excreted as a harmless substance. It has been established empirically—as exemplified by Woodwell's study, cited above—that these two processes produce an equilibrium concentration in fish CF 10-100 times larger than the concentration in the plankton upon which they feed.[44]

The body concentration of DDT following a sudden cessation in the uptake of DDT is known from experiments with goldfish[45] and with bluegills and goldfish[46] to decrease approximately exponentially, indicating that the excretion rate from fish EXF is roughly proportional to the amount of DDT still stored in the fish F.

The average excretion halflife EXHL for DDT from goldfish is reported to be 29 days by Grzenda, while Gakstatter and Weiss obtained somewhat larger values for bluegills and goldfish.[47] From their curves it seems that there are in fact two superimposed exponential decays, one with a short halflife ($\approx$ days) and one with a much longer halflife ($\approx$ months). Durham finds an excretion halflife of the

[43] Ibid.

[44] Woodwell, "DDT Residues."

[45] A. R. Grzenda et al., "The Uptake, Metabolism, and Elimination of Chlorinated Residues by Goldfish Fed a C-DDT Contaminated Diet," *Transactions of the American Fisheries Society,* vol. 102 (1970), p. 385.

[46] J. H. Gakstatter and C. M. Weiss, "The Elimination of DDT-C, Dieldrin-C, and Lindane-C from Fish Following a Single Sublethal Exposure in Aquaria," ibid., vol. 96 (1967), p. 301.

[47] Grzenda, "The Uptake," and Gakstatter and Weiss, "The Elimination of DDT-C."

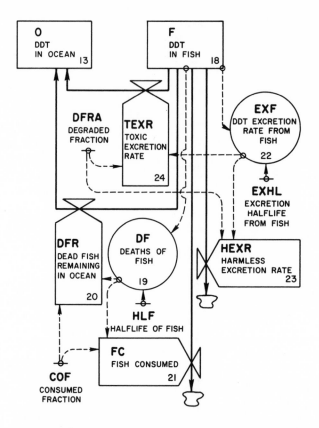

Figure 3-10   DDT movements from fish to the ocean

order of 100 days for rats, while the U.S. Department of Health, Education, and Welfare, in a review of existing results, reports halflives on the order of one year for rhesus monkeys and steers.[48] The excretion halflife for DDT in man is about 180 days.[49]

We chose an excretion halflife EXHL for fish of 0.3 years but realize that the correct value may be anywhere between 0.05 years and 0.7 years.

Even less is known about whether DDT is excreted as toxic DDT molecules or as harmless degradation products. However, given the fact that the degradation halflife of DDT in soil DHLS is as long as 10 years, it seems reasonable to assume that most of the DDT excreted from fish is still not degraded to harmless material. Instead, it simply goes back into the reservoir of DDT already in the ocean. Undoubtedly, some fraction of the DDT is degraded to harmless material before excretion, and we hypothesize that the degraded fraction DFRA is 0.1. It should

[48] See New York Academy of Sciences, *Biological Effects of Pesticides in Mammalian Systems*, Annals of the New York Academy of Sciences, vol. 160 (1969), p. 184, and HEW, *Continuing Need for DDT*, pp. 275-294.

[49] Hayes, "Monitoring Food and People."

be stressed that this is nothing but a guess. However, it is quite satisfactory to rely on a guess in this case because the value of the degraded fraction DFRA is without importance for our simulations. This conclusion follows from SCEP's estimate that only 600 tons of DDT are currently stored in the world's fish while 500,000 tons exist in the world's oceans.[50] Thus even over a fifty-year period only a very small fraction of the total ocean DDT moves from the ocean into fish. Hence, as far as the total ocean concentration of DDT is concerned, it does not matter whether the small amount returned from fish to the ocean is in the form of DDT or harmless degradation products.

The same type of consideration holds for the amount of DDT lost by deaths of fish DF. This rate of loss of DDT includes the fish caught by fish-eating birds and the human consumption of fish. Based on Ryther's estimates that the annual production of fish is 240 million tons, of which man catches 60 million tons and birds catch an equivalent amount,[51] we put the consumed fraction COF—the fraction of dead fish that does not remain in the ocean—equal to 0.5.

Again, because it is unimportant, we chose to assume that all the DDT in dead fish remaining in the sea is returned to the ocean and is not degraded. The amount lost by deaths of fish DF is determined by the average halflife of fish HLF, which would typically be 3 years (1 year to 10 years).

The final segment of our flow diagram is shown in Figure 3-10.

DDT in Higher Animals. The fish consumed FC includes the fish caught by fish-eating birds and the human consumption of fish, and it is in part by this mechanism that DDT enters higher animals and man.

The concentration of DDT reaches still higher values in this next level of the food chain. Through feeding on fish contaminated with DDT, birds can acquire a concentration of DDT in their own bodies higher by a factor of 10-100 than the concentration in the fish. The same effect occurs in man. This final link in the food chain was not explicitly included in our simulation, although it is the most important to man, because there is still so much disagreement about the actual effect of DDT in the bodies of higher organisms. It is urgent that the short-term and long-term effects of DDT on human health and on other animals be clarified soon. In the meantime we have refrained from making quantitative statements about the accumulation of DDT beyond the level of fish. It can be safely assumed, however, that the DDT accumulation outlined here for fish will be magnified by further biological concentration, after further time delays, in all fish-eating animals, from birds to human beings.

The Complete Model of the DDT System

In Figure 3-11 we have put together all the flow diagram segments developed in earlier sections to obtain a complete model of the flow of DDT in the environment.

---

[50] SCEP, *Man's Impact,* p. 135.
[51] Ryther, "Photosynthesis."

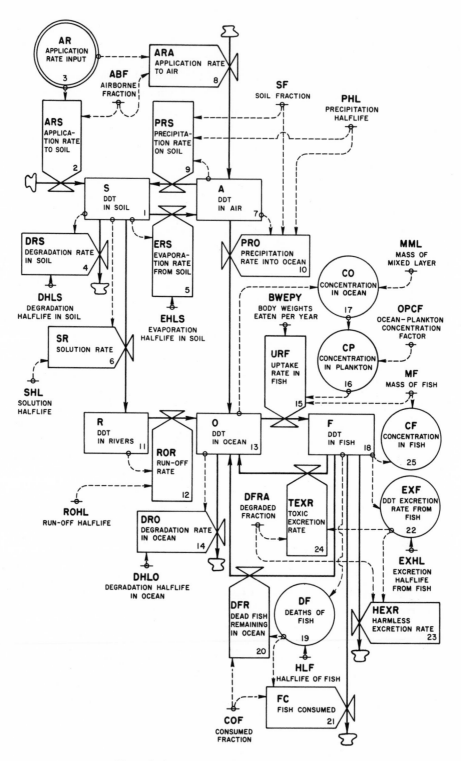

Figure 3-11 The flow of DDT in the environment

To avoid getting lost in all the details, it is probably worthwhile at this point to emphasize that the flow diagram is nothing but a schematic representation of the verbal description of the "DDT system" presented in earlier sections. Each element in the flow diagram can be defined by a simple mathematical equation that expresses the relationship between that element and other connecting elements. An example of such an equation is the expression for the level of DDT in the air (see Figure 3-12).

A.K=A.J+(DT)(ARA.JK+ERS.JK−PRS.JK−PRO.JK)

A	– DDT IN AIR (TONS)
ARA	– APPLICATION RATE TO AIR (TONS/YEAR)
ERS	– EVAPORATION RATE FROM SOIL (TONS/YEAR)
PRS	– PRECIPITATION RATE ON SOIL (TONS/YEAR)
PRO	– PRECIPITATION RATE INTO OCEAN (TONS/YEAR)
DT	– TIME INCREMENT IN COMPUTATION (YEARS)

This equation specifies that the level of DDT in the air at any time K (A.K) is equal to the level at the previous time J (A.J) plus the amount that has entered the atmosphere through evaporation and application minus the amount precipitated on soil or into the ocean in the intervening time period. The amount evaporated equals the current evaporation rate (ERS.JK) multiplied by the length of time that rate has pertained (DT—the time difference between times J and K). The amount applied directly to the air through spraying equals the current appli-

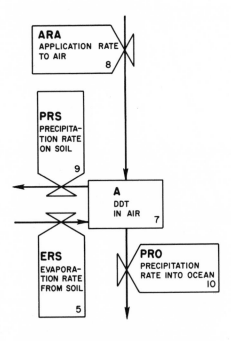

Figure 3-12 The flows of DDT to and from
the atmosphere

cation rate to air (ARA.JK), again multiplied by the time interval DT. Similarly, the amounts removed through precipitation on soil and into the ocean equal the appropriate rates (PRS.JK and PRO.JK) multiplied by DT.

A list of the simulation equations is given in the appendix to this chapter. The role of the computer is simply to begin with the level of DDT in each part of the ecosystem (soil, air, ocean, fish) at the initial time specified (1940) and then, on the basis of a given world DDT application rate, to follow the flow of DDT through each level as a function of time. Thus the levels and the flow rates are constantly changing throughout the simulation run. The levels are dependent on the past accumulation in that level and on the inflow and outflow rates. The rates in turn are dependent on the accumulations in the levels and on the numerical values assumed for halflives, airborne fraction, concentration fractions, and so forth.

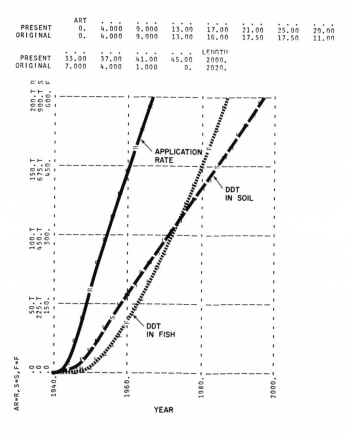

Figure 3-13 The effect of continually increasing the use of DDT

Note: In this and the following runs, the vertical axis gives the amounts of DDT in soil S (in metric tons) and in fish F (in tons) for the plotted application rate R (in tons per year). The letter T on the vertical axis represents 1,000 metric tons.

Simulation Results. Four examples of simulation outputs are shown in Figures 3-13 through 3-16. For each run, a different world application rate of DDT was assumed after 1971. Before 1971 the actual world application rate was taken, as illustrated previously in Figure 3-2. Because of the uncertainty in many of the model coefficients and because of the high level of aggregation (not representing the probable higher concentrations of DDT in coastal waters, for example), the results are not useful as precise predictions. Much more meaningful than the absolute levels or the precise timing of maximums in the different DDT concentrations are the relative magnitude and timing of responses to different policies. For all its imperfections it is fair to state that this model of DDT flow is at least superior to the intuitive estimates on which current DDT policy is based.

In Run 1 (Figure 3-13) the application rate of DDT continues to rise indefinitely, at roughly the same rate it has risen over the past decade. The levels of DDT in soil and in fish lag behind the application rate because of the time delays inherent in the DDT distribution processes. Both levels increase rapidly, however, and run off the scale of the graph. With this pattern of DDT application, the level

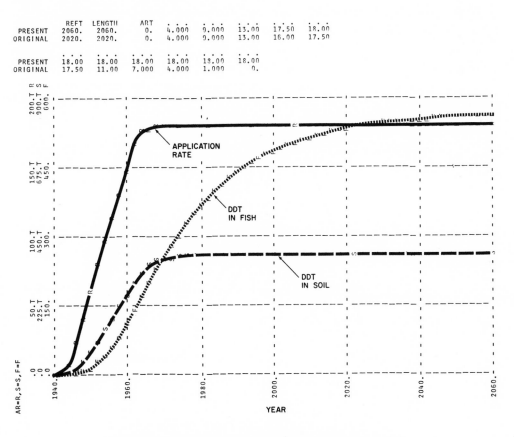

Figure 3-14 The effect of constant annual use of DDT from 1971

of DDT in fish doubles between 1971 and 1980 and reaches four times the 1971 level by 1990.

What would happen if the world decided to level off the application rate of DDT, holding it constant at about the present rate? Such a decision is simulated in Figure 3-14.

The amount of DDT in the soil levels off nearly as quickly as the application rate, but the DDT in fish continues to rise for more than fifty years after the application rate becomes constant. The final equilibrium value of DDT in fish is more than twice the 1971 value.

In Figure 3-15 the result of a world decision to phase out the use of DDT is depicted. The application rate decreases, starting in 1971, and reaches zero by the year 2000. However, because of the delays inherent in the numerous pathways DDT takes through the environment, the level in fish goes on rising for more than a decade after DDT usage reaches its peak. DDT in fish does not come back down to the 1971 level until 1995—a quarter of a century after the decision was made to decrease the application rate.

Suppose the use of DDT were stopped completely in 1971, all around the world. The result would be similar to that shown in Figure 3-16. The level of DDT in the soil would drop almost immediately. The level in fish would rise slightly for a few years and then gradually decrease. Even after fifty years there would still be

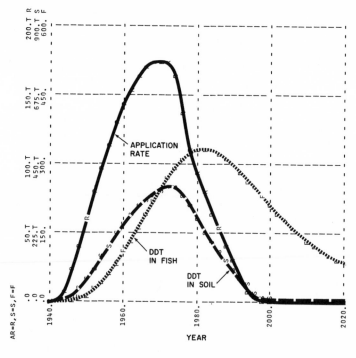

Figure 3-15 The effect of a gradual reduction, starting in 1971, in the use of DDT. The usage rate is assumed to reach zero by the year 2000.

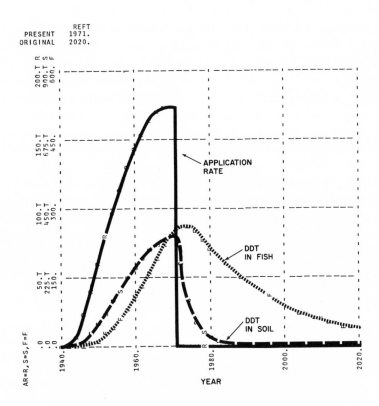

Figure 3-16   The effect of a complete ban on DDT in 1971

a measurable amount of DDT in fish, as the last long-lived molecules circulate through the natural distribution processes and into the food chain.

Sensitivity of Results to Parameter Changes.   In the discussion of the detailed steps of the distribution of DDT, we stressed the many uncertainties in the measurement of numerical values used in the simulation model. Given all these uncertainties, how confident can one be that the results shown in Figure 3-13 through 3-16 are relatively correct? We can answer that question by conducting a sensitivity analysis, by changing various numbers in the calculations within the total range of possible values suggested by the data. If a simple change in numbers alters the entire behavior pattern of the DDT model, one must regard the simulation results with suspicion until more certain data are obtained. If, on the other hand, an adjustment in numerical values has little effect on the behavior of the model, one can be more confident of the results and begin to use the simulation model as an input to policy decisions. In any case, the numbers used should be continually refined to increase confidence in the model.

The three runs shown in Figures 3-17, 3-18, and 3-19 provide an indication of the adequacy of the current knowledge about DDT flows. All three runs make the same assumption about future application rates. Figure 3-19 uses the average or best estimate value for each parameter, as described in the previous detailed presentation of DDT flows and summarized in Figure 3-20. Figure 3-17 shows the result of consistently choosing the "optimistic" extreme for every value in the model. It assumes that the halflife of DDT in each level is the minimum ever suggested, that concentration factors are minimized, while degradation into harmless products is maximized. Figure 3-18, on the other hand, takes the opposite extreme. It assumes the maximum possible halflife for DDT in each medium and chooses the most "pessimistic" value for all other constants. It should be emphasized that most scientists would agree on numbers very close to the "best estimate" run. The "optimistic" and "pessimistic" runs are included here only to demonstrate the most extreme results that are at all compatible with current knowledge. Thus they provide an indication of the reliability of the present "best estimate" model.

It is clear from Figures 3-17, 3-18, and 3-19 that the general behavior of the model is similar under all three sets of assumptions. In each case the level of DDT in fish continues to increase after the application of DDT has decreased. The time lag from the peak in application rate to the peak in accumulation of DDT in fish

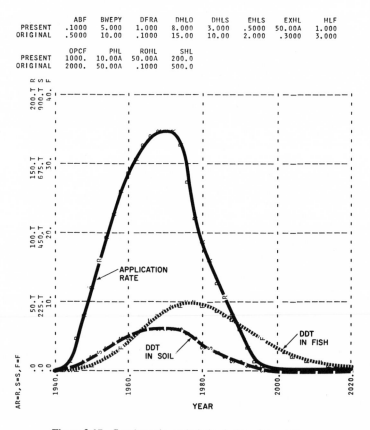

Figure 3-17   Consistently optimistic choice of parameters

ranges from 8 years in the "optimistic" run to 24 years in the "pessimistic" run. With the "optimistic" assumptions, the level of DDT in fish increases by 10 percent of the 1972 value before it begins to decline; with the "pessimistic" assumptions, it increases by 100 percent. In the "best estimate" run, which is probably the closest to reality, the DDT level in fish rises for 11 years after the cutback in application, and it increases by about 50 percent of the 1971 value before declining.

The overall similarity of the runs in Figures 3-17, 3-18, and 3-19 would suggest that our knowledge about the DDT system is indeed adequate to begin discussing the longer-term implications of DDT use. Some of these implications are listed in the following section. On the other hand, the figures also indicate that one must still be cautious about making exact quantitative predictions of future DDT levels. In particular, the actual value of the DDT level in fish is quite sensitive to the numerical assumptions made. (The vertical scales in Figures 3-17, 3-18, and 3-19 are the same for the DDT application rate and DDT in soil but very different for DDT in fish. The final maximum value of the DDT level in fish is 33,000 times greater in the "pessimistic" run than in the "optimistic" run.) Thus,

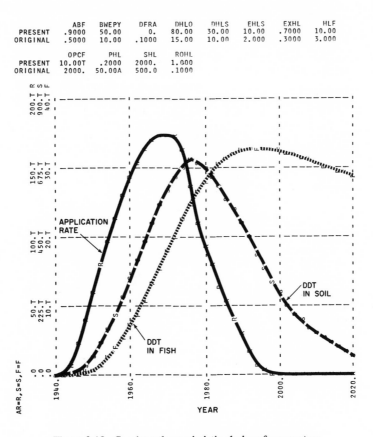

Figure 3-18 Consistently pessimistic choice of parameters

although we are able now to understand the general dynamic behavior of DDT in the biosphere, we are far from being able to make exact predictions of its future levels of accumulation. This dynamic model cannot be a refined predictive tool until better data become available on the actual dispersion and metabolic break-down of DDT in the various levels of the system.

The Policy Implications of the DDT Model. The main conclusions that can be drawn at this point about the movement of DDT in the environment are

1. Because of its dispersal, by means of soil erosion, air currents, ocean current, and the movements of fish, DDT can spread long distances from its point of application.
2. Because of its great stability and because of the delays inherent in natural processes, DDT appears in significant concentrations in the ocean-based food chain only several years after its original application on land.
3. Most important, the level of DDT concentrations in the food chain will continue to increase for several years after action is taken to decrease the rate of application.

The last point has profound policy implications. Suppose, for example, that the "best estimate" run is an accurate representation of the DDT system. Suppose also that damage to fish or to fish-eating birds (a function of the DDT level in

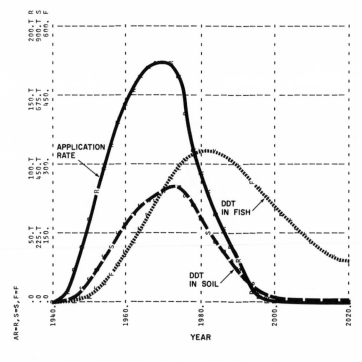

Figure 3-19   Best estimates used for all parameters

fish) finally became sufficient in 1971 to make society agree on a gradual elimination of the chemical as in Figure 3-19. In such a case, the level of DDT in fish would not decrease below the 1971 level for twenty-five years, long enough to exterminate any bird species whose fertility was already substantially decreased by the 1971 levels of DDT. This delayed response of DDT levels to corrective action calls for extreme caution. The time lags in the natural processes of DDT dispersal and degradation imply that extensive damage will be wrought on a species if reductions in the rate of DDT application are postponed until damage is first observed in the species' general population.

As already mentioned, these conclusions are generally applicable to other kinds of long-lived pollutants that can be concentrated biologically. In fact, the basic simulation model diagramed in Figure 3-11 could be used for most of this class of pollutants, with appropriate changes in all numerical constants, such as halflives in various levels. For example, a detailed system dynamics model of global mercury flows is presented in Chapter 4 of this volume.

The beneficial effects of DDT are immediate and local. Crop-eating pests and malarial mosquitoes are subdued, and there are gains in agricultural productivity or in the health of the populace. On the other hand, the harmful effects of DDT are widespread and delayed. The insecticide residues cross international boundaries and enter the food chains of the oceans, which are regarded as the common property of all nations. The total harmful effects to organisms other than those initially sprayed are not perceived until many years after the spraying. Thus it would seem that DDT, and other global pollutants of its class, might be the obvious first subjects for discussion by international environmental regulating

		Optimistic	Best Estimate	Pessimistic
ABF	Airborne fraction (dimensionless)	0.1	0.5	0.9
BWEPY	Body weights eaten per year (per year)	5	10	50
COF	Consumed fraction (dimensionless)	0.5	0.5	0.5
DFRA	Degraded fraction (dimensionless)	1	0.1	0
DHLO	Degradation halflife in ocean (years)	8	15	80
DHLS	Degradation halflife in soil (years)	3	10	30
EHLS	Evaporation halflife from soil (years)	0.5	2	10
EXHL	Excretion halflife from fish (years)	0.05	0.3	0.7
HLF	Halflife of fish (years)	1	3	10
MF	Mass of fish (tons)	6×10^8	6×10^8	6×10^8
MML	Mass of mixed layer (tons)	3×10^{16}	3×10^{16}	3×10^{16}
OPCF	Ocean-plankton concentration factor (dimensionless)	1000	2000	10000
PHL	Precipitation halflife (years)	0.01	0.05	0.2
ROHL	Runoff halflife (years)	0.05	0.1	1
SF	Soil fraction (dimensionless)	0.3	0.3	0.3
SHL	Solution halflife (years)	200	500	2000

Figure 3-20 Range of values used to test the sensitivity of the model

bodies. Since most long-lived pollutants are presently being released into the environment in enormous amounts and at exponentially increasing rates, the following steps should be carefully considered:

1. A temporary ceiling, fixing all emissions at or below their present rate until a final decision is made on permissible emission rates.

2. A detailed research effort to ascertain the real costs and benefits of use of the polluting substances and possible substitutes and to clarify their paths through the ecosystem.

3. An agreement on the safe level, if any, of the pollutant allowable at each point in the system, including air, fresh water, ocean water, and each trophic level of the food chain.

4. A careful determination of a scheme of pollutant usage, based on a dynamic analysis of the sort presented here, to assure that all immediate and future accumulations of the pollutant do not exceed safe standards.

5. A just distribution of the acceptable annual consumption of pollutant among those who must use it.

Appendix: Computer Program for the DDT Model

```
DDT IN SOIL

S.K=S.J+(DT)(ARS.JK+PRS.JK-DRS.JK-ERS.JK-SR.JK)        1, L
S=SI                                                   1.1, N
SI=0                                                   1.2, C
     S        - DDT IN SOIL (TONS)
     DT       - TIME INTERVAL BETWEEN EACH CALCULATION
                  (YEARS)
     ARS      - APPLICATION RATE TO SOIL (TONS/YEAR)
     PRS      - PRECIPITATION RATE ON SOIL (TONS/YEAR)
     DRS      - DEGRADATION RATE IN SOIL (TONS/YEAR)
     ERS      - EVAPORATION RATE FROM SOIL (TONS/YEAR)
     SR       - SOLUTION RATE (TONS/YEAR)

ARS.KL=AR.K*(1-ABF)                                    2, R
     ARS       - APPLICATION RATE TO SOIL (TONS/YEAR)
     AR        - APPLICATION RATE (TONS/YEAR)
     ABF       - AIRBORNE FRACTION (DIMENSIONLESS)

AR.K=TABHL(ART,TIME.K,1943,1998,5)*1E4*CLIP(0,1,       3, A
   TIME.K,REFT)
ART=0/4/9/13/16/17.5/17.5/11/7/4/1/0                   3.1, T
REFT=2020                                              3.2, C
ABF=.5                                                 3.3, C
     AR        - APPLICATION RATE (TONS/YEAR)
     TIME      - YEAR IN WHICH SIMULATION RUN INITIATES
                  (YEARS)
     ABF       - AIRBORNE FRACTION (DIMENSIONLESS)

DRS.KL=S.K/(1.5*DHLS)                                  4, R
DHLS=10                                                4.1, C
     DRS       - DEGRADATION RATE IN SOIL (TONS/YEAR)
     S         - DDT IN SOIL (TONS)
     DHLS      - DEGRADATION HALFLIFE IN SOIL (YEARS)

ERS.KL=S.K/(1.5*EHLS)                                  5, R
EHLS=2                                                 5.1, C
     ERS       - EVAPORATION RATE FROM SOIL (TONS/YEAR)
     S         - DDT IN SOIL (TONS)
     EHLS      - EVAPORATION HALFLIFE IN SOIL (YEARS)
```

```
SR.KL=S.K/(1.5*SHL)                                    6, R
SHL=500                                                6.1, C
     SR       - SOLUTION RATE (TONS/YEAR)
     S        - DDT IN SOIL (TONS)
     SHL      - SOLUTION HALFLIFE (YEARS)
```

DDT IN AIR

```
A.K=A.J+(DT)(ARA.JK+ERS.JK-PRS.JK-PRO.JK)              7, L
A=AI                                                   7.1, N
AI=0                                                   7.2, C
     A        - DDT IN AIR (TONS)
     DT       - TIME INTERVAL BETWEEN EACH CALCULATION
                 (YEARS)
     ARA      - APPLICATION RATE TO AIR (TONS/YEAR)
     ERS      - EVAPORATION RATE FROM SOIL (TONS/YEAR)
     PRS      - PRECIPITATION RATE ON SOIL (TONS/YEAR)
     PRO      - PRECIPITATION RATE INTO OCEAN (TONS/YEAR)
```

```
ARA.KL=AR.K*ABF                                        8, R
     ARA      - APPLICATION RATE TO AIR (TONS/YEAR)
     AR       - APPLICATION RATE (TONS/YEAR)
     ABF      - AIRBORNE FRACTION (DIMENSIONLESS)
```

```
PRS.KL=A.K*SF/(1.5*PHL)                                9, R
SF=.3                                                  9.1, C
PHL=.05                                                9.2, C
     PRS      - PRECIPITATION RATE ON SOIL (TONS/YEAR)
     A        - DDT IN AIR (TONS)
     SF       - SOIL FRACTION (DIMENSIONLESS)
     PHL      - PRECIPITATION HALFLIFE (YEARS)
```

```
PRO.KL=A.K*(1-SF)/(1.5*PHL)                            10, R
     PRO      - PRECIPITATION RATE INTO OCEAN (TONS/YEAR)
     A        - DDT IN AIR (TONS)
     SF       - SOIL FRACTION (DIMENSIONLESS)
     PHL      - PRECIPITATION HALFLIFE (YEARS)
```

DDT IN RIVERS

```
R.K=R.J+(DT)(SR.JK-ROR.JK)                             11, L
R=RI                                                   11.1, N
RI=0                                                   11.2, C
     R        - DDT IN RIVERS (TONS)
     DT       - TIME INTERVAL BETWEEN EACH CALCULATION
                 (YEARS)
     SR       - SOLUTION RATE (TONS/YEAR)
     ROR      - RUN-OFF RATE (TONS/YEAR)
```

```
ROR.KL=R.K/(1.5*ROHL)                                  12, R
ROHL=.1                                                12.1, C
     ROR      - RUN-OFF RATE (TONS/YEAR)
     R        - DDT IN RIVERS (TONS)
     ROHL     - RUN-OFF HALFLIFE (YEARS)
```

DDT IN OCEAN

```
O.K=O.J+(DT)(PRO.JK+ROR.JK+DFR.JK+TEXR.JK-DRO.JK-      13, L
  URF.JK)
O=OI                                                   13.1, N
OI=0                                                   13.2, C
     O        - DDT IN OCEAN (TONS)
     DT       - TIME INTERVAL BETWEEN EACH CALCULATION
                 (YEARS)
     PRO      - PRECIPITATION RATE INTO OCEAN (TONS/YEAR)
     ROR      - RUN-OFF RATE (TONS/YEAR)
     DFR      - DEAD FISH REMAINING IN OCEAN (TONS/YEAR)
     TEXR     - TOXIC EXCRETION RATE (TONS/YEAR)
     DRO      - DEGRADATION RATE IN OCEAN (TONS/YEAR)
     URF      - UPTAKE RATE IN FISH (TONS/YEAR)
```

```
DRO.KL=O.K/(1.5*DHLO)                                    14, R
DHLO=15                                                  14.1, C
     DRO    - DEGRADATION RATE IN OCEAN (TONS/YEAR)
     O      - DDT IN OCEAN (TONS)
     DHLO   - DEGRADATION HALFLIFE IN OCEAN (YEARS)


URF.KL=CP.K*MF*BWEPY                                     15, R
     URF    - UPTAKE RATE IN FISH (TONS/YEAR)
     CP     - CONCENTRATION IN PLANKTON (DIMENSIONLESS)
     MF     - MASS OF FISH (TONS)
     BWEPY  - BODY WEIGHTS EATEN PER YEAR (1/YEAR)


CP.K=OPCF*CO.K                                           16, A
OPCF=2000                                                16.1, C
     CP     - CONCENTRATION IN PLANKTON (DIMENSIONLESS)
     OPCF   - OCEAN-PLANKTON CONCENTRATION FACTOR
                (DIMENSIONLESS)
     CO     - CONCENTRATION IN OCEAN (DIMENSIONLESS)


CO.K=O.K/MML                                             17, A
MML=3E16                                                 17.1, C
MF=6E8                                                   17.2, C
BWEPY=10                                                 17.3, C
     CO     - CONCENTRATION IN OCEAN (DIMENSIONLESS)
     O      - DDT IN OCEAN (TONS)
     MML    - MASS OF MIXED LAYER (TONS)
     MF     - MASS OF FISH (TONS)
     BWEPY  - BODY WEIGHTS EATEN PER YEAR (1/YEAR)


  DDT IN FISH


F.K=F.J+(DT)(URF.JK-DFR.JK-FC.JK-HEXR.JK-TEXR.JK)        18, L
F=FI                                                     18.1, N
FI=0                                                     18.2, C
     F      - DDT IN FISH (TONS)
     DT     - TIME INTERVAL BETWEEN EACH CALCULATION
                (YEARS)
     URF    - UPTAKE RATE IN FISH (TONS/YEAR)
     DFR    - DEAD FISH REMAINING IN OCEAN (TONS/YEAR)
     FC     - FISH CONSUMED (TONS/YEAR)
     HEXR   - HARMLESS EXCRETION RATE (TONS/YEAR)
     TEXR   - TOXIC EXCRETION RATE (TONS/YEAR)


DF.K=F.K/(1.5*HLF)                                       19, A
HLF=3                                                    19.1, C
     DF     - DEATHS OF FISH (TONS/YEAR)
     F      - DDT IN FISH (TONS)
     HLF    - HALFLIFE OF FISH (YEARS)


DFR.KL=DF.K*(1-COF)                                      20, R
COF=.5                                                   20.1, C
     DFR    - DEAD FISH REMAINING IN OCEAN (TONS/YEAR)
     DF     - DEATHS OF FISH (TONS/YEAR)
     COF    - CONSUMED FRACTION (DIMENSIONLESS)


FC.KL=DF.K*COF                                           21, R
     FC     - FISH CONSUMED (TONS/YEAR)
     DF     - DEATHS OF FISH (TONS/YEAR)
     COF    - CONSUMED FRACTION (DIMENSIONLESS)


EXF.K=F.K/(1.5*EXHL)                                     22, A
EXHL=.3                                                  22.1, C
     EXF    - DDT EXCRETION RATE FROM FISH (TONS/YEAR)
     F      - DDT IN FISH (TONS)
     EXHL   - EXCRETION HALFLIFE FROM FISH (YEARS)


HEXR.KL=EXF.K*DFRA                                       23, R
DFRA=.1                                                  23.1, C
     HEXR   - HARMLESS EXCRETION RATE (TONS/YEAR)
     EXF    - DDT EXCRETION RATE FROM FISH (TONS/YEAR)
     DFRA   - DEGRADED FRACTION (DIMENSIONLESS)
```

```
TEXR.KL=EXF.K*(1-DFRA)                              24, R
    TEXR   - TOXIC EXCRETION RATE (TONS/YEAR)
    EXF    - DDT EXCRETION RATE FROM FISH (TONS/YEAR)
    DFRA   - DEGRADED FRACTION (DIMENSIONLESS)

CF.K=F.K/MF                                         25, A
    CF     - CONCENTRATION IN FISH (DIMENSIONLESS)
    F      - DDT IN FISH (TONS)
    MF     - MASS OF FISH (TONS)

 CONTROL STATEMENTS

TIME=1940                                           25.4, N
LENGTH=2020                                         25.5, C
PLTPER=2                                            25.6, C
DT=.02                                              25.7, C
    TIME   - YEAR IN WHICH SIMULATION RUN INITIATES
             (YEARS)
    LENGTH - YEAR IN WHICH SIMULATION RUN TERMINATES
             (YEARS)
    PLTPER - TIME INTERVAL BETWEEN EACH SET OF PLOTTED
             OUTPUTS (YEARS)
    DT     - TIME INTERVAL BETWEEN EACH CALCULATION
             (YEARS)

PLOT  AR=R(0,20E4)/S=S(0,90E4)/F=F(0,600)
NOTE
NOTE MODEL RUN CONTROL CARDS
NOTE
T   ART=0/4/9/13/17/21/25/29/33/37/41/45
C   LENGTH=2000
RUN INCREASING USE
T   ART=0/4/9/13/17.5/17.5/17.5/17.5/17.5/17.5/17.5/17.5
C   LENGTH=2060
RUN CONSTANT USE
*   NO CHANGE NEEDED
RUN DECREASING USE
C   REFT=1972
RUN DDT BANNED 1972
C   ABF=.1
C   BWEPY=5
C   DFRA=1
C   DHLO=8
C   DHLS=3
C   EHLS=.5
C   EXHL=.05
C   HLF=1
C   OPCF=1000
C   PHL=.01
C   ROHL=.05
C   SHL=200
PLOT  AR=R(0,20E4)/S=S(0,90E4)/F=F(0,40)
RUN OPTIMISTIC PARAMETERVALUES
*   NO CHANGE NEEDED
RUN BEST PARAMETERVALUES
C   ABF=.9
C   BWEPY=50
C   DFRA=0
C   DHLO=80
C   DHLS=30
C   EHLS=10
C   EXHL=.7
C   HLF=10
C   OPCF=10000
C   PHL=.2
C   ROHL=1
C   SHL=2000
PLOT  AR=R(0,20E4)/S=S(0,90E4)/F=F(0,40E3)
RUN PESSIMISTIC PARAMETERVALUES
```

4
System Simulation to Identify Environmental Research Needs: Mercury Contamination

Alison A. Anderson and Jay Martin Anderson

World3 employs a single dynamic structure to represent the persistent pollutants generated by industry and agriculture. Implicit in this approach are certain general assumptions about the geographic distribution and the delayed appearance of materials from both sectors. To test the extent to which these assumptions are generally applicable to different pollutants, a study of mercury flows through the environment was conducted, as a comparison with the DDT study described in Chapter 3. The mercury report also illustrates the use of formal models to identify the areas in which our lack of data most seriously limits our ability to understand the behavior of a complex system.

The research described in this chapter was begun at Bryn Mawr College with Miss Lydia Mayer and was supported during the summer of 1971 by an Undergraduate Research Participation grant from the National Science Foundation. A shortened version of this chapter has been published as "System Simulation to Identify Environmental Research Needs: Mercury Contamination," by A. A. Anderson, J. M. Anderson, and L. E. Mayer, in Oikos: Acta Oecologica Scandinavica.

4
System Simulation to Identify Environmental Research Needs: Mercury Contamination

Introduction

The problem of mercury pollution has attracted concern in the United States and abroad. Human fatality through contamination of food has been discussed and reported in the "environmental press."[1] The discovery of high concentrations of mercury in tuna and swordfish in the United States and mercury contamination of fish and birds in Sweden and elsewhere has been reported in the technical literature.[2] These reports contain some information on the distribution of mercury in the environment; they indicate that man's use of mercury may have a wider impact on himself and on his environment than he had expected.

On the other side of the debate, it has been suggested that the high levels of mercury, especially in marine life, are due to natural concentrations of mercury in the global system, and that while the consumption of some fish may need to be restricted, there is no threat to the balance of nature.[3] This side argues that the hazards of mercury are at most confined to sites of local effluents, mercury in the air near mines or smelters, and the careless use of mercurials.

In this paper we summarize the data on the distribution and translocation of mercury in the environment, both by natural processes and by man's activities. We then ask if the data are sufficient to support either side of the debate and, if not, where further environmental research is needed. A simulation model for the flow of mercury proves to be a particularly useful tool for the identification of research needs, an assessment of the persistence of mercury as a pollutant, and an analysis of policies for the control of mercury pollution.

The model, similar to one constructed to analyze the flow of DDT in the global system,[4] traces the path of mercury from its natural sources to its natural sinks. By superimposing on the natural flow of mercury the discharge of mercury from man's activity, we can examine how the consumption and dispersal of mercury by industry and agriculture contribute to mercury contamination of the world system.

Rather than offer a final, complete model here, we hope to begin a modeling process that can suggest what new data are needed, easily accommodate those data as they become available, and examine new policies for the control of mercury pollution as they are formulated.

[1] See, for example, Katherine Montague and Peter Montague, *Mercury* (San Francisco: Sierra Club, 1971); Neville Grant, "Mercury in Man," *Environment,* vol. 13 (1971), no. 4, p. 2; and Terri Aaronson, "Mercury in the Environment," ibid., p. 16.

[2] See Arne Jernelöv, "Conversion of Mercury Compounds," in *Chemical Fallout,* ed. Martin W. Miller and George G. Berg (Springfield, Ill.: Charles C. Thomas, 1969); Gunnel Westöö, "Methylmercury Compounds in Animal Foods," in ibid.; Alf G. Johnels and T. Westermark, "Mercury Contamination of the Environment in Sweden," in ibid.; Robin A. Wallace, William Fulkerson, Wilbur D. Shults, and William S. Lyon, *Mercury in the Environment: The Human Element,* report ORNL NSF-EP-1 (Oak Ridge, Tenn.: Oak Ridge National Laboratory, 1971) (hereafter cited as Wallace et al., *Mercury: Human Element*); Göran Löfroth, *Methylmercury,* Swedish Natural Science Research Council, Bulletin no. 4, 2nd ed. Ecological Research Committee, (Stockholm, 1970); and Study Group on Mercury Hazards, "Hazards of Mercury," *Environmental Research,* vol. 4 (1971), p. 1.

[3] Leonard J. Goldwater, "Mercury in the Environment," *Scientific American,* vol. 224 (1971), no. 5, p. 15, and Allen L. Hammond, "Mercury in the Environment: Natural and Human Factors," *Science,* vol. 171 (1971), p. 788.

[4] Jørgen Randers, "DDT Movement in the Global Environment," chap. 3 in this volume.

System Dynamics: A Modeling Methology

Our model of the flow of mercury in the world has been developed by using the techniques of system dynamics, a theory of system structure that permits an analyst to represent, symbolically and mathematically, the interactions governing the long-term behavior of complex social, economic, and physical systems.

The system dynamics methodology demands that all assumptions about the behavior of mercury in the environment be made explicit and precise. The relationships among the elements of the system are represented simply in graphical form. With both the data and the structure of the model thus exposed to critical view, it is easy to see if any factors have been neglected, if any relationships have been erroneously quantified, and if the model behavior is sensitive to the precision of the data.

The model is displayed graphically using a simple symbolic language, and it is expressed mathematically in an equally simple user-oriented computer language, each called DYNAMO. DYNAMO flow diagrams make use of the symbols and concepts described in Chapter 2 and summarized in Figure 2-2.

The Natural Flow of Mercury in the Environment

We shall represent the flow of two different chemical forms of mercury in the environment: metal-inorganic (M) and organomercurials (O). This disaggregation of the model into two parallel tracks is important because the two forms are interconvertible by means of dynamically distinct processes and because organomercury compounds, such as the methylmercuric ion, are more toxic than the metal or its inorganic ions.

The model calculates the amount of mercury in five sectors of the environment: air, soil, fresh water and sediments, oceans, and fish (the food chain). The local differences in the concentration of metal-inorganic or organic mercury in each sector are less important than the global mercury levels that build up over the time span of interest in the model. That time span is 150 years, from 1900 to 2050.

The time scale of 150 years and the five-by-two disaggregation determine the model's structure. Short-term transients in the concentration of mercury in a specific sector were ignored. We sought only those interactions that are important over decades and globally significant. A physical flow diagram is shown in Figure 4-1.

In the natural system, mercury enters the air through the weathering of mercury-containing rocks and through volcanic activity. The possibility of a large-scale mercury influx into the air through degassing of the earth's crust has been suggested.[5] Mercury can also be introduced into the stream-sediment sector by the erosion of cinnabar and other mercury-bearing rocks.

From the air, rainfall will carry mercury compounds to the soil or upper (mixed) layer of the ocean. Mercury in the soil is slowly washed into streams, and

---

[5] Edward D. Goldberg, private communication; see also Herbert V. Weiss, Minoru Koide, and Edward D. Goldberg, "Mercury in a Greenland Ice Sheet: Evidence of Recent Input by Man," *Science,* vol. 172 (1971), p. 692.

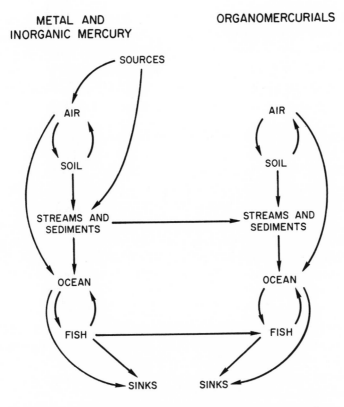

METAL AND
INORGANIC MERCURY   ORGANOMERCURIALS

Figure 4-1 The natural physical flow of mercury in the environment. The only natural sources of mercury introduce
the metal and inorganic compounds into the air and
water. The sources of organomercurials are discussed in
the text.

again into the ocean. Once in the ocean it may be taken up by fish, from which it
may be transferred to other animals and man, or it may precipitate and be
deposited on the ocean floor.

We assumed that the several physicochemical equilibria governing the inter-
conversion of mercury salts and their solubility are rapid compared with the
150 year time span of the model. Thus we did not consider it necessary to
distinguish in the model among various mercury salts or between mercury in
streams and mercury in sediments.

The major sections of the model are described in detail in the following pages.
The entire model, both in flow diagram form and in DYNAMO equations, is given
in the appendix to this chapter.

Steady-State or Background Levels. We base our model on the major premise
that in the presence of natural sources and sinks alone a simulation of the model
should yield constant levels of mercury in the ten sectors. Several of our choices
of parameters and some of our arguments depend on this assumption.

It follows that the natural input of mercury must be balanced by an equal natural output and that all sectors of the model must maintain this same throughput. We know that about 250 tons per year[6] of mercury are injected into the atmosphere by weathering and volcanic activity, although this figure is subject to some debate, as discussed later. We assume that an equal amount of mercury is introduced into streams from erosion. The total input of 500 tons per year must be counterbalanced by an equal deposition in the sink—the ocean floor. This estimate is in good agreement with our knowledge that about 6×10^4 tons per year of lead are deposited on the ocean floor,[7] and that the concentration of lead is about one hundred times that of mercury in marine sediments.[8]

Our choice of rate parameters for the translocation of mercury has been made consistent with a throughput of about 500 tons per year.

Air, Soil, and Stream-Sediment Sectors.[9] We first considered the levels of mercury in the air, soil, and stream-sediment (mud) sectors of the model and the translocation rates between these sectors. The DYNAMO flow diagram for this portion of the model is shown in Figure 4-2.

To begin a simulation of the flow of mercury from its natural sources to its natural sink, we needed to supply an initial, or background, value for each level. These levels should be those existing in 1900, and they should remain unchanged—in the absence of man-made inputs—until 2050.

Some references indicate that the average atmospheric mercury concentration lies in the range 2-20 ng m^{-3}.[10] Given the volume of the "standard atmosphere," 4×10^{18} cubic meters, the atmosphere must carry between 8,000 and 80,000 tons of mercury. However, this level of mercury in the atmosphere cannot be sustained with the modest input of mercury from nature alone—the 500 tons per year suggested earlier—in view of the estimated time constant for precipitation from air of 0.4 yr^{-1}.[11] We are therefore faced with an inconsistency in the available data: the given translocation rates and mechanisms, the measured background level of mercury in the air, and the assumed natural rate of mercury input to the air cannot all be correct.

For example, we estimate that an input of mercury of 15,000 tons per year into the air is required to sustain a level of mercury in the air between 8,000 and

---

[6] Oiva I. Joensuu, "Fossil Fuels as a Source of Mercury Pollution," ibid., vol. 172 (1971), p. 1027.

[7] Roy Chester, "Elemental Geochemistry of Marine Sediments," in *Chemical Oceanography,* by John Price Riley and Geoffrey Skirrow (New York: Academic Press, 1965).

[8] Quoted from K. K. Turekian by D. H. Klein and Edward D. Goldberg, "Mercury in the Marine Environment," *Environmental Science and Technology,* vol. 4 (1970), p. 765.

[9] Throughout this report, tons are metric tons, or 1,000 kilograms. Concentrations are measured in nanograms per cubic meter, ng m^{-3} (a nanogram is one billionth of a gram); parts per billion, ppb; or parts per million, ppm.

[10] Alfred Stock and Friedrich Cucuel, "Die Verbreitung des Quecksilbers," *Naturwissenschaften,* vol. 22 (1934), p. 390; Samuel H. Williston, "Mercury in the Atmosphere," *Journal of Geophysical Research,* vol. 73 (1968), p. 7051; and U.S. Geological Survey, *Mercury in the Environment,* Professional Paper no. 713 (Washington, D.C.: Government Printing Office, 1970).

[11] See Randers, "DDT Movement"; Goldberg, private communication; Weiss, Koide, and Goldberg, "Mercury in a Greenland Ice Sheet"; U.S. Geological Survey, *Mercury In the Environment;* and Eric Ericksson, private communication quoted by Study Group on Mercury Hazards, in *Environmental Research.*

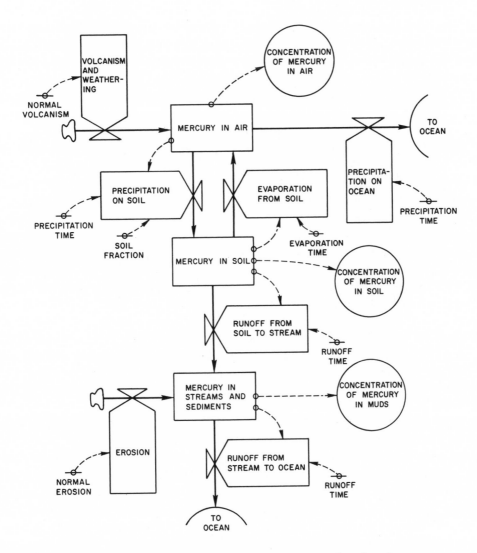

Figure 4-2 DYNAMO flow diagram of mercury in the aír, soil, and stream-sediment (mud) sectors of the environment

80,000 tons, whereas Joensuu claims that but 250 tons per year can enter the air from weathering and volcanic activity.[12] We therefore suggest that the level of mercury in the air cannot be on the order of 2-20 ng m^{-3}. If only 250 tons per year of mercury are naturally released into the air, we find that a global load of 2,000 tons or a concentration of 0.5 ng m^{-3} can be sustained, in agreement with Williston's data.[13]

This point of view also agrees with those who question that the atmospheric mercury measurements made near ground level in industrial Germany in 1934[14]

[12] Joensuu, "Fossil Fuels."
[13] Williston, "Mercury in the Atmosphere."
[14] Stock and Cucuel, "Die Verbreitung."

were free of man-made mercury and were therefore true background measurements.[15] In fact, given that the atmosphere mixes and circulates effectively in about two weeks,[16] one wonders how any recent measure of atmospheric mercury can be truly "background."

On the other hand, Goldberg argues that the earth's crust degasses approximately 25,000 tons of mercury annually, a rate of mercury input to the air that is quite sufficient to sustain an atmospheric load of 8,000-80,000 tons.[17]

This inconsistency prompts our first recommendation for new research: how can background, natural levels of mercury in the air be measured precisely in an age of atmospheric mercury pollution? Are there mechanisms that naturally inject upward of 15,000 tons of mercury into the air annually?

We built our model on the assumption that 250 tons per year of mercury are injected naturally into the air, that the background concentration of mercury in the air is 0.5 ng m^{-3} and that this amount is sustained by very slow translocation rates out of the soil and stream sectors. If these assumptions are in error, our model will be pessimistic by predicting a larger effect of man-made mercury in the air but optimistic by predicting a smaller effect of man-made mercury in the stream sector. The sensitivity of the model to this assumption is reported later in this chapter.

The soil includes the earth's land area, 1.7×10^{14} m^2, to a depth of 5 cm and with an average density of 5 g per cm^3, for a global mass of 4.2×10^{13} tons. The U.S. Geological Survey reports a natural mercury concentration in soil of 50-100 ppb, with occasional values (for example, near mercury deposits) much higher.[18] We chose to set the initial soil concentration, that is, in the year 1900, at 100 ppb, or a background mass of 4.2×10^6 tons of mercury.

The mud includes an area of 1.4×10^{13} m^2, representing all freshwater systems and estuaries, to a depth of 5 cm and with an average density of 4 g per cm^3, for a total mass of 2.8×10^{12} tons.[19] The U.S. Geological Survey indicates a mercury concentration of 100 ppb in this sector also, or a global total of 2.8×10^5 tons.[20] We do not include mercury levels in the streams themselves because most of the mercury is in the sediments and because a simple and rapid equilibrium ratio relates stream to mud concentrations. Since the mud-stream equilibrium is reached very rapidly (relative to the model's time span), there is no dynamic difference between stream and mud.

To generate the flow of mercury through this sector, we needed estimates of rates of translocation of mercury. We have already noted that weathering and

[15] Williston, "Mercury in the Atmosphere," and U.S. Geological Survey, *Mercury in the Environment.*

[16] W. E. Langlois, H. C. W. Kwok, and R. A. Ellefson, "Numerical Simulation of Weather and Climate. IV. Global Transport of Carbon Monoxide from Automotive Sources" (San José, Calif.: IBM Research Laboratory, n.d.).

[17] Weiss, Koide, and Goldberg, "Mercury in a Greenland Ice Sheet."

[18] U.S. Geological Survey, *Mercury in the Environment.*

[19] Roger Revelle, "Water," in *Man and the Ecosphere* (San Francisco: W. H. Freeman and Company, 1971).

[20] U.S. Geological Survey, *Mercury in the Environment*

volcanism contribute 250 tons per year to the atmosphere,[21] and we assumed a similar input from erosion into the streams. For precipitation from the atmosphere we assumed that one-quarter of all precipitated airborne mercury falls on land and three-quarters on the oceans; the time constant for precipitating insoluble airborne materials is estimated to be 0.4 year, with a range one order of magnitude to each side.[22] Through this paper, the phrase "time constant" is the constant τ in the linear differential equation.

$$dL/dt = -L/\tau$$

τ is the time in which some level L will have adjusted 63 percent of the way from its initial value to its final value; it equals 1.45 times the halflife for the process.

Although the rate of evaporation of inorganic mercury compounds from a clean surface is characterized by a time constant of 13 years,[23] we note that two reports call attention to the tight adsorption of mercury on clay and humus.[24] The evaporation of inorganic mercury must therefore be slower by a factor of the equilibrium ratio of free to adsorbed mercury. Although this equilibrium ratio is unknown, we can use the requirement that the model simulations be consistent with a steady-rate throughput of 500 tons per year to assign a value of 0.01 to this ratio, or an *effective* evaporation time constant of 1300 years. The sensitivity of the model to this assumption is shown in Figure 4-12. The assumption of very long translocation times in the soil and mud sectors may be invalid under certain conditions: for example, as the pH of rain, ground, or surface water falls, we may expect mercury-clay complexes to break up more easily and the runoff rates to be greater. Although our model does not include such effects, we call attention to the possible synergism operating between pollutants that increase the acidity of rain or freshwater systems and mercury pollution.

The same assumptions about the adsorption of mercury to soils were made to estimate the runoff time constant for translocation from soil to stream. Although 36 years is suggested,[25] based on the volume of water that percolates from soil to stream annually, we applied our estimated equilibrium ratio of free to adsorbed mercury and used an effective runoff time constant of 3,600 years. Finally, the same kind of reasoning led us to suggest that the time constant for runoff from stream sediments to ocean is 500 years.

Ocean and Fish Sectors.   Mercury enters the mixed layer of the ocean via stream runoff and precipitation. Within the ocean, mercury is ingested by microorganisms and passed up the food chain to larger marine biota. In the model we represent this process simply by one rate of absorption from ocean to fish, where concentrations have been measured. Mercury is lost from the mixed layer to the

[21] Joensuu, "Fossil Fuels."
[22] See fn. 11.
[23] Ericksson, private communication.
[24] Wallace et al., *Mercury: Human Element,* and U.S. Geological Survey, *Mercury in the Environment.*
[25] Ericksson, private communication.

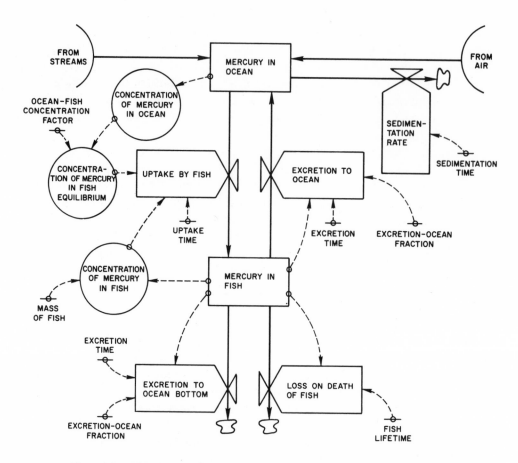

Figure 4-3　DYNAMO flow diagram of mercury in the ocean and fish (food chain) sectors of the environment

ocean bottom by the death of fish, through fish excreta, and by sedimentation. This sector of the model is shown in Figure 4-3.

The ocean refers to the upper 300 meters, called the "mixed layer," which has a mass of 2.7×10^{16} tons.[26] Hammond has indicated a conservative estimate of 0.1 ppb mercury in the ocean, which corresponds to a global burden of about 2×10^6 tons.[27]

The mass of fish in the ocean is taken to be 5.5×10^8 tons.[28] A value of 0.2 ppm seems to be generally accepted for background mercury levels in fish;[29] therefore, the total mercury in fish is about 100 tons.

The dynamic behavior of these two sectors is determined by the uptake of mercury by fish, the excretion of mercury by fish, and the death of fish. We assume that mercury is ingested at a rate proportional to the difference between

[26] Randers, "DDT Movement."

[27] Hammond, "Mercury in the Environment: Natural and Human Factors."

[28] Randers, "DDT Movement."

[29] Wallace et al., *Mercury: Human Element,* and U.S. Geological Survey, *Mercury in the Environment.*

the mercury level in the fish and the equilibrium mercury level in fish. The latter concentration is about 3,000 times (range, 1,000 to 10,000 times) that in the surrounding ocean.[30] The time constant is taken to be the time for fish to consume 63 percent of their weight, or 0.1 year.[31] These assumptions are admittedly crude but are consistent with the available data.

We guess that one-half of the fish excreta are returned to the mixed layer of the ocean and one-half to the ocean depths; the mercury-excretion time constant for fish has been measured to be about two-thirds of a year.[32] The average lifetime of fish is about three years.[33] The quantity of mercury in fish is but a small fraction of the total; therefore, errors in the assumptions just made have little effect on the behavior of the other sectors of the model.

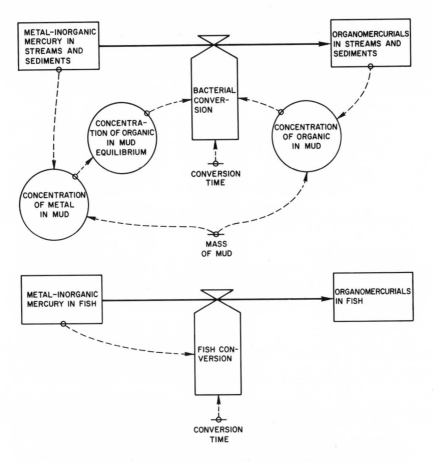

Figure 4-4 DYNAMO flow diagrams for the conversion of metal-inorganic mercury to organomercurials in stream sediments by bacteria (upper) and by fish (lower)

[30] Löfroth, *Methylmercury.*
[31] Randers, "DDT Movement."
[32] Montague and Montague, *Mercury.*
[33] Randers, "DDT Movement."

Metal-Organic Conversions.   The organic side of the model has the same structure as the metal-inorganic side. The only natural source of organomercurials is the action of bacteria on metal-inorganic mercury. We assigned evaporation and run-off time constants for organomercurials five times smaller than those of metal-inorganic mercury because organomercurials are more soluble and more volatile than the inorganic mercury compounds.

Bacteria methylate inorganic mercury to organomercurials in stream sediments,[34] and inorganic mercury is methylated in fish as well.[35] The structures that model these conversions are shown in Figure 4-4.

The bacterial methylation of mercury has only recently been studied. The maximum methylmercury output for a given metal-inorganic input has been charted by several workers,[36] and is reproduced in Figure 4-5 in the log-linear form used in the DYNAMO model. The rate at which the maximum methylation is achieved is very rapid—on the order of days—and is made equal to 0.05 years in our model.

The conversion of mercury from inorganic to organic compounds in fish is less well studied; the data indicate a first-order process with a time constant of two years for the conversion.[37]

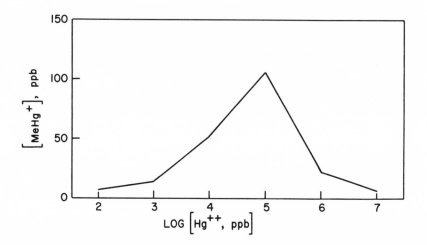

Figure 4-5   Maximum concentration of methylmercury (MeHg$^+$) produced from a given concentration of mercuric ion [Hg^{++}]
After S. Jensen and Arne Jernelöv, in Nature, vol. 223 (1969), p. 753

[34] S. Jensen and Arne Jernelöv, "Biological Methylation of Mercury in Aquatic Organisms," *Nature,* vol. 223 (1969), p. 753, and J. M. Wood, F. Scott Kennedy, and C. G. Rosen, "Synthesis of Methyl-mercury Compounds by Extracts of a Methanogenic Bacterium," ibid., vol. 220 (1968), p. 173.

[35] C. A. Bache, W. H. Gutemann, and D. J. Lisk, "Residues of Total Mercury and Methylmercuric Salts in Lake Trout as a Function of Age," *Science,* vol. 172 (1971), p. 951.

[36] Jensen and Jernelöv, "Biological Methylation," and Wood, Kennedy, and Rosen, "Synthesis of Methyl-mercury Compounds."

[37] Bache, Gutemann, and Lisk, "Residues of Total Mercury."

The conversion from metal-inorganic to organic mercury compounds by soil bacteria is highly likely; it is presently under investigation in Sweden.[38] Likewise, the possibility of methylation in the ocean also exists, but it has not yet been detected. Finally, the reversibility of methylation reactions becomes possible at high organomercury concentrations and low pH.[39] Although organomercury concentrations do not build up to the point where the reverse of the methylation reaction would constitute a serious perturbation to the system, the possibility of a reverse reaction under more acid conditions should be considered in some local areas. We have omitted these processes until more data become available.

We set the initial levels of organic mercury to zero in all model sectors except fish. Since fish probably convert ingested mercury rapidly to an organic form, we assumed that the background load of 100 tons of mercury in fish is distributed 60:40 between the organic and inorganic sides of the model.

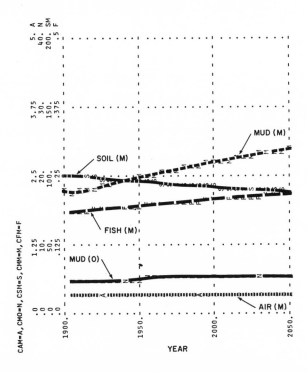

Figure 4-6 Simulation of the natural flow of mercury through the global system from 1900 to 2050
The scales, as noted, are different for each curve. (M) means metal-inorganic mercury; (O) means organomercurials

[38] Arne Andersson, private communication; see also idem "Något om Kvicksilvrets geokemi," *Grundföbättring,* vol. 23 (1970), p. 31.
[39] Bache, Gutemann, and Lisk, "Residues of Total Mercury."

Simulations of the "Natural" Mercury Flow Model. A 150-year simulation of the model is shown in Figure 4-6. The plot of concentrations of metal-inorganic mercury and organomercurials in air, mud, soil, oceans, and fish is generated by the DYNAMO computer program. Figure 4-6 shows that the parameter set chosen yields a nearly steady-state distribution of mercury in the environment.

Although one might quarrel with our use of "steady state" in describing the simulation shown in Figure 4-6, the precision of available data hardly warrants more care in assigning parameters for a steady-state simulation. As better data become available, refinements in the model and its assumptions can easily be made, and the validity of the model simulating the natural flow of mercury can be tested and confirmed.

Using Figure 4-6 as a starting point, while remembering the uncertainty in the assumptions underlying its structure and parameter values, we may examine the consequences of the introduction of mercury into the environment through man's activities.

Mercury Pollution

We shall define a pollutant as a material that persists in remaining out of its natural place in the environment and depresses the normal functions of living species. The "natural place" of mercury is defined for us by the concentrations in the ten levels given by the simulation shown in Figure 4-6, and it is the task of this section to examine the dynamics of man's translocation of mercury and its persistence out of its natural place.

To estimate the input of mercury from man's activity, we must know what fraction of man's yearly consumption of mercury is discharged into the several

Use	Consumption	Of the 82 Percent Dissipated, Mercury Goes to the		
		Air	Soil	Streams
Electrical, laboratory, control uses	41% used $\left(\dfrac{18\% \text{ recycled}}{23\% \text{ dissipated}}\right)$	14% (M)		14% (M)
Chlor-alkali plants	33%	20% (M)		20% (M)
Dental and catalysts	6%	3% (M)		5% (M)
Pulp and paper, drugs, paints, agriculture	20%	9% (O)	7% (O)	8% (O)
Total consumption		37% (M) 9% (O)	7% (O)	39% (M) 8% (O)

Figure 4-7 Consumption of mercury and its environmental impact for the United States in 1968
Source: R. A. Wallace et al., Mercury in the Environment: The Human Element, *report ORNL-NSF-EP-1 (Oak Ridge, Tenn.: Oak Ridge National Laboratory, 1971).*
Note: (M) indicates metal-inorganic mercury; (O) indicates organomercurials.

sectors of the environment. However, the available data cover only the total consumption of mercury in the world with a breakdown of U.S. mercury consumption by use. Consequently, we have made the assumption that the fraction of mercury consumption in each of several broad categories is constant over the world and over time. Figure 4-7 gives the use of mercury in the United States in

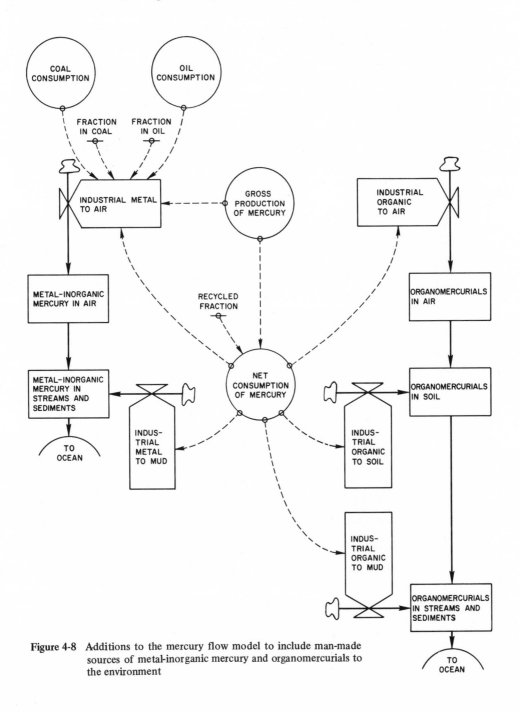

Figure 4-8 Additions to the mercury flow model to include man-made sources of metal-inorganic mercury and organomercurials to the environment

1968 and indicates the assumed disposal of mercury into the environment. The usefulness of this assumption is increased because we are not interested in the specific uses of the metal but only in the fraction of gross mercury consumption that is disposed of in each sector of the environment. Beyond 1970, we have used the projected production values of the Bureau of Mines,[40] and have assumed that production is constant from 2000 until 2050. The later values may be too high, inasmuch as the exponential reserve life index for mercury is estimated to be only 41 years,[41] even if undiscovered reserves are five times larger than known reserves.

We therefore added to the model flows of man-made mercury into the environment, as shown in Figure 4-8. These flows are based on the projected consumption of mercury and, as will be explained, of coal and oil. The historical and projected consumption data for mercury, together with discharges of mercury when coal or oil is combusted, are shown in Figure 4-9.

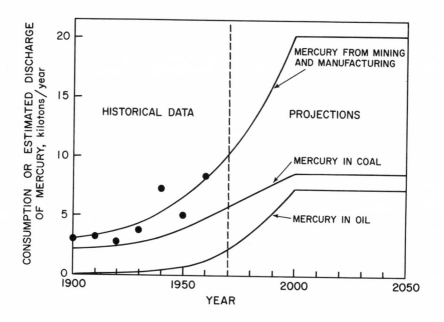

Figure 4-9   Consumption of mercury, and estimated discharge of mercury from the combustion of coal and oil. From 1900-1970, historical data; from 1970-2000, projected data, each from the Bureau of Mines. Estimates of mercury discharge by the combustion of coal and oil are based on 1 ppm mercury in oil and 2 ppm mercury in coal (see text). *See G. N. Greenspoon, in* Mineral Facts and Problems, 1970, *U.S. Department of the Interior, Bureau of Mines, Bulletin 650 (Washington, D.C., 1970).*

[40] G. N. Greenspoon, in U.S. Bureau of Mines, *Mineral Facts and Problems, 1970,* U.S. Department of the Interior, Bureau of Mines, Bulletin 650 (Washington, D.C., 1970).

[41] Donella H. Meadows, Dennis L. Meadows, Jorgen Randers, and William W. Behrens III, *The Limits to Growth* (New York: Universe Books, 1972).

About 3 percent of gross mercury production is lost to the air in mining and smelting. Of this production, less the mercury that is conserved by recycling, 37 percent is discharged to the air as metallic or inorganic compounds, and 9 percent to the air as organic compounds. Another 39 percent is discharged to streams as metal-inorganic compounds and 8 percent to the streams as organomercurials. Finally, 7 percent of net production is applied to the soil as organomercurials. These figures are taken from Figure 4-7.

The effect of man's mercury production on the global environment is simulated in Figure 4-10. Mercury in the air rises steadily; the concentration reaches a plateau in the year 2000, when we have assumed that production ceases to increase. Metal-inorganic mercury in the soil undergoes little change; the soil serves as a massive and slow buffer to the air and mud sectors. Organomercurials in the soil rise, but, because toxicity levels have not yet been established for this sector, the biocidal consequences are difficult to assess. Presumably, agricultural areas are richer in organo-mercurials than other areas, but the model does not reflect local concentrations higher or lower than average.

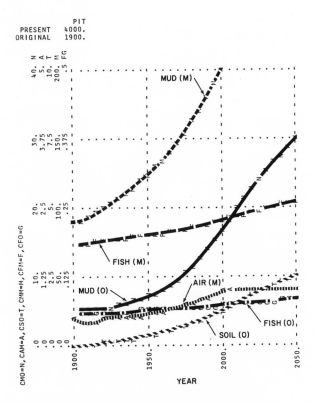

Figure 4-10 Simulation of the mercury flow model including man-made sources of mercury from the world consumption of mercury
See notes to Figure 4-6.

Mercury in freshwater systems rises rapidly. Mercury levels in the mud sector are primarily due to man-made discard of mercury directly into freshwater and not to precipitation into the freshwater sector from the air, as indicated by simulations of the system with input only to the air and precipitation from the air to the freshwater system. The problem of mercury pollution in lakes and streams, like that of the soil, is aggravated in local areas where mercurial effluents are large and unregulated. Therefore, mercury pollution in the freshwater sector is a local problem, not a global problem.

Because the mud-soil pathway is a very slow translocation route, mercury in the ocean appears most immediately from direct precipitation of airborne mercury. Mercury flow through the air-ocean sectors poses the most immediate global threat. Mercury in fish follows the level in the ocean with only a slight delay. It is impossible with this model to identify mercury levels in any particular species of fish, such as tuna. Nonetheless, we can expect mercury concentrations to increase with the length of the food chain.

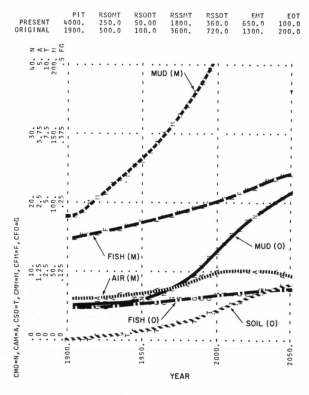

Figure 4-11 Sensitivity of the model to the choice of translocation rate parameters. Simulation of the model as in Figure 4-10, except that all runoff and evaporation time constants are one-half as large.

We can now examine the sensitivity of the model to uncertainties in the parameters. For example, Figure 4-11 shows the same simulation as Figure 4-10, but with all the soil and stream translocation time constants decreased by half. In some sectors the model is sensitive to the choice of translocation parameters, indicating that more precise data would be helpful in analyzing the problem of mercury pollution.

The effect of more efficient recycling can be modeled by increasing the recycling fraction from the present-day 18 percent to 50 percent in 1980. A comparison of Figures 4-10 and 4-12 indicates that recycling has only a very slight effect on global pollution, although it may have an economic effect as mercury grows more and more scarce. The soil and stream sectors are insensitive to large changes in mercury discharge because of the large natural concentrations of mercury in these sectors and the slow flows through them. The levels of mercury in the air change more drastically because the background levels are low and the response in this sector is rapid.

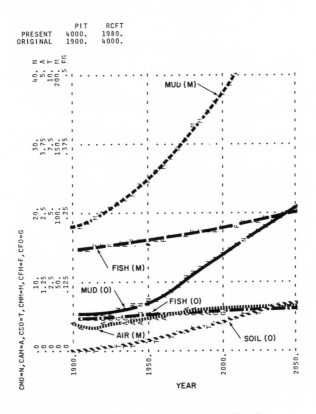

Figure 4-12 The effect of greater recycling. In 1980 a policy of 50 percent recycling of mercury is implemented, superceding the current 18 percent recycling fraction shown in Figure 4-10.

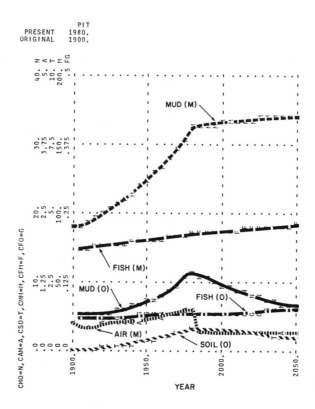

Figure 4-13   The persistence of mercury in the environment. The change of mercury concentrations in response to total cessation of mercury consumption in 1980.

The persistence of mercury as a global pollutant can be tested by ceasing consumption of the metal in 1980, as simulated in Figure 4-13. Organomercury in the streams does not return to its 1950 level until 2050, seventy years after consumption ceases, and the level of metal-inorganic mercury in streams and sediments is permanently raised over the 150-year time span shown here.

Mercury in Fuels. The foregoing discussion indicates how mercury placed in the environment as a result of man's use of the metal moves through the global system. However, man's consumption of fossil fuels also injects mercury into the air in proportion to the consumption of fuels and to their mercury content. The pollution by trace contaminants in major resources is particularly insidious. In addition to the discharge of mercury associated with the combustion of coal and oil, mercury is released in the combustion of natural gas and the roasting of limestone to produce lime. The amount of mercury discharged as a trace contaminant in major resources may exceed that discharged in the use of the metal itself. We included in this model only mercury discharged by the

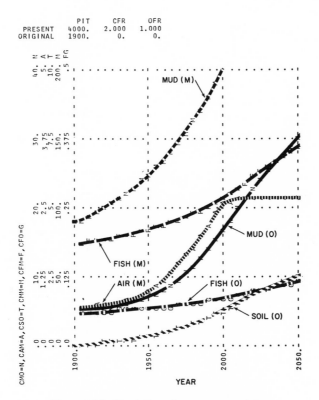

Figure 4-14 Simulation of mercury concentrations in the environment in response both to man's consumption of mercury itself and to estimated discharges of mercury by the combustion of coal and oil.

combustion of coal and oil. Data on the mercury content of fuels suggest an average of about 2 ppm in coal;[42] from the sparse data for oil,[43] we chose a value of 1 ppm in our model, even though estimates range from 0.05 to 10 ppm. Mercury discharged by the combustion of coal and oil in the world has been included in Figure 4-9, using historical data to 1970 and Bureau of Mines projections to 2000 for the use of these fuels.

Figure 4-14 shows the simulation of the added effect of mercury released from fuel combustion. At least for the air and ocean sectors, this source of mercury is clearly more important than mercury consumption itself. Figure 4-14 indicates the possibility that by the end of the century the global average level of mercury in fish could rise above the U.S. Food and Drug Administration maximum level of 0.5 ppm.[44] This conclusion rests on the assumption that oil

[42] Wallace et al., *Mercury: Human Element,* and Meadows et al., *Limits to Growth.*
[43] Joensuu, "Fossil Fuels."
[44] Montague and Montague, *Mercury.*

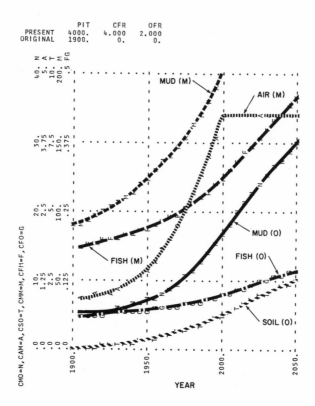

Figure 4-15 Sensitivity of the model to the choice of fraction of mercury in coal and oil. Simulation of the model is as in Figure 4-14, except that the fraction of mercury in both coal and oil is twice as large.

contains on the order of 1 ppm of mercury. Here is another area where new research is needed: more and better data on traces of mercury in fuels and other resources will help to substantiate or refute the prediction of Figure 4-14. The model is clearly sensitive to this parameter. Figure 4-15 shows the results of a simulation in which it was assumed that coal and oil contain twice as much mercury as was assumed in Figure 4-14.

Technological change, of course, can ameliorate the mercury pollution problem. Removal of mercury from coal and oil, similar to desulfurization to reduce pollution of the air by sulfur dioxide, might be implemented, together with recycling, to reduce the hazard of mercury pollution.

Summary

Mercury pollution of soils and streams is primarily a local problem, requiring careful monitoring and regulation of effluents. Mercury is translocated to the sea only very slowly from soil and stream but rapidly by precipitation from the air.

Mercury levels in marine fish may rise above acceptable levels if the combustion of fossil fuels with a high (≥ 1 ppm) mercury content continues.

In the ocean and marine biota, mercury can persist for several decades after pollution stops. To be effective, the control of mercury pollution must anticipate mercury movements up to sixty years in the future.

Further experimental research is needed to obtain data on the mercury content of fossil fuels, on possible natural mechanisms for the release of mercury into the air, and on conversion mechanisms for methylation of mercury in the soil, ocean, and fish sectors.

Appendix: Flow Diagram and Computer Program for the Mercury Model

The DYNAMO flow diagram for the full mercury model and the DYNAMO computer program for the model follow. Symbols appearing on the flow diagram are referenced by number to the equations, where definitions for each element as it appears in each equation are given.

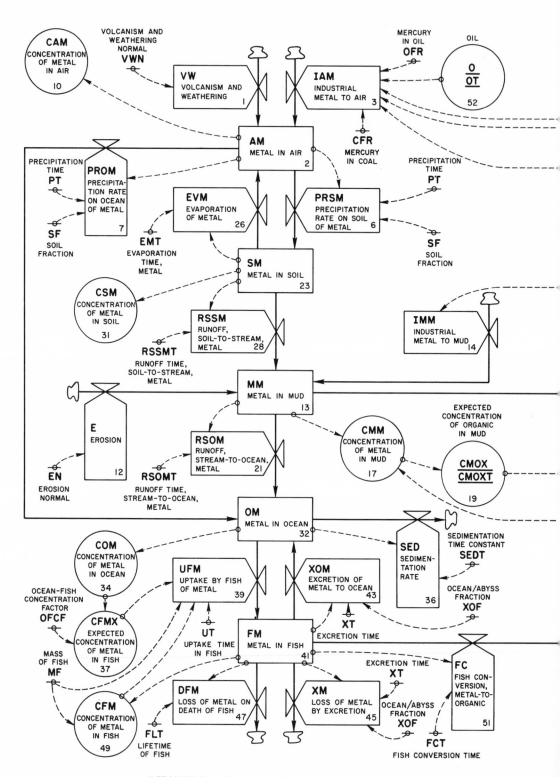

DYNAMO flow diagram for full mercury model

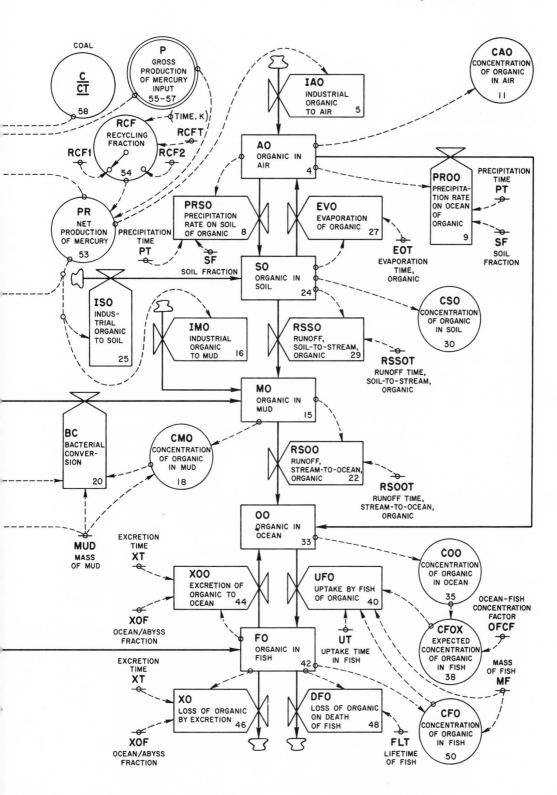

```
VW.KL=VWN                                            1, R
VWN=250                                              1.1, C
     VW     - VOLCANISM AND WEATHERING, TON/YR
     VWN    - VOLCANISM AND WEATHERING NORMAL, TON/YR


AM.K=AM.J+DT*(VW.JK+EVM.JK-PRSM.JK-PROM.JK+IAM.JK)   2, L
AM=AMB                                               2.1, N
AMB=2E3                                              2.2, C
     AM     - METAL IN AIR, TON
     VW     - VOLCANISM AND WEATHERING, TON/YR
     EVM    - EVAPORATION OF METAL, TON/YR
     PRSM   - PRECIPITATION RATE ON SOIL OF METAL, TON/YR
     PROM   - PRECIPITATION RATE ON OCEAN OF METAL, TON/
              YR
     IAM    - INDUSTRIAL METAL TO AIR, TON/YR
     AMB    - BACKGROUND METAL IN AIR, TON


IAM.KL=0.37*PR.K+CFR*C.K+OFR*O.K+0.03*P.K            3, R
CFR=0                                                3.1, C
OFR=0                                                3.2, C
     IAM    - INDUSTRIAL METAL TO AIR, TON/YR
     PR     - NET PRODUCTION OF MERCURY, TON/YR
     CFR    - MERCURY IN COAL, PPM
     C      - COAL, MILLIONS OF TON/YR
     OFR    - MERCURY IN OIL, PPM
     O      - OIL, MILLIONS OF TON/YR
     P      - GROSS PRODUCTION OF MERCURY, TON/YR


AO.K=AO.J+DT*(EVO.JK-PRSO.JK-PROO.JK+IAO.JK)         4, L
AO=AOB                                               4.1, N
AOB=0                                                4.2, C
     AO     - ORGANIC IN AIR, TON
     EVO    - EVAPORATION OF ORGANIC, TON/YR
     PRSO   - PRECIPITATION RATE ON SOIL OF ORGANIC, TON/
              YR
     PROO   - PRECIPITATION RATE ON OCEAN OF ORGANIC,
              TON/YR
     IAO    - INDUSTRIAL ORGANIC TO AIR, TON/YR
     AOB    - BACKGROUND ORGANIC IN AIR, TON


IAO.KL=0.09*PR.K                                     5, R
     IAO    - INDUSTRIAL ORGANIC TO AIR, TON/YR
     PR     - NET PRODUCTION OF MERCURY, TON/YR


PRSM.KL=AM.K*SF/PT                                   6, R
SF=.25                                               6.1, C
PT=.4                                                6.2, C
     PRSM   - PRECIPITATION RATE ON SOIL OF METAL, TON/YR
     AM     - METAL IN AIR, TON
     SF     - SOIL FRACTION, DIMENSIONLESS
     PT     - PRECIPITATION TIME, YR


PROM.KL=AM.K*(1-SF)/PT                               7, R
     PROM   - PRECIPITATION RATE ON OCEAN OF METAL, TON/
              YR
     AM     - METAL IN AIR, TON
     SF     - SOIL FRACTION, DIMENSIONLESS
     PT     - PRECIPITATION TIME, YR


PRSO.KL=AO.K*SF/PT                                   8, R
     PRSO   - PRECIPITATION RATE ON SOIL OF ORGANIC, TON/
              YR
     AO     - ORGANIC IN AIR, TON
     SF     - SOIL FRACTION, DIMENSIONLESS
     PT     - PRECIPITATION TIME, YR


PROO.KL=AO.K*(1-SF)/PT                               9, R
     PROO   - PRECIPITATION RATE ON OCEAN OF ORGANIC,
              TON/YR
     AO     - ORGANIC IN AIR, TON
     SF     - SOIL FRACTION, DIMENSIONLESS
     PT     - PRECIPITATION TIME, YR
```

```
CAM.K=AM.K/4E3                                          10, A
    CAM    - CONCENTRATION OF METAL IN AIR, NG/M**3
    AM     - METAL IN AIR, TON


CAO.K=AO.K/4E3                                          11, A
    CAO    - CONCENTRATION OF ORGANIC IN AIR, NG/M**3
    AO     - ORGANIC IN AIR, TON


  MUD-STREAM SECTOR

E.KL=EN                                                12, R
EN=250                                                 12.1, C
    E      - EROSION, TON/YR
    EN     - EROSION NORMAL, TON/YR


MM.K=MM.J+DT*(E.JK+RSSM.JK-BC.JK-RSOM.JK+IMM.JK)       13, L
MM=MMB                                                 13.1, N
MMB=2.5E5                                              13.2, C
    MM     - METAL IN MUD, TON
    E      - EROSION, TON/YR
    RSSM   - RUNOFF, SOIL-TO-STREAM, METAL, TON/YR
    BC     - BACTERIAL CONVERSION, METAL-TO-ORGANIC,
               TON/YR
    RSOM   - RUNOFF, STREAM-TO-OCEAN, METAL, TON/YR
    IMM    - INDUSTRIAL METAL TO MUD (STREAM), TON/YR
    MMB    - BACKGROUND METAL IN MUD, TON


IMM.KL=0.39*PR.K                                       14, R
    IMM    - INDUSTRIAL METAL TO MUD (STREAM), TON/YR
    PR     - NET PRODUCTION OF MERCURY, TON/YR


MO.K=MO.J+DT*(BC.JK+RSSO.JK-RSOO.JK+IMO.JK)            15, L
MO=MOB                                                 15.1, N
MOB=4000                                               15.2, C
    MO     - ORGANIC IN MUD, TON
    BC     - BACTERIAL CONVERSION, METAL-TO-ORGANIC,
               TON/YR
    RSSO   - RUNOFF, SOIL-TO-STREAM, ORGANIC, TON/YR
    RSOO   - RUNOFF, STREAM-TO-OCEAN, ORGANIC, TON/YR
    IMO    - INDUSTRIAL ORGANIC TO MUD (STREAM), TON/YR
    MOB    - BACKGROUND ORGANIC IN MUD, TON


IMO.KL=0.08*PR.K                                       16, R
    IMO    - INDUSTRIAL ORGANIC TO MUD (STREAM), TON/YR
    PR     - NET PRODUCTION OF MERCURY, TON/YR


CMM.K=MM.K*1E9/MUD                                     17, A
MUD=2.8E12                                             17.1, C
    CMM    - CONCENTRATION OF METAL IN MUD, PPB
    MM     - METAL IN MUD, TON
    MUD    - MASS OF MUD, TON


CMO.K=MO.K*1E9/MUD                                     18, A
    CMO    - CONCENTRATION OF ORGANIC IN MUD, PPB
    MO     - ORGANIC IN MUD, TON
    MUD    - MASS OF MUD, TON


CMOX.K=TABHL(CMOXT,LOGN(CMM.K)/2.3,2,7,1)              19, A
CMOXT=5/12/50/110/20/5                                 19.1, T
    CMOX   - EXPECTED CONCENTRATION OF ORGANIC IN MUD,
               PPB
    CMOXT  - METAL-ORGANIC CONVERSION TABLE
    CMM    - CONCENTRATION OF METAL IN MUD, PPB


BC.KL=MAX(0,(CMOX.K-CMO.K)/DT)*(MUD/1E9)               20, R
    BC     - BACTERIAL CONVERSION, METAL-TO-ORGANIC,
               TON/YR
    CMOX   - EXPECTED CONCENTRATION OF ORGANIC IN MUD,
               PPB
    CMO    - CONCENTRATION OF ORGANIC IN MUD, PPB
    MUD    - MASS OF MUD, TON
```

```
RSOM.KL=MM.K/RSOMT                                    21, R
RSOMT=500                                             21.1, C
    RSOM   - RUNOFF, STREAM-TO-OCEAN, METAL, TON/YR
    MM     - METAL IN MUD, TON
    RSOMT  - RUNOFF TIME, STREAM-OCEAN, METAL, YR


RSOO.KL=MO.K/RSOOT                                    22, R
RSOOT=100                                             22.1, C
    RSOO   - RUNOFF, STREAM-TO-OCEAN, ORGANIC, TON/YR
    MO     - ORGANIC IN MUD, TON
    RSOOT  - RUNOFF TIME, STREAM-OCEAN, ORGANIC, YR


  SOIL SECTOR

SM.K=SM.J+DT*(PRSM.JK-EVM.JK-RSSM.JK)                 23, L
SM=SMB                                                23.1, N
SMB=4.2E6                                             23.2, C
    SM     - METAL IN SOIL, TON
    PRSM   - PRECIPITATION RATE ON SOIL OF METAL, TON/YR
    EVM    - EVAPORATION OF METAL, TON/YR
    RSSM   - RUNOFF, SOIL-TO-STREAM, METAL, TON/YR
    SMB    - BACKGROUND METAL IN SOIL, TON


SO.K=SO.J+DT*(PRSO.JK-EVO.JK-RSSO.JK+ISO.JK)          24, L
SO=SOB                                                24.1, N
SOB=0                                                 24.2, C
    SO     - ORGANIC IN SOIL, TON
    PRSO   - PRECIPITATION RATE ON SOIL OF ORGANIC, TON/
             YR
    EVO    - EVAPORATION OF ORGANIC, TON/YR
    RSSO   - RUNOFF, SOIL-TO-STREAM, ORGANIC, TON/YR
    ISO    - INDUSTRIAL ORGANIC TO SOIL, TON/YR
    SOB    - BACKGROUND ORGANIC IN SOIL, TON

ISO.KL=0.07*PR.K                                      25, R
    ISO    - INDUSTRIAL ORGANIC TO SOIL, TON/YR
    PR     - NET PRODUCTION OF MERCURY, TON/YR


EVM.KL=SM.K/EMT                                       26, R
EMT=1300                                              26.1, C
    EVM    - EVAPORATION OF METAL, TON/YR
    SM     - METAL IN SOIL, TON
    EMT    - EVAPORATION TIME, METAL, YR


EVO.KL=SO.K/EOT                                       27, R
EOT=200                                               27.1, C
    EVO    - EVAPORATION OF ORGANIC, TON/YR
    SO     - ORGANIC IN SOIL, TON
    EOT    - EVAPORATION TIME, ORGANIC, YR


RSSM.KL=SM.K/RSSMT                                    28, R
RSSMT=3600                                            28.1, C
    RSSM   - RUNOFF, SOIL-TO-STREAM, METAL, TON/YR
    SM     - METAL IN SOIL, TON
    RSSMT  - RUNOFF TIME, SOIL-STREAM, METAL, YR


RSSO.KL=SO.K/RSSOT                                    29, R
RSSOT=720                                             29.1, C
    RSSO   - RUNOFF, SOIL-TO-STREAM, ORGANIC, TON/YR
    SO     - ORGANIC IN SOIL, TON
    RSSOT  - RUNOFF TIME, SOIL-STREAM, ORGANIC, YR


CSO.K=SO.K/4.2E4                                      30, A
    CSO    - CONCENTRATION OF ORGANIC IN SOIL, PPB
    SO     - ORGANIC IN SOIL, TON


CSM.K=SM.K/4.2E4                                      31, A
    CSM    - CONCENTRATION OF METAL IN SOIL, PPB
    SM     - METAL IN SOIL, TON
```

OCEAN SECTOR

```
OM.K=OM.J+DT*(RSOM.JK+PROM.JK-UFM.JK+XOM.JK-SED.JK) 32, L
OM=OMB                                              32.1, N
OMB=2E6                                             32.2, C
    OM      - METAL IN OCEAN, TON
    RSOM    - RUNOFF, STREAM-TO-OCEAN, METAL, TON/YR
    PROM    - PRECIPITATION RATE ON OCEAN OF METAL, TON/
              YR
    UFM     - UPTAKE BY FISH OF METAL, TON/YR
    XOM     - EXCRETION OF METAL TO OCEAN, TON/YR
    SED     - SEDIMENTATION RATE (METAL-INORGANIC ONLY),
              TON/YR
    OMB     - BACKGROUND METAL IN OCEAN, TON


OO.K=OO.J+DT*(RSOO.JK+PROO.JK-UFO.JK+XOO.JK)        33, L
OO=OOB                                              33.1, N
OOB=4E4                                             33.2, C
    OO      - ORGANIC IN OCEAN, TON
    RSOO    - RUNOFF, STREAM-TO-OCEAN, ORGANIC, TON/YR
    PROO    - PRECIPITATION RATE ON OCEAN OF ORGANIC,
              TON/YR
    UFO     - UPTAKE BY FISH OF ORGANIC, TON/YR
    XOO     - EXCRETION OF ORGANIC TO OCEAN, TON/YR
    OOB     - BACKGROUND ORGANIC IN OCEAN, TON


COM.K=OM.K/2.7E7                                    34, A
    COM     - CONCENTRATION OF METAL IN OCEAN, PPB
    OM      - METAL IN OCEAN, TON


COO.K=OO.K/2.7E7                                    35, A
    COO     - CONCENTRATION OF ORGANIC IN OCEAN, PPB
    OO      - ORGANIC IN OCEAN, TON


SED.KL=OM.K/SEDT                                    36, R
SEDT=4000                                           36.1, C
    SED     - SEDIMENTATION RATE (METAL-INORGANIC ONLY),
              TON/YR
    OM      - METAL IN OCEAN, TON
    SEDT    - SEDIMENTATION TIME CONSTANT, YEAR


CFMX.K=COM.K*OFCF                                   37, A
OFCF=3                                              37.1, C
    CFMX    - EXPECTED CONCENTRATION OF METAL IN FISH,
              PPM
    COM     - CONCENTRATION OF METAL IN OCEAN, PPB
    OFCF    - OCEAN-FISH CONCENTRATION FACTOR, PPM/PPB


CFOX.K=COO.K*OFCF                                   38, A
    CFOX    - EXPECTED CONCENTRATION OF ORGANIC IN FISH,
              PPM
    COO     - CONCENTRATION OF ORGANIC IN OCEAN, PPB
    OFCF    - OCEAN-FISH CONCENTRATION FACTOR, PPM/PPB


UFM.KL=MAX(0,(CFMX.K-CFM.K)*MF/(UT*1E6))            39, R
MF=5.5E8                                            39.1, C
UT=.1                                               39.2, C
    UFM     - UPTAKE BY FISH OF METAL, TON/YR
    CFMX    - EXPECTED CONCENTRATION OF METAL IN FISH,
              PPM
    CFM     - CONCENTRATION OF METAL IN FISH, PPM
    MF      - MASS OF FISH, TON
    UT      - UPTAKE TIME IN FISH, YR

UFO.KL=MAX(0,(CFOX.K-CFO.K)*MF/(UT*1E6))            40, R
    UFO     - UPTAKE BY FISH OF ORGANIC, TON/YR
    CFOX    - EXPECTED CONCENTRATION OF ORGANIC IN FISH,
              PPM
    CFO     - CONCENTRATION OF ORGANIC IN FISH, PPM
    MF      - MASS OF FISH, TON
    UT      - UPTAKE TIME IN FISH, YR
```

```
FISH SECTOR

FM.K=FM.J+DT*(UFM.JK-XOM.JK-XM.JK-FC.JK-DFM.JK)        41, L
FM=FMB                                                 41.1, N
FMB=40                                                 41.2, C
     FM        - METAL IN FISH, TON
     UFM       - UPTAKE BY FISH OF METAL, TON/YR
     XOM       - EXCRETION OF METAL TO OCEAN, TON/YR
     XM        - LOSS OF METAL BY EXCRETION, TON/YR
     FC        - FISH CONVERSION, METAL-TO-ORGANIC, TON/YR
     DFM       - LOSS OF METAL ON DEATH OF FISH, TON/YR
     FMB       - BACKGROUND METAL IN FISH, TON

FO.K=FO.J+DT*(UFO.JK-XOO.JK-XO.JK-DFO.JK+FC.JK)        42, L
FO=FOB                                                 42.1, N
FOB=60                                                 42.2, C
     FO        - ORGANIC IN FISH, TON
     UFO       - UPTAKE BY FISH OF ORGANIC, TON/YR
     XOO       - EXCRETION OF ORGANIC TO OCEAN, TON/YR
     XO        - LOSS OF ORGANIC BY EXCRETION, TON/YR
     DFO       - LOSS OF ORGANIC ON DEATH OF FISH, TON/YR
     FC        - FISH CONVERSION, METAL-TO-ORGANIC, TON/YR
     FOB       - BACKGROUND ORGANIC IN FISH, TON

XOM.KL=FM.K*XOF/XT                                     43, R
XOF=.5                                                 43.1, C
XT=.8                                                  43.2, C
     FM        - METAL IN FISH, TON
     XOF       - OCEAN/ABYSS FRACTION
     XT        - EXCRETION TIME, YR

XOO.KL=FO.K*XOF/XT                                     44, R
     FO        - ORGANIC IN FISH, TON
     XOF       - OCEAN/ABYSS FRACTION
     XT        - EXCRETION TIME, YR

XM.KL=FM.K*(1-XOF)/XT                                  45, R
     FM        - METAL IN FISH, TON
     XOF       - OCEAN/ABYSS FRACTION
     XT        - EXCRETION TIME, YR

XO.KL=FO.K*(1-XOF)/XT                                  46, R
     FO        - ORGANIC IN FISH, TON
     XOF       - OCEAN/ABYSS FRACTIONS
     XT        - EXCRETION TIME, YR

DFM.KL=FM.K/FLT                                        47, R
FLT=3                                                  47.1, C
     DFM       - LOSS OF METAL ON DEATH OF FISH, TON/YR
     FM        - METAL IN FISH, TON
     FLT       - LIFETIME OF FISH, YR

DFO.KL=FO.K/FLT                                        48, R
     DFO       - LOSS OF ORGANIC ON DEATH OF FISH, TON/YR
     FO        - ORGANIC IN FISH, TON
     FLT       - LIFETIME OF FISH, YR

CFM.K=FM.K*1E6/MF                                      49, A
     CFM       - CONCENTRATION OF METAL IN FISH, PPM
     FM        - METAL IN FISH, TON
     MF ·      - MASS OF FISH, TON

CFO.K=FO.K*1E6/MF                                      50, A
     CFO       - CONCENTRATION OF ORGANIC IN FISH, PPM
     FO        - ORGANIC IN FISH, TON
     MF        - MASS OF FISH, TON

FC.KL=FM.K/FCT                                         51, R
FCT=2                                                  51.1, C
     FC        - FISH CONVERSION, METAL-TO-ORGANIC, TON/YR
     FM        - METAL IN FISH, TON
     FCT       - FISH CONVERSION TIME, YR
```

MAN-MADE SECTOR

```
O.K=100*TABLE(OT,TIME.K,1900,2050,10)                52, A
OT=.2/.5/1/2/3/5/11/21/36/53/75/75/75/75/75/75       52.1, T
     O      - OIL, MILLIONS OF TON/YR
     OT     - OIL PRODUCTION TABLE, MILLIONS OF TON/YR


PR.K=0.97*P.K*(1-RCF.K)                               53, A
     PR     - NET PRODUCTION OF MERCURY, TON/YR
     P      - GROSS PRODUCTION OF MERCURY, TON/YR
     RCF    - RECYCLING FRACTION, DIMENSIONLESS


RCF.K=CLIP(RCF2,RCF1,TIME.K,RCFT)                     54, A
RCF1=.18                                              54.1, C
RCF2=.50                                              54.2, C
RCFT=4000                                             54.3, C
     RCF    - RECYCLING FRACTION, DIMENSIONLESS
     RCF2   - RECYCLING FRACTION, SECOND VALUE
     RCF1   - RECYCLING FRACTION, FIRST VALUE
     RCFT   - RECYCLING IMPLEMENTATION TIME


P.K=100*CLIP(P2.K,P1.K,TIME.K,PIT)                    55, A
PIT=1900                                              55.1, C
     P      - GROSS PRODUCTION OF MERCURY, TON/YR
     P2     - P, SECOND VALUE
     P1     - P, FIRST VALUE
     PIT    - POLICY IMPLEMENTATION TIME



P1.K=TABLE(P1T,TIME.K,1900,2050,10)                   56, A
P1T=31/33/36/43/55/68/83/104/132/170/202/202/202/     56.1, T
   202/202/202
     P1     - P, FIRST VALUE
     P1T    - P1 TABLE


P2.K=0                                                57, A
     P2     - P, SECOND VALUE


C.K=100*TABLE(CT,TIME.K,1900,2050,10)                 58, A
CT=11/12/13/14/16/19/25/30/34/39/44/44/44/44/44/44    58.1, T
     C      - COAL, MILLIONS OF TON/YR
     CT     - COAL PRODUCTION TABLE, MILLIONS OF TON/YR
```

DIRECTIONS

```
TIME=1900                                             58.5, N
PRINT 1)CAM,CAO/2)CSM,CSO/3)CMM,CMO/4)CFM,CFO/5)COM,COO
PLOT CAM=A(0,5)/CMO=N(0,40)/CSM=S,CMM=M(0,200)/
X    CFM=F(0,.5)
SPEC   DT=.1/LENGTH=2050/PRTPER=0/PLTPER=5
RUN FIGURE 6.   BACKGROUND
```

5

The Eutrophication of Lakes

Jay Martin Anderson

Pollution damage may theoretically be controlled in two ways: by decreasing the rate of pollution generation or by removing the pollutant from those areas in which it causes harm. DDT and mercury are primarily subject to the first approach. Eutrophication is one pollution problem in which the second response may be effective. Thus a simulation study of eutrophication was conducted to test the relative effectiveness of alternative removal policies.

The analysis supports one conclusion derived from the global model: no control policy based on removal can succeed indefinitely in holding pollution to acceptable levels when the generation of pollutants grows exponentially.

A shortened version of this chapter has been published as "System Simulation to Test Environmental Policy: The Eutrophication of Lakes," Environmental Letters, *vol. 3(1972), p. 203.*

5
The Eutrophication of Lakes

The Process of Eutrophication

The trophic state of lakes and water impoundments and, to a lesser extent, streams and estuaries is a measure of the support the nutrient supply of the lake affords primary producers such as algae.[1] Lakes with low nutrient resources are *oligotrophic;* those with high nutrient resources are *eutrophic. Eutrophication* refers to the process of enriching the lake medium with nutrient factors necessary to the growth of primary producers. Eutrophication can be *natural,* for it is possible that, through normal runoff and precipitation, nutrients are washed into or deposited in the lake. *Cultural* eutrophication refers to the accelerated enrichment of the limnetic medium through discharge and runoff of the wastes of man's activity.

A lake's trophic state is characterized not only by its nutrient content but also by the quantity and type of biota it supports. An oligotrophic lake supports only a small population of primary producers such as algae. A eutrophic lake supports such a large algal population that the lake becomes opaque, and thick mats of algae decrease the recreational potential of the lake and interfere with industrial and municipal water-handling equipment.

The oxygen content of a lake can also be used as an index of its trophic state. The algae generate oxygen and fix inorganic carbon into the biomass by photosynthesis. Part of this oxygen is released into the atmosphere, part into the lake. Following the death of algae, the algal detritus sinks to the bottom of the lake, where oxygen-requiring decay processes decompose the detrital sediments and return the nutrient to the lake. Consequently, if the algal population grows, leading to the accumulation of a mass of detritus on the lake bottom, the oxygen concentration in the lake can be depleted. Whereas oligotrophic lakes are nearly saturated with oxygen, the oxygen content of eutrophic lakes may decline to 30 percent of saturation or less, especially in the lower regions (hypolimnion) of the lake.[2] The ability of the lake to maintain a high oxygen concentration depends on the rate of solubility of oxygen in water and the rate of dispersion of oxygen through the lake, especially to the lake bottom.

With the reduction in oxygen the population of "noble" fish, popular for sport and eating, declines and is replaced by that of less popular scavenger fish, which can adapt to low levels of oxygen. Mats of dead and decaying algae give off the offensive odors characteristic of partially decayed matter. Low oxygen levels retard the lake's natural ability to clean itself so that it can no longer dilute and dispose of municipal organic wastes.

The evolution from oligotrophy to eutrophy is characteristic of many lakes. As nutrients gradually flow or fall into lakes, algae grow, and life on the lake bottom increases until the lake becomes a swamp or bog. The swamp evolves

[1] This discussion is excerpted from the International Symposium on Eutrophication, *Eutrophication: Causes, Consequences, Correctives* (Washington, D.C.: National Academy of Sciences, 1969), which contains a thorough bibliography.

[2] A. M. Beeton, "Eutrophication of the St. Lawrence Great Lakes," *Limnology and Oceanography*, vol. 10 (1965), p. 240.

ultimately into a meadow and finally a forest. Natural eutrophication takes place on the geologic time scale of thousands of years. Cultural eutrophication, however, can accelerate this transition to a few decades. Many of man's activities are responsible for the enrichment of the freshwater environment. Nitrogen and phosphorus nutrients from fertilizers run off from soil to stream; detergents in municipal water discharges add to the supply of nutrients in the lake; human wastes and animal wastes from feedlots are discharged in municipal water systems.[3] Once started, the process can be irreversible, and a source of clean water for municipal, industrial, commercial, or recreational use may be permanently lost or impaired.

Artificial eutrophication has been arrested and reversed to some extent, however, in some notable examples in the United States and abroad.[4] Strategies for combating eutrophication include:

1. Further treatment of sewage discharges to remove nutrients that would accelerate eutrophication;
2. Dilution of municipal and industrial effluents, or diversion of effluents away from lakes and into rapidly running streams;
3. Treatment with algicide;
4. Removing detritus from the lake bottom by dredging;
5. Harvesting the algal crop for use as a foodstuff;
6. Manipulating the limnetic environment by isolating the hypolimnion or by preventing seasonal turnover of the lake.

A System Dynamics Model for Eutrophication

Simulation modeling of environmental systems facilitates both the understanding of environmental problems and the testing of alternative policies for the survival and maintenance of the system. In fact, the American Chemical Society's Subcommittee on Environmental Improvement recommends:

> Investigations should be pursued of the fundamental chemical and biological parameters of eutrophication and its effects. Development of effective and economic long-term controls will depend on considerably improved knowledge of factors such as mass balances for significant nutrients; the forms in which those nutrients exist in water; natural population dynamics; potentially limiting nutrients in specific situations; and algal, bacterial, and plant physiology in general.[5]

---

[3] See, for example, Robert J. Butscher, "Eutrophication and Nutrient Sources," in *Environmental Side Effects of Rising Industrial Output,* ed. A. J. Van Tassel (Lexington, Mass.: Heath-Lexington Books, 1970).

[4] See R. T. Oglesby and W. Thomas Edmondson, "Control of Eutrophication," *Journal of the Water Pollution Control Federation,* vol. 38 (1966), p. 1452; W. T. Edmondson, "Water-Quality Management and Lake Eutrophication: The Lake Washington Case," in *Water Resources Management and Public Policy,* ed. T. H. Campbell and D. O. Sylvester (Seattle: University of Washington Press, 1968); F. A. Ferguson, "A Nonmyopic Approach to the Problem of Excess Algal Growth," *Environmental Science and Technology,* vol. 2 (1968), p. 188; and Arthur D. Hasler, "Cultural Eutrophication is Reversible," *Bioscience,* vol. 19 (1969), p. 425.

[5] American Chemical Society, Committee on Chemistry and Public Affairs, Subcommittee on Environmental Improvement, *Cleaning Our Environment: The Chemical Basis for Action* (Washington, D.C., 1969), p. 152.

Leonard Dworsky, contributing to a symposium on eutrophication in large lakes and impounds notes these advantages of system modeling:

> The principal benefit arising out of the "system" approach is to allow the formulation and comparative examination of a wider range of alternative solutions. . . . An added benefit is the identification of areas of needed knowledge towards which research efforts and resources will need to be applied.[6]

Two models have been proposed for the growth of biotic communities in the lake environment.[7] These models paid particular attention to the several trophic levels of the lake food chain, but they did not study oxygen levels nor did they allow policies for the control of eutrophication to be tested.

This chapter, using the methodology of system dynamics,[8] develops an extremely simple formal model for the eutrophication of lakes. The model is used to trace the behavior of lakes under conditions of natural and cultural eutrophication, and to evaluate alternative policies for arresting eutrophication and maintaining oligotrophy.

In developing a formal model for a system, be it physical or social, one must begin by defining the system boundary in time and in space. The boundary is chosen in response to the questions the model seeks to answer.

For example, if I wished to study the problem of food supply, my responses would be quite different if I were thinking of a twenty-four-hour period or a five-century period. In the former case, the system would include my kitchen, immediate household, and local food shops; in the latter, it would include the world population, climate modification, and the global availability of arable land.

The present model for eutrophication seeks to answer the question, how can cultural eutrophication effectively be arrested? Its time scale is therefore long—on the order of centuries—to preserve the distinction between natural and cultural processes. At once, therefore, we can rule out seasonal or diurnal fluctuations as unimportant perturbations in the development of a lake over the course of two hundred years. At the same time, we cannot neglect effects that, although small, could be amplified by the model simulation and lead to erroneous conclusions about the state of the system after a century.

The system boundary includes those variables, and only those variables, that are necessary to construct an answer to our principal question. We have identified four such variables: a nutrient, a biotic population, decaying detritus, and oxygen. We shall discuss further the validity of restricting the system to these four variables and suggest directions in which the model could be extended.

---

[6] Leonard B. Dworsky, "Lakes as a Part of the Total Water System," in *Eutrophication in Large Lakes and Impounds,* ed. C. P. Milway, from the symposium on that subject at Uppsala, May 1968 (Paris: OECD, 1970).

[7] Frederick E. Smith, "Effects of Enrichment in Mathematical Models," in International Symposium on Eutrophication, *Eutrophication,* and Loren W. Mitchell and Michael O. Breitmeyer, "Generalized Simulation of a Temperate Eutrophic Lake," *1971 Proceedings of Summer Computer Simulation Conference* (Denver: Board of Simulation Conferences, 1971), p. 1046.

[8] The system dynamics flow diagram symbols are described in Chapter 2 and summarized in Figure 2-2.

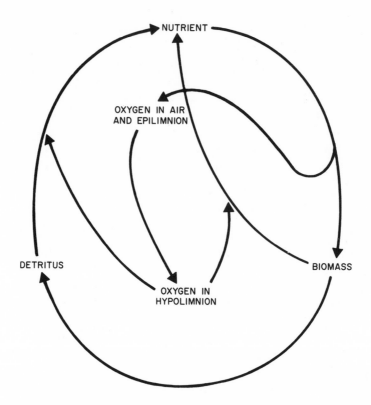

Figure 5-1 The flow of nutrient and of oxygen in the lake environment

A conceptual model such as this is not designed to propose specific engineering solutions for arresting eutrophication in a particular lake. It is designed to capture the most basic causes and consequences of the process of eutrophication so that these processes can be easily understood and policies to alter them can be considered. This simple model could be extended and specialized to examine the details of any particular lake, given an adequate data base. The extended model could then be used to test specific engineering recommendations for arresting eutrophication in that lake. But to aid in acquiring a basic understanding of the process, we began by omitting many known biological and limnological variables. We focused only on the minimum set of variables necessary to reproduce the gross trophic development of all lakes.

Having defined the system boundary, the system dynamics modeling effort continues with the identification of flows of matter and the cause-and-effect relationships modifying these flows. Figure 5-1 shows the basic cycle of nutrient flow in a lake, from inorganic nutrient pool to biomass to detritus and back to nutrient pool, as well as the flow of oxygen that is coupled to the nutrient cycle.

Nutrient Cycling.   The flow of a nutrient through biomass, detritus, and back to nutrient pool is a closed loop; thus biotic growth is limited by nutrient availabil-

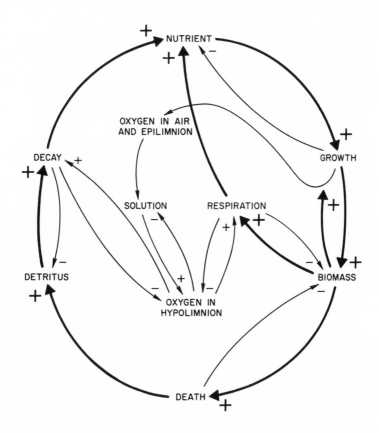

Figure 5-2 A causal-loop diagram for eutrophication. Arrows indicate cause-and-effect relationships; the sign at each
arrowhead indicates the sense of the relationship. For
example, an increase in nutrients causes an increase in
growth, but an increase in growth depletes nutrients.
The three positive feedback loops that cycle nutrient
through the system are heavily outlined.

ity. The system is not static even in steady state, however, for nutrient is cycled
by three positive feedback loops as shown in Figure 5-2. The rate of nutrient
cycling is restrained or controlled at the same time by the four negative feedback
loops shown in Figure 5-3.

The DYNAMO equations for the cycling of nutrient are listed and discussed
later, together with the assumptions on which they are based. Throughout, concentrations are expressed as milligrams of nutrient element per liter, and times are
in years.

The size of the biotic community is governed by its growth rate, death rate,
and respiration rate. Growth fixes nutrient into biomass, whereas death deposits
this element in the detrital pool. Metabolic processes such as respiration or excretion also return the element to the nutrient pool from biomass. The rate FARM
will be discussed in the section on policy alternatives.

```
B.K=B.J+DT*(GR.JK-DR.JK-FARM.JK-RR.JK)              2, L
B=BI                                                2.1, N
BI=0.2                                              2.2, C
     B       - BIOMASS, MG/L
     GR      - GROWTH RATE, MG/L-YR
     DR      - DEATH RATE, MG/L-YR
     FARM    - FARMING RATE, MG/L-YR
     RR      - RESPIRATION RATE, MG/L-YR
     BI      - BIOMASS, INITIAL, MG/L


GR.KL=K1*N.K*B.K                                    10, R
K1=0.2                                              10.1, C
     GR      - GROWTH RATE, MG/L-YR
     K1      - GROWTH-RATE CONSTANT, L/MG-YR
     N       - NUTRIENT, MG/L
     B       - BIOMASS, MG/L
```

The growth rate is first order in both biomass B* and nutrient N, which is equivalent to saying that the growth of the biomass is limited by the nutrient available. Smith's model makes a similar assumption.[9] The model could of course be modified to include a gradual transition from a rate first-order in nutrient to a rate zeroth-order in nutrient, as is suggested by Michaelis-Menton enzyme kinetics.[10] That is, if the medium were saturated by nutrient, the growth rate would be proportional to biomass concentration but independent of nutrient concentration.

If the rate of growth were independent of any given nutrient, then some other factor would become limiting to growth. The model assumes that only one specific nutrient is limiting throughout the entire growth process. An obvious extension of the model would examine the possibility that, as one nutrient is increased, some other nutrient becomes the growth-limiting factor.[11] Carbon is thought to be the limiting nutrient in some limnetic systems, although nitrogen and phosphorous are the more common suspects. In some lakes, mineral or organic micronutrients—trace metals or vitamins—may be the growth-limiting factors. The model structure could be modified to represent these cases, but the basic behavior modes would remain those exhibited by this model.

The relative flows of a specific nutrient in the relationship between growth (nutrient assimilation) and oxygen production, and between respiration and decay and oxygen consumption, are calculated in the model by simple stoichiometric requirements. Because the stoichiometric relationship between fixation of inorganic carbon (carbon dioxide, bicarbonate ion, or carbonate ion) and oxygen production is known from the chemical equation of photosynthesis, carbon has been used as the limiting nutrient in this conceptual model. One gram of carbon is stoichiometrically equivalent to 2.67 grams of oxygen, so the oxygen-nutrient

---

[9] Smith, "Effects of Enrichment."

[10] These terms are explained in modern physical chemistry textbooks such as Walter J. Moore, *Physical Chemistry* (Englewood Cliffs, N.J.: Prentice Hall, 1962).

[11] Eugene P. Odum, *Fundamentals of Ecology* (Philadelphia, Pa.: W. B. Saunders, 1971), p. 107.

*Eds. note—Whenever we use a term that corresponds to a variable in the simulation model, the variable name (as it appears in the model equations in the appendix to this chapter) is printed immediately following that term.

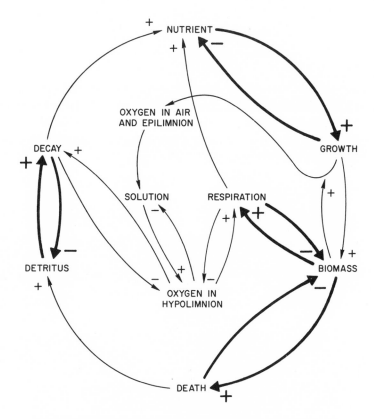

Figure 5-3 The causal-loop diagram of Figure 5-2 with four negative, or goal-seeking, feedback loops heavily outlined.

ratio ONR = 2.67. Specific stoichiometric and mechanistic changes would be required to adapt the model to a nutrient other than carbon.

An oligotrophic lake fixes approximately 7.5 grams of carbon per square meter per year[12] or, for a typical lake,[13] about 1.6 mg L^{-1} yr^{-1}.[14] In the same lake, the nutrient pool contains about 40 mg L^{-1} of carbon (as carbonate). Since aquatic primary producers fix about eight times their own mass per year,[15] biomass B stands initially at about 0.2 mg L^{-1}. The growth rate constant K1 must therefore be 0.2 L mg^{-1} yr^{-1}.

In a given year, approximately half the carbon in the biomass is respired, and half "dies."[16] The death rate must be proportional to the biomass; the rate constant for this process is K2 = 4 yr^{-1}.

[12] Wilhelm Rohde, "Eutrophication Concepts in Northern Europe," in the symposium cited in fn. 1.

[13] Data are for the Zürichsee, taken from Eugene A. Thomas, "The Process of Eutrophication in Central European Lakes," in the symposium cited in fn. 1.

[14] Throughout this paper, concentrations of nutrient and oxygen are measured in milligrams per liter, abbreviated mg L^{-1}. Rates of change of these concentrations are measured in milligrams per liter per year, or mg L^{-1} yr^{-1}.

[15] Bert Bolin, "The Carbon Cycle," *Scientific American,* September 1970, p. 124.

[16] Ibid.

```
DR.KL=K2.K*B.K                                              11, R
   DR     - DEATH RATE, MG/L-YR
   K2     - DEATH-RATE CONSTANT, 1/YR
   B      - BIOMASS, MG/L
```

Respiration depends on both biomass and oxygen. Initially, the respiration rate must, like the death rate, be about half the growth rate, or 0.8 mg L^{-1} yr^{-1}; therefore, if the initial oxygen level is 9 mg L^{-1}, the respiration rate constant K4 must be 0.445 L mg^{-1} yr^{-1}. If a nutrient other than carbon were represented, this equation would reflect excretion rather than respiration.

```
RR.KL=K4*B.K*OH.K                                          15, R
K4=0.445                                                   15.1, C
   PR     - RESPIRATION RATE, MG/L-YR
   K4     - RESPIRATION-RATE CONSTANT, L/MG-YR
   B      - BIOMASS, MG/L
   OH     - OXYGEN IN HYPOLIMNION, MG/L
```

The death of biota transfers material from the biomass to the detritus, and decay completes the cycle by transferring the material back to the inorganic nutrient pool.

```
D.K=D.J+DT*(DR.JK-DEC.JK-DREDG.JK)                         3, L
D=DI                                                       3.1, N
DI=2                                                       3.2, C
   D      - DETRITUS, MG/L
   DR     - DEATH RATE, MG/L-YR
   DEC    - DECAY RATE, MG/L-YR
   DREDG  - DREDGING RATE, MG/L-YR
   DI     - DETRITUS, INITIAL, MG/L

DEC.KL=K3*D.K*OH.K                                         14, R
K3=0.0445                                                  14.1, C
   DEC    - DECAY RATE, MG/L-YR
   K3     - DECAY-RATE CONSTANT, L/MG-YR
   D      - DETRITUS, MG/L
   OH     - OXYGEN IN HYPOLIMNION, MG/L

N.K=N.J+DT*(FR.JK-GR.JK+RR.JK+DEC.JK)                      1, L
N=NI                                                       1.1, N
NI=40                                                      1.2, C
   N      - NUTRIENT, MG/L
   FR     - FEEDING RATE, MG/L-YR
   GR     - GROWTH RATE, MG/L-YR
   RR     - RESPIRATION RATE, MG/L-YR
   DEC    - DECAY RATE, MG/L-YR
   NI     - NUTRIENT, INITIAL, MG/L
```

The rates FR and DREDG are discussed in the section on policy alternatives.

The rate of detritus decay depends on both the detritus and the oxygen supply. Because we have no knowledge of the amount of decaying organic matter in an oligotrophic lake, we know only that (initially) K3 [D] [O] must be 0.8 mg L^{-1} yr^{-1}, so K3 [D] = 0.08 yr^{-1}. Sample values might be K3 = 0.01, D = 8, for example. The choice of these parameters can affect the behavior of the model.

Oxygen Consumption and Production. The flow of oxygen in and out of a lake is a complex superposition of many effects, including the diurnal cycle of photosynthetic production, the seasonal overturn of lakes, solution, diffusion, and the effects of temperature fluctuations. We seek here, without recourse to hydro-dynamic models of the flux and gradients of dissolved species, to isolate the behavior of oxygen flow over the course of centuries.

Most lakes are divided into two vertical strata, the epilimnion and the hypo-limnion. The epilimnion, or upper portion of the lake, is two to five meters deep, contains most of the primary producers, and is rich in oxygen. The lower level, or hypolimnion, is separated from the epilimnion by the thermocline, a boundary between cold and warm water. With the seasonal turnover of the lake, oxygen is mixed into the hypolimnion, and nutrients are returned to the epilimnion.

As a first approximation, then, oxidation of detritus takes place in the hypo-limnion. The oxygen in this region is replaced very slowly from the epilimnion by diffusion and convection,[17] and seasonally by the lake overturn. In the epilim-nion, photoproduction of oxygen keeps the oxygen level near saturation, that is, about 10 mg L^{-1}. If more oxygen is produced than can be dissolved in the epilim-nion, this oxygen is rapidly released into the atmosphere; if the oxygen level in the epilimnion falls below saturation, it is rapidly replenished from the atmos-phere. That the epilimnion rapidly adjusts toward saturation is supported by the rate equation for oxygen dissolution, including entrance and exit coefficients,[18] which indicates that up to 5,400 mg $L^{-1}yr^{-1}$ of oxygen can be exchanged with the atmosphere.

The rapid exchange of oxygen from the epilimnion to the atmosphere and the slow exchange of oxygen from the epilimnion to the hypolimnion suggest that a model with a two-hundred-year time span can assume that the epilimnion remains in equilibrium with the atmosphere but that oxygen is depleted from the hypo-limnion by respiration and decay processes and is replenished from the epilimnion by seasonal turnover.

If seasonal turnover were the only mechanism for oxygen replenishment, the maximum rate of oxygen influx to the hypolimnion (averaged over one year) would be

$$(\text{seasonal turnovers per year}) \times \frac{(\text{oxygen in epilimnion})}{(\text{volume of lake})} =$$

$$(2 \text{ yr}^{-1})(10 \text{ mg } L^{-1})\frac{V_e}{V_l}$$

If the ratio of the volume of the epilimnion to total lake, $V_e/V_l \cong 0.1$, then the rate of oxygen influx would be 2 mg $L^{-1} yr^{-1}$. Values less than 2 mg $L^{-1} yr^{-1}$ would be obtained if the hypolimnion itself contained some source of oxygen, and values greater than 2 mg $L^{-1} yr^{-1}$ would be obtained if other dispersive mecha-nisms, such as convection and diffusion, were efficient. Since these mechanisms

[17] G. E. Hutchinson, *A Treatise on Limnology* (New York: John Wiley & Sons, 1957).
[18] Ibid.

are not well understood,[19] for the purposes of this conceptual model, the oxygen levels in the lake were taken to be governed by the following assumptions:

1. The oxygen level was computed as a weighted average of oxygen in the epilimnion OE and oxygen in the hypolimnion OH, using a ratio of epilimnion to hypolimnion volume EHR:

```
O.K=EHR*OE+(1-EHR)*OH.K                                    5, S
EHR=.1                                                    5.1, C
    O        - AVERAGE OXYGEN IN LAKE, MG/L
    EHR      - EPILIMNION/HYPOLIMNION VOLUME RATIO,
               DIMENSIONLESS
    OE       - OXYGEN IN EPILIMNION, MG/L
    OH       - OXYGEN IN HYPOLIMNION, MG/L
```

2. Oxygen in the epilimnion is constant and equal to the saturated oxygen concentration.

3. Oxygen is consumed from the hypolimnion by respiration and decay and is replenished from the epilimnion at a rate proportional to the difference between epilimnion and hypolimnion concentrations, but not exceeding 20 mg L^{-1} yr^{-1}.

```
OH.K=OH.J+DT*(SR.JK-CR.JK+AER.JK)                         4, L
OH=OE-1                                                   4.1, N
OE=10                                                     4.2, C
    OH       - OXYGEN IN HYPOLIMNION, MG/L
    SR       - SOLUTION RATE, OXYGEN TO HYPOLIMNION, MG/L-
               YR
    CR       - OXYGEN-CONSUMPTION RATE, MG/L-YR
    AER      - AERATION RATE, MG/L-YR
    OE       - OXYGEN IN EPILIMNION, MG/L

CR.KL=(RR.JK+DEC.JK)*ONR                                  16, R
ONR=2.67                                                  16.1, C
    CR       - OXYGEN-CONSUMPTION RATE, MG/L-YR
    RR       - RESPIRATION RATE, MG/L-YR
    DEC      - DECAY RATE, MG/L-YR
    ONR      - OXYGEN-NUTRIENT RATIO, DIMENSIONLESS

SR.KL=MIN(20,K5*(OE-OH.K))                                17, R
K5=4.27                                                   17.1, C
    SR       - SOLUTION RATE, OXYGEN TO HYPOLIMNION, MG/L-YR
    K5       - SOLUTION RATE CONSTANT, 1/YR
    OE       - OXYGEN IN EPILIMNION, MG/L
    OH       - OXYGEN IN HYPOLIMNION, MG/L
```

Summary. The model was initialized with steady-state conditions:

$$GR = DR + RR = 1.6 \text{ mg (carbon) } L^{-1} yr^{-1}$$

$$DEC = DR = 0.8 \text{ mg (carbon) } L^{-1} yr^{-1}$$

and

$$CR = SR = (2.67)(1.6) = 4.27 \text{ mg (oxygen) } L^{-1} yr^{-1}.$$

[19] Ibid.

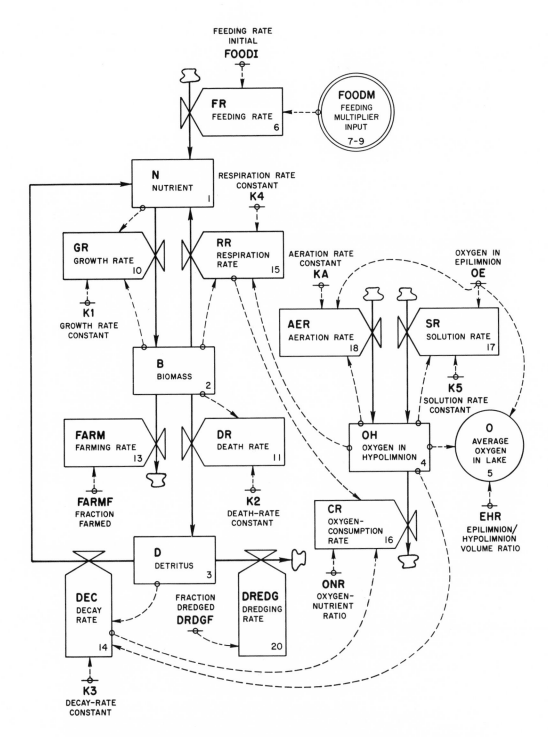

Figure 5-4 DYNAMO flow diagram of eutrophication. K1, K3, and K4 are second-order rate constants; K2 and K5 are first-order rate constants.

Quantity	Value	Reference
Nutrient N	40 mg L^{-1}	a
Biomass B	0.2 mg L^{-1}	b c
Oxygen O	10 mg L^{-1} in epilimnion	d
Growth constant K1	0.2 L mg^{-1} yr^{-1}	b
Death constant K2	4 yr^{-1}	c
Respiration constant K4	0.445 L mg^{-1} yr^{-1}	c
Solution constant K5	4.27 yr^{-1}	steady state
Although neither initial detritus D nor the decay constant K3 are known, the product K3 [D] is	0.08 yr^{-1}	steady state
Oxygen-nutrient ratio ONR	2 .67	stoichiometry
Epilimnion-hypolimnion ratio EHR	0.1	estimate

[a]Eugene A. Thomas, "The Process of Eutrophication in Central European Lakes," in International Symposium on Eutrophication, *Eutrophication: Causes, Consequences, Correctives* (Washington, D.C.: National Academy of Sciences, 1969).
[b]Wilhelm Rohde, "Eutrophication Concepts in Northern Europe," in ibid.
[c]Bert Bolin, "The Carbon Cycle," *Scientific American,* September 1970, p. 124.
[d]G. E. Hutchinson, *A Treatise on Limnology* (New York: John Wiley & Sons, 1957).

Figure 5-5   Parameters and initial conditions for the eutrophication model

The full DYNAMO flow diagram for the model is shown in Figure 5-4. Figure 5-5 summarizes the parameters used in the model, and the appendix to this paper gives the DYNAMO equations for the model.

Behavior of the System
To exhibit the property of oligotrophy, we have simulated the lake system with the model just described, using a constant nutrient input of 1 μg L^{-1} yr^{-1}.

```
FR.KL=FOODI*FOODM.K                                    6, R
FOODI=.001                                             6.1, C
     FR     - FEEDING RATE, MG/L-YR
     FOODI  - FEEDING RATE, INITIAL, MG/L-YR
     FOODM  - FEEDING MULTIPLIER, DIMENSIONLESS


FOODM.K=SWITCH(FOODM2.K,FOODM1.K,FSW)                  7, A
FSW=1                                                  7.1, C
     FOODM   - FEEDING MULTIPLIER, DIMENSIONLESS
     FOODM2  - FEEDING MULTIPLIER, SECOND VALUE,
                  DIMENSIONLESS
     FOODM1  - FEEDING MULTIPLIER, FIRST VALUE,
                  DIMENSIONLESS
     FSW     - FEEDING-MULTIPLIER SWITCH
```

```
FOODM1.K=TABHL(FOODM1T,TIME.K,0,200,20)              8, A
FOODM1T=1/1/1/1/1/1/1/1/1/1/1                        8.1, T
    FOODM1 - FEEDING MULTIPLIER, FIRST VALUE,
                DIMENSIONLESS
    FOODM1T- FEEDING-MULTIPLIER TABLE, FIRST VALUES

FOODM2.K=TABHL(FOODM2T,TIME.K,0,200,20)              9, A
FOODM2T=1/1.44/2.06/2.96/4.25/6.15/8.82/12.70/      9.1, T
  18.29/26.34/37.93
    FOODM2 - FEEDING MULTIPLIER, SECOND VALUE,
                DIMENSIONLESS
```

In the equations for feeding rate FR, this operating condition is selected by resetting the "switch" FSW to choose FOODM1T, the constant feeding multiplier, and by resetting the initial feeding rate FOODI to 0.001.

The results of this simulation are shown in Figure 5-6. Biomass B and detritus D rise only slightly, and the depletion of oxygen over the course of two centuries is very slight.

The ability of the limnetic environment to recover after a period of eutrophication is examined in Figure 5-7. The feeding rate is reset so that 10 μg L^{-1} yr^{-1} of nutrient are applied to the lake for forty years, and thereafter the oligotrophic 1 μg L^{-1} yr^{-1} is applied. It is clear that the lake system, as modeled here, does not recover; that is, it does not return to the initial nutrient-biomass-detritus state.

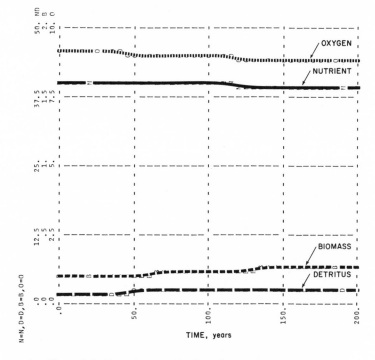

Figure 5-6   Natural eutrophication. A very slow buildup of biomass and depletion of oxygen in the response to an enrichment of 1 μg L^{-1} yr^{-1}.

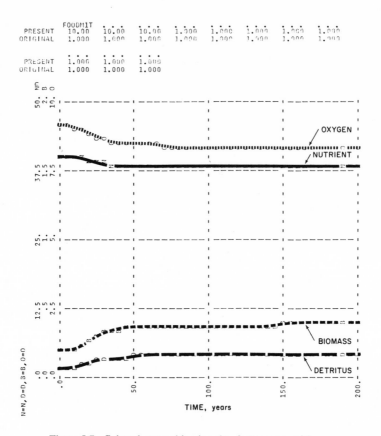

Figure 5-7 Cultural eutrophication for forty years, with an
enrichment rate of 10 μg L⁻¹ yr⁻¹, followed by a
return to natural eutrophication, as in Figure 5-6

Rather, a new steady state with an elevated biomass B and detritus D budget is
achieved. Because of the delays in the system, this new state is not reached until
several years after the return to a low feeding rate. We conclude from this simulation that, in the absence of a specific recovery action on the part of water-
resource planners or in the absence of an efficient autorestoration mechanism for
the lake, lakes cannot recover from an initial nutrient overload; once nutrient has
been deposited in the lake it can only be cycled from the biomass to the detritus
to the inorganic pool. It cannot disappear. Second, we conclude that a policy to
arrest eutrophication must anticipate nutrient loads ten or more years in advance
because of the inherent delays in the system response to any policy.

The rate of discharge of nutrients into the waterways of the nation is increasing at about 2 percent per year.[20] If we assume that an input ten times the
oligotrophic background, or 10 μg L⁻¹ yr⁻¹, is a conservative estimate for eutro-
phicating lakes, and that that input grows exponentially at 2 percent per year,

[20] Butscher, "Eutrophication and Nutrient Sources."

then severe oxygen depletion becomes likely, as shown in Figure 5-8. The rapid growth of biomass B and detritus D is accompanied by a decline in oxygen in the hypolimnion OH to about 50 percent of saturation. Other simulations indicate that oxygen can be depleted to less than a third of saturation in only thirty years if the feeding rate is one hundred times the background rate, or 100 μg L^{-1} yr^{-1}.

Policies for the Control of Eutrophication.

Various solutions have been proposed to reverse or halt lake eutrophication, and some have been successfully implemented. The dilution or diversion of effluents is intended to maintain enrichment rates at or near the natural rate. The diluted or diverted effluents are cleaned in the more rapidly flowing outlet stream of the lake. Recovery to the extent indicated in Figure 5-7 is possible. This solution policy attacks the problem where nutrients enter the lake, but it places a greater burden on water users downstream.

Figures 5-9–5-12 are simulations of the system with exponentially growing nutrient discharge (2 percent per year) as in Figure 5-8 but under four radical policy alternatives, each applied at year 100.

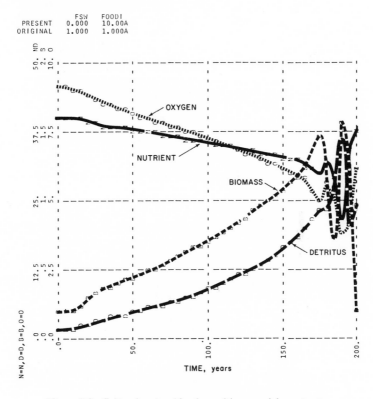

Figure 5-8 Cultural eutrophication with an enrichment rate beginning at 10 μg L^{-1} yr^{-1} and increasing at an annual rate of 2 percent

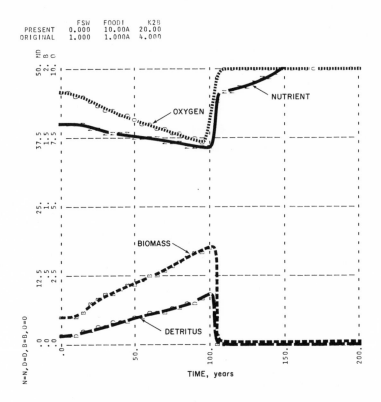

Figure 5-9 The effect of applying algicide to a lake undergoing cultural eutrophication at the rate shown
in Figure 5-8. Algicide is applied *continuously*
beginning at year 100.

Algicide has been used to purge lakes of algal biomass. Figure 5-9 indicates that the lake can be maintained in an oligotrophic state by increasing the death rate of algae fivefold. It is important to understand, however, that the algicide would have to be applied continuously to achieve the limited goal of oligotrophy. At the same time, of course, repercussions of this biocidal policy through the food chain must be considered; they do not appear explicitly in the model. This model does not trace the effect of algicide on other trophic levels, nor the effect of an exponentially increasing nutrient concentration N on the environment. To represent all the implications of the policy of algicide application, the system boundary would have to be extended to include these factors. Therefore, on the basis of this model, we cannot justify simultaneously discharging wastes and applying algicide as a solution to the problem of eutrophication.

Aeration of the lake by bubbling air into the water can restore the oxygen level of the lake, but only for a short time, as shown in Figure 5-10. This process was modeled by including an aeration rate at year 100.

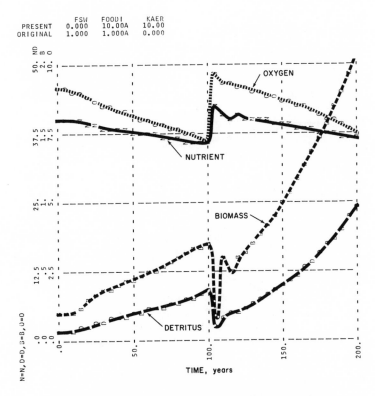

Figure 5-10 The effect of aeration on a lake undergoing cultural eutrophication at the rate shown in Figure 5-8. Aeration begins and continues from year 100.

```
AER.KL=KA.K*(OE-OH.K)                                    18, R
     AER    - AERATION RATE, MG/L-YR
     KA     - AERATION-RATE CONSTANT, 1/YR
     OE     - OXYGEN IN EPILIMNION, MG/L
     OH     - OXYGEN IN HYPOLIMNION, MG/L

KA.K=CLIP(KAER,0,TIME.K,PIT)                             19, A
KAER=0                                                   19.1, C
     KA     - AEPATION-RATE CONSTANT, 1/YR
     KAER   - AERATION-RATE CONSTANT, SECOND VALUE
     PIT    - POLICY-IMPLEMENTATION TIME, YEAR
```

The aeration rate is more than twice the natural dissolution rate for oxygen. Even though aeration is maintained, continued enrichment is still manifested as eutrophication. In fact, the exogenous oxygen supply enhances the positive feedback loops and drives the system at an even faster rate. Thus aeration appears to be effective only in the short term.

Dredging the lake bottom of the detrital sediments each year is also a successful method, as Figure 5-11 shows. The dredging rate is proportional to the amount of detritus, beginning at year 100.

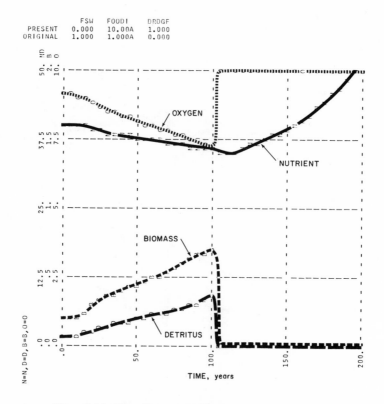

Figure 5-11　The effect of dredging detrital sediments on a lake undergoing cultural eutrophication at the rate shown in Figure 5-8. Dredging begins and continues from year 100.

```
DREDG.KL=CLIP(MAX(0,DRDGF*D.K),0,TIME.K,PIT)          20, R
DRDGF=0                                               20.1, C
     DREDG   - DREDGING RATE, MG/L-YR
     DRDGF   - FRACTION DREDGED PER YEAR, 1/YR
     D       - DETRITUS, MG/L
     PIT     - POLICY-IMPLEMENTATION TIME, YEAR
```

Although dredging may also have repercussions in the lake environment by removing benthic organisms, the sediment removed can be returned to the land as fertilizer.

Finally, Figure 5-12 shows the effect of farming the algal crop twice a year. This material is reported to be a good source of protein and of some vitamins, and it could be marketed as a valuable foodstuff.

```
FARM.KL=CLIP(MAX(0,FARMF*B.K),0,TIME.K,PIT):          13, R
FARMF=0                                               13.1, C
     FARM    - FARMING RATE, MG/L-YR
     FARMF   - FRACTION FARMED PER YEAR, 1/YR
     B       - BIOMASS, MG/L
     PIT     - POLICY-IMPLEMENTATION TIME, YEAR
```

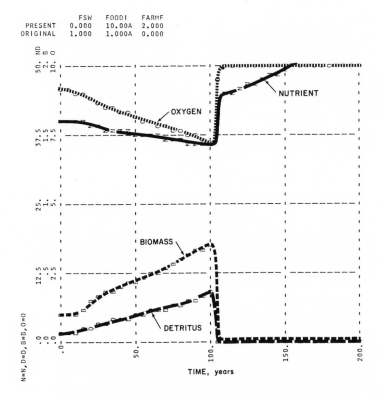

Figure 5-12   The effect of harvesting algae on a lake undergoing cultural eutrophication at the rate shown
in Figure 5-8. The algal crop is harvested four
times a year, beginning in year 100.

It is clear that the only policies with long-term continued success are those
that remove nutrients from the lake by restricting or diverting inputs, dredging
sediments, or harvesting algae. Other policies do not attack the problem—nutrient
enrichment—at its root. They will be unsuccessful in the long run.

Conclusions

A simple model of nutrient recycling and oxygen consumption explains the
transition from oligotrophy to eutrophy in lakes. The model can be improved and
extended by adding specific representation of the stratification of the lake and
seasonal turnover, higher trophic levels, and multiple or micronutrients. Further
research on how different nutrients affect biotic growth is important for extensions of the model.

The danger of destroying the aquatic environment through the continued
expansion of man's activities is clearly traced in Figure 5-8. The premature evolution of lakes such as Lake Erie in the United States is an established fact. Manipulating the limnetic environment leads only to a brief delay of eutrophy, but man

can reverse the process, both by arresting unnatural enrichment of the lakes at the source and by removing this material as biomass or detritus.

Appendix: Computer Program for the Eutrophication Model

```
N.K=N.J+DT*(FR.JK-GR.JK+RR.JK+DEC.JK)                    1, L
N=NI                                                      1.1, N
NI=40                                                     1.2, C
     N      - NUTRIENT, MG/L
     FR     - FEEDING RATE, MG/L-YR
     GR     - GROWTH RATE, MG/L-YR
     RR     - RESPIRATION RATE, MG/L-YR
     DEC    - DECAY RATE, MG/L-YR
     NI     - NUTRIENT, INITIAL, MG/L

B.K=B.J+DT*(GR.JK-DR.JK-FARM.JK-RR.JK)                   2, L
B=BI                                                      2.1, N
BI=0.2                                                    2.2, C
     B      - BIOMASS, MG/L
     GR     - GROWTH RATE, MG/L-YR
     DR     - DEATH RATE, MG/L-YR
     FARM   - FARMING RATE, MG/L-YR
     RR     - RESPIRATION RATE, MG/L-YR
     BI     - BIOMASS, INITIAL, MG/L

D.K=D.J+DT*(DR.JK-DEC.JK-DREDG.JK)                       3, L
D=DI                                                      3.1, N
DI=2                                                      3.2, C
     D      - DETRITUS, MG/L
     DR     - DEATH RATE, MG/L-YR
     DEC    - DECAY RATE, MG/L-YR
     DREDG  - DREDGING RATE, MG/L-YR
     DI     - DETRITUS, INITIAL, MG/L

OH.K=OH.J+DT*(SR.JK-CR.JK+AER.JK)                        4, L
OH=OE-1                                                   4.1, N
OE=10                                                     4.2, C
     OH     - OXYGEN IN HYPOLIMNION, MG/L
     SR     - SOLUTION RATE, OXYGEN TO HYPOLIMNION, MG/L-
              YR
     CR     - OXYGEN-CONSUMPTION RATE, MG/L-YR
     AER    - AERATION RATE, MG/L-YR
     OE     - OXYGEN IN EPILIMNION, MG/L

O.K=EHR*OE+(1-EHR)*OH.K                                  5, S
EHR=.1                                                    5.1, C
     O      - AVERAGE OXYGEN IN LAKE, MG/L
     EHR    - EPILIMNION/HYPOLIMNION VOLUME RATIO,
              DIMENSIONLESS
     OE     - OXYGEN IN EPILIMNION, MG/L
     OH     - OXYGEN IN HYPOLIMNION, MG/L

FR.KL=FOODI*FOODM.K                                      6, R
FOODI=.001                                                6.1, C
     FR     - FEEDING RATE, MG/L-YR
     FOODI  - FEEDING RATE, INITIAL, MG/L-YR
     FOODM  - FEEDING MULTIPLIER, DIMENSIONLESS

FOODM.K=SWITCH(FOODM2.K,FOODM1.K,FSW)                    7, A
FSW=1                                                     7.1, C
     FOODM  - FEEDING MULTIPLIER, DIMENSIONLESS
     FOODM2 - FEEDING MULTIPLIER, SECOND VALUE,
              DIMENSIONLESS
     FOODM1 - FEEDING MULTIPLIER, FIRST VALUE,
              DIMENSIONLESS
     FSW    - FEEDING-MULTIPLIER SWITCH

FOODM1.K=TABHL(FOODM1T,TIME.K,0,200,20)                  8, A
FOODM1T=1/1/1/1/1/1/1/1/1/1/1                             8.1, T
     FOODM1 - FEEDING MULTIPLIER, FIRST VALUE,
              DIMENSIONLESS
     FOODM1T- FEEDING-MULTIPLIER TABLE, FIRST VALUES
```

```
FOODM2.K=TABHL(FOODM2T,TIME.K,0,200,20)                    9, A
FOODM2T=1/1.44/2.06/2.96/4.25/6.15/8.82/12.70/             9.1, T
    18.29/26.34/37.93
    FOODM2 - FEEDING MULTIPLIER, SECOND VALUE,
             DIMENSIONLESS

GR.KL=K1*N.K*B.K                                           10, R
K1=0.2                                                     10.1, C
    GR       - GROWTH RATE, MG/L-YR
    K1       - GROWTH-RATE CONSTANT, L/MG-YR
    N        - NUTRIENT, MG/L
    B        - BIOMASS, MG/L

DR.KL=K2.K*B.K                                             11, R
    DR       - DEATH RATE, MG/L-YR
    K2       - DEATH-RATE CONSTANT, 1/YR
    B        - BIOMASS, MG/L

K2.K=CLIP(K2B,K2A,TIME.K,PIT)                             12, A
K2A=4                                                     12.1, C
K2B=4                                                     12.2, C
PIT=100                                                   12.3, C
    K2       - DEATH-RATE CONSTANT, 1/YR
    K2B      - DEATH-RATE CONSTANT, SECOND VALUE
    K2A      - DEATH-RATE CONSTANT, FIRST VALUE
    PIT      - POLICY-IMPLEMENTATION TIME, YEAR

FARM.KL=CLIP(MAX(0,FARMF*B.K),0,TIME.K,PIT):             13, R
FARMF=0                                                   13.1, C
    FARM     - FARMING RATE, MG/L-YR
    FARMF    - FRACTION FARMED PER YEAR, 1/YR
    B        - BIOMASS, MG/L
    PIT      - POLICY-IMPLEMENTATION TIME, YEAR

DEC.KL=K3*D.K*OH.K                                        14, R
K3=0.0445                                                 14.1, C
    DEC      - DECAY RATE, MG/L-YR
    K3       - DECAY-RATE CONSTANT, L/MG-YR
    D        - DETRITUS, MG/L
    OH       - OXYGEN IN HYPOLIMNION, MG/L

RR.KL=K4*B.K*OH.K                                         15, R
K4=0.445                                                  15.1, C
    RR       - RESPIRATION RATE, MG/L-YR
    K4       - RESPIRATION-RATE CONSTANT, L/MG-YR
    B        - BIOMASS, MG/L
    OH       - OXYGEN IN HYPOLIMNION, MG/L

CR.KL=(RR.JK+DEC.JK)*ONR                                  16, R
ONR=2.67                                                  16.1, C
    CR       - OXYGEN-CONSUMPTION RATE, MG/L-YR
    RR       - RESPIRATION RATE, MG/L-YR
    DEC      - DECAY RATE, MG/L-YR
    ONR      - OXYGEN-NUTRIENT RATIO, DIMENSIONLESS

SR.KL=MIN(20,K5*(OE-OH.K))                               17, R
K5=4.27                                                  17.1, C
    SR       - SOLUTION RATE, OXYGEN TO HYPOLIMNION, MG/L-YR
    K5       - SOLUTION RATE CONSTANT, 1/YR
    OE       - OXYGEN IN EPILIMNION, MG/L
    OH       - OXYGEN IN HYPOLIMNION, MG/L

AER.KL=KA.K*(OE-OH.K)                                    18, R
    AER      - AERATION RATE, MG/L-YR
    KA       - AERATION-RATE CONSTANT, 1/YR
    OE       - OXYGEN IN EPILIMNION, MG/L
    OH       - OXYGEN IN HYPOLIMNION, MG/L

KA.K=CLIP(KAER,0,TIME.K,PIT)                             19, A
KAER=0                                                    19.1, C
    KA       - AERATION-RATE CONSTANT, 1/YR
    KAER     - AERATION-RATE CONSTANT, SECOND VALUE
    PIT      - POLICY-IMPLEMENTATION TIME, YEAR
```

```
DREDG.KL=CLIP(MAX(0,DRDGF*D.K),0,TIME.K,PIT)        20, R
DRDGF=0                                             20.1, C
     DREDG   - DREDGING RATE, MG/L-YR
     DRDGF   - FRACTION DREDGED PER YEAR, 1/YR
     D       - DETRITUS, MG/L
     PIT     - POLICY-IMPLEMENTATION TIME, YEAR

PLOT N=N,D=D(0,50)/B=B(0,2)/O=O(0,10)
SPEC DT=.05/LENGTH=200/PRTPER=0/PLTPER=5
RUN NATURAL EUTROPHICATION
T FOODM1T=10/10/10/1/1/1/1/1/1/1/1
RUN RECOVERY
CP FSW=0
CP FOODI=.01
RUN GROWTH
C K2B=20
RUN ALGICIDE
C KAER=10
RUN AERATION
C   DRDGF=1
RUN DREDGING
C FARMF=2
RUN FARMING
```

6

The Dynamics of Natural Resource Utilization

William W. Behrens III

In World3 nonrenewable resource depletion is an important potential limit to material growth. In the resource sector of the global model, technology is presented as an exogenous influence that may decrease the costs of obtaining resources or increase the efficiency of their use. An important assumption of the global model is that as the unexploited reserves of any resource decline in quality, a greater and greater fraction of the industrial capital base must be allocated to locating, extracting, processing, and distributing that resource. The result of this assumption is a gradual decrease in the total material output that can be obtained from a given amount of capital stock.

It has been noted empirically that the cost of obtaining resources over the past several decades has in fact held constant or declined slightly, even in the face of decreasing resource quality. Technology clearly has had a major influence upon the cost of obtaining resources. An important question thus becomes the extent to which technological advances in the future may continue to hold down the costs of using ever-poorer resources. The substudy by William Behrens examines the potential influence of substitution technology and technical advances in the extraction and processing of virgin resources.

World3 does not explicitly include the price of raw materials. It is assumed that a material's relative cost is closely determined by the amount of industrial capital that must be employed in obtaining the material. Each of the three resource studies presented in this collection does explicitly represent price, its determinants, and its implications for production and consumption. Even with these more detailed representations, each substudy presented here indicates a depletion life cycle analogous to that exhibited by the resource sector of the global model. It is significant that in each case the resource price also reflects real-world behavior: price is held low by technology until near the end of the depletion cycle, at which time the price rises rather suddenly and steeply. Thus models whose behaviors are consistent with declining historical price trends can still suggest abrupt price increases in the future.

6
The Dynamics of Natural
Resource Utilization

Introduction

A regular supply of mineral resources is essential to the viability of industrial societies. In the past, society has not had to concern itself with long-term resource availability, primarily because the amount of resources in the earth appeared to be nearly infinite. Annual usage rates were such a small fraction of the supply that one could not foresee any shortages.

Within the last decade, however, two trends have changed this picture. The usage of resources has been growing at exponential rates of about 6 percent per year.[1] Also, nations are beginning to expand their planning horizons, approaching plans for twenty or thirty years hence instead of only two years hence. These two trends have forced nations to realize that the mineral resources of the globe are indeed finite and nonrenewable. Stocks that are sufficient for the next two years will be wholly deficient in thirty years.

The situation becomes even more critical when one considers the resources within one national boundary. In a recent issue of *Chemical and Engineering News,* it is pointed out that the United States is a net importer of 26 of the 36 "critical" raw materials, while the USSR is a net importer of only 7.[2] Public and private awareness of potential resource shortages has indicated the need for a rational, comprehensive scheme within which we can plan the management of our nonrenewable resources.

The Static Reserve Life Index

The need for a measure of resource availability has led to the use of the static reserve life index (SRLI), which indicates the number of years current known reserves could support consumption at its present level. For example, if estimates indicate that we have 200 tons of some material remaining, and the current consumption rate is 10 tons per year, then the SRLI for that resource would be twenty years. This measure, while useful as a very rough approximation to resource availability, does not reflect the complex interactions that govern actual availability.

The shortcomings of the static reserve life index stem from the assumptions about reserves and usage rates that underlie its formulation. These assumptions are:

1. Consumption will remain constant. This implies that changes in per capita consumption and population, if any, must offset one another. If costs change, they are not expected to change overall consumption.

2. The grade of minable ores will not decrease. The SRLI is based on the known reserves of the metal located in deposits of currently economical grade.

[1] National Academy of Sciences, National Research Council (NAS-NRC), *Resources and Man: A Study and Recommendations by the Committee on Resources and Man* (San Francisco: W. H. Freeman and Company, 1970), p. 119.

[2] Raymond Ewell, "US Will Lag USSR in Raw Materials," *Chemical and Engineering News,* August 24, 1970, p. 43.

3. No new discoveries will be made.

4. There will be no changes in extraction technology.

5. There will be no changes in substitution technology.

An index based on these assumptions is not an accurate reflection of the real world system. Every important resource probably violates all of them.

The Impact of Exponential Demand on the Reserve Index.   The failure to recognize the well-documented exponential growth in demand for resources introduces large errors into the static reserve life index. If one assumes a growth rate of 3 percent

Mineral	Static Index (in years)	Exponential Index at 3 Percent Growth Rate (in years)
Coal	900	110
Chromium	560	96
Iron	400	86
Manganese	180	62
Aluminum	175	60
Cobalt	155	58
Nickel	140	55
Molybdenum	100	46
Petroleum	70	35
Copper	40	26
Tungsten	40	26
Natural gas	35	24
Tin	25	19
Platinum	20	16
Silver	20	16
Zinc	18	14
Gold	17	14
Lead	15	12
Mercury	13	11

Figure 6-1   Comparison of static and exponential reserve life indices for various minerals for the world. By calculus,

$$e = \frac{\ln(r \times s + 1)}{r}$$

where e = exponential reserve life index, s = static reserve life index, r = annual fractional growth rate.

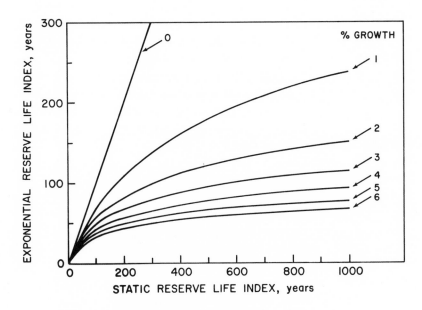

Figure 6-2 Exponential versus static reserve life indices as a function of annual growth rate

per year, the resultant reduction of the static reserve life index is shown in Figure 6-1.[3]

Figure 6-1 indicates that the static reserve life index is an inadequate measure of resource availability if demand is increasing exponentially. The estimate of a 3 percent growth rate is not critical; Figure 6-2 illustrates the relationship between the static and the exponential indices at various rates of growth. As long as demand is exponentially increasing, even by as little as 1 percent per year, the exponential index is significantly lower than the static index, especially when one considers time spans on the order of decades.

This figure also points out another implication of exponentially growing usage rates. New discoveries increase the exponential reserve life index substantially less than one might expect. For example, at a 3 percent rate of growth, a static index of 40 years corresponds to an exponential index of 26 years. If the static index were increased to 400, corresponding to a discovery that increased the known reserves by a factor of 10, the exponential index increases only to 86, a factor of less than 3.5. Given an exponentially rising demand, new discoveries of even the largest magnitude may increase the long-term availability only slightly.

The Impact of Other Factors on the Reserve Index.   Errors in other assumptions underlying the static reserve life index may make it slightly conservative. Ores of

---

[3] A 3 percent annual growth in consumption is used as an average estimate for illustration only. For Bureau of Mines Projections, see U.S. Bureau of Mines, *Mineral Facts and Problems, 1970,* U.S. Department of the Interior, Bureau of Mines, Bulletin 650 (Washington, D.C., 1970).

lower grades than those mined at present will certainly be mined in the future. As any resource is depleted and its price rises, ores of lower and lower grade become profitable to mine. This fact will partially counteract the effect of exponential demand on the static index. However, resources of continually falling grade will not be able to afford a supply into the indefinite future, as some have proposed.[4]

Other factors will also compensate partially for exponential growth in demand. As the grade of the ore exploited falls, prices will rise, which may restrict demand and spur technological change. There are two types of technological change that could modify usage. One is in the technology of resource extraction, processing, and distribution. The other is in the technology governing the substitution of alternative resources for that in question. Recycling technology is a special case of the latter.[5] Optimists who anticipate no resource problems in the future expect sufficient improvements in these two technologies to avoid any resource shortages. It is essential to include the causes and effects of technological change in any index of resource availability.

Realistically, no mineral resource will ever be completely exhausted. Most minerals are elements that cannot be destroyed. Rather, the resources will come to exist only in such remote or dilute forms that substantial quantities cannot be economically obtained. Even current ore bodies will not be completely exhausted. As the costs rise, the demand for the resource will become essentially zero. The static and exponential reserve life indices imply a point in the future at which a resource will be completely depleted. It would be more realistic and useful to have an index relating price, extraction rates, and ore body stocks over time.

The Need for a Dynamic Model.   The shortcomings of the static and exponential reserve life indices dictate the need for a more realistic index of resource availability. The task of generating that index is complicated by the interrelated nature of the elements that must be included in it. Costs are dependent on the resources remaining; the resources remaining depend on past extraction rates; and extraction rates are dependent on costs. Technological advances are stimulated by rising costs, and these advances affect costs and usage. There is no way to determine the ultimate effect of each element on the reserve index unless one knows the behavior of the other elements and the inherent delays in the system.

The complex interdependence of all these factors precludes the possibility of being able to transform the static index into a dynamic index merely by adding to or subtracting from it a set of constant conversion factors. These factors are themselves dynamic (changing through time), so that no unique relationship exists between the static and the dynamic reserve life indices of a given material.

---

[4] The A/G (arithmetic/geometric) ratio, or the Lasky ratio, introduced by the geologist S. G. Lasky in 1950 ("How Tonnage-Grade Relations Help Predict Ore Reserves," *Engineering Mining Journal,* vol. 151 (1950), no. 4, pp. 81-85), stated that as the average grade of ore mined decreased arithmetically, the tonnage increased geometrically. Unfortunately, this has been shown to hold only for a few minerals, such as porphyry coppers, and only over a small range of grades.

[5] For a complete discussion of the factors governing resource recycling, see Jørgen Randers and Dennis L. Meadows, "The Dynamics of Solid Waste Generation," chap. 7 in this volume.

Thus we need a conceptual framework within which these elements are allowed to operate on each other through time as they do in the real world. A dynamic model of the system would allow one to examine the interrelationships and foresee the effects of different policies on the future availability of resources. A model will be limited by what we know and can assume about the important relationships; it is certain, however, that a dynamic model will afford a better understanding than the inadequate static reserve life index.

A Dynamic Model of Resource Utilization

Figure 6-3 gives a simplified causal-loop diagram of such a dynamic resource model, formulated using the method of system dynamics. This diagram indicates major system variables interconnected in feedback loops by lines of influence. The signs at the end of each arrow represent the polarity of effect; for example, as the average grade decreases, the actual cost increases.

Three interlocking feedback loops are shown in the diagram. Loop 1 is a negative loop, or goal-seeking loop, which relates the remaining stocks to the cost of extracting those resources. As the resources are depleted, the average grade of the resource remaining declines. A declining grade causes a rise in costs, which will depress demand and thus depress the usage rate, slowing down the depletion of natural resources. Loop 2 is a negative loop that acts to maintain actual cost at a constant level. If costs should rise, the investment in research and development will rise in an attempt to keep costs down. Continued investments in research and development will produce technological improvements that bring actual cost

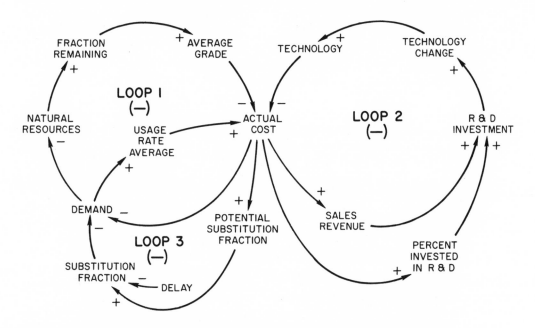

Figure 6-3 Causal-loop diagram for the dynamic model of resource utilization

down. Loop 3 is a negative loop that tends to restrain the demand for the resource. As actual cost rises, the potential substitution fraction rises, which, after the delay inherent in technological advance, allows a larger fraction of the demand for the resource to be satisfied by substitutes. This relationship assumes that alternatives are available at that cost, which is the case for most natural resources, where the potential role of substitution in alleviating shortages is of critical importance.

Each loop can be examined separately to illustrate its detailed relationships and behavior.

Loop 1: Resource Reserves and Actual Cost. Feedback Loop 1, Figure 6-4, describes the effects of the actual physical flow of natural resources on costs and usage. Resources are defined by an initial stock of material that is depleted by the usage rate UR.[*] They are assumed not to be renewable, as their geologic replacement time is outside the scope of this study.[6] We assume that we know, or can at least estimate for planning purposes, the entire present stock of the resource, including ores of all grades and those not yet discovered.

As resources are depleted, the natural resource fraction remaining NRFR declines. We assume that resources are exploited in an order of declining grade

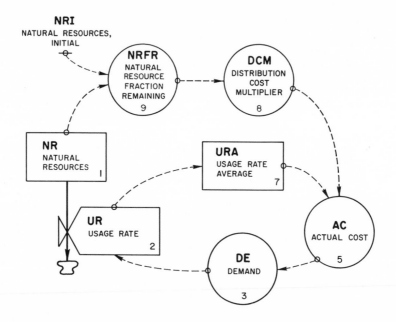

Figure 6-4 Loop 1: Resource reserves and actual cost

[6] Some resources can be recycled, of course. The dynamics of recycling have been studied in a complementary model by Randers and Meadows (ibid.).

[*] Eds. note—Whenever we use a term that corresponds to a variable in the simulation model, the variable name (as it appears in the model equations in the appendix to this chapter) is printed immediately following that term.

and increasingly inconvenient distribution. Figure 6-5 empirically illustrates this assumption in the case of copper within the United States.

The interactions among firms are unimportant for the dynamics of resource usage over 100 years or more. One may thus view all firms involved in the use of a resource as a single industry engaged in the continuous processing of a natural

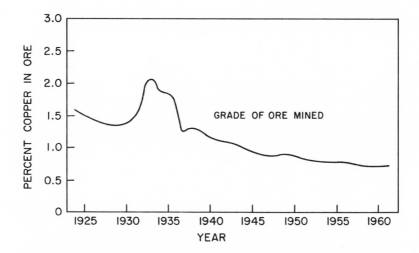

Figure 6-5   Grade of copper ore mined in the United States, 1925-1960
Adapted from Resources and Man: *A Study and Recommendations by the Committee on Resources and Man of the Division of Earth Sciences, National Academy of Sciences-National Research Council, with the cooperation of the Division of Biology and Agriculture. W. H. Freeman and Company. Copyright © 1969, p. 124.*

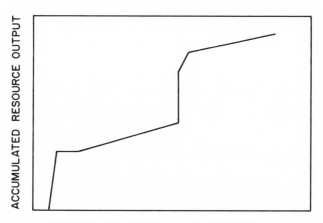

FRACTION OF CAPITAL BASE DEVOTED TO
EXTRACTION, PROCESSING, AND DISTRIBUTION

Figure 6-6   Resource conversion path
Source: Adapted from H. J. Barnett and C. F. Morse, Scarcity and Growth *(Baltimore: Johns Hopkins Press, 1963).*

resource from the mine to the finished product. A certain fraction of the industry's capital base will be devoted to extracting, processing, and distributing the resource before it is incorporated in the final product. As the grade of the material declines, or as its spatial distribution becomes more inconvenient, that fraction of the capital base will increase along a "resource conversion path," as illustrated in Figure 6-6. This will result in a rising cost of the resource, represented in the model by the distribution cost multiplier DCM. This phenomenon is already apparent in some resources, most notably mercury, which has exhibited the relationship shown in Figure 6-7.

The effect of the factors causing the behavior in Figure 6-7 is represented in the model as a normalized multiplicative factor on the actual cost AC. The actual cost AC, as shown in Figure 6-8 is a curve relating the annual usage rate UR to the production costs at that usage rate UR. This is analogous to the short run supply curve of the industry. The effect of the distribution cost multiplier DCM is to shift the curve upward so that the cost at any level of production is increased. The actual cost AC depends on the usage rate average URA, a delayed version of the usage rate UR. This delay represents the combined effects of short-run delays in capital allocation, employment levels, and the opening and closing of economically marginal mines.

Two factors determine the demand DE in this feedback loop. If the actual cost AC were constant, we assume that demand DE would increase exponentially because of growth in both population and per capita consumption. However, changing costs also have an effect on demand. This impact is represented by a

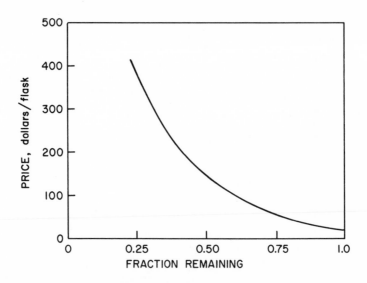

Figure 6-7   Mercury: The relationship between the fraction
of the resource remaining and the cost
Data from the U.S. Bureau of Mines Minerals
Yearbook *(Washington, D.C.: Government Printing Office, 1941-1970).*

downward sloping demand curve; as cost AC increases, the level of demand DE at that cost decreases. The level of demand DE indicated by the demand curve, multiplied by the exponential growth factor, gives the demand DE at any cost. We assume that there are no restrictions on the usage rate UR other than the market consideration of cost. The usage rate UR in any year is thus taken to be equal to the demand in that year.

The simulation of Loop 1, separated from the rest of the model, produces the behavior shown in Figure 6-9. The usage rate UR grows exponentially until the depletion of natural resources causes a rise in actual cost AC. As costs rise, the usage rate falls, until costs become high enough to suppress usage completely. At

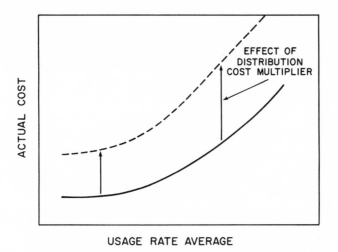

Figure 6-8   Actual cost as a function of the usage rate

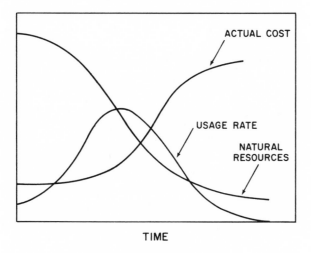

Figure 6-9   Behavior of Loop 1

that point, the remaining natural resources are too uneconomical to extract. Most resources today are exhibiting the behavior characteristic of the period before the rise in costs.

Loop 2: Extraction Technology. Many resources today exhibit declining costs because of the factors represented in Loop 2, even while depletion (Loop 1) should be raising costs. This feedback loop, Figure 6-10, demonstrates the endogenous (system-induced) advances in technology that tend to keep down costs.

Technology is not easily quantified. We know that technology represents accumulated research and knowledge, so it can be modeled as a level variable. We know that changes in technology will produce cost decreases. We assume that changes in the technology of the extracting, processing, and distributing activities result only from investments in research and development. Research and development investment RDI each year is a variable percentage of the annual sales revenue SR. The percent invested in research and development PIRD is a function of the elasticity of demand ED. If the industry perceives that by lowering its price it could increase its sales, given a constant profit margin, it would invest in research and development to improve technology T and lower costs. If it perceives the elasticity of demand ED to be less than unity, it will invest only a nominal

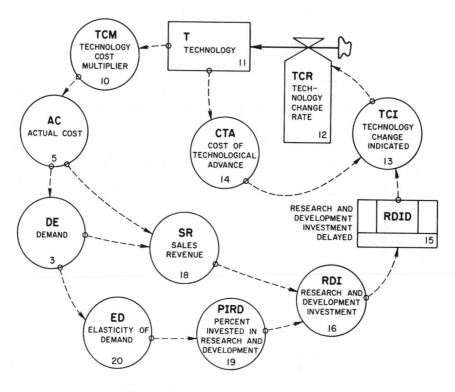

Figure 6-10 Loop 2: extraction technology

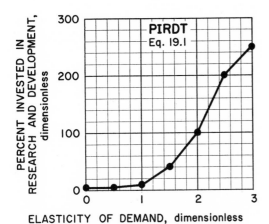

Figure 6-11 Percent invested in research and development PIRD as a function of elasticity of demand ED

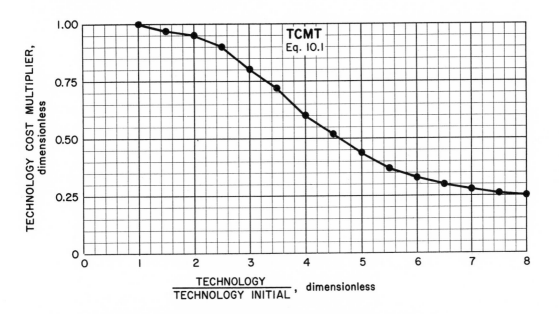

Figure 6-12 Technology cost multiplier TCM as a function of technology T

fraction in research and development. This relationship models the economic incentive of the industry to invest in research. As illustrated in Figure 6-11, the percentage can exceed 100 percent of sales revenue, representing research to enter a new market where revenue is still low.

Investment in research does not immediately produce technological advance.[7] There is a delay of about twenty years between the investment in research and an actual change in implemented technology. In this model, changes in technology

---

[7] See Peter F. Drucker, *The Age of Discontinuity* (New York: Harper & Row, 1968), pp. 44ff.

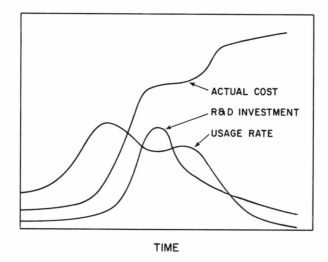

TIME

Figure 6-13   Behavior of Loops 1 and 2

T are important because of their effect on actual cost AC. Figure 6-12 shows the technology cost multiplier TCM as a fraction of the ratio of current to initial technology T. Any increase in technology T yields a corresponding decrease in cost. The multiplier acts in a manner similar to the distribution cost multiplier DCM, except that it shifts the actual cost AC curve down. Figure 6-12 shows the general direction of this relationship but does not purport to be an exact curve.[8]

The cost of technological advance CTA in the flow diagram represents the cost of effecting an incremental advance in technology T. This cost is assumed to decrease as technology T first develops, then gradually to increase as more investment is required for each marginal increase in technology T.

The behavior of Loop 2 is most meaningful when viewed in conjunction with Loop 1. Figure 6-13 illustrates a simulation of these two loops independent of Loop 3. As actual cost AC rises, investment in research and development RDI rises, which, after a delay, produces advances in technology T, causing cost AC to remain constant or fall and allowing the usage rate UR to rise. As resources near depletion, technology T is not sufficient to make extraction economical, so the usage rate UR falls to zero.

Loop 3: Substitution Technology.   Loop 3 of the model incorporates the factors in the system that influence the technology allowing other resources to be substituted for the natural resource examined in the study. (See Figure 6-14.)

---

[8] It is often true in complex systems that the structure and the direction of relationships are more important than the actual parameter values. If one were concerned with describing the precise behavior of a specific resource, this and other curves would have to be estimated more closely. To determine whether the exact shape of the curve is important, one may test the sensitivity of the model results to changes in the curve.

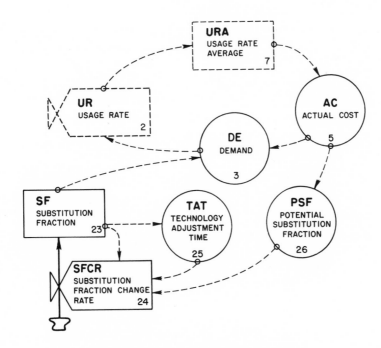

Figure 6-14   Loop 3: substitution technology

If one considers the resource as a factor input to some production process, then that resource can be substituted to some degree by other factor inputs, such as other minerals, energy, or capital. The extent of possible substitution depends on the characteristics of the products in which the material is used and on the relative composition of the total product mix. These factors define the maximum substitution fraction possible, which for most materials will be less than 1. As costs rise, there is a rise in the potential for substitution, implying that it would be economical to satisfy some fraction of the demand of the resource by other inputs. Figure 6-15 illustrates this relationship.

The actual substitution fraction SF will be equal to the potential substitution fraction PSF only after the technology of substitution has been developed and implemented. The model formulates the substitution fraction SF by taking the difference between the actual fraction and the potential fraction, and making up that difference through time. This time is represented in the model by the constant technology adjustment time TAT.

The ultimate effect of increased substitution will be a decrease in the demand DE for the resource at any cost. Total demand DE will thus equal the level of demand indicated by the demand curve, multiplied by the exponential growth factor, and multiplied by 1 minus the substitution fraction SF.

The behavior of this feedback loop is best seen in conjunction with Loop 1, independent of Loop 2. When the actual cost AC is low, the substitution fraction SF is low because there is no economic incentive to increase substitution. As the

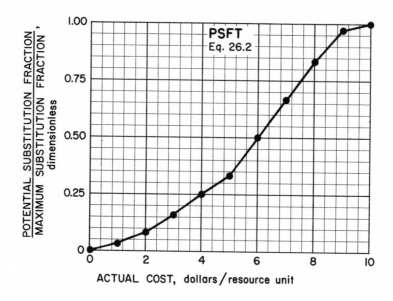

Figure 6-15 Potential substitution fraction PSF as a function of actual cost AC

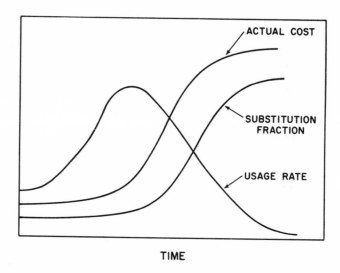

Figure 6-16 Behavior of Loops 1 and 3

cost of the primary resource rises, it becomes increasingly profitable to invest in the production of substitute materials. The substitution fraction SF will rise after the delay required to develop and implement the necessary substitution technology (see Figure 6-16).

System Behavior

Model Sensitivity. The objective of this study was to develop a better tool for analyzing the factors that will control future resource availability. An important part of the study focused on the inclusion of technology as an endogenous response to changes in cost over the life cycle of a mineral resource.

Because technology is not easily quantified, the exact gains in Loops 2 and 3 cannot be easily specified. It is possible to specify quite accurately the values of the delays. It would aslo be possible and useful to conduct case analyses of the technology for specific resources. However, one can only speculate about the loop gains in the future. The simulation model will allow one to make assumptions about insufficiently quantified relationships and to test the system for its sensitivity to those assumptions.

An example of this type of relationship is the technology cost multiplier TCM (Figure 6-12). We chose the current situation as our reference, so this function must start as 1. Further improvements in technology T will lower costs, but not below zero. One can often bound a relationship in this manner with more confidence than one can specify its precise values. One could then test the system to see if it matters whether that function is concave, convex, s-shaped, or linear. One could also test the other assumptions in the model by an analogous sensitivity test. Combining the results of these tests with those elements one can quantify, one would obtain a good understanding of what controls future resource availability.

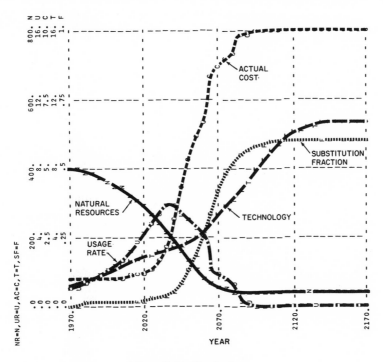

Figure 6-17   Standard run

Model Behavior.   One could specify the parameters in this model to represent any particular resource, because the relationships in the model are characteristic of all nonrenewable resources. The techniques of system dynamics have allowed a focus on those relationships that will govern the long-term availability of all mineral resources. This general understanding is considerably more powerful than the narrow insights that would result from a study of one particular resource. The computer runs in this paper are illustrative of a generic resource that in 1970 had a static reserve life index of 400 years.

Figure 6-17 illustrates the standard run of the model. This is the run against which alternate runs will be evaluated. Time is plotted along the bottom axis, beginning in 1970. The line on the left side below the heading gives the plot symbols, and to the immediate left of the graph are the scales for the variables.

This run would be the expected behavior of the resource system if demand is assumed to grow at 3 percent per year, all else being equal. During the period before 2020, actual cost AC remains fairly constant, even though the grade of the resource is declining, because of the advance of technology T (plot symbol T). The advance of technology T is not fast enough to counteract the forces of declining grade after the year 2020. As costs begin to rise, the substitution fraction SF (plot symbol F) rises, and increased substitution coupled with increasing

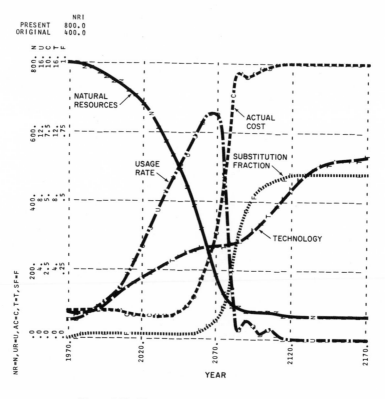

Figure 6-18   New discovery that doubles reserves

costs forces the usage rate UR to decline. Renewed effort in research and development is not sufficient to halt the rise in costs. In about 2100 the actual cost AC has risen to a level 10 times the level in 1970 (noninflated), so that usage declines essentially to zero. The substitution fraction SF has risen to its maximum feasible level, here taken as 60 percent. The remaining resources, about 5 percent of the initial supply, are available only at a prohibitively high cost. After the year 2120 any demand for this particular resource must be satisfied by recycled resources. This situation was reached after 125 years, even though the static reserve life index had predicted supplies for 400 years.

Figure 6-18 illustrates the effect of a discovery in 1970 that doubles the remaining reserves. The static reserve life index in this run is 800 years in 1970, as opposed to 400 years in the previous run. Observe that the larger initial stock of resources allows costs to remain constant for about 35 years longer than in the standard run, which allows the usage rate UR to continue its exponential growth for another 35 years. Note that the time at which usage falls to zero, 2115, is only 20 years later than the time at which usage reached zero in the standard run. The lifetime, or dynamic reserve life index, was increased by only 20 years, even though the simulated discovery increased the static reserve life index from 400 to 800 years.

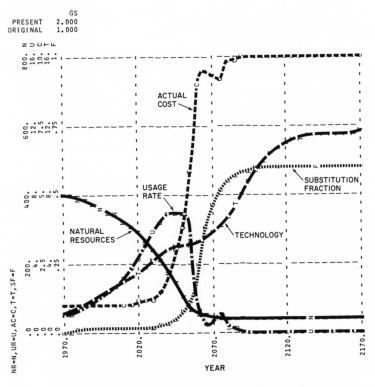

Figure 6-19 Subsidy of research and development investment

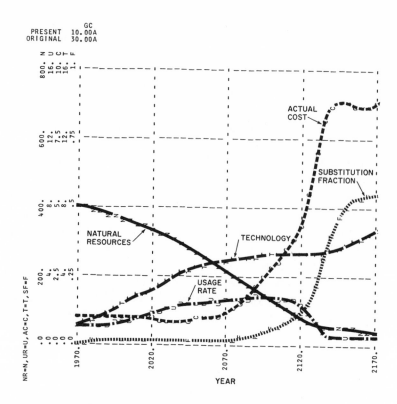

Figure 6-20   1 percent annual growth in demand

Extensive research is normally undertaken only in response to economic pressures. These pressures may be rising costs, as in extraction technology; the potential for profit, as in substitution; or price or tax incentives from the government. The process of implementing technology, however, is a long undertaking. It is many years before a technological breakthrough results in a significant market impact. A current example of this can be seen in nuclear power. The technology required to generate electricity from nuclear sources was available before 1950. The first commercial plant was installed before 1960. In 1969, nuclear power was contributing only 1 percent of the electric power of the United States, or 0.25 percent of the total power consumed.[9]

The computer runs in Figures 6-17 and 6-18 illustrate that in neither case is technology advancing rapidly enough to have an impact on the cost. One possible response to this dilemma might be to subsidize investment in research and development. Figure 6-19 illustrates the same conditions as the standard run except that research and development investment RDI is doubled, simulating the impact of a matching funds subsidy. The effect of this subsidy in the long run is

[9] John Holdren and Philip Herrera, *Energy* (San Francisco: Sierra Club, 1971).

counter to that desired. The increased investment is able to keep costs down for approximately 10 years longer. The result is that the usage rate UR is permitted to grow even higher, reaching a maximum value about 20 percent higher than in the standard run. The ultimate effect is to drive costs to a prohibitive level at least as fast as without a subsidy.

One could examine a number of other policies to determine their impact on resource availability. The purpose of this paper is not to design a perfect natural resource policy but to develop a dynamic theory of resource utilization and to demonstrate the usefulness of a simulation model in long-term planning. The process of formulating the model is a source of significant insight into the system. In the case of resources, this model illustrates that adequate long-term supplies are impossible to achieve if one continues to promote growth in usage over the short run. The model illustrates the relative insensitivity of the system to any increase in reserves. It also suggests that efforts should be directed to reducing short-term consumption of nonrenewable resources.

Figure 6-20 illustrates the impact of reducing the growth in demand from 3 percent per year to 1 percent per year. Because resources are used more slowly in the short run, the usage rate UR stays above zero for at least 75 years longer than in the standard run. A comparison of Figures 6-17 and 6-20 demonstrates that the adequacy of long-term supplies of resources depends heavily on the ability to restrain usage in the short run.

Conclusion

The static reserve life index is a poor measure of resource availability. We currently lack a better index, not because of lack of information but because of a lack of the structure required to interrelate that information. This paper has shown how a simulation model can provide that structure and how a model can provide the understanding required to begin formulating long-term policies.

Appendix: Computer Program for the Resource Model

The following is a listing of the equations of the computer model, with the definitions and dimensions of the model variables. The equations are in the DYNAMO simulation language.

```
NR.K=NR.J+(DT)(-UR.JK)                              1, L
NR=NRI                                              1.1, N
NRI=400                                             1.2, C
    NR    - NATURAL RESOURCES (RESOURCE UNITS)
    UR    - USAGE RATE (RESOURCE UNITS/YEAR)
    NRI   - NATURAL RESOURCES, INITIAL (RESOURCE UNITS)

UR.KL=DE.K                                          2, R
    UR    - USAGE RATE (RESOURCE UNITS/YEAR)
    DE    - DEMAND (RESOURCE UNITS/YEAR)
```

```
DE.K=(TABHL(DET,AC.K/ACN,0,10,1))*URN.K*(1-SF.K)      3, A
DET=2.5/1/.89/.78/.67/.56/.45/.34/.23/.12/1E-6        3.1, T
      DE      - DEMAND (RESOURCE UNITS/YEAR)
      DET     - DE TABLE
      AC      - ACTUAL COST (DOLLARS/RESOURCE UNIT)
      ACN     - ACTUAL COST NORMAL (DOLLARS/RESOURCE UNIT)
      URN     - USAGE RATE NORMAL (RESOURCE UNITS/YEAR)
      SF      - SUBSITITUTION FRACTION (FRACTION)


URN.K=URI*EXP(GC*(TIME.K-1970))                       4, A
URI=1                                                 4.1, C
GC=.03                                                4.2, C
      URN     - USAGE RATE NORMAL (RESOURCE UNITS/YEAR)
      URI     - USAGE RATE, INITIAL (RESOURCE UNITS/YEAR)
      GC      - GROWTH CONSTANT (FRACTION/YEAR)
      TIME    - TIME (YEARS)


AC.K=(TABHL(ACT,URA.K/URN.K,0,3,.5))*DCM.K*TCM.K*     5, A
  CN.K
ACT=1.5/1.2/1/1.5/2.2/3.5/6                           5.1, T
      AC      - ACTUAL COST (DOLLARS/RESOURCE UNIT)
      ACT     - AC TABLE
      URA     - USAGE RATE AVERAGE (RESOURCE UNITS/YEAR)
      URN     - USAGE RATE NORMAL (RESOURCE UNITS/YEAR)
      DCM     - DISTIRBUTION COST MULTIPLIER (D'LESS)
      TCM     - TECHNOLOGY COST MULTIPLIER (D'LESS)
      CN      - COST NORMAL (DOLLARS/RESOURCE UNIT)


CN.K=CLIP(ACN,ACN1,SWT1,TIME.K)                       6, A
ACN1=1                                                6.1, C
ACN=1                                                 6.2, C
SWT1=1970                                             6.3, C
      CN      - COST NORMAL (DOLLARS/RESOURCE UNIT)
      ACN     - ACTUAL COST NORMAL (DOLLARS/RESOURCE UNIT)
      ACN1    - ACN, ALTERNATE VALUE (DOLLARS/RESOURCE
                UNIT)
      SWT1    - SWITCH TIME ONE (YEARS)
      TIME    - TIME (YEARS)


URA.K=SMOOTH(UR.JK,URST)                              7, A
URA=1                                                 7.1, N
URST=3                                                7.2, C
      URA     - USAGE RATE AVERAGE (RESOURCE UNITS/YEAR)
      UR      - USAGE RATE (RESOURCE UNITS/YEAR)
      URST    - USAGE RATE SMOOTHING TIME (YEARS)


DCM.K=TABHL(DCMT,NRFR.K,0,1,.1)                       8, A
DCMT=100/20/9.5/7/5/3/2/1.5/1.2/1.08/1                8.1, T
      DCM     - DISTIRBUTION COST MULTIPLIER (D'LESS)
      DCMT    - DCM TABLE
      NRFR    - NATURAL RESOURCE FRACTION REMAINING (D'
                LESS)


NRFR.K=NR.K/NRI                                       9, A
      NRFR    - NATURAL RESOURCE FRACTION REMAINING (D'
                LESS)
      NR      - NATURAL RESOURCES (RESOURCE UNITS)
      NRI     - NATURAL RESOURCES, INITIAL (RESOURCE UNITS)


TCM.K=TABHL(TCMT,T.K/TI,1,8,.5)                       10, A
TCMT=1/.97/.95/.90/.8/.72/.6/.52/.44/.37/.33/.30/     10.1, T
  .28/.26/.25
      TCM     - TECHNOLOGY COST MULTIPLIER (D'LESS)
      TCMT    - TCM TABLE
      T       - TECHNOLOGY (TECHNOLOGY UNITS)
      TI      - TECHNOLOGY, INITIAL (TECHNOLOGY UNITS)


T.K=T.J+(DT)(TCR.JK)                                  11, L
T=TI                                                  11.1, N
TI=1                                                  11.2, C
      T       - TECHNOLOGY (TECHNOLOGY UNITS)
      TCR     - TECHNOLOGY CHANGE RATE (TECHNOLOGY UNITS/
                YEAR)
      TI      - TECHNOLOGY, INITIAL (TECHNOLOGY UNITS)
```

```
TCR.KL=TCI.K                                          12, R
     TCR   - TECHNOLOGY CHANGE RATE (TECHNOLOGY UNITS/
                 YEAR)
     TCI   - TECHNOLOGY CHANGE INDICATED (TECHNOLOGY
                 UNITS/YEAR)


TCI.K=TCIN*(1/CTA.K)*RDID.K*TI                         13, A
TCIN=.1                                               13.1, C
     TCI   - TECHNOLOGY CHANGE INDICATED (TECHNOLOGY
                 UNITS/YEAR)
     TCIN  - TECHNOLOGY CHANGE INDICATED NORMAL
                 (TECHNOLOGY UNITS/YEAR)
     CTA   - COST OF TECHNOLOGICAL ADVANCE (DOLLARS/
                 TECHNOLOGY UNIT-YEAR)
     RDID  - RESEARCH AND DEVELOPMENT INVESTMENT DELAYED
                 (DOLLARS/YEAR)
     TI    - TECHNOLOGY, INITIAL (TECHNOLOGY UNITS)


CTA.K=TABHL(CTAT,T.K/TI,1,6,.5)                        14, A
CTAT=1/.9/.82/.75/.82/.9/1/1.5/3/9/20                 14.1, T
     CTA   - COST OF TECHNOLOGICAL ADVANCE (DOLLARS/
                 TECHNOLOGY UNIT-YEAR)
     CTAT  - CTA TABLE
     T     - TECHNOLOGY (TECHNOLOGY UNITS)
     TI    - TECHNOLOGY, INITIAL (TECHNOLOGY UNITS)


RDID.K=DELAY3(RDI.K,TD)                                15, A
TD=30                                                 15.1, C
     RDID  - RESEARCH AND DEVELOPMENT INVESTMENT DELAYED
                 (DOLLARS/YEAR)
     RDI   - RESEARCH AND DEVELOPMENT INVESTMENT
                 (DOLLARS/YEAR)
     TD    - TECHNOLOGY DELAY (YEARS)


RDI.K=SR.K*PIRD.K*GSRD.K                               16, A
     RDI   - RESEARCH AND DEVELOPMENT INVESTMENT
                 (DOLLARS/YEAR)
     SR    - SALES REVENUE (DOLLARS/YEAR)
     PIRD  - PERCENT INVESTED IN RESEARCH AND
                 DEVELOPMENT (D'LESS)
     GSRD  - GOVERNMENT SUBSIDY OF RESEARCH AND
                 DEVELOPMENT (D'LESS)


GSRD.K=CLIP(1,GS,SWT1,TIME.K)                          17, A
GS=1                                                  17.1, C
     GSRD  - GOVERNMENT SUBSIDY OF RESEARCH AND
                 DEVELOPMENT (D'LESS)
     GS    - GOVERNMENT SUBSIDY (D'LESS)
     SWT1  - SWITCH TIME ONE (YEARS)
     TIME  - TIME (YEARS)


SR.K=AC.K*DE.K                                         18, A
     SR    - SALES REVENUE (DOLLARS/YEAR)
     AC    - ACTUAL COST (DOLLARS/RESOURCE UNIT)
     DE    - DEMAND (RESOURCE UNITS/YEAR)


PIRD.K=TABHL(PIRDT,ED.K,0,3,.5)                        19, A
PIRDT=.05/.05/.1/.4/1/2/2.5                            19.1, T
     PIRD  - PERCENT INVESTED IN RESEARCH AND
                 DEVELOPMENT (D'LESS)
     PIRDT - PIRD TABLE
     ED    - ELASTICITY OF DEMAND (D'LESS)


ED.K=(AC.K/DE.K)*(DD.K/DAC.K)                          20, A
     ED    - ELASTICITY OF DEMAND (D'LESS)
     AC    - ACTUAL COST (DOLLARS/RESOURCE UNIT)
     DE    - DEMAND (RESOURCE UNITS/YEAR)
     DD    - DIFFERENTIAL OF DEMAND (RESOURCE UNITS/
                 YEAR)
     DAC   - DIFFERENTIAL OF ACTUAL COST (DOLLARS/
                 RESOURCE UNIT)
```

```
DAC.K=.1*AC.K                                              21, A
     DAC    - DIFFERENTIAL OF ACTUAL COST (DOLLARS/
                 RESOURCE UNIT)
     AC     - ACTUAL COST (DOLLARS/RESOURCE UNIT)

DD.K=(TABHL(DET,.9*AC.K/ACN,0,10,1))*URN.K*(1-SF.K) 22, A
   -DE.K
     DD     - DIFFERENTIAL OF DEMAND (RESOURCE UNITS/
                 YEAR)
     DET    - DE TABLE
     AC     - ACTUAL COST (DOLLARS/RESOURCE UNIT)
     ACN    - ACTUAL COST NORMAL (DOLLARS/RESOURCE UNIT)
     URN    - USAGE RATE NORMAL (RESOURCE UNITS/YEAR)
     SF     - SUBSITITUTION FRACTION (FRACTION)
     DE     - DEMAND (RESOURCE UNITS/YEAR)

SF.K=SF.J+(DT)(SFCR.JK)                                    23, L
SF=SFI                                                     23.1, N
SFI=0                                                      23.2, C
     SF      - SUBSITITUTION FRACTION (FRACTION)
     SFCR    - SUBSTITUTION FRACTION CHANGE RATE
                  (FRACTION/YEAR)
     SFI     - SUBSITITUTION FRACTION, INITIAL (FRACTION)

SFCR.KL=(PSF.K-SF.K)/TAT.K                                 24, R
     SFCR    - SUBSTITUTION FRACTION CHANGE RATE
                  (FRACTION/YEAR)
     PSF     - POTENTIAL SUBSTITUTION FRACTION (FRACTION)
     SF      - SUBSITITUTION FRACTION (FRACTION)
     TAT     - TECHNOLOGY ADJUSTMENT TIME (YEARS)

TAT.K=TABHL(TATT,SF.K,0,.6,.1)                             25, A
TATT=10/10/10/10/10/10/10                                  25.1, T
     TAT     - TECHNOLOGY ADJUSTMENT TIME (YEARS)
     TATT    - TAT TABLE
     SF      - SUBSITITUTION FRACTION (FRACTION)

PSF.K=MSF*TABHL(PSFT,AC.K,0,10,1)                          26, A
MSF=.6                                                     26.1, C
PSFT=0/.033/.083/.16/.25/.33/.5/.66/.83/.97/1              26.2, T
TIME=1970                                                  26.3, N
LENGTH=2170                                                26.4, C
DT=1                                                       26.5, C
PLTPER=5                                                   26.6, C
     PSF     - POTENTIAL SUBSTITUTION FRACTION (FRACTION)
     MSF     - MAXIMUM SUBSTITUTION FRACTION (FRACTION)
     PSFT    - PSF TABLE
     AC      - ACTUAL COST (DOLLARS/RESOURCE UNIT)
     TIME    - TIME (YEARS)
PLOT   NR=N(0,800)/UR=U(0,16)/AC=C(0,10)/T=T(0,16)/SF=F(0,1)
RUN    STANDARD
C   NR1=800
RUN    DISCOVERY
C   GS=2
RUN    R&D SUBSIDY
C   GC=.01
RUN    GROWTH
```

7

The Dynamics of Solid Waste Generation

Jørgen Randers and Dennis L. Meadows

The generation and disposal of solid wastes involve relationships that are relevant to two sectors of the global model. First, solid waste represents a sink for natural resources. To the extent that solid wastes accumulate in a form that cannot be reused, natural resources are depleted. Second, because of the minimal reuse of waste, solid waste must be regarded as a pollutant. Solid waste disposal constitutes a growing environmental problem on a local level and, in some forms, on a global level.

New technical capabilities will certainly be developed in response to the resource and pollution problems projected by World3. For example, recycling is a technical development that has been proposed to decrease both resource depletion and the rate of solid waste generation. The following paper summarizes a study undertaken to determine the potential contribution of technical advances in recycling to the solution of resource and pollution problems. In the process the model provides an explicit picture of how social and political factors interact with technical capabilities to determine the rate at which resources are depleted. The conclusions illustrate the necessity of coupling social and economic change with technical advance in the solution of an important ecological problem.

A shortened version of this chapter appeared under the same title in Technology Review, *April 1972 (Cambridge, Mass.: Massachusetts Institute of Technology) pp. 20-32.*

7
The Dynamics of Solid Waste Generation

Introduction

The Solid Waste Problem.   All industrialized countries have an urgent solid waste problem. The problem, an ever-increasing rate of disposal of domestic and industrial trash, has two aspects: a pressing shortage of waste dumping areas and an irreversible depletion of nonrenewable resources.

Many facts may be cited to suggest the urgency of the solid waste problem. Figure 7-1 presents data on the actual magnitude of the present solid waste production in the United States and its effects upon the environment. In less abstract form, the present situation is such that every person in the United States yearly discards 188 pounds of paper, 250 metal cans, 133 bottles and jars, and 388 caps and crowns. On a national basis 7 million cars and 100 million tires are discarded every year.[1]

This enormous solid waste generation rate of course leads to problems that are especially accentuated in densely populated areas:

> For years, sanitation officials have been exploring exotic schemes to rid their cities of garbage . . . precious little has been achieved. New York relies on three stinking dumps that will be filled up by 1976, leaving the city with 15,000 tons of trash each day and nowhere to put it. Houston, whose garbage dump is now the highest point on the Texas coastal plain, has already passed the saturation point. . . . .

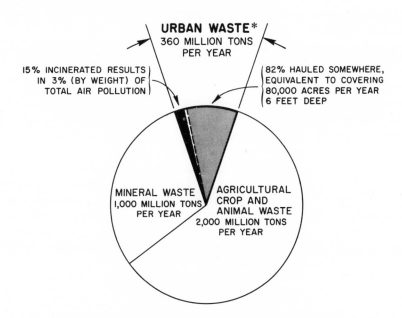

Figure 7-1 Production and disposal of solid waste in the
United States
*Data for year 1967

---

[1] P. C. George, "Solid Waste: America's Neglected Pollutant," *Nation's Cities*, June 1970, p. 8.

The fact is that with garbage now being jettisoned by Americans at the rate of 360 million tons a year—a rate that will double by 1980—the capacity of cities to cope with the problem is shrinking fast. And the dangers posed to the urban environment are rising at a concomitant rate. Seventy per cent of the 300 incinerators maintained by U. S. cities have no pollution controls whatsoever. Ninety-four per cent of the country's landfills are still breeding grounds for rats and disease and have been declared unsanitary by the U. S. Public Health Service.[2]

It is also easy to show that natural resources are being depleted at a considerable rate. The day is near when many critical resources will be in short supply even at substantially higher prices than today's. In the words of the Council on Environmental Quality:

Even taking into account such economic factors as increased prices with decreasing availability, it would appear at present that the quantities of platinum, gold, zinc, and lead are not sufficient to meet demands. At the present rate of expansion of about 6 percent a year, silver, tin, and uranium may be in short supply even at higher prices by the turn of the century. By the year 2050, several more minerals may be exhausted if the current rate of consumption continues.[3]

To estimate the world's reserve supply of mineral resources is an extremely difficult task.[4] An estimate may be made, however, by assuming that demand will not increase in the future. Figure 7-2 presents the resulting values of this "static world reserve index" for some mineral resources.

It is a fact, however, that the per capita consumption of metals in the United States increased by a factor of 9.6 in the period from 1870 to 1965.[5] This is equivalent to an increase in demand of 2.5 percent per year or a doubling time of 29 years. If we hypothesize a continued increase in demand of 2.5 percent per year (which actually is significantly lower than many present predictions, as in the preceding quotation) we derive the figures shown in the last column in Figure 7-2. It should be clear that the static world reserve index is a conservative estimate of the world's resources because it neglects the likely exponential increase in demand. New reserves will be found, of course, but the potential is limited:

Despite spectacular recent discoveries, there are only a limited number of places left to search for most minerals. Geologists disagree about the prospects for finding large, new, rich ore deposits. Reliance on such discoveries would seem unwise in the long term. Extraction of minerals from some large reserves of very low-grade ores may become economically feasible in the future. However, the techniques of extraction themselves may pose significant environmental problems. For example, the power requirements for extraction may be immense. That would add to thermal pollution. In addition, the yield of waste products can be substantial.[6]

---

[2] *Newsweek,* June 29, 1970, p. 77.

[3] Council on Environmental Quality, *Environmental Quality: First Annual Report* (Washington, D.C.: Government Printing Office, 1970), p. 158; hereafter cited as *Environmental Quality.*

[4] A dynamic world reserve index that accounts for the impact of changes in grade, demand, and technology on the reserves of nonrenewable natural resources is developed by William W. Behrens III, "The Dynamics of Natural Resource Utilization," chap. 6 in this volume.

[5] P. T. Flawn, *Mineral Resources* (Skokie, Ill.: Rand McNally, 1966), p. 246.

[6] *Environmental Quality*, p. 158.

	Static World Reserve Index $=\dfrac{\text{Known Reserves}}{\text{Present Annual Consumption}}$ (in years)	World Reserve Index, (Assuming 2.5 Percent Annual Increase in Consumption (in years)
Chromium	420	98
Iron	240	78
Nickel	150	62
Cobalt	110	53
Aluminum	100	50
Manganese	97	49
Molybdenum	79	44
Tungsten	40	28
Copper	36	26
Lead	26	20
Zinc	23	18
Tin	17	15
Silver	16	13
Mercury	13	11
Gold	11	10

Figure 7-2 World reserve indices (1970) with and without correction for increased consumption
Source: Donella H. Meadows et al., The Limits to Growth *(New York: Universe Books, 1972), p. 56.*

Possible Solutions.   Feasible solutions for the solid waste problem are very few. The goal is twofold: to slow down the consumption of natural resources and to reduce the rate of growth of material in dumps. Thus an approach such as the use of biodegradable products is not a good solution. It alleviates only one-half of the problem, the dump growth rate. In principle, there is only *one* satisfactory approach, to reduce the rate at which natural resources are transformed into solid waste by the production of intermediate products. The *flow* of materials from natural resources to solid waste (see Figure 7-3) must be reduced.

To speak precisely about controlling this flow, we need a quantitative expression for its magnitude (measured in tons per year). If we assume that the equilibrium number of products in use is P, and the average lifetime of the product (that is, the time it is used) is L, then the number of products discarded per time unit (the discard rate) is

$$P/L.$$

Assuming that the amount of waste in each product is w, the solid waste generation rate S is

$$S = Pw/L.$$

Thus there are only three ways of reducing the solid waste generation rate:

1. To reduce P, the actual number of products in use.
2. To increase L, the product's lifetime.
3. To reduce w, the amount of solid waste in each product.

Let us discuss these alternatives in more detail.

Since the material standard of living is related to the actual number of products in use per capita, the first approach implies a deliberate reduction in the average material standard of living. This may be necessary in the long run but is probably not politically feasible at present.

Proposal two—to increase the useful lifetime of products—represents an attempt at curbing the "throw away-no return" and "planned obsolescence" tendencies of the present economic system. There are many ways in which the useful lifetime of a product can be increased. The most obvious way, of course, is to construct the product so that it lasts longer. But a second alternative is to design products to be easily and cheaply repaired. (Included in this scheme must be an adequate number of easily accessible repairmen and service centers.)

A third alternative would be deliberate economic and social incentives inducing people to keep products for longer periods than normal. This might, however, have little impact. Though many people sell or throw away products before they break down, simply because they like to have new and exciting things and can afford them, the usage of many products does not end until the product is beyond repair. Products discarded by the primary user are often picked up and used by secondary and tertiary consumers until the product is completely useless. Inducing the primary user to hold on to the product longer might then decrease only the number of users and not the total product lifetime.

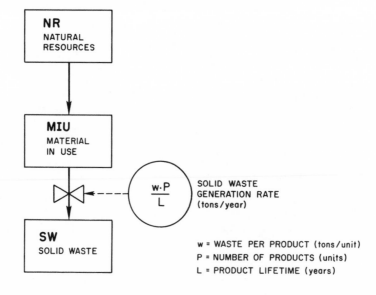

Figure 7-3 The flow of resources to waste

In any event this approach would not be useful for one important category of products: items that are explicitly produced for a single use followed by disposal. These products (for instance, soft-drink bottles) cannot be used by a secondary consumer, and hence seem destined for the dump. This very rapid flow of resources into solid waste can be avoided, of course, by reuse of the product by the producer, who can refill the bottle and sell it anew. Each refilling of the bottle in fact corresponds to an increase of its product lifetime—which can be multiplied by a factor of 20-30 by such procedures. The approach is unfortunately increasingly difficult to implement:

> Undeniably, housewives in growing numbers don't want to be bothered with carting bottles back to the store. The number of trips made by the average returnable bottle has declined drastically—from 31 trips twenty years ago to 19 in the case of beer bottles. And just two years ago, the Pepsi Cola Co. put 14.4 million new Pepsi bottles in circulation in New York City and raised the deposit to 5 cents to encourage their return. Six months later, all the bottles had disappeared.[7]

In spite of Pepsi Cola's experience, there is little doubt that the road to increased product lifetime in the case of reusable products is through increased incentives to the consumer to return the used product instead of throwing it away and through increased incentives to the producer to reuse it.

It is important to realize that one does not necessarily have to increase the production rate to increase the material standard of living, that is, the number of products in use. One can obtain the same increase in material prosperity by maintaining the production rate and increasing product lifetimes. At equilibrium the number of products in use equals the average life of the item multiplied by its production rate. Instead of increasing the throughput, one can obtain the same large stock of products in use by increasing the product lifetime:

> Minimizing the rate of throughput which maintains a stock is equivalent to maximizing the life expectancy or durability of the stock. This can be done in two ways: increasing the durability of the individual commodities (instead of planning for obsolescence and self-destruction), and designing commodities and distribution channels so that the "corpse" of commodities can be recycled and "reincarnated" in a new commodity (the opposite of throw-away technology). . . . It is not the increase of production but the increase of capital stock which makes us rich.[8]

At first glance, the third proposal—to reduce the amount of raw material in each product—looks like an effective way of reducing the solid waste generation rate. However, one ought to consider the fact that the durability of the product in many cases depends on the amount of raw material used in its construction. Hence the lifetime L of the product (the time before it becomes useless) may decrease when the amount of material in the product w decreases. The result might be that w/L does not decrease as w is reduced, and that the solid waste generation rate (which is proportional to w/L) under certain conditions might even *increase* as a consequence of reducing w.

[7] *Newsweek,* September 21, 1971, p. 70.
[8] H. E. Daly, *New York Times,* October 14, 1970.

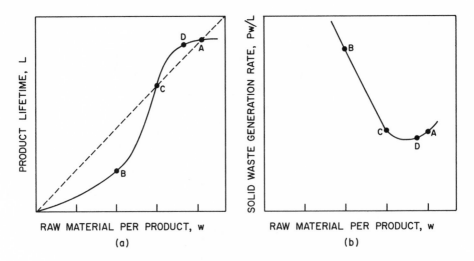

Figure 7-4 The dependency of product lifetime on raw material per product

As an example of this phenomenon, Figure 7-4(a) presents a hypothetical relationship between the amount of raw material in a product and its lifetime. The lifetime is very small when only a little raw material is used; it then increases steeply as the amount of raw material per unit is raised. Finally, a point is reached where one has to increase the raw material usage by large factors to achieve barely perceivable improvements in the lifetime of the product.

Figure 7-4(b) shows the solid waste generation rate Pw/L for a constant number P of products in use as the construction weight w of the product is changed. It is derived directly from Figure 7-4(a) by dividing the weight w by the lifetime L at each point. If we are initially at point A on the figure, a 50 percent reduction in w will move us to point B, and we will experience no decrease in w/L. To the contrary, w/L will double because of the large decrease in L.

Point C, corresponding to a 25 percent decrease in w, is seen to result in no change in the value of w/L, whereas a reduction of only 10 percent has the desired effect: a reduction in the value of w/L and hence in the waste generation rate (point D). It is reasonable to assume that producers already cut costs by using minimal amounts of raw materials in their products. Hence it might be detrimental to introduce general taxes on the weight of the discarded product. Such a tax would probably lead producers to reduce the weight of their products by lowering raw material inputs even further. In unhappy circumstances the result could be increased waste problems. Such a tax would be very beneficial, however, in the case of packaging. The tax would probably reduce much of the excess packaging, a reduction that can easily be made without impairing the utility of the packaging and with no effect whatsoever on the useful lifetime of the product inside the package. It is of interest to note that packaging constitutes most of the litter and 70 percent of the household wastes collected in the United States.[9]

[9] *Nation's Cities,* June 1970, p. 12.

Recycling. There exists, however, another way of effectively reducing the amount of material in a product w that does not simultaneously result in changes in product lifetime. The material in the discarded product can be recycled. Because recycling can reduce to a small fraction the part of w that actually is thrown away, it can potentially reduce the solid waste generation rate substantially.

Thus it appears that the most practical way to reduce the solid waste generation rate with substantial and long-lasting results is through recycling the discarded products. Preferably this method should be coupled with a general increase in product lifetime through better construction of appliances and the reuse of containers and other single-use products, when disproportionate increases in material per product are not required.

> It seems desirable from the conservation point of view to obtain large fractions of our mineral supplies from recycling metals. . . .
>
> Recycling of minerals would also appear to be desirable in view of a lessened environmental impact. The amount of waste products that must be disposed of is reduced, and the energy requirements of recycling appear to be less than those required for primary production. In the long term, there appears to be no adequate substitute to recycling.[10]

President Nixon in August 1970 stated:

> The prospect of increasing population density adds urgency to the need for greater emphasis on recycling of "waste" products. More people means greater consumption—and thus more rapid depletion—of scarce natural resources; greater consumption means more "waste" to dispose of—whether in the form of solid wastes, or of the pollutants that foul our air and water. . . .
>
> We can no longer afford the indiscriminate waste of our natural resources; neither should we accept as inevitable the mounting costs of waste removal. We must move increasingly toward closed systems that recycle what now are considered wastes back into useful and productive purposes. This poses a major challenge—and a major opportunity—for private industry.[11]

Resistance to Change. But to effect a transition from the present wasteful society to a society that recycles most of its wastes is easier in theory than in practice.

First of all, numerous technical problems must be solved. The most obvious of these is: how does one go about collecting and sorting billions of tons of waste? Not only must these processes be automated but the recycling must be done in such a way that the resulting pollution (odors, seepage, heat, and so on) is kept low. And in the waste refining processes, entirely new types of impurities in the recycled material will have to be dealt with.

But even when these technical problems are solved (and vigorous efforts are underway to solve them[12]), one is left with a seemingly impossible task, namely,

---

[10]*Environmental Quality,* p. 158.

[11] Richard M. Nixon, Message to the Congress, August 1970.

[12] D. G. Wilson, "Present and Future Possibilities of Reclamation from Solid Wastes," *New Directions in Solid Waste Processing* (Amherst: University of Massachusetts, 1970).

to change the behavior of today's manufacturers, investors, consumers, and mining companies. The enormous investment in present-day technology based on the present consumption pattern is the basis of a significant resistance to change. So is the habit of the consumer to purchase anything he wants—regardless of whether it is feasible for disposal or recycling—and to throw it away afterward, more or less wherever he pleases, and at no cost.

A forced change to a situation with less solid waste generation and more recycling clearly will affect society in many important ways. Changes will occur in the consumption of raw materials, in the prices of products, in the demand for finished products, in the amount of mining that will continue, and in the inventories of processed raw materials. In face of the opposition such a forced change is likely to meet, it would be highly desirable to be able to test the different possible policies in advance, to eliminate at least the most obvious mistakes.

Is it, for instance, more effective to start by taxing the mining industry or by subsidizing the recycling industry? How important is it to encourage recycling now rather than wait until material shortages make it profitable for individual firms to recycle? When the cost of raw materials is low relative to the price of the finished good, will economic incentives work to conserve resources for the long run?

To answer these and other questions and to substantiate the points considered earlier in this chapter, we made a comprehensive model of the interconnected relationships governing the use of raw materials and the generation of solid waste.

In the following sections, we present this mathematical system dynamics model of the solid waste system and show how it can be used to simulate the behavior of the system through time.[13] We then present some sample policy experiments—that is, studies of the effects of different policies on the behavior of the system.

A Dynamic Model of Solid Waste Generation

Questions to Be Answered by the Model.   Before making a model of a phenomenon, it is essential to know exactly what questions the model should address. When that is unclear, it is impossible to decide which variables and relationships to include in the model and which to omit.

The preceding discussion identified a general area of study, but it was not sufficiently limiting to provide the focus required for constructing a useful and meaningful model. The questions we chose to address in this study center upon the process of material flow from natural resources to solid waste over a time span of about one hundred years. This lengh of time was chosen because it exceeds the world reserve indices for many minerals and metals, and one can foresee significant changes in the cost of extraction and in usage and recycling patterns over

---

[13] The system dynamics flow diagram symbols are described in Chapter 2 and summarized in Figure 2-2.

such a time period. On the other hand, in choosing such a long time horizon, we excluded from the study all kinds of short-term variations, such as the daily fluctuations in the price of resources or seasonal fluctuations in production. What we retained is the general evolution of the system, that is, the trends in the system and their behavior over a long period of time.

The type of questions we wanted to answer were: What determines the size of the flow of material from resources to waste? What determines the composition of virgin and recycled material in the flow? How can one increase the recycled fraction? How can one slow down the solid waste generation rate? What advantages are there to increasing the recycled fraction now above that dictated by purely economic incentives?

The Model Boundary. After the important questions and the time horizon had been specified for the study, we turned to determining a "system boundary," that is, to selecting those quantities and relationships that are both necessary and sufficient to answer the questions we posed.

First, we decided to focus on the dynamics of a single nonrenewable resource. Throughout this paper, copper is used as an example, but it is important to realize that the underlying model structure is appropriate for any nonrenewable commodity that can be recycled. Thus if one wants to study a different resource—such as iron, mercury, gold, or aluminum—one only has to change the values of the parameters in the model, not the model structure of interlocking feedback loops.

We decided to model the production, consumption, disposal, and possible recycling of the one raw material chosen for study. The limitation to one raw material means that our "product" is defined as the usual mixture of objects made from one ton of raw material. In the case of copper this is 36 percent wire, 48 percent tubes and sheets, 15 percent castings, and one percent powder.[14]

Second, we decided to look at the copper-production market as a whole. We were concerned neither with the competition among individual firms producing the same product nor with the behavior of individual consumers. The model includes longer-term relationships binding together an industry, its sources of processed raw material, the consumers of the industry's product, and the resulting stock of solid waste.

Third, we assumed that the level of the industry's output is determined only by the demand for the product. In reality this demand is a function of the product's quality, price, and convenience in use. It also depends on factors such as marketing efforts and the average affluence of the consumer. To focus on the influence of resource constraints, we assumed that all these factors, except the price of the product, are constants. That is, we assumed that, for a given product price, there exists a specific demand for the product. This demand does not vary with time if the price stays constant.

---

[14]Charles River Associates, Inc., *Economic Analysis of the Copper Industry* (Cambridge, Mass., March 1970), p. 9.

This demand assumption is similar to that made in microeconomics and is reasonable in the short run. In the longer run, growth in population and buying power per capita would shift the demand curve. Such effects can easily be built into the model; they were eliminated from the basic model only because the direct effect of waste generation becomes clearer if we assume a constant demand function.

We also assumed that all the production factors (energy, managers, stores, and others) except the raw material are abundant. This is to say that if there is enough raw material the industry will produce enough to satisfy demand after the delay necessary for expansions or layoffs. This assumption was made only to clarify the results. The production sector of the model could easily be expanded for a more detailed analysis of a specific material.

Finally, the model does not explicitly include changes in extraction or recycling technology. Advances in technology are important, but their effects on this particular system may adequately be studied by changes in parameter values.[15]

The Important Feedback Loops in the Model.   These assumptions permitted us to separate a small, well-defined system from the immense totality of interactions involved in the flow of nonrenewable resources.

This system is limited by a "boundary." Outside the boundary are the factors or elements that do not affect the behavior of the system, in addition to the elements that affect the system in a constant manner throughout the simulation period. Inside the boundary, on the other hand, are all the variables or elements whose values change through time due to mutual interaction with the other variables inside the boundary. Thus a two-way causal relationship exists—a feedback loop—between each of these variables and the rest of the system: these variables *change* the rest of the system and *are changed by* the rest of the system.

The values of the exogenous variables—those outside the system boundary—can be specified by the analyst at any time during the simulation. That, however, is not the case for the variables inside the system boundary. The values of these endogenous variables are determined by their mutual interactions, that is, by the way in which they are organized or interrelated in what one calls the structure of the system. It is this network of interrelations among the endogenous or state variables that determines the time evolution of the system. Given the initial conditions (the initial values) for the state variables and their interrelationships (the system structure), the subsequent variations in values of the state variables in the simulation are determined for all the future.

What is the structure of the solid waste system? The cardinal assumption of system dynamics is that system behavior derives primarily from feedback-loop relationships. A system dynamics study consequently begins by identifying the

---

[15] Technological change may be modeled as an endogenous response to increasing scarcity and cost where these relationships are important. See Behrens, chap. 6.

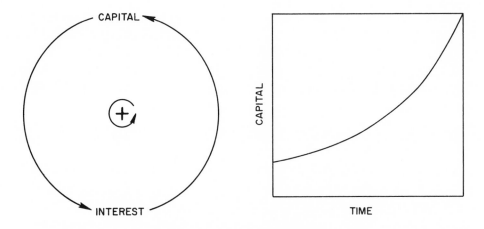

Figure 7-5   A positive feedback loop

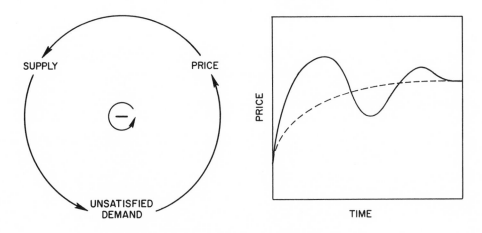

Figure 7-6   A negative feedback loop

feedback loops that are assumed to determine the real world behavior of the system.

There are only two types of feedback loops: positive and negative. The positive feedback loop is a closed chain of cause-and-effect relationships that amplify any disturbance occurring in the chain. Positive feedback loops show explosive behavior either toward plus infinity or toward minus infinity. An example of a positive feedback loop is the capital-interest loop shown in Figure 7-5. A certain capital placed in a bank account earns a certain interest, which we assume is also placed on the same account. This increases the capital, which in turn results in increased interest and so on ad infinitum. The behavior of capital versus time is shown in the diagram on the right in the figure. The growth rate is determined by the interest rate.

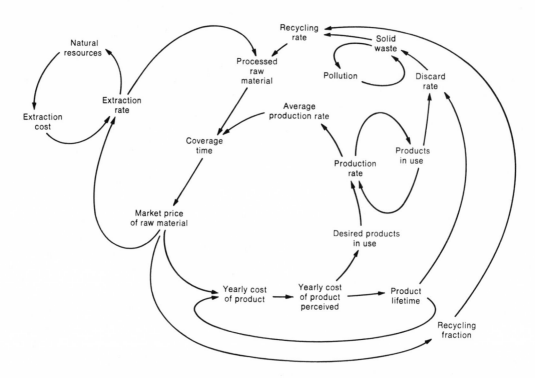

Figure 7-7 Causal-loop diagram for the solid waste model
Figures 7-7,8,11,12,13,15,17 and 19 courtesy of Technology Review *edited at the Massachusetts Institute of Technology.*

The negative feedback loop is goal seeking. The cause-and-effect relationships around the loop are such that the loop will respond to a disturbance not by explosive growth or decay but by motion toward a finite value—the goal. An example of a negative feedback loop is the price determination loop shown in Figure 7-6. Given a certain unsatisfied demand for a product, the price will tend to increase. This increase will increase the profitability of producing the product; as a consequence more manufacturers will enter the market. Thus the supply of the product increases and the final result is that the manufacturers can cover the market. The unsatisfied demand decreases, the price falls, and if the manufacturers have overreacted to the price increase the result is the oscillatory behavior shown by the solid line in the diagram on the right in Figure 7-6. The frequency of the oscillation is determined by reaction delays around the loop. If the manufacturers expanded exactly enough to cover the increased demand, the result is the smooth adjustment of price shown by the dashed line in Figure 7-6.

The feedback-loop structure of the natural resources-solid waste system is shown in the causal-loop diagram in Figure 7-7. We shall now discuss the individual loops one by one and describe in detail all the assumptions made.

Loop 1: The Natural Resources-Extraction Cost Loop.   Loop 1 is shown in Figure 7-8. It is negative and represents the fact that a decrease in the amount of

Figure 7-8 Loop 1: the natural resources extraction cost loop

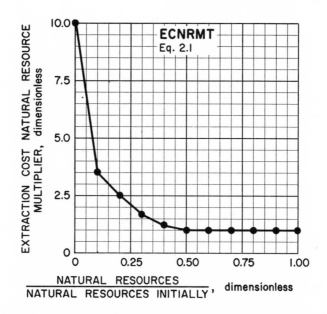

Figure 7-9 The increase in extraction cost caused by depletion of natural resources
The figure is a graphical representation of the tabular relationship used in the computer model. The relationship is denoted by the symbol, $\overline{ECNRMT}$ in the DYNAMO flow diagram in Figure 7-21.

natural resources NR[16] remaining results in an increase in the extraction cost EC per ton of copper when no new extraction techniques are being used. Figure 7-9 shows the assumed relationship between the natural resources NR remaining and the extraction cost EC. The increase in cost results from the fact that, as the amount of raw material left decreases, one has to go deeper in the mines, to mine poorer grades of ore, and to use mines that are farther away. The extraction cost EC influences the extraction rate ER, which is the number of tons mined per year. The quantity with which the mining industry compares the extraction cost

[16] Whenever we use a term that corresponds to a variable in the simulation model, the variable name—as it appears in the model equations (see the appendix to this chapter)—is printed next to the term. For example, the variable "natural resources" is referred to as natural resources NR, while "products in use" is products in use PIU.

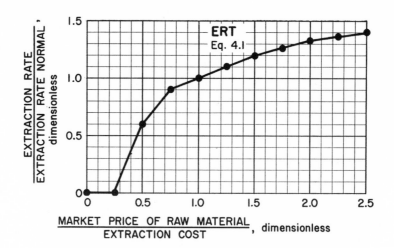

Figure 7-10   The dependence of extraction rate on the market price
of raw material

EC is the market price of raw material MPRM. The extraction rate ER will be high when the extraction cost EC is low compared with the market price of raw material MPRM. The extraction rate ER will be low when the opposite is true (see Figure 7-10). The extraction rate ER, of course, depletes the natural resource stock NR, closing the feedback loop.

Comment on Technology.   At this point it is useful to comment briefly on the role of technology. When future resource problems are predicted, it is common to suggest that technological advance will solve the problem. Historically, new techniques have provided less and less expensive means of mining existing reserves and more efficient ways of finding new reserves. Copper is a good illustration. The grade of copper ore mined has been steadily decreasing (see Figure 7-11). However, the price has increased only slightly in the same period because technical progress managed to increase the mining efficiency in the same period. But the efficiency was improved by using much more energy per ton of copper extracted (see Figure 7-12). Thus technology has not saved total resources; it has merely substituted other nonrenewable resources, oil and gas, for manpower costs. As a consequence the cost of mining one ton of copper is ultimately going to increase when energy resources become scarce and expensive, if not before. This is the relationship postulated in the model.

Since we are interested in the relative effectiveness of alternative policies, it is not very important to know exactly how far technology may postpone cost increases. For this reason the determinants of technology were omitted as explicit variables in the model. As mentioned before, any hypothesized improvement in technology can be taken into account exogenously by an appropriate change in the extraction cost EC. However, such a change will have little effect on the overall behavior of the model, unless one is willing to postulate techniques to

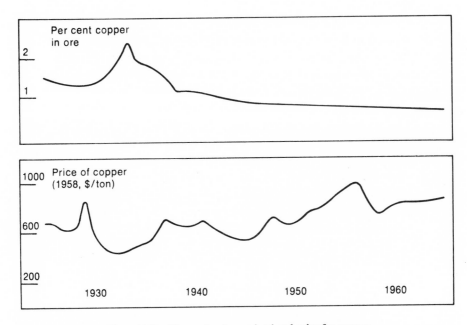

Figure 7-11 The grade of ore mined and price for copper
Adapted from Resources and Man; *op. cit,*

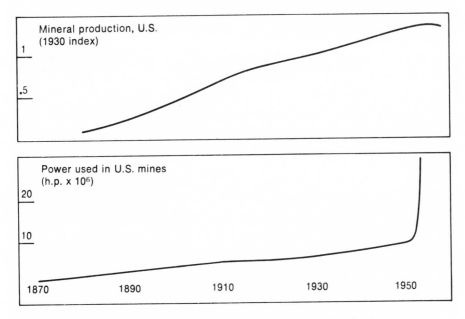

Figure 7-12 Increases in energy do not increase metal production
Adapted from Resources and Man *op. cit.*

extract copper (or a substitute) cheaply for all the foreseeable future. Such techniques would solve the resource depletion problem, but they would certainly exacerbate the solid waste problem.

Loop 2: The Market Price of Raw Material-Extraction Rate Loop.   Loop 2 interrelates the extraction rate ER, the stock of processed raw material PRM (that is, the amount of natural resources that has already been extracted, or recycled, and refined to the point where it is ready for use by the producer) and the market price of raw material MPRM (see Figure 7-13). When the market price of raw material MPRM increases, the extraction rate ER increases, and one gets a larger flow of material into the stock of processed raw material PRM (Figure 7-10).

Given the raw material price, storage costs, the present consumption of raw material, chances for labor strikes, and losses during storage, there exists an optimum stock size—that is, a stock size that is most profitable to the producer. The size of this desired stock of processed raw material PRM can be represented in terms of the corresponding normal coverage time CTN. This is the period of time

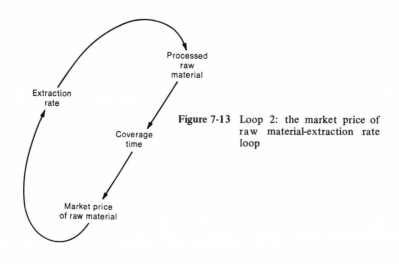

Figure 7-13 Loop 2: the market price of raw material-extraction rate loop

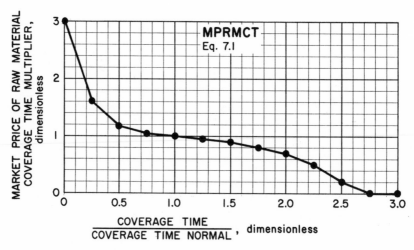

Figure 7-14 The determination of market price from coverage time

the desired stock would supply the current average consumption rate (equal to the average production rate APR, that is, the average rate at which new products are produced). Thus

$$\text{normal coverage time} = \frac{\text{desired stock of processed raw materials}}{\text{average production rate}} .$$

The market price of raw material MPRM is determined by the relative sizes of the desired normal coverage time and the actual coverage time CT, that is, the actual stock of processed raw material PRM divided by the average production rate APR. If the coverage time CT becomes too large, holders of the stock will lower the price paid for raw material. Thus the market price of raw material MPRM will decrease when the coverage time CT increases. The assumed relationship is shown in Figure 7-14.[17]

Loop 2 in effect adjusts the market price of raw material MPRM to the supply of raw material in such a way that the coverage tends toward its optimum value, determined by the present average production rate APR. Loop 2 is also negative.

Loop 3: The Market Price of Raw Material-Recycling Rate Loop.   However, there is another process by which the stock of processed raw material PRM can be increased, namely, by recycling. This possibility is shown as Loop 3 (see Figure 7-15). In this loop the market price of raw material MPRM determines the recycling fraction RCF. The recycling fraction RCF represents the fraction of the existing stock of solid waste SW that is recycled per year. Thus a recycling fraction RCF equal to 0.05 per year indicates that 5 percent of the total inventory of copper scrap—be it localized in dumps, in junkyards, or in radiators in abandoned cars—is recycled per year. The flow of recycled material, the recycling rate RCR, equals the recycling fraction RCF multipled by the current amount of solid waste SW. Note that a recycling fraction of 0.05 per year does not indicate that 5 percent of all copper used in producing new products is recycled. To obtain this quantity, that is, the fraction of material used in production that is recycled, one must compare the recycling rate RCR with the production rate PR.

The recycling fraction RCF is determined by comparing the market price of raw material MPRM with the actual cost of recycling the waste (see Figure 7-16). This recycling cost RCC consists mainly of the cost of collecting and sorting the waste, work that is still labor intensive. Typically, a ton of urban waste in the United States contains 7 percent by weight of metals.[18] The cost of collecting this ton of waste is roughly $20,[19] and the cost of hand-sorting it is *very* roughly

[17] An extensive explanation of this relation for commodity systems is given in a system dynamics-econometric study: F. Helmut Weymar, *The Dynamics of the World Cocoa Market* (Cambridge, Mass.: The M.I.T. Press, 1968), p. 32-55.

[18] American Chemical Society, *Cleaning Our Environment* (Washington, D.C., 1969), p. 167.

[19] *Environmental Quality,* p. 109.

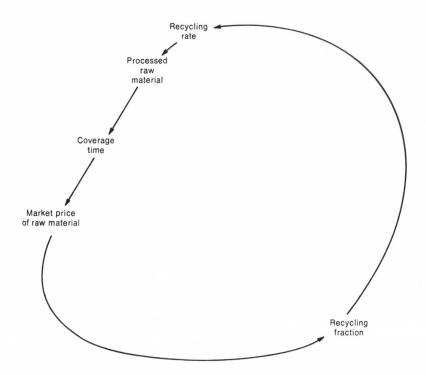

Figure 7-15   Loop 3: the market price of raw material-recycling
rate loop

$10.[20] Hence, if there is only one percent copper in the waste and the rest of the garbage has no significant value, it would cost about $3,000 per ton to recycle copper. The market price of one ton of copper is typically $700 per ton. For this reason urban waste is not effectively recycled at present. It is cheaper to extract virgin natural resources because the mining process has been automated.

Not all solid waste comes from urban refuse, however. Industrial waste is important because it is less expensive to recycle. Even at low market prices it is economic to recycle some waste—like mill scrap, for instance, which is easily and inexpensively recycled. As prices rise, more and more dumps (for example, radiators in abandoned cars) become profitable sources of material, and the recycling fraction RCF increases as suggested in Figure 7-16.

Implicit in this discussion is the assumption that the solid waste composition is the same in each dump category at all times. Of course, this is not true. The cheapest sources will be used first, so there is probably a tendency for a greater and greater fraction of the solid waste to lie in high-cost dump categories as time goes on. We chose to ignore this effect in the basic model because it does not affect the general conclusions sought. The actual size of the flow of recycled

[20] U.S. Department of Health, Education, and Welfare, *Solid Waste Processing* (Washington, D.C.: Government Printing Office, 1969), p. 13.

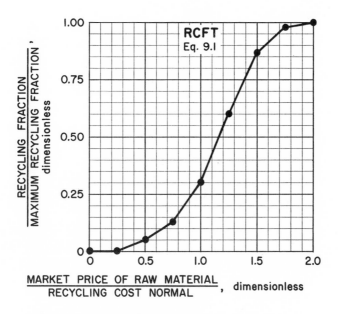

Figure 7-16   The dependence of the recycling fraction on the market price of raw material

material into processed raw material PRM (the recycling rate RCR) is the product of the recycling fraction RCF and the existing amount of solid waste SW. Thus a large recycling rate RCR requires both a large recycling fraction RCF and a large amount of solid waste SW.

To summarize, the effect of Loops 2 and 3 is to adjust the price of raw material in such a way that the resulting extraction and recycling supply exactly enough processed raw material PRM to give the optimum coverage for the given price and average production rate APR.

The Gross Behavior of the System.   These three interconnected loops (1, 2, and 3) are sufficient for understanding the main processes governing the behavior of the solid waste system. At the present time, for most resources the market price of raw material MPRM is low and the demand for raw material is satisfied primarily by extraction. As time goes on, the natural resource NR is gradually depleted and the extraction cost EC increases steadily. The cost of recycling, on the contrary, stays relatively constant; it may even decrease as solid waste SW accumulates, providing more recyclable material. As the price rises, it becomes profitable to satisfy a larger fraction of the demand for processed raw material by recycling. In the end, extraction will essentially stop when the cost of extracting the small part of the natural resources NR that remains in the ground becomes prohibitive. At this point, the use of this material will depend solely on the recycling of waste.

Although these three loops are sufficient to give the general behavior of the system, the questions we posed require the inclusion of several other factors. For example, since recycling is inevitably less than 100 percent effective, eventually even a constant annual demand for a material cannot be satisfied by recycling. Whenever a ton of copper is put through a use cycle, there is some loss; some part of the material becomes so finely dispersed in either water, air, or soil that it is lost forever. For this reason it is important to realize that what one calls solid waste is the part of society's waste *that is recoverable.* The part of the waste that is irretrievably lost—as, for example, the copper that is dissolved in water or exists as dust in the air—is generally considered to be pollution. Obviously, it is important to keep this part of the waste as small as possible. As long as the material remains as solid waste, it is still possible to recycle it; only when it ends up in the pollution category is recovery no longer possible. Thus in our model pollution POLL represents lost natural resources NR.

It is also important to represent in the model the dynamics of the resource demand structure. Changes in the market price of raw material MPRM affect the prices of the products that are finally produced from the raw material. A change in the market price of the product MPP is important because it affects the demand for the product. One should note that changes in price affect the demand for a product in two very different ways.

First, a lower price results in a tendency among consumers to stock more of the product; it increases the number of products in use at any point in time. An example is the demand for automobiles. A lower price leads a family to desire more cars. But there is another effect of a lower price, namely, a tendency among users to place less emphasis on repairs. Thus cars deteriorate faster and are junked sooner. Therefore when prices are lower—their lifetime decreases. So, when the price of cars decreases, one not only tends to scrap cars sooner but one also tends to have more cars in one's garage at any time.

The relative strength of the two effects does vary, however, from product to product. In the case of products typically produced for a single use—like paper towels, razor blades, packaging materials, and other types of disposable products—the price effect on the product lifetime PLT will be strong while the effect on the amount of the product one wants to store probably will be low. The price will determine how willingly one uses the products, the product lifetime being very sensitive to changes in price. The opposite is true for houses, cars, and appliances, which typically are made for sustained use. For these items, the product lifetime PLT is only weakly dependent on price because the product tends to be inherited by secondary, tertiary, and other users if the primary user throws it out before it has deteriorated completely. On the other hand, people often accumulate large stocks of such durable products when prices go down. The copper products we are studying here (electrical wiring and tubes) seem to belong to the second class of products. Copper products are bought for sustained use, and their effective lifetime is probably not strongly affected by prices. If the model parameters are changed to represent a different material, however, the relationship between price and lifetime might be quite different.

It should be noted further that price does not basically determine the amount of a product one wants to use at any point in time (the desired products in use DPIU) and the time one wants to keep the product before discarding it (the product lifetime PLT). Rather, the significant quantity is the cost per time unit of using the product (the yearly cost of product YCOP). One is willing to pay more for a product that lasts longer. The yearly cost of product YCOP is found by dividing the market price of product MPP by the product lifetime PLT (the unit of time in the model is years).

However, it is some time before a change in the yearly cost of the product YCOP is perceived by the consumer, because it obviously requires one product lifetime PLT to decide on the durability of the product. The perception delay will be of variable length: short for products like pop bottles and longer for cars and appliances. Hence it is not the yearly cost of product YCOP but a delayed version of the same quantity—the yearly cost of product perceived YCOPP—that determines the demand for the product.

In the case of our copper product, the product lifetime PLT is defined as the average time it takes between production and discard for the representative set of products produced from one ton of copper. This average lifetime is about 20 years,[21] since most of the copper is used in wires and tubes. The perception delay between an actual change in the yearly cost of a product and a change in the perceived cost is found by econometric studies to be around 15 years for copper.[22]

Loop 4: The Yearly Cost of Product-Production Rate Loop. The effect of price on the desired number of products in use DPIU is represented in Loop 4 (Figures 7-17 and 7-18). The market price of raw material MPRM affects the market price

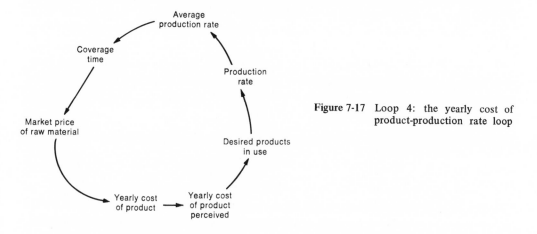

Figure 7-17 Loop 4: the yearly cost of product-production rate loop

[21] H. Brown, "Human Materials Production as a Process in the Biosphere," *Scientific American,* September 1970, p. 205.
[22] Charles River Associates, *Economic Analysis of the Copper Industry,* p. 40.

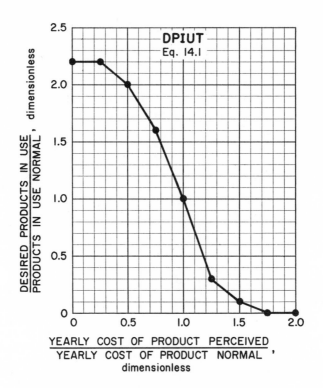

Figure 7-18   The demand curve for the product

of the product MPP, which, together with the product lifetime PLT, determines the yearly cost of product YCOP and also the yearly cost of product perceived YCOPP. The yearly cost of product perceived YCOPP determines the desired products in use DPIU. Subtracting the number of products actually in use at the present time (products in use PIU) from the desired products in use DPIU gives the number of additional products the market will absorb before it is saturated. Our earlier assumption was that the industry simply tries to satisfy the existing demand for its product. Consistent with this, we now assume that the industry decides to saturate the market in a specific period of time (the market saturation time MST). The resulting production rate is:

$$\text{production rate} = \frac{\text{desired products in use} - \text{products in use}}{\text{market saturation time}}.$$

This, then, is the rate at which the industry as a whole is turning processed raw material PRM into finished products. Finally, this rate is averaged over a certain time period (the averaging time AT) to arrive at the average production rate APR, which is the quantity required to compute the coverage time CT provided by the stock of processed raw material PRM.

Thus Loop 4 also acts to affect the market price of raw material MPRM. Its implicit goal is to alter the desired products in use DPIU so that the production rate PR meshes with the stock of processed raw material PRM and produces a stable price.

Loop 5: The Yearly Cost of Product-Discard Rate Loop.   The effect of price on the product lifetime PLT is portrayed in Loop 5 (Figures 7-19 and 7-20), which also shows how the yearly cost of product YCOP is obtained.

The product lifetime PLT is important because it determines the rate at which products are discarded (the discard rate DR). The average number of products discarded every year is:

discard rate = products in use/product lifetime.

Since a low yearly cost of product YCOP results in a short product lifetime PLT, its effect is ultimately a faster generation of solid waste SW. This branch of the feedback-loop structure closes back into the recycling rate RCR.

The Flow Diagram

We have discussed the causal links or feedback loops that we think determine the behavior of every natural resources-solid waste system. The next step is to draw logically consistent conclusions from the assumptions, that is, to analyze the detailed behavior of the system of feedback loops outlined. To do this we specified the assumptions more precisely so that they could be represented in a computer program. So far we have specified only the structure of the system; that is, we have indicated which variables affect which. Now we must specify these interactions quantitatively.

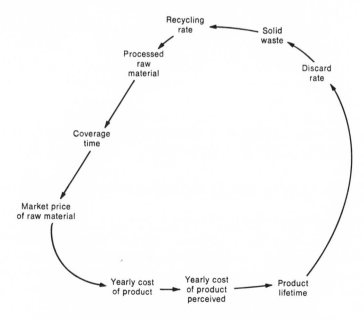

Figure 7-19   Loop 5: The yearly cost of product-discard rate loop

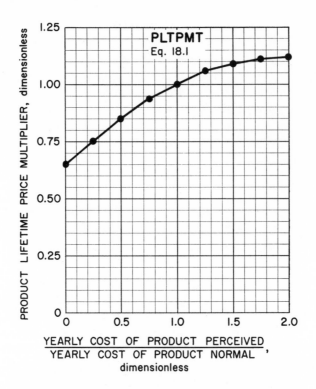

Figure 7-20   Product lifetime as a function of yearly cost of
product

The first step was to express the feedback loops in the DYNAMO flow diagram shown in Figure 7-21. This flow diagram is simply a formalized and detailed representation of the causal-loop diagram (Figure 7-7). Its elements correspond one to one with the statements in the final computer program (shown in the appendix to the chapter). As in most system dynamics studies we used the DYNAMO computer language. The names of quantities in the flow diagram are the same as those used in describing the causal-loop diagram.

The graphical relationships discussed earlier all appear in the flow diagram. Each of these "table functions" is represented by a circle where the variable name has horizontal lines above and below it. The relationships chosen for the table functions were the ones displayed in the previous sections.

Use of the Model to Simulate the Effects of Different Policies

In the following simulation runs made with the model, the parameters and table functions were set to represent the copper industry. It is important to remember at this point, however, that, since variations in demand and technology have been excluded, the actual point predictions are not significant. What is important, and consequently what one should concentrate on when studying the runs, is the relative behavior modes, that is, the change in general trends produced by a policy or technological change.

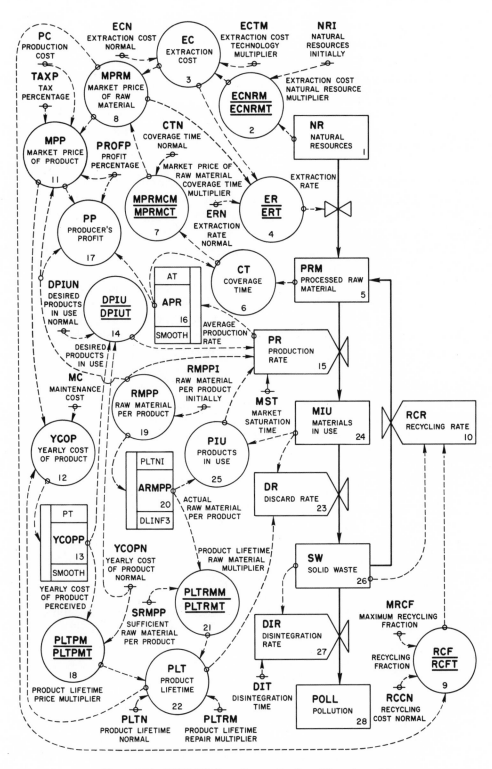

Figure 7-21 DYNAMO flow diagram for the solid waste model

For example, if the result of a particular run is a doubling of the recycling rate RCR over the next twenty years, one is not justified, looking at this run only, to infer that the simulated policy actually would double the recycling in the real world. This is so because, among other things, we have neglected to include the fact that demand is increasing exponentially. But if simulation of another policy results in a fourfold increase in the recycling rate RCR over the same period, one can say with some certainty that the latter policy enhances recycling more strongly than the former.

The initial conditions in all the runs are identical and chosen so that a *rough* approximation to today's conditions on the copper market is reached around year 20 of each model run. Today's market is characterized by a production rate PR $\approx$ 6×10^6 tons per year, consisting of roughly 70 percent virgin and 30 percent recycled material,[23] a world reserve index of approximately 40 years,[24] a copper price MPRM $\approx$ \$660 per ton,[25] and an inventory of materials in use MIU *very* roughly equal to 120×10^6 tons.[26]

Although this model is perfectly capable of reproducing past resource behavior, it should again be emphasized that this choice of values was made only to ensure that the model starts off in a reasonably realistic way. The runs should not be interpreted as predictions for the copper industry but as general indications of how the natural resources-solid waste system responds to alternative policies. The general conclusions are in fact valid for any nonrenewable natural resource that can be recycled.

In the runs, all changes in parameters are made in year 25 except when otherwise indicated.

Figure 7-22 shows a typical output from a simulation run. Several important variables are plotted on the vertical axes against time on the horizontal axis. Explanations of the symbols used in the plot are given to the left of the vertical axis. The magnitude of each variable at a given point in time can be read from the vertical axis using the correct scale, which is the one where the plot symbol for the variable occurs at the top of the scale (M meaning 10^6 and A meaning 10^{-3}). All runs use the same vertical scales. The three lines in the upper left corner indicate which parameters have been changed from the values occurring in the basic model as given in the appendix. Definitions of the symbols used in the plots can be found to the left of the vertical axis.

The computer prints only the individual characters (for example, the string of P's indicating pollution POLL) in the plots. To improve the readability of the graphs, the curves were drawn manually connecting the individual, identical symbols. To avoid crowding the plots with too many curves, we drew such trend

---

[23] *Metal Statistics, 1968*, pp. 20-30.

[24] See Figure 7-2.

[25] National Academy of Sciences, National Research Council, *Resources and Man: A Study and Recommendations by the Committee on Resources and Man* (San Francisco: W. H. Freeman and Company, 1970), p. 124.

[26] Brown, "Human Materials Production," p. 205.

lines for just four variables: natural resources NR (in tons), products in use PIU (in units), solid waste SW (in tons), and pollution POLL (in tons). Occasionally, a dotted trend-line was drawn for a fifth variable to demonstrate a specific point.

Policies to Increase Recycling.   Looking at Run 1 (Figure 7-22), where we assumed that there is *no* recycling during the entire run, one sees that it shows the expected behavior. Natural resources NR are depleted while solid waste SW and pollution POLL increase. Solid waste SW decreases after year 100. After that year there is a larger flow of material from solid waste SW to pollution POLL than into solid waste SW from products in use PIU. The level of products in use PIU is seen to fall rapidly from its initial level once the natural resources NR approach zero. This is caused by the diminishing extraction rate ER, which no longer can keep up with the discard rate, even though the latter decreases as a consequence of the increased product lifetime PLT. The increase in product lifetime PLT is caused by the increase in the market price of raw material MPRM, which increases when the natural resource NR gets scarce. The producer's profit PP, that is, the profit of the industry transforming the raw material into finished products falls catastrophically with declining products in use PIU.

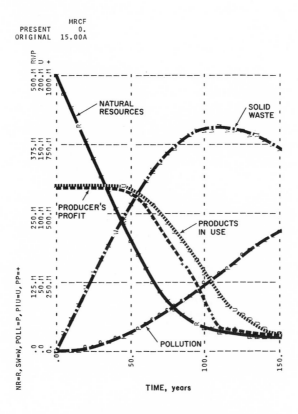

Figure 7-22   Run 1: no recycling

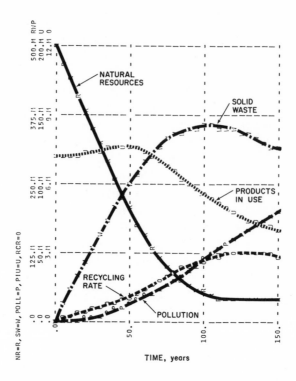

Figure 7-23   Run 2: standard run

The situation looks much less gloomy in Run 2 (Figure 7-23), where we assume a maximum recycling fraction MRCF of 1.5 percent per year, which is close to the actual value.[27] One gets a nonzero recycling rate RCR, and the advantages are obvious when compared with the no-recycling case in Run 1. First, the solid waste SW and pollution POLL are somewhat smaller; further, more natural resources NR are left at the end of the run. The difference is not enormous, however, because the availability of raw material through recycling leads to a much higher products in use PIU (or material standard of living) throughout the run. The market price of raw material MPRM is lower and the product lifetime PLT is somewhat lower as a consequence. The producer's profit PP, however, is gigantic compared to Run 1—a fact that would spur manufacturers' interest in recycling programs if future cash flows were not discounted with such a large interest rate.

It thus seems clear that recycling has all the advantages we expected, both for consumer and for producer and both in the short and in the long run. The following runs investigate the possibility of increasing the recycling rate RCR at an early point in the depletion of the natural resources NR.

---

[27] J. W. Shuster, "Copper Price Behavior in the Short Run" (Master's thesis, M.I.T., Sloan School of Management, 1968), p. 28.

Numerous authorities have stressed the immediate importance of initiating or increasing recycling efforts for specific materials and also for waste in general. There have also been specific suggestions about exactly how one should go about increasing the recycling. Proposals have varied from subsidizing train shipment rates for trash, to taxing the use of virgin material, to opening research institutes for recycling. In principle, however, all the different proposals may be reduced to the question of whether one wants to enhance recycling by subsidies or to discourage extraction by taxes. This model clarifies the implications of each approach.

As a first attempt at enhancing the recycling, we introduced a 50 percent tax on extraction (that is, the extraction cost EC was increased by 50 percent) in year 25. Run 3 (Figure 7-24) shows that the effect is to reduce the extraction rate ER and hence to save natural resources NR, as one would expect.

However, the effect is much less than one would anticipate because the system responds very quickly to the increase in the market price of raw material MPRM at year 25 and drives the price down nearly to its level in Run 2. (See the peak in the market price of raw material MPRM curve). The mechanisms that restore the market price to its former value are increased recycling and lower

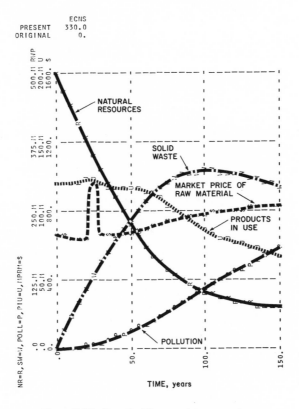

Figure 7-24 Run 3: 50 percent tax on extraction introduced in year 25

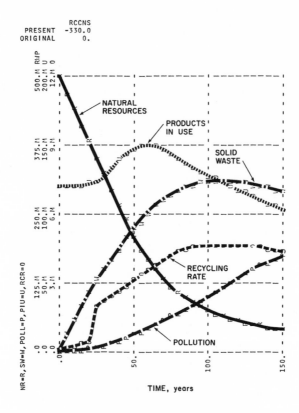

Figure 7-25   Run 4: 50 percent subsidy for recycling introduced in year 25

demand. This is a good example of the unexpected results one generally experiences in complex systems. One can always anticipate that the system will compensate internally for the changes imposed on it. In conclusion, then, the tax on extraction saves some natural resources NR and also reduces the solid waste SW and pollution POLL somewhat, but it is paid for by a slight reduction in products in use PIU.

In Run 4 (Figure 7-25) we reduced the recycling cost RCC by 50 percent, simulating a hypothetical subsidy, a breakthrough in the recycling technology, or a reduction in the recycling labor cost. As a result the recycling rate RCR increases significantly. The effect of this is an increased supply of raw material, lower prices, higher demand, and consequently a very high products in use PIU. All this is done without increases in solid waste SW and pollution POLL; in fact, the two are smaller in Run 4 than in the standard run (Figure 7-23) in spite of the much higher products in use PIU. The producer's profit PP is very large.

The natural resources NR are depleted approximately as fast as before, however. As an attempt to remedy this situation (and also to raise money to pay for the subsidizing of recycling) we tried in Run 5 (Figure 7-26) to combine the 50 percent reduction of the recycling cost RCC with a 50 percent tax on extraction.

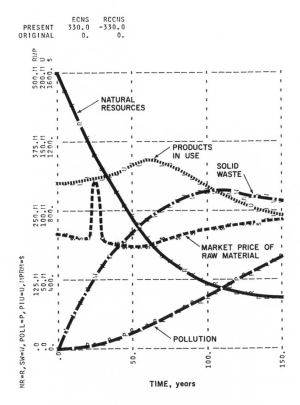

Figure 7-26 Run 5: 50 percent tax on extraction and 50 percent subsidy for
recycling

The effect is to save natural resources NR, but there is also a reduction of
products in use PIU because the market price of raw materials MPRM increases
slightly. The solid waste SW and pollution POLL are still lower than in Run 4,
and, since products in use PIU never falls much below the initial value, this
solution must be said to be the best yet.

In another run we simply assumed that one starts making products in such a
way that they are more easily recycled, an example being to make beer cans solely
of aluminum, avoiding the presently used steel bottom that results in a difficult
impurity in aluminum recycling. Changing the maximum recycling fraction MRCF
from 0.015 to 0.03 doubles the amount of solid waste SW recycled each year at
any market price. The result of the change is similar to what was obtained in Run
4 by subsidies.

It is important to remember that the success of the recycling scheme depends
on the existence of recyclable solid waste SW. In the runs described so far, the
quantities of solid waste SW have been ample to sustain large recycling rates RCR
for the time period studied. This is so because the "leakage" of material from
solid waste SW to the unrecoverable pollution POLL was assumed to be very slow.

(We assumed that the time for disintegration of all the solid waste SW into pollution POLL, the disintegration time DIT, is 200 years.)

The disintegration time DIT is determined by society's use of raw materials. In the case of copper the disintegration time DIT will be much longer if one uses all the material in thick-walled tubes, which are easily recycled, than if it is used in microelectronic circuits from which the copper will quite certainly never be recovered.

A run not shown demonstrated quite clearly that it is extremely important to use and dispose of used nonrenewable natural resources in such ways that they can be recovered at a later time. In this run we maintained the 50 percent subsidy for recycling from Run 4 (Figure 7-25) but assumed, in addition, a pattern of consumption and disposal of copper that produced a disintegration time DIT equal to 20 years.

The result was that even though the market price of raw material MPRM went very high, the recycling rate RCR did not increase, since the solid waste stockpile never became very large. The material standard of living was low and the pollution POLL very high—a dismal situation indeed.

Policies to Reduce the Solid Waste Generation Rate.   It is appropriate now to ask how one can reduce the solid waste generation rate. As mentioned in the introduction, the three possible approaches are to

1. reduce the actual number of products in use;

2. increase the product lifetime; and

3. reduce the amount of solid waste in each product.

An obvious, but politically infeasible, solution would be to tax the use of products to such an extent that people could not afford to use them. We demonstrated that such an action (approach 1) would indeed succeed by increasing the yearly cost of product YCOP approximately 20 percent through a tax on the market price of the product MPP. A run showed that the tax led to a substantial decrease both in the products in use PIU and in the solid waste SW and made the natural resources NR last much longer.

There are, however, other more realistic possibilities. Approach 2 is investigated in Run 6 (Figure 7-27), where the product lifetime PLT was increased. Such an increase could come about from better construction of the product. It could also result from better maintenance if repairs could be more easily and inexpensively made. A reduction of labor cost relative to machine/energy costs would probably have the effect of increasing product lifetime PLT. Run 6 clearly shows how one can substantially increase the material standard of living (that is, the products in use PIU) by increasing the product lifetime PLT.

The effects of increasing the product lifetime PLT are quite involved, however. Initially, a higher product lifetime PLT leads to a lower yearly cost of product YCOP. This causes higher demand and consequently a higher market price of raw material MPRM. This higher price leads to an increase in the yearly

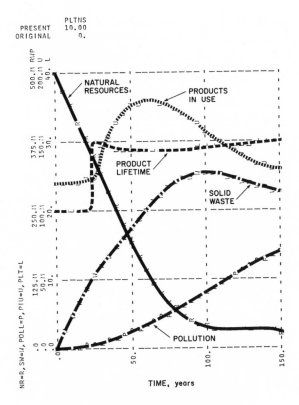

Figure 7-27   Run 6: introduction of 50 percent
better products in year 25

cost of product YCOP. But given the model assumptions, this increase is not large enough to counteract the cost reduction caused by the longer product lifetime PLT. And in response to the falling yearly cost of product YCOP the product lifetime PLT starts to fall after the initial rise in year 25. If the dependence of the product lifetime PLT on the yearly cost of the product perceived YCOPP had been stronger, one might have seen the effect of making better products being counteracted by the tendency of faster consumption when price decreases. But because of the assumptions made in Run 6 there is only a weak tendency toward such a relaxation of the product lifetime. The producer's profit PP is exceptionally large in this case because of the high demand coupled with the high prices.

We then turn to approach 3, namely, to reduce the amount of raw material per product RMPP. Run 7 (Figure 7-28) shows the effect of doing this when it is assumed that the reduction has no effect on product lifetime PLT or on the market price of the product MPP. (In some way the run simulates a decision to eliminate some completely unessential part of the product—for instance, the packaging.) The results shown by Run 7 are surprising, to say the least, when compared with the standard run (Figure 7-23). A reduction of the waste in each product by 40 percent does not lead to any measurable reduction of the solid waste SW. The reason is simple. The decreased demand for the raw material that occurs when the producers cut their use of the raw material by 40 percent results in a substantial (30 percent) decrease in the market price of raw material MPRM. As a consequence the price of the product also decreases, and the demand increases, resulting in a much larger products in use PIU than before the elimination of the waste. This larger stock of products in use PIU is capable of producing the previous amount of solid waste SW, even with a smaller amount of waste in each product.

The effects of reducing the raw material per product RMPP (as demonstrated by Figures 7-28 and 7-23) are indeed unexpected; they demonstrate clearly the deceptive behavior so often displayed by complex systems. It is this kind of behavior that is in fact the raison d'être for the system dynamics approach. It also explains why many well-intended past laws and regulations have not worked out as planned.

The effects of reducing the amount of raw material per product RMPP when it affects both the market price of the product MPP (which becomes less when

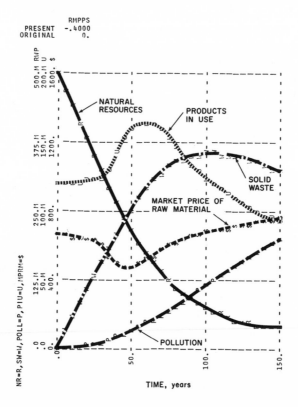

Figure 7-28   Run 7: reduction of raw material per product by 40 percent without any effect on market price of product or product lifetime

less raw material is employed) and the product lifetime PLT (which becomes less when less than a sufficient amount of raw material per product RMPP is used) were also tested. We assumed the relationship between product lifetime PLT and raw material per product RMPP to be as shown in Figure 7-29. We then experimented with decreases in raw material per product RMPP, chosen so that the new values of

$$\frac{w}{L} = \frac{\text{raw material per product}}{\text{product lifetime}} = \frac{RMPP}{PLT}$$

were, respectively, 0.9, 1, and 2 times the original value. The three new values represent the three possible cases that the decrease in product lifetime PLT is (a) larger than, (b) equal to, and (c) less than the decrease in the raw material per product RMPP. When simulations of these changes were compared with the standard run (Figure 7-23), it turned out that only case (c) represented any advantage, and that advantage was merely an increase in products in use PIU. Quite contrary to our expectations, neither solid waste SW nor pollution POLL decreased measurably. This occurred because as products get cheaper—when there is less raw material in them—demand increases. The same amount of waste is thus generated even though the amount of garbage per product is less. People simply have more to throw away.

In both of the other cases—(a) and (b)—the result was a short period of high products in use PIU (caused by high demand for the cheaper products before

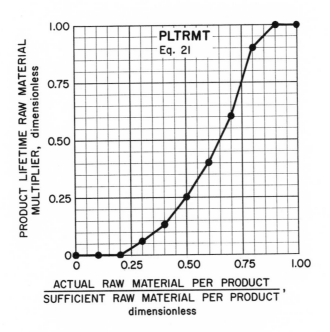

Figure 7-29 The dependence of product lifetime on the amount of raw material per product

people realize the shorter lifetime), followed by a decline to situations with less products in use PIU and more solid waste SW and pollution POLL (caused by the actual short lifetime of the new products). The situation is especially bad in case (a), where the resulting reduction in product lifetime PLT is so large that the yearly cost of product YCOP soars, even though the market price of raw material MPRM decreases.

Hence it seems that a reduction of the raw material per product RMPP should be undertaken only if it leads to a less than proportional decrease in product lifetime PLT.

A Solution. From the runs just described, one could be tempted to draw the conclusion that it is impossible to do anything significant about the natural resources-solid waste problem. It seems that the solid waste generation rate soars regardless of countermeasures.

To show that this pessimism is not necessary, we include Run 8 (Figure 7-30), which shows a policy leading to a high material standard of living (products in use PIU), low solid waste SW and pollution POLL, and fair reserves of natural resources NR.

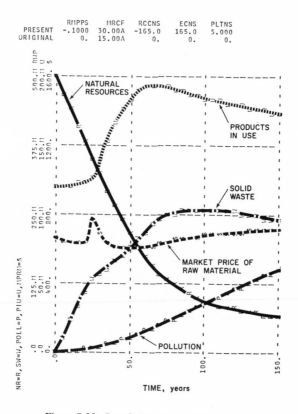

Figure 7-30   Run 8: how to beat the system

What kind of policy is it that has such advantageous effects? It is nothing but a combination of the policies we have already tried and found successful in certain respects. The following policies were all imposed simultaneously to produce Run 8:

1. a 25 percent tax on extraction;
2. a 25 percent subsidy to recycling;
3. a 25 percent increase in the product lifetime;
4. a doubling of the maximum recycling fraction; and
5. a reduction of the raw material per product in such a way that w/L changes from 1 to 0.9.

In combination, these changes create the desirable situation shown in Run 8 (Figure 7-30). The run demonstrates that it *is* possible to improve the system behavior by applying policies at several different points in the system at once.

Discussion of Real-Life Implications of the Study

A Practical Solution.   The logical question is, how does one go about implementing these changes in the real world?

Taxing extraction and subsidizing recycling are straightforward policies that could be enacted in several ways. Increasing the maximum recycling fraction, reducing the amount of raw material per product, and at the same time increasing the product lifetime are more difficult to achieve.

One basic consideration is that the user of a product should reasonably bear the cost of disposal. One might want to have the producer pay, but this is, of course, in the long run equivalent to making the user bear the cost. Paying for disposal is equivalent to introducing the price mechanism on the disposal market, that is, for the consumption of scarce dumping grounds. Since both materials and dumping areas are in short supply, it would seem equitable and efficient to have the consumer pay for the disposal of his discarded products.

The price of disposal would become the presently missing feedback between the solid waste generation rate and the consumer's high demand for products. However, it is important to introduce this feedback in such a way that it represents an incentive to the producer to make products that create fewer problems when they end up as solid waste. In other words, the feedback must lead to products that can easily be recycled, contain little waste, and have a long lifetime. Can such a feedback be found?

Luckily, a simple regulatory mechanism exists that would fulfill all the necessary feedback functions. This mechanism would be a tax on products (and thus ultimately paid by the consumer) that is proportional to the waste in the product divided by the product lifetime, namely, a tax proportional to

$$w/L.$$

Here w is the amount of waste that actually reaches the dump. In other words, it is the actual amount of raw material in the products minus the amount that is recycled. Such a tax would thus be an incentive both to decrease the amount of raw material per product and to manufacture the product in such a way that large parts of it can be recycled. However, by making the tax inversely proportional to the product lifetime, one avoids the problem of having the producer reduce the raw material to the extent that the product lifetime falls more than proportionally. Moreover, a tax levied in this way becomes an incentive to increase the product lifetime (that is, the time between production and discard) by any method: by making better products, by making reusable products, by giving better repair service, and so forth.

In practice, the product lifetime of a product could be assessed from a statistical investigation by some bureau, as could the amount of raw material in the product and its amenability to recycling. Such a bureau might find it appropriate to increase the tax somewhat for products made of materials especially troublesome in the dump.

The tax proportional to w/L is both a theoretically pleasing solution and also of interest from a practical point of view.

Current Policy Suggestions. Although the tax system just discussed might be among the most effective in solving the natural resources-solid waste problem, many other policies have been suggested that would in fact be quite useful in

Policy Proposal	Equivalent Parameter Change
Remove depletion allowances in mining industries	Increase extraction cost EC
Remove deductions for cost of exploration	Increase extraction cost EC
Remove capital-gains tax treatment in mining industries	Increase extraction cost EC
Make freight rates as low for scrap as for virgin raw material	Decrease recycling cost RCC
Remove federal government stipulations that prohibit use of anything but virgin material	Decrease recycling cost RCC (through the economies of scale which larger demand makes possible)
Make people sort their own wastes in their homes	Decrease recycling cost RCC
Prohibit nonreturnable containers	Increase product lifetime PLT (for the substitute returnable containers)
Reduce packaging	Reduce raw material per product RMPP.

Figure 7-31 Possible policies intended to solve the natural resources-solid waste problem

diminishing the problem. The effects of most of these alternative policies can be simulated by the solid waste model. To study the effects of a specific policy, one must first determine what changes in the parameters of the model best represent the impact of that policy on real-world relationships. Figure 7-31 indicates the changes in the model's parameters that must be made to simulate the effects of several frequently proposed policies to relieve the natural resources-solid waste problem.

As can be seen from Figure 7-31, all the policies ultimately influence the system by changing precisely the same parameters already changed in the runs of the preceding sections. Thus the relative effects of the various policies can be studied simply by examining the simulation runs in which specific parameters were changed.

The Urgency of the Problem.   Given the model assumptions, all the runs implied that society has something like forty years to come to grips with the copper solid waste problem. This is approximately the time, according to the standard run (Figure 7-23), before the standard of living (or at least the usage of copper) really

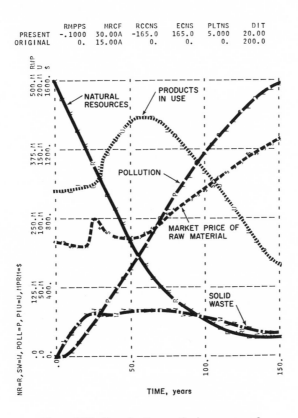

Figure 7-32 Run 9: the continuing success of
the policy in Run 8 when the disintegration time is 20 years

starts decreasing because of lack of natural resources NR. (Remember that present conditions correspond roughly to year 25 in the runs.)

Several of the assumptions underlying the model, however, are such that they result in an overestimate of the time span available. For instance, we assumed a disintegration time DIT for solid waste SW of 200 years. Considering the way in which solid waste SW is presently buried (for example, under golf courses, new housing complexes, and highways) or dumped in the oceans, it is likely that the solid waste SW becomes inaccessible for future recycling in just 20 years.

Run 9 (Figure 7-32) explores the success of our "beat-the-system" policy (shown in Run 8, Figure 7-30) when faced with a short disintegration time. As one can see, the policy still is successful: it increases the products in use PIU significantly over an extended period of time.

If, however, one chose to postpone the implementation of the policies until the material standard of living had already started its decrease, that is, until year 70 according to the standard run (Figure 7-23), the situation becomes much more

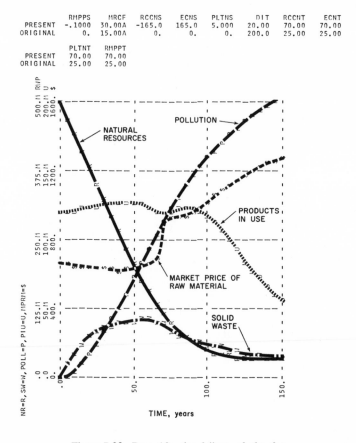

Figure 7-33 Run 10: the failure of the for-
merly successful policy when implemented too late (in year 70)

critical. This can be seen from Run 10 (Figure 7-33), where we implemented the "beat-the-system" policies in year 70 instead of year 25 (that is, 45 years from now instead of today). As the run shows, these very strong countermeasures fail to have any significant effect when employed at this late time. In the natural resources-solid waste system it is too late to react when the decline has started. To avoid the decline, one must start changing the policies many decades in advance.

Finally, the reader must not forget that all the runs assume constant population and income per capita. In fact, both of these are growing exponentially, with a resulting increase in the consumption of minerals of roughly 2.5 percent per year (for the past one hundred years). This growth results in a 300 percent increase in demand over a forty-year period and thus naturally increases the urgency of the necessary change.

Appendix: Computer Program for the Solid Waste Model

```
NR.K=NR.J+(DT)(-ER.JK)                              1, L
NR=NRI                                              1.1, N
NRI=500E6                                           1.2, C
    NR      - NATURAL RESOURCES (TONS)
    DT      - TIME INTERVAL BETWEEN EACH CALCULATION
              (YEARS)
    ER      - EXTRACTION RATE (TONS/YEAR)
    NRI     - NATURAL RESOURCES INITIALLY (TONS)

ECNRM.K=TABHL(ECNRMT,NR.K/NRI,0,1,.1)               2, A
ECNRMT=10/3.5/2.5/1.7/1.2/1/1/1/1/1/1               2.1, T
    ECNRM   - EXTRACTION COST NATURAL RESOURCE MULTIPLIER
              (DIMENSIONLESS)
    TABHL   - TERM DENOTING A TABULAR RELATIONSHIP
    ECNRMT  - EXTRACTION COST NATURAL RESOURCE MULTIPLIER
              TABLE
    NR      - NATURAL RESOURCES (TONS)
    NRI     - NATURAL RESOURCES INITIALLY (TONS)

EC.K=(ECNI+STEP(ECNS,ECNT))*ECTM*ECNRM.K            3, A
ECNI=660                                            3.1, C
ECNS=0                                              3.2, C
ECNT=25                                             3.3, C
ECTM=1                                              3.4, C
    EC      - EXTRACTION COST ($/TON)
    ECNI    - EXTRACTION COST NORMAL INITIALLY ($/TON)
    STEP    - FUNCTION CAUSING A STEP CHANGE IN A
              VARIABLE
    ECNS    - EXTRACTION COST NORMAL STEP ($/TON)
    ECNT    - EXTRACTION COST NORMAL TIME (YEAR)
    ECTM    - EXTRACTION COST TECHNOLOGY MULTIPLIER
              (DIMENSIONLESS)
    ECNRM   - EXTRACTION COST NATURAL RESOURCE MULTIPLIER
              (DIMENSIONLESS)

ER.KL=TABHL(ERT,MPRM.K/EC.K,0,2.5,.25)*ERN          4, R
ERT=0/0/.6/.9/1/1.1/1.2/1.27/1.33/1.37/1.4          4.1, T
ERN=6E6                                             4.2, C
    ER      - EXTRACTION RATE (TONS/YEAR)
    TABHL   - TERM DENOTING A TABULAR RELATIONSHIP
    ERT     - EXTRACTION RATE TABLE (TONS/YEAR)
    MPRM    - MARKET PRICE OF RAW MATERIAL ($/TON)
    EC      - EXTRACTION COST ($/TON)
    ERN     - EXTRACTION RATE NORMAL (TONS/YEAR)
```

```
PRM.K=PRM.J+(DT)(ER.JK+RCR.JK-PR.JK)              5, L
PRM=PRMI                                          5.1, N
PRMI=6E6                                          5.2, C
    PRM    - PROCESSED RAW MATERIAL (TONS)
    DT     - TIME INTERVAL BETWEEN EACH CALCULATION
             (YEARS)
    ER     - EXTRACTION RATE (TONS/YEAR)
    RCR    - RECYCLING RATE (TONS/YEAR)
    PR     - PRODUCTION RATE (TONS/YEAR)
    PRMI   - PROCESSED RAW MATERIAL INITIALLY (TONS)


CT.K=PRM.K/APR.K                                  6, A
    CT     - COVERAGE TIME (YEARS)
    PRM    - PROCESSED RAW MATERIAL (TONS)
    APR    - AVERAGE PRODUCTION RATE (TONS/YEAR)


MPRMCM.K=TABHL(MPRMCT,CT.K/CTN,0,3,.25)           7, A
MPRMCT=3/1.6/1.18/1.05/1/.95/.9/.8/.7/.5/.2/0/0   7.1, T
CTN=1                                             7.2, C
    MPRMCM - MARKET PRICE OF RAW MATERIAL COVERAGE TIME
             MULTIPLIER (DIMENSIONLESS)
    TABHL  - TERM DENOTING A TABULAR RELATIONSHIP
    MPRMCT - MARKET PRICE OF RAW MATERIAL COVERAGE TIME
             MULTIPLIER TABLE
    CT     - COVERAGE TIME (YEARS)
    CTN    - COVERAGE TIME NORMAL (YEARS)


MPRM.K=EC.K*MPRMCM.K                              8, A
    MPRM   - MARKET PRICE OF RAW MATERIAL ($/TON)
    EC     - EXTRACTION COST ($/TON)
    MPRMCM - MARKET PRICE OF RAW MATERIAL COVERAGE TIME
             MULTIPLIER (DIMENSIONLESS)


RCF.K=TABHL(RCFT,MPRM.K/(RCCNI+STEP(RCCNS,RCCNT)) 9, A
 ,0,2,.25)*MRCF
RCFT=0/0/.05/.13/.3/.6/.87/.98/1                  9.2, T
MRCF=.015                                         9.3, C
RCCNI=660                                         9.4, C
RCCNS=0                                           9.5, C
RCCNT=25                                          9.6, C
    RCF    - RECYCLING FRACTION (1/YEAR)
    TABHL  - TERM DENOTING A TABULAR RELATIONSHIP
    RCFT   - RECYCLING FRACTION TABLE (1/YEAR)
    MPRM   - MARKET PRICE OF RAW MATERIAL ($/TON)
    RCCNI  - RECYCLING COST NORMAL INITIALLY ($/TON)
    STEP   - FUNCTION CAUSING A STEP CHANGE IN A
             VARIABLE
    RCCNS  - RECYCLING COST NORMAL STEP ($/TON)
    RCCNT  - RECYCLING COST NORMAL TIME (YEAR)
    MRCF   - MAXIMUM RECYCLING FRACTION (1/YEAR)


RCR.KL=RCF.K*SW.K                                 10, R
    RCR    - RECYCLING RATE (TONS/YEAR)
    RCF    - RECYCLING FRACTION (1/YEAR)
    SW     - SOLID WASTE (TONS)


MPP.K=(PC+MPRM.K*RMPP.K)/(1-PROFP/(1-TAXP))       11, A
PC=140                                            11.1, C
PROFP=.1                                          11.2, C
TAXP=.5                                           11.3, C
    MPP    - MARKET PRICE OF PRODUCT ($/UNIT)
    PC     - PRODUCTION COST ($/UNIT)
    MPRM   - MARKET PRICE OF RAW MATERIAL ($/TON)
    RMPP   - RAW MATERIAL PER PRODUCT (TON/UNIT)
    PROFP  - PROFIT PERCENTAGE (DIMENSIONLESS)
    TAXP   - TAX PERCENTAGE (DIMENSIONLESS)


YCOP.K=(MPP.K/PLT.K)+MC                           12, A
MC=0                                              12.1, C
    YCOP   - YEARLY COST OF PRODUCT ($/UNIT*YEAR)
    MPP    - MARKET PRICE OF PRODUCT ($/UNIT)
    PLT    - PRODUCT LIFETIME (YEARS)
    MC     - MAINTENANCE COST ($/YEAR*UNIT)
```

```
YCOPP.K=SMOOTH(YCOP.J,PT)                          13, L
YCOPP=50                                           13.1, N
PT=15                                              13.2, C
    YCOPP  - YEARLY COST OF PRODUCT PERCEIVED ($/UNIT*
                  YEAR)
    SMOOTH - FIRST ORDER EXPONENTIAL SMOOTHING FUNCTION
    YCOP   - YEARLY COST OF PRODUCT ($/UNIT*YEAR)
    PT     - PERCEPTION TIME (YEARS)


DPIU.K=TABHL(DPIUT,YCOPP.K/YCOPN,0,2,.25)*DPIUN     14, A
DPIUT=2.2/2.2/2/1.6/1/.3/.1/0/0                     14.1, T
YCOPN=50                                            14.2, C
DPIUN=126E6                                         14.3, C
    DPIU   - DESIRED PRODUCTS IN USE (UNITS)
    TABHL  - TERM DENOTING A TABULAR RELATIONSHIP
    DPIUT  - DESIRED PRODUCTS IN USE TABLE (UNITS)
    YCOPP  - YEARLY COST OF PRODUCT PERCEIVED ($/UNIT*
                  YEAR)
    YCOPN  - YEARLY COST OF PRODUCT NORMAL ($/UNIT*YEAR)
    DPIUN  - DESIRED PRODUCTS IN USE NORMAL (UNITS)


PR.KL=MAX(((DPIU.K-PIU.K)*RMPP.K/MST),0)            15, R
MST=1                                               15.1, C
    PR     - PRODUCTION RATE (TONS/YEAR)
    DPIU   - DESIRED PRODUCTS IN USE (UNITS)
    PIU    - PRODUCTS IN USE (UNITS)
    RMPP   - RAW MATERIAL PER PRODUCT (TON/UNIT)
    MST    - MARKET SATURATION TIME (YEARS)


APR.K=SMOOTH(PR.JK,AT)                              16, A
AT=3                                                16.1, C
    APR    - AVERAGE PRODUCTION RATE (TONS/YEAR)
    SMOOTH - FIRST ORDER EXPONENTIAL SMOOTHING FUNCTION
    PR     - PRODUCTION RATE (TONS/YEAR)
    AT     - AVERAGING TIME (YEARS)


PP.K=MPP.K*PROFP*APR.K/RMPP.K                       17, A
    PP     - PRODUCER'S PROFIT ($/YEAR)
    MPP    - MARKET PRICE OF PRODUCT ($/UNIT)
    PROFP  - PROFIT PERCENTAGE (DIMENSIONLESS)
    APR    - AVERAGE PRODUCTION RATE (TONS/YEAR)
    RMPP   - RAW MATERIAL PER PRODUCT (TON/UNIT)


PLTPM.K=TABHL(PLTPMT,YCOPP.K/YCOPN,0,2,.25)         18, A
PLTPMT=.65/.75/.85/.94/1/1.06/1.09/1.11/1.12        18.1, T
    PLTPM  - PRODUCT LIFETIME PRICE MULTIPLIER
                  (DIMENSIONLESS)
    TABHL  - TERM DENOTING A TABULAR RELATIONSHIP
    PLTPMT - PRODUCT LIFETIME PRICE MULTIPLIER TABLE
                  (DIMENSIONLESS)
    YCOPP  - YEARLY COST OF PRODUCT PERCEIVED ($/UNIT*
                  YEAR)
    YCOPN  - YEARLY COST OF PRODUCT NORMAL ($/UNIT*YEAR)


RMPP.K=RMPPI+STEP(RMPPS,RMPPT)                      19, A
RMPPI=1                                             19.1, C
RMPPS=0                                             19.2, C
RMPPT=25                                            19.3, C
    RMPP   - RAW MATERIAL PER PRODUCT (TON/UNIT)
    RMPPI  - RAW MATERIAL PER PRODUCT INITIALLY (TON/
                  UNIT)
    STEP   - FUNCTION CAUSING A STEP CHANGE IN A
                  VARIABLE
    RMPPS  - RAW MATERIAL PER PRODUCT STEP (TON/UNIT)
    RMPPT  - RAW MATERIAL PER PRODUCT TIME (YEAR)


ARMPP.K=DLINF3(RMPP.K,PLTNI)                        20, A
    ARMPP  - ACTUAL RAW MATERIAL PER PRODUCT (TONS/UNIT)
    DLINF3 - THIRD ORDER EXPONENTIAL DELAY FUNCTION
    RMPP   - RAW MATERIAL PER PRODUCT (TON/UNIT)
    PLTNI  - PRODUCT LIFETIME NORMAL INITIALLY (YEARS)
```

```
PLTRMM.K=TABHL(PLTRMT,ARMPP.K/SRMPP,0,1,.1)          21, A
PLTRMT=0/0/0/.06/.13/.25/.4/.6/.9/1/1                21.1, T
SRMPP=1                                              21.2, C
     PLTRMM - PRODUCT LIFETIME RAW MATERIAL MULTIPLIER
              (DIMENSIONLESS)
     TABHL  - TERM DENOTING A TABULAR RELATIONSHIP
     PLTRMT - PRODUCT LIFETIME RAW MATERIAL MULTIPLIER
              TABLE (DIMENSIONLESS)
     ARMPP  - ACTUAL RAW MATERIAL PER PRODUCT (TONS/UNIT)
     SRMPP  - SUFFICIENT RAW MATERIAL PER PRODUCT (TONS/
              UNIT)


PLT.K=(PLTNI+STEP(PLTNS,PLTNT))*PLTRM*PLTPM.K*       22, A
  PLTRMM.K
PLTNI=20                                             22.2, C
PLTNS=0                                              22.3, C
PLTNT=25                                             22.4, C
PLTRM=1                                              22.5, C
     PLT    - PRODUCT LIFETIME (YEARS)
     PLTNI  - PRODUCT LIFETIME NORMAL INITIALLY (YEARS)
     STEP   - FUNCTION CAUSING A STEP CHANGE IN A
              VARIABLE
     PLTNS  - PRODUCT LIFETIME NORMAL STEP (YEARS)
     PLTNT  - PRODUCT LIFETIME NORMAL TIME (YEARS)
     PLTRM  - PRODUCT LIFETIME REPAIR MULTIPLIER
              (DIMENSIONLESS)
     PLTPM  - PRODUCT LIFETIME PRICE MULTIPLIER
              (DIMENSIONLESS)
     PLTRMM - PRODUCT LIFETIME RAW MATERIAL MULTIPLIER
              (DIMENSIONLESS)


DR.KL=MIU.K/PLT.K                                    23, R
     DR     - DISCARD RATE (TONS/YEAR)
     MIU    - MATERIALS IN USE (TONS)
     PLT    - PRODUCT LIFETIME (YEARS)


MIU.K=MIU.J+(DT)(PR.JK-DR.JK)                        24, L
MIU=MIUI                                             24.1, N
MIUI=120E6                                           24.2, C
     MIU    - MATERIALS IN USE (TONS)
     DT     - TIME INTERVAL BETWEEN EACH CALCULATION
              (YEARS)
     PR     - PRODUCTION RATE (TONS/YEAR)
     DR     - DISCARD RATE (TONS/YEAR)
     MIUI   - MATERIALS IN USE INITIALLY (TONS)


PIU.K=MIU.K/ARMPP.K                                  25, A
     PIU    - PRODUCTS IN USE (UNITS)
     MIU    - MATERIALS IN USE (TONS)
     ARMPP  - ACTUAL RAW MATERIAL PER PRODUCT (TONS/UNIT)


SW.K=SW.J+(DT)(DR.JK-RCR.JK-DIR.JK)                  26, L
SW=SWI                                               26.1, N
SWI=0                                                26.2, C
     SW     - SOLID WASTE (TONS)
     DT     - TIME INTERVAL BETWEEN EACH CALCULATION
              (YEARS)
     DR     - DISCARD RATE (TONS/YEAR)
     RCR    - RECYCLING RATE (TONS/YEAR)
     DIR    - DISINTEGRATION RATE (TONS/YEAR)
     SWI    - SOLID WASTE INITIALLY (TONS)


DIR.KL=SW.K/DIT                                      27, R
DIT=200                                              27.1, C
     DIR    - DISINTEGRATION RATE (TONS/YEAR)
     SW     - SOLID WASTE (TONS)
     DIT    - DISINTEGRATION TIME (YEARS)
```

```
POLL.K=POLL.J+(DT)(DIR.JK)                          28, L
POLL=POLLI                                          28.1, N
POLLI=0                                             28.2, C
LENGTH=150                                          28.4, C
PLTPER=5                                            28.5, C
DT=.05                                              28.6, C
    POLL   - POLLUTION (TONS)
    DT     - TIME INTERVAL BETWEEN EACH CALCULATION
             (YEARS)
    DIR    - DISINTEGRATION RATE (TONS/YEAR)
    POLLI  - POLLUTION INITIALLY (TONS)
    LENGTH - YEAR IN WHICH SIMULATION RUN TERMINATES
             (YEARS)
    PLTPER - TIME INTERVAL BETWEEN EACH SET OF PLOTTED
             OUTPUTS (YEARS)

PLOT  NR=R,SW=W,POLL=P(0,500E6)/PIU=U(0,200E6)
NOTE
NOTE  MODEL RUN CONTROL CARDS
NOTE
C     MRCF=0
PLOT  NR=R,SW=W,POLL=P(0,500E6)/PIU=U(0,200E6)/PP=+(0,1000E6)
RUN 1 NO RECYCLING
*     NO CHANGES NEEDED
RUN 2 STANDARD
PLOT  NR=R,SW=W,POLL=P(0,500E6)/PIU=U(0,200E6)/RCR=0(0,12E6)
RUN 2 STANDARD
C     ECNS=-330
PLOT  NR=R,SW=W,POLL=P(0,500E6)/PIU=U(0,200E6)/MPRM=$(0,1600)
RUN 3 EXTRACTION TAX
C     RCCNS=-330
PLOT  NR=R,SW=W,POLL=P(0,500E6)/PIU=U(0,200E6)/RCR=0(0,12E6)
RUN 4 RECYCLING SUBSIDY
C     ECNS=330
C     RCCNS=-330
PLOT  NR=R,SW=W,POLL=P(0,500E6)/PIU=U(0,200E6)/MPRM=$(0,1600)
RUN 5 EXTRACTION TAX AND RECYCLING SUBSIDY
C     PLTNS=10
PLOT  NR=R,SW=W,POLL=P(0,500E6)/PIU=U(0,200E6)/PLT=L(0,40)
RUN 6 BETTER PRODUCTS
C     RMPPS=-.4
PLOT  NR=R,SW=W,POLL=P(0,500E6)/PIU=U(0,200E6)/MPRM=$(0,1600)
*     THE FOLLOWING CHANGES MUST BE MADE IN EDIT MODE:
*     RMPP.K MUST BE CHANGED TO RMPPI IN EQUATIONS 11,A AND 17,A
*     ARMPP.K MUST BE CHANGED TO RMPPI IN EQUATION 21,A
RUN 7 LESS PACKAGING
C     RMPPS=-.1
C     MRCF=.03
C     ECNS=165
C     RCCNS=-165
C.    PLTNS=5
PLOT  NR=R,SW=W,POLL=P(0,500E6)/PIU=U(0,200E6)/MPRM=$(0,1600)
RUN 8 HOW TO BEAT THE SYSTEM
C     DIT=20
C     RMPPS=-.1
C     MRCF=.03
C     ECNS=165
C     RCCNS=-165
C     PLTNS=5
PLOT  NR=R,SW=W,POLL=P(0,500E6)/PIU=U(0,200E6)/MPRM=$(0,1600)
RUN 9 FASTER DISINTEGRATION
C     DIT=20
C     RMPPS=-.1
C     RMPPT=70
C     MRCF=.03
C     ECNS=165
C     ECNT=70
C     RCCNS=-165
C     RCCNT=70
C     PLTNS=5
C     PLTNT=70
PLOT  NR=R,SW=W,POLL=P(0,500E6)/PIU=U(0,200E6)/MPRM=$(0,1600)
RUN 10 TOO LATE IMPLEMENTATION
```

8
The Discovery Life Cycle of a Finite Resource: A Case Study of U.S. Natural Gas

Roger F. Naill

The resource sector of the global model deals with those resources that exist in finite and nonrenewable supply. An important question relevant to the global model is the extent to which currently unsuspected reserves might alter the model's projections. A secondary issue concerns the extent to which legislative changes and tax incentives might be used to alter the rate at which those unsuspected reserves are discovered and utilized. Both issues are addressed in the following paper.

The natural gas industry is currently experiencing greater shortages and higher growth rates than any other resource industry in the United States. Domestic proven reserves are sufficient to last less than fifteen years at the current annual rate of consumption, and that consumption rate is still increasing rapidly. Because the combustion of natural gas provides 33 percent of the total power currently produced in the United States, national policies with respect to this resource are extremely important.

The following paper focuses on the economic processes that transfer unknown gas reserves to the proven reserve category and provide for the subsequent exploitation of those reserves. Legislative, technical, and other policies are introduced to determine the degree to which they can alleviate long-term gas shortages and regulate the role of natural gas in the energy economy. An extended version of the model, a survey of related literature on gas production, and a discussion of the statistical inference techniques that may be used with dynamic, nonlinear models are presented in a 1972 M.I.T. Sloan School of Management M.S. thesis by Naill, "Managing the Discovery Life Cycle of a Finite Resource: A Case Study of U.S. Natural Gas."

213

8
The Discovery Life Cycle
of a Finite Resource:
A Case Study of U.S. Natural Gas

*For the first time in history, the nation's energy sup-
ply is failing to keep ahead of the ever-growing demand. America's factories and consumers are
increasing use of electricity, natural gas, coal and
other fuels faster than the suppliers of energy can
boost their output. Some analysts see the problem as
temporary, but others view it as a historical turning
point in which the energy resources that always have
been taken for granted become a limiting factor in
national growth.*

Wall Street Journal, June 2, 1970

Introduction

The United States today depends on fossil fuels for 96 percent of its energy supply.[1] The total amount of fossil fuels within United States territory is finite and nonrenewable during time periods of less than millions of years. Coal is still in relative abundance, for it has been estimated that the U.S. coal reserves will be sufficient for another four centuries at current rates of consumption.[2] M. K. Hubbert has also estimated, however, that more than half the originally existing U.S. supplies of petroleum have been depleted, and demand will soon outstrip the exploration and development of new reserves.

The natural gas industry seems to be facing the most imminent crisis of fossil fuel depletion. Although it has been estimated that from 400 to 900 trillion cubic feet of natural gas still remain undiscovered in the United States,[3] proven reserves are falling rapidly. The discovery rate, currently less than the production rate, is decreasing, while the production of natural gas is rising at almost 7 percent per year.[4] The trends in the discovery and production of natural gas over the past decade are shown in Figure 8-1.

The producers of natural gas cite price regulation as the major cause for decreasing discoveries: " 'Frankly, there is no incentive for wildcatting,' says W. W. Keeler, chairman of Phillips Petroleum Co., a major gas producer. 'Until there is a break in these FPC regulations,' he adds, 'I don't think we'll spend a lot of money trying to find gas.' "[5] Others outside the industry contend that shortages in the overall supply of gas are beginning to have an impact on rates of discovery.

What are the major factors controlling the discovery of supplies of fossil fuel and other resources? It is immediately apparent that, if a resource is finite and

[1] *Statistical Abstract of the United States, 1970* (Washington, D.C.: U.S. Government Printing Office, 1970) p. 506.

[2] M. K. Hubbert, "Energy Resources," in National Academy of Sciences, National Research Council, *Resources and Man*: A Study and Recommendations by the Committee on Resources and Man (San Francisco: W. H. Freeman and Company, 1969), p. 205; hereafter cited as Hubbert, in *Resources and Man.*

[3] Ibid., p. 188.

[4] M. K. Hubbert, "Energy Resources," in *Environment: Resources, Pollution and Society,* ed. W. W. Murdoch (Stamford, Conn.: Sinauer Associates, 1971), p. 97; hereafter cited as Hubbert, in *Environment.*

[5] *Wall Street Journal,* April 12, 1971.

Year	Reserves (trillion ft.^{3})	Discovery (Plus Extensions and Revisions) (trillion ft.^{3})	Production (trillion ft.^{3})	R/P Ratio (years)
1960	262.3	13.9	13.0	20.2
1961	266.3	17.2	13.4	20.0
1962	272.3	19.5	13.6	20.0
1963	276.2	18.2	14.5	19.2
1964	281.3	20.3	15.3	18.4
1965	286.5	21.3	16.3	17.6
1966	289.3	20.2	17.5	16.5
1967	292.9	21.8	18.4	15.9
1968	287.3	13.7	19.4	14.9
1969	275.2	8.5	20.7	13.3

Figure 8-1   Discovery and production of U.S. natural gas
Source: American Gas Association, Gas Facts, 1970 *(New York, 1970).*

nonrenewable, a trade-off between short-term and long-term goals is implied. With a finite resource one can enjoy a high usage rate for a relatively short period of time, depleting resources quickly, or one can sustain a lower usage rate over a longer period. What, then, are the effects of governmental policies such as ceiling price regulations or tax incentives on the short-term and long-term supply of a resource?

The answer to these questions depends on many factors, including, for example, the estimate of existing reserves in the United States, the cost of exploration, investment in exploration, price of the resource, sales revenue, proven reserves, demand, and usage rate. Rather good data are available on each of these factors, but their interaction over time is not intuitively obvious.[6]

In this paper, a system dynamics model of the natural resource discovery process is presented, and the model is applied to the natural gas industry as an example. This model permits one to test, through simulation, the probable effects of alternative regulatory policies. The following section describes in detail the functional relationships among the variables included in the system. The implications of various possible and existing policies on the supply of natural gas and other fossil fuels are next discussed. The final section presents the major conclusions to be drawn from the work to date and the potentials for further research.

A Dynamic Model of the Natural Resource Discovery Process

The natural gas industry in the United States seems to be at a turning point, for it is having more and more difficulty supplying the resources needed to continue past trends in growth of consumption. The goal of the model presented

[6] See Jay W. Forrester, "Counterintuitive Behavior of Social Systems," chap. 1 in this volume.

here is to represent and examine the implications of the factors controlling the supply of nonrenewable resources such as the fossil fuels, to determine the nature of the turning point in supply, and to examine the effectiveness of various policies in alleviating the problem.

To present a clear example of the system's behavior, the parameter values and estimates pertinent to the natural gas industry in the United States will be used, but it is important to recognize that the underlying model structure is appropriate for any finite nonrenewable resource. The end use of fossil fuels dictates that the process of recycling be excluded from this model. The impact of recycling on a recyclable mineral resource has been analyzed in Chapter 7. The results of that study could be incorporated in an application of this model to a mineral resource. Thus if one wishes to study the dynamics of the coal, oil, or copper industry's discovery process, only the values of the parameters would have to be changed. In the case of copper a recycling loop would be added, but the general structure of the model would remain the same.

Model Assumptions.   The model assumes that the natural gas industry is composed of many firms, all producing one undifferentiated product, natural gas. The interdependency between the oil and gas industries has been ignored for the purposes of this study. Although this assumption certainly affects the specific behavior of the model in the early stages of natural gas discovery, it does not affect overall behavior or the relative effects of policies. Furthermore, this assumption is becoming more and more valid at present. Directional drilling for either gas or oil is becoming more successful, and over 70 percent of all gas wells are now unassociated with oil.[7]

The model includes the relationships that govern the behavior of the industry as a whole; the separate producers' actions in discovery and production are aggregated together to obtain this industry behavior. The producers of natural gas are taken as those engaged in the discovery of natural gas and in the preparation of gas for use. Pipeline distribution companies are considered consumers, not producers. The gas is sold at the wellhead, usually under long-term contracts.

The cost of exploration is assumed to rise monotonically as resources are depleted. Of course, in reality the cost of exploration contains random fluctuations, and an example of the model's response to random fluctuations in cost is shown in the next section. However, we are interested only in the long-term behavior of costs as a function of the fraction of total resources remaining to be discovered.

Natural gas companies also exhibit eight- to fifteen-year cyclical variations in their reserve-production ratio caused by capacity acquisition delays in building pipelines. It is not the concern of this paper to model this effect; however, a complete analysis of this behavior can be found in Meadows and Swanson.[8]

---

[7] M. A. Adelman, *The Supply and Price of Natural Gas,* supplement to *Journal of Industrial Economics* (Oxford: Basil Blackwell, 1962).

[8] D. L. Meadows and C. V. Swanson, "Policy Design for Gas Reserves Acquisition Using Industrial Dynamics" (Paper presented at the 1969 Transmission Conference of the American Gas Association, Louisiana, Mississippi, May 26, 1969).

In the model, demand is assumed to be an endogenous function of product price, with other determinants such as growth in population and per capita consumption causing growth in demand at any given price. This rate of growth in potential demand is determined exogenously to the model, and in the case of natural gas it is assumed to be 6.57 percent per year.[9]

The model does not explicitly include changes in extraction technology, substitution effects, or the effects of imports in its structure. These effects can, however, be implicitly studied by their influence on existing parameter values in the model. The process of testing the effects of extraction technology and imports on the behavior of the model will be discussed later in this paper. The dynamic structure and the effects of technology and substitution are treated by William W. Behrens III in Chapter 6 of this volume.

General Description of the Model.   Figure 8-2 is a causal-loop diagram that illustrates the major feedback loops of the natural gas model. The model contains only two major state variables, or levels, corresponding to unproven reserves UPR and proven reserves PR.* Loop 1 is a negative feedback loop relating the level of

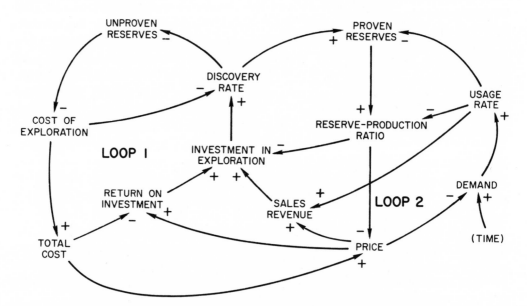

Figure 8-2 Causal-loop diagram of the natural resource discovery model
Note: The algebraic sign, plus or minus, at the head of each arrow expresses the polarity of influence between the two variables linked by that arrow. For example, as PRICE increases, SALES REVENUE increases (a positive relationship), and as PRICE increases, DEMAND decreases (a negative relationship).

[9] Hubbert, in *Environment*, p. 97.

*Eds. note—Whenever we use a term that corresponds to a variable in the simulation model, the variable name (as it appears in the model equations in the appendix to this chapter) is printed immediately following that term.

unproven reserves, the cost of exploration, and the discovery rate. As unproven reserves are depleted, the cost of exploration rises because less of the resource is found per exploration and because producers must look in more inaccessible places. The rising cost of exploration decreases the discovery rate, slowing the depletion of unproven reserves. A rise in the cost of exploration also increases the total unit cost of production, which decreases the return on investment in exploration, causing a decrease in investment in exploration.

Loop 2 is the demand loop, relating the level of proven reserves, price, demand, and usage rate. An increase in proven reserves increases the reserve-production ratio, which decreases price because of excess coverage.[10] A price decrease results in an increase in demand, which increases the usage rate and thus decreases proven reserves. The increase in usage rate also increases sales revenue, which in turn increases investment in exploration, for it is assumed that the industry allocates its investment proportional to revenues. Investment in exploration is decreased when the reserve-production ratio exceeds a desired coverage because the need for further discoveries is momentarily diminished.

Figure 8-3 shows the variables in the model as related by a system dynamics flow diagram. The following section describes the important relationships among the system elements and presents the mathematical equations that express these relationships in a form suitable for processing by the computer.

Loop 1: Discovery Loop.   Loop 1, the discovery loop, is a negative feedback loop representing the long-term effects of depletion of unproven reserves on the cost and discovery rate of natural gas. Each variable in the loop is described separately in this section, and each description includes justification for the parameters chosen in the model.

1. Unproven reserves **UPR**. Perhaps the simplest and yet most important concept of the model is that the total amount of unproven reserves UPR in the system is finite. The total extent of the reserves will be unknown initially, existing largely as unproven reserves UPR. Even after those reserves are discovered they may not be economically exploited, but the total quantity is fixed. Thus unproven reserves UPR begin with some initial value UPRI and can only decrease over time as unproven reserves are discovered.

There has been much controversy over the estimation of the value of initial unproven reserves. Because of the close relationship between gas and oil finds, most gas estimates are based on the results of existing extensive oil analyses. Estimates of 2,000 trillion cubic feet or more have been made on the basis of the Zapp hypothesis,[11] which is based on the assumption that "oil to be discovered per foot of exploratory drilling in any given petroliferous region will remain

---

[10] Coverage is the number of years you can support current production out of your current inventories; it is equal to the reserve-production ratio RPR.

[11] T. A. Hendricks, *Resources of Oil, Gas, and Natural Gas Liquids in the United States and the World*, U.S. Geological Survey Circular no. 522 (1965).

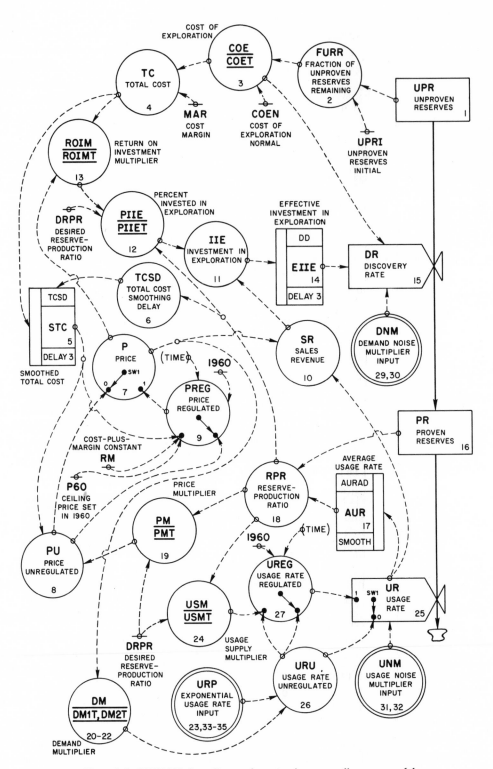

Figure 8-3   DYNAMO flow diagram for natural resource discovery model

essentially constant until an areal density of about one exploratory well per two square miles has been achieved."[12] Hubbert shows that discoveries per foot drilled have in fact fallen off exponentially with the cumulative footage drilled. He estimates an initial level of unproven reserves of gas for the United States, excluding Alaska and Hawaii, of 1,040 trillion cubic feet on the basis of this hypothesis.[13] Because the Hubbert estimate is derived from the discovery data, his value of 1,040 trillion cubic feet of initial unproven reserves is used in the model. This value can, however, be changed easily from one simulation run to the next to determine the dynamic implications of alternative possible unproven reserve bases, as discussed in the following section. The value of a simulation model lies in its flexibility to examine such variations in model assumptions.

```
UPR.K=UPR.J+(DT)(-DR.JK)                              1, L
UPR=UPRI                                              1.1, N
UPRI=1.04E15                                          1.2, C
     UPR    - UNPROVEN RESERVES (CUBIC FEET)
     DT     - TIME INCREMENT BETWEEN CALCULATIONS (YEARS)
     DR     - DISCOVERY RATE (CUBIC FEET/YEAR)
     UPRI   - UNPROVEN RESERVES INITIAL (CUBIC FEET)
```

2. Fraction of unproven reserves remaining **FURR**.   As unproven reserves are depleted, the level of unproven reserves at any given time divided by the initial amount of unproven reserves UPRI gives the fraction of unproven reserves remaining to be discovered FURR:

```
FURR.K=UPR.K/UPRI                                     2, A
     FURR   - FRACTION OF UNPROVEN RESERVES REMAINING
              (DIMENSIONLESS)
     UPR    - UNPROVEN RESERVES (CUBIC FEET)
     UPRI   - UNPROVEN RESERVES INITIAL (CUBIC FEET)
```

3. Cost of exploration **COE**.   It has been found that for all nonrenewable natural resources the cost of exploration is a decreasing function of reserves remaining: as reserves are depleted, the cost of exploration increases.[14] Initially, when the fraction of unproven reserves remaining FURR is one, the industry will explore for new gas reserves in the most accessible places and exploit the largest fields available, making the cost of exploration relatively low. As most of the larger deposits are discovered, producers must look in less accessible places, such as the sea bottom or Alaska, causing the cost of exploration to rise. In addition, both the size of the reserves found and the success ratio of wildcat wells drilled decrease, further increasing costs as the fraction of unproven reserves diminishes. Finally, as the fraction of unproven reserves remaining FURR approaches zero, the cost of exploration approaches infinity as no more gas can be found at any

[12] Hubbert, in *Resources and Man,* p. 185. For the original formulation by Zapp, see A. D. Zapp, "Future Petroleum Producing Capacity of the United States," *U.S. Geological Survey Bulletin,* no. 1142-H (1962).

[13] Hubbert, in *Resources and Man,* p. 188.

[14] See, for example, the discussion of costs in H. J. Barnett and C. F. Morse, *Scarcity and Growth* (Baltimore, Md.: Johns Hopkins Press, 1963).

cost. The graph of the cost of exploration COE as a function of the fraction of unproven reserves remaining FURR is given in Figure 8-4. Equations 3 and 3.1 in the printout are simply shorthand notations expressing the relationship between COE and FURR shown in Figure 8-4.

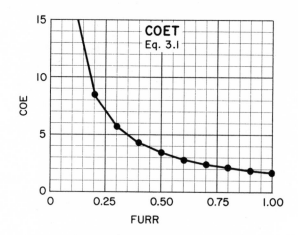

Figure 8-4 Cost of exploration versus fraction
of resources remaining

```
COE.K=TABHL(COET,FURR.K,0,1,.1)*COEN                        3, A
COET=1E4/9.97/5/3.32/2.48/1.99/1.67/1.42/1.25/1.1/1   3.1, T
COEN=1.7E-5                                                3.2, C
     COE    - COST OF EXPLORATION (DOLLARS/CUBIC FOOT)
     TABHL  - TERM DENOTING A TABULAR RELATIONSHIP
     COET   - COST OF EXPLORATION TABLE
     FURR   - FRACTION OF UNPROVEN RESERVES REMAINING
              (DIMENSIONLESS)
     COEN   - COST OF EXPLORATION NORMAL (DOLLARS/CUBIC
              FOOT)
```

The long-run relationship shown in Figure 8-4 was derived from data given in *Resources and Man* relating the rate of discovery of oil per foot drilled as a function of the cumulative feet drilled (Figure 8-5).[15] Hubbert notes that the rate of gas discovered to oil discovered has averaged about 6,000 cubic feet per barrel over the past twenty years.[16] The trend toward directional drilling tends to increase this ratio for the future. We assume, however, that the gains are largely offset by recently rising costs of drilling because of the increasing average well depths.[17] With this assumption, one can derive the cost of exploration COE versus fraction of unproven reserves remaining FURR curve (Figure 8-4) from the curve in Figure 8-5.

The cost of exploration normal COEN is a constant that serves to fit the cost of exploration curve to the actual data.[18] These data, as noted by Adelman, are

[15] Hubbert, in *Resources and Man,* fig. 8.19, p. 186.
[16] Ibid.
[17] American Petroleum Institute, Independent Petroleum Association of America, Mid-Continent Oil and Gas Association, "Joint Association Survey of Industry Drilling Costs," 1959-1967.
[18] Ibid.

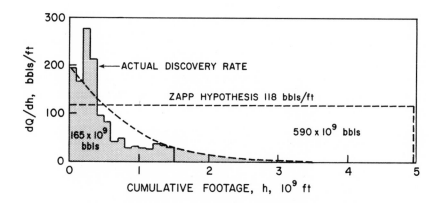

Figure 8-5 Oil per foot drilled versus cumulative feet drilled
Adapted from Resources and Man; *op. cit.*

extremely difficult to obtain because of the problem of allocating costs between oil and gas or between exploration and development.[19] An estimate was made by multiplying total exploration expenditures for oil and gas by the percentage of gas wells, weighted by the cost per well drilled (see the appendix to this chapter). The shape of the cost of exploration curve, not the actual values on the curve (as determined by COEN), is the important factor in determining system behavior. According to Adelman's study, there is little doubt that these costs are rising: "We must be content with the limited but firm conclusion that finding cost has almost certainly been on the increase from the late 1940's to the middle 1960's."[20]

4. Total cost **TC**. During the period 1955-1967, exploration costs remained relatively constant, at 30 percent of the total exploration, development, and production costs for the oil and gas industry.[21] Included in the cost margin is a profit percentage of 12 percent over costs to cover normal return on investment. Thus cost is assumed to be a constant multiple of 3.7 times the cost of exploration for the natural gas industry.

```
TC.K=(MAR)(COE.K)                                          4, A
MAR=3.7                                                    4.1, C
     TC      - TOTAL COST (DOLLARS/CUBIC FOOT)
     MAR     - COST MARGIN (DIMENSIONLESS)
     COE     - COST OF EXPLORATION (DOLLARS/CUBIC FOOT)
```

5. Smoothed total cost **STC**. The response of price to total cost is delayed by a smoothing delay to represent the fact that, although the discovery cost of an

[19] M. A. Adelman, "Trends in Cost of Finding and Developing Oil and Gas in the U.S.," *Essays in Petroleum Economics,* Proceedings of the 1967 Rocky Mountain Petroleum Economics Institute, Colorado School of Mines, 1967, p. 58.

[20] Ibid., p. 65.

[21] U.S. Energy Study Group, *Energy R & D and National Progress* (Washington, D.C.: Government Printing Office, 1964), p. 147, and American Petroleum Institute, "Joint Association Survey (Section II)," 1967, p. 5.

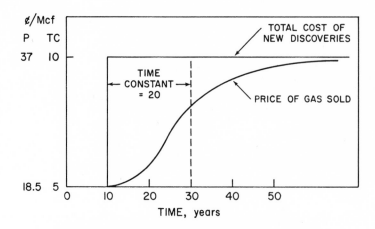

Figure 8-6 Effects on price of step rise in total cost

additional unit of gas may be high, its impact on the price of proven reserves must be weighted by the fraction of total proven reserves with the higher price. This can be represented with a delay on total cost, as shown in Figure 8-6. If total cost were to rise in year 10 from five cents per thousand cubic feet (Mcf) to ten cents per Mcf, the response of a third-order delay with a time constant of twenty years is shown in Figure 8-6. This representation is not as precise as one that would keep track of each different cost category of gas and would specify the usage and discovery rates for each. However, the error introduced by this simplification has no influence on the conclusions derived from this model. It might, however, be important in short-term studies of the natural gas industry.

```
STC.K=DELAY3(TC.K,TCSD.K)                                    5, A
    STC   - SMOOTHED TOTAL COST (DOLLARS/CUBIC FOOT)
    DELAY3 - TERM DENOTING A LAGGED RELATIONSHIP
    TC    - TOTAL COST (DOLLARS/CUBIC FOOT)
    TCSD  - TOTAL COST SMOOTHING DELAY (YEARS)
```

6. Total cost smoothing delay **TCSD**. The length of the smoothing delay TCSD depends on the relative magnitudes of the discovery rate DR, the level of proven reserves PR, and the usage rate UR. The reserve-production ratio RPR gives a measure of the average time gas remains in the proven reserve category. If the discovery rate DR and the usage rate UR were equal, the time delay on cost that would give the average price would be the reserve-production ratio RPR divided by two. If the discovery rate were nearly zero, this time delay would be best represented simply by the value of the reserve-production ratio RPR. This difference in delay representation becomes significant in relation to model behavior only when the discovery rate DR is near zero, so the total cost smoothing delay is assumed equal to the reserve-production ratio RPR.

One can see the effects of this cost delay in the price data for natural gas in Figure 8-7, which show that the average new contract price is consistently higher than the average wellhead price over time.

```
TCSD.K=RPR.K                                              6, A
     TCSD    - TOTAL COST SMOOTHING DELAY (YEARS)
     RPR     - RESERVE-PRODUCTION RATIO (YEARS)
```

Year	Average Wellhead Price (¢/Mcf)	Weighted Average New Contract Price (¢/Mcf)
1960	15.5	18.5
1961	16.3	17.5
1962	16.5	17.9
1963	16.5	16.8
1964	16.6	16.8
1965	16.7	16.8
1966	16.7	17.8
1967	17.0	18.6
1968	17.2	19.4
1969	17.5	19.7

Figure 8-7   Average price and new contract price of gas
Source: Federal Power Commission, Sales by Producers
of Natural Gas to Interstate Pipeline Companies,
1960-1969 (Washington, D.C.).

7. Price **P**. The model assumes one price for gas, which influences both supply and demand, corresponding roughly to an average wellhead price. This price is set by the producer on a cost-plus basis, modified for cases of relative abundance or scarcity of the product, and perhaps influenced by government regulation. Price is controlled by a switch function that permits the analyst to choose in a given run either a regulated or an unregulated price.

The regulated price PREG is assumed to be a function only of cost, while the unregulated price PU is a function both of cost and of the reserve-production ratio RPR of gas. When price is a function of the quantity supplied (through the reserve-production ratio RPR), it is free to seek an equilibrium level depending on the quantity supplied and the quantity demanded. Price regulation upsets this process, for price is then set on a cost-plus margin basis and no longer responds to shortages in supply indicated by a low reserve-production ratio RPR.

```
P.K=SWITCH(PU.K,PREG.K,SW1)                              7, A
SW1=0                                                    7.1, C
     P       - PRICE (DOLLARS/CUBIC FOOT)
     SWITCH  - FUNCTION WHOSE VALUE IS SET INITIALLY BY
               ANALYST
     PU      - PRICE UNREGULATED (DOLLARS/CUBIC FOOT)
     PREG    - PRICE REGULATED (DOLLARS/CUBIC FOOT)
     SW1     - REGULATION SWITCH
```

8. Unregulated price **PU**. The unregulated price equals the smoothed total cost STC modified by a price multiplier that reflects the relative abundance or

scarcity of reserves. If the reserve-production ratio RPR is above that desired by the industry, the margin above cost that producers will charge will be relatively small, for the producers wish to avoid the costs of carrying excess inventory and will therefore sell at a lower price. In the natural gas industry, reserves are sold to a pipeline or other distribution company under a long-term contract, usually valid for twenty years. Thus if the reserve-production ratio RPR is below 20, the producers run the risk of not being able to fulfill a future committed delivery if they choose to sell additional gas now. The alternative is to tap marginally productive reserves with higher costs so that in any case a low reserve-production ratio RPR forces the producers to charge a higher price for gas.

```
PU.K=(STC.K)(PM.K)                                          8, A
      PU    - PRICE UNREGULATED (DOLLARS/CUBIC FOOT)
      STC   - SMOOTHED TOTAL COST (DOLLARS/CUBIC FOOT)
      PM    - PRICE MULTIPLIER (DIMENSIONLESS)
```

9. Regulated price **PREG**. As a result of the Supreme Court decision in the Phillips Petroleum Company v. Wisconsin case in 1954,[22] the natural gas industry has been subject to price ceiling regulation by the Federal Power Commission (FPC), based on operating costs. As an approximation of this regulation the price is taken as unregulated up to 1960, at which time a ceiling price of 18.5¢ per Mcf was set for all pre-1960 contracts.[23] This price was set above the FPC cost-plus margin guideline, but it was explained as a move to take care of uncertainties during the changeover period and to provide added stimulus for exploratory activity.[24] Then, if the cost-plus margin were to rise above the 1960 price, the FPC would raise the ceiling accordingly. Thus the regulated price is formulated in the model as a function whose value equals the unregulated price PU before 1960 and whose value after 1960 is the larger of the 1960 price or the cost-plus margin price. The margin is set at 12 percent, as determined by the FPC.[25] The regulated price PREG is therefore presumed to be equal to the smoothed total cost STC as STC rises above the 1960 price level.

```
PREG.K=CLIP(MAX(P60,RM*STC.K),PU.K,TIME.K,1960)      9, A
P60=1.85E-4                                          9.1, C
RM=1                                                 9.2, C
     PREG   - PRICE REGULATED (DOLLARS/CUBIC FOOT)
     CLIP   - FUNCTION WHOSE VALUE CHANGES DURING RUN
     MAX    - FUNCTION WHICH CHOOSES THE MAXIMUM OF TWO
              ARGUMENTS
     P60    - CEILING PRICE SET IN 1960 (DOLLARS/CUBIC
              FOOT)
     RM     - COST-PLUS-MARGIN CONSTANT (DIMENSIONLESS)
     STC    - SMOOTHED TOTAL COST (DOLLARS/CUBIC FOOT)
     PU     - PRICE UNREGULATED (DOLLARS/CUBIC FOOT)
     TIME   - TIME (YEARS)
```

[22] Phillips Petroleum Company v. Wisconsin, 347 U.S. 672 (1954).
[23] R. S. Spritzer, "Changing Elements in the Natural Gas Picture: Implications for the Federal Regulatory Scheme," in Resources for the Future, Inc. (RFF), forthcoming volume, ed. Keith Brown, first draft, p. 11.
[24] Ibid., p. 12.
[25] Ibid.

10. Sales revenue **SR**. Sales revenue is simply the product of usage rate and price, reflecting the total revenue obtained from the sale of the resource. The industry's ability to invest in exploration for new reserves is assumed to be proportional to its current revenue. Thus growth in sales revenue provides the positive impetus that increases the discovery rate DR through increased investment in exploration during the growth phase of the industry.

```
SR.K=(UR.JK)(P.K)                                    10, A
    SR      - SALES REVENUE (DOLLARS/YEAR)
    UR      - USAGE RATE (CUBIC FEET/YEAR)
    P       - PRICE (DOLLARS/CUBIC FOOT)
```

11. Investment in exploration **IIE**. The total amount invested in exploration per year is given by the sales revenue for that year multiplied by the percentage of sales revenue invested in exploration. From historical data it appears that the industry tends to limit its investment in exploration to about 35 percent of sales revenue.[26] Deviations dependent on the apparent return on investment and relative coverage or abundance of reserves are reflected in the function PIIE described next.

```
IIE.K=(PIIE.K)(SR.K)                                 11, A
    IIE     - INVESTMENT IN EXPLORATION (DOLLARS/YEAR)
    PIIE    - PERCENT INVESTED IN EXPLORATION (FRACTION)
    SR      - SALES REVENUE (DOLLARS/YEAR)
```

12. Percent invested in exploration **PIIE**. As stated by C. A. Hawkins, "the decision to spend money in drilling for oil or gas is a capital investment decision. . . . Capital will be shifted away from exploration if there is the expectation of a higher return in other investments; the decision to drill for oil or gas is no different from any other type of investment decision."[27]

As represented in the model, the decision to invest in exploration contains two components: (1) A return on investment multiplier ROIM that encourages investment when the return on investment is adequate and that decreases investment when the return is low. The measure for return on investment is taken as current price/average cost. (2) A function of the reserve-production ratio RPR, which states that when the reserve-production ratio RPR exceeds a desired ratio (assumed to be 20 years for the gas industry), investment in discovery will be reduced. This action is caused by the high inventory costs of maintaining a reserve larger than needed. The percentage invested in discovery as a function of RPR/DRPR is given in Figure 8-8. Producers are expected to limit their investment in discovery to 35 percent when the return on investment is normal and the

[26] American Petroleum Institute, "Joint Association Survey," and American Gas Association, *Gas Facts, 1969* (New York, 1969).
[27] C. A. Hawkins, "Structure of the Natural Gas Producing Industry," in RFF forthcoming volume, first draft, p. 29.

reserve-production ratio RPR is 20, for this has been the normal cost of exploration as a percentage of average revenue. When reserves become higher than desired, producers will reduce the investment in exploration to discourage new discoveries. Such a reduction happened in 1939, for example, when the percentage invested in discovery fell to about 15 percent at a high reserve-production ratio RPR of 28 years.[28] If the reserve-production ratio RPR falls below the desired ratio, producers are assumed to increase their investment in exploration up to a maximum of 40-45 percent of sales revenue, assuming that the expected return on investment is high.

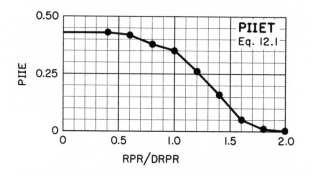

Figure 8-8   Investment in exploration versus
reserve-production ratio/desired
reserve-production ratio

```
PIIE.K=TABHL(PIIET,RPR.K/DRPR,.2,2.0,.2)*(ROIM.K)    12, A
PIIET=.43/.43/.42/.38/.35/.26/.16/.05/.01/0          12.1, T
    PIIE   - PERCENT INVESTED IN EXPLORATION (FRACTION)
    TABHL  - TERM DENOTING A TABULAR RELATIONSHIP
    PIIET  - PERCENT INVESTED IN EXPLORATION TABLE
    RPR    - RESERVE-PRODUCTION RATIO (YEARS)
    DRPR   - DESIRED RESERVE-PRODUCTION RATIO (YEARS)
    ROIM   - RETURN ON INVESTMENT MULTIPLIER
             (DIMENSIONLESS)
```

13. Return on investment multiplier **ROIM**. The percentage invested in exploration is a function of not only the reserve-production ratio RPR but also the return on investment. It is assumed that when the average price P is lower than total cost TC, or price/total cost P/TC is less than one, investors would greatly decrease their capital investment in exploration (Figure 8-9). As price/total cost P/TC rises above one, producers will increase their investment in exploration. When the price P is 40 percent above total cost TC, producers invest the full amount indicated by the relative coverage of reserves, or RPR/DRPR.

[28]Estimated from data in U.S., Bureau of the Census, *Census of Mineral Industries: 1963,* vol. 1 (Washington, D.C.: Government Printing Office, 1967), p. 13B-67.

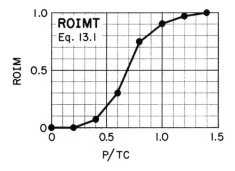

Figure 8-9 Return on investment multiplier

```
ROIM.K=TABHL(ROIMT,P.K/TC.K,0,1.8,.2)              13, A
ROIMT=0/0/.07/.3/.75/.9/.97/1/1/1                  13.1, T
    ROIM   - RETURN ON INVESTMENT MULTIPLIER
             (DIMENSIONLESS)
    TABHL  - TERM DENOTING A TABULAR RELATIONSHIP
    ROIMT  - RETURN ON INVESTMENT MULTIPLIER TABLE
    P      - PRICE (DOLLARS/CUBIC FOOT)
    TC     - TOTAL COST (DOLLARS/CUBIC FOOT)
```

14. Effective investment in exploration **EIIE**. The outcome of an investment in exploration is generally not known for four to five years due to the time involved in finding a prospective site for drilling, setting up and drilling the wells, and making an accurate estimate of the size of discovery. M. A. Adelman cites, as a rule of thumb, that four to five years of development time are required for wells.[29] J. Daniel Khazzoom has determined, on the basis of lagged regression

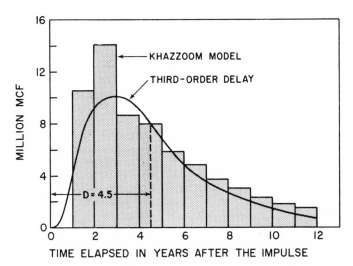

Figure 8-10 Khazzoom model response of discoveries to a one-cent impulse rise in price
Source: J. D. Khazzoom, "FPC Gas Model," Bell Journal of Economics and Management, *Spring 1971.*

[29] Adelman, *Supply and Price of Natural Gas,* p. 6.

```
EIIE.K=DELAY3(IIE.K,DD)                                          14, A
DD=4.5                                                           14.1, C
     EIIE   - EFFECTIVE INVESTMENT IN EXPLORATION
              (DOLLARS/YEAR)
     DELAY3 - TERM DENOTING A LAGGED RELATIONSHIP
     IIE    - INVESTMENT IN EXPLORATION (DOLLARS/YEAR)
     DD     - DISCOVERY DELAY (YEARS)
```

analyses, the response of gas discoveries in subsequent years as a function of a one-year impulse rise in the price of gas.[30] The subsequent output he presents (shown in Figure 8-10) describes a third-order delay with a delay time of 4.5 years.

15. Discovery rate **DR**. The amount of gas discovered per year, the discovery rate DR, is equal to the industry's effective investment in exploration EIIE per year divided by the cost of exploration COE in dollars per cubic foot of gas discovered. As sales revenue rises with rising usage, investment in exploration and thus the discovery rate DR also rise.

```
DR.KL=(EIIE.K/COE.K)*(DNM.K)                                     15, R
     DR    - DISCOVERY RATE (CUBIC FEET/YEAR)
     EIIE  - EFFECTIVE INVESTMENT IN EXPLORATION
             (DOLLARS)
     COE   - COST OF EXPLORATION (DOLLARS/CUBIC FOOT)
     DNM   - DEMAND NOISE MULTIPLIER (DIMENSIONLESS)
```

Loop 2: Demand Loop. The demand loop (Figure 8-11) is a negative or goal-seeking loop that works to establish an equilibrium between proven reserves PR, usage rate UR, and price P. The reserve-production ratio RPR is a measure of the relative levels of supply (proven reserves PR) and demand (usage rate UR). Producers work to stabilize this ratio by raising the price when the reserve-production ratio RPR is lower than the desired reserve-production ratio DRPR and vice versa.

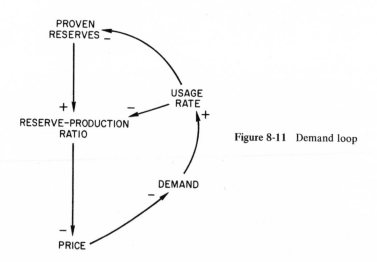

Figure 8-11   Demand loop

[30]J. D. Khazzoom, "FPC Gas Model," *Bell Journal of Economics and Management Science*, vol. 2, no. 1 (Spring 1971), p. 71.

Consumers respond through the demand multiplier DM by reducing consumption at higher prices, thus lowering the usage rate UR. A lower usage rate UR acts to raise the reserve-production ratio RPR toward the desired level. Note that a rising total cost TC constantly drives the price equilibrium level upward. Each of these variables is described in detail in the following pages.

1. Proven reserves **PR**. Proven reserves PR are increased by the discovery rate DR and decreased by the usage rate UR. The level of proven reserves PR corresponds to the natural gas already discovered by drilling but not yet used. Since in most cases it remains in its original reservoir in the ground, it is extremely difficult to obtain an accurate estimate of the reserves discovered when a new field is first drilled. Thus each year a large fraction of the discoveries (in most years over half) may be attributed to extensions and revisions of the reserves in previously located fields.

```
PR.K=PR.J+(DT)(DR.JK-UR.JK)                        16, L
PR=PRI                                             16.1, N
PRI=5.8E12                                         16.2, C
      PR      - PROVEN RESERVES (CUBIC FEET)
      DT      - TIME INCREMENT BETWEEN CALCULATIONS (YEARS)
      DR      - DISCOVERY RATE (CUBIC FEET/YEAR)
      UR      - USAGE RATE (CUBIC FEET/YEAR)
      PRI     - PROVEN RESERVES INITIAL (CUBIC FEET)
```

2. Average usage rate **AUR**. The average usage rate AUR is determined as an exponential average of the usage rate UR during the most recent year, which tends to smooth out short-term variations in usage, reflecting only the longer-term trends. This averaging process corresponds also with the industry's accounting practices: usage rates and levels of reserves are calculated year by year.

```
AUR.K=SMOOTH(UR.JK,AURAD)                          17, A
AUR=AURI                                           17.1, N
AURI=2.9E11                                        17.2, C
AURAD=1                                            17.3, C
      AUR     - AVERAGE USAGE RATE (CUBIC FEET/YEAR)
      SMOOTH  - FIRST-ORDER EXPONENTIAL SMOOTHING FUNCTION
      UR      - USAGE RATE (CUBIC FEET/YEAR)
      AURAD   - AVERAGE USAGE RATE ADJUSTMENT DELAY (YEARS)
      AURI    - AVERAGE USAGE RATE INITIAL (CUBIC FEET/
                YEAR)
```

3. Reserve-production ratio **RPR**. The reserve-production ratio RPR has traditionally been the industry's measure of how long current reserves can supply current consumption. The usage rate UR, however, has been climbing at about 7 percent per year, making the reserve-production ratio RPR a gross overestimate of the reserves' actual expected life. Figure 8-12 shows the relationship between the reserve-production ratio RPR and the actual time before reserves are depleted at various growth rates of usage. When there is no growth, the relationship is linear. At a 6.5 percent growth rate, a 20-year reserve-production ratio RPR actually

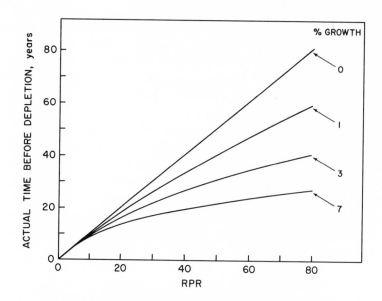

Figure 8-12 Actual time before depletion versus reserve-production ratio at various growth rates

```
RPR.K=PR.K/AUR.K                                          18, A
DRPR=20                                                   18.1, C
    RPR    - RESERVE-PRODUCTION RATIO (YEARS)
    PR     - PROVEN RESERVES (CUBIC FEET)
    AUR    - AVERAGE USAGE RATE (CUBIC FEET/YEAR)
    DRPR   - DESIRED RESERVE-PRODUCTION RATIO (YEARS)
```

lasts only 12.7 years. The reserve-production ratio RPR continues, however, to be used by producers as a measure of the relative abundance of the resource.[31]

4. Price multiplier **PM**. The price multiplier PM (Figure 8-13) represents the response of producers to changes in the reserve-production ratio RPR and defines the producer supply curve in the unregulated case. The price never drops below 0.9 times the cost-plus margin determined by the cost of exploration COE, for it is assumed that producers would never sell below cost. As the usage rate UR or the quantity demanded increases, the reserve-production ratio RPR decreases, and the price at which producers are willing to sell rises. This is caused by the nature of the selling process in the industry. Because reserves are normally committed to long-term contracts, in which the producer agrees to deliver a prescribed quantity at a given price for as long as 20 years, a producer runs a certain risk by selling reserves now that he may need to fulfill contracts in the future. If he sells now, and further reduces his reserve-production ratio RPR, he must either discover new reserves to replace those sold or tap more costly known reserves. In either case, the effect is to cause the producer to sell reserves at a higher price when the reserve-production ratio RPR is low.

---

[31] Industry practices cited in Adelman, *Supply and Price of Natural Gas*, pp. 66-68.

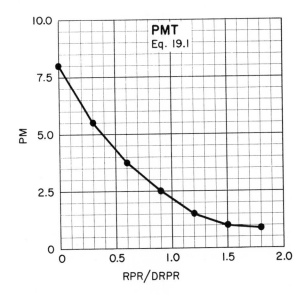

Figure 8-13 Price multiplier

```
PM.K=TABHL(PMT,RPR.K/DRPR,0,1.8,.3)                     19, A
PMT=8/5.5/3.75/2.5/1.5/1/.9                             19.1, T
    PM      - PRICE MULTIPLIER (DIMENSIONLESS)
    TABHL   - TERM DENOTING A TABULAR RELATIONSHIP
    PMT     - PRICE MULTIPLIER TABLE
    RPR     - RESERVE-PRODUCTION RATIO (YEARS)
    DRPR    - DESIRED RESERVE-PRODUCTION RATIO (YEARS)
```

The price multiplier PM acts to define the reaction of producers in setting prices according to changing conditions of supply and demand. The traditional economic approach is to define a static industry supply and demand curve, valid at only one point in time. The system dynamics approach recognizes the importance of changing economic conditions when modeling long-term behavior, including the dynamic responses of producers and consumers to changing conditions of supply and price. System dynamics extends the ability of static theory to capture real-world behavior. Producers react to changing conditions in supply by charging a higher or lower price (corresponding to an industry supply schedule), and their response in turn affects the quantity demanded (demand curve) and thus the usage rate UR, which again changes the conditions of supply. This is a goal-seeking process that gradually approaches the static economic concept of equilibrium. Eventually, a price is reached where supply and demand are balanced, if nothing else in the system changes. The equilibrium price is usually changing, however, for producers are faced with changing costs, and potential demand is exponentially increasing.

5. Demand multiplier **DM**. The demand multiplier reflects the consumer response to changes in gas prices. This static demand curve (Figure 8-14) is an extremely difficult curve to estimate empirically, but the precise values on the curve do not affect the general behavior modes of the model or the various relative effects of the policies. The model is sensitive only to the assumption that

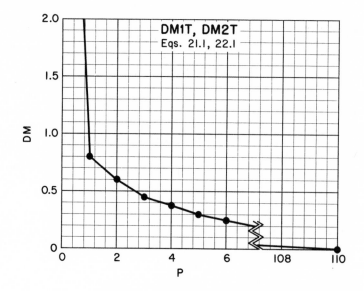

Figure 8-14 Demand multiplier*

```
DM.K=CLIP(DM2.K,DM1.K,P.K,1E-3)                              20, A
     DM    - DEMAND MULTIPLIER (DIMENSIONLESS)
     CLIP  - FUNCTION WHOSE VALUE CHANGES DURING RUN
     DM2   - DEMAND MULTIPLIER TWO (DIMENSIONLESS)
     DM1   - DEMAND MULTIPLIER ONE (DIMENSIONLESS)
     P     - PRICE (DOLLARS/CUBIC FOOT)

DM1.K=TABHL(DM1T,P.K,0,1E-3,1E-4)                           21, A
DM1T=6.5/.8/.6/.45/.38/.3/.25/.2/.15/.12/.1               21.1, T
     DM1   - DEMAND MULTIPLIER ONE (DIMENSIONLESS)
     TABHL - TERM DENOTING A TABULAR RELATIONSHIP
     DM1T  - DEMAND MULTIPLIER TABLE ONE
     P     - PRICE (DOLLARS/CUBIC FOOT)

DM2.K=TABHL(DM2T,P.K,1E-3,1.1E-2,1E-3)                     22, A
DM2T=.1/.05/.025/.018/8.8E-3/4.4E-3/2.2E-3/1.1E-3/        22.1, T
     5.5E-4/2.8E-4/0
     DM2   - DEMAND MULTIPLIER TWO (DIMENSIONLESS)
     TABHL - TERM DENOTING A TABULAR RELATIONSHIP
     DM2T  - DEMAND MULTIPLIER TABLE TWO
     P     - PRICE (DOLLARS/CUBIC FOOT)
```

the response of consumer demand to increasing price is negative. DM1 and DM2 are two parts of the same continuous curve, describing the response of demand in detail at lower prices, and at wider intervals when prices become higher.

6. Usage rate potential **URP**. The potential usage rate URP represents the rate of use of natural gas that consumers would demand each year, given that the price were held constant and the supply were unlimited.[32] Up to the 1960s the natural gas usage rate exhibited an average exponential growth in demand of 6.57 percent per year[33] due to rising population and increasing per capita energy con-

---

[32] Equation no. 23 is DYNAMO notation for $URP(t) = URI*e^{GC1\,(t-1900)}$.
[33] Hubbert, in *Environment*, p. 97.

*This relationship could also have been shown as a logarithmic table function rather than as two table functions with different value ranges.

sumption. The latter is a result both of increased income per capita and of increased substitution of natural gas for other fossil fuels because of its clean burning properties. The model assumes that the growth in *potential* demand will continue at 6.57 percent per year, while other market forces such as a higher price or restrictions in supply will eventually limit the growth in the *actual* usage rate UR.

```
URP1.K=URI*EXP(GC1*(TIME.K-1900))                    23, A
GC1=.0657                                            23.1, C
URI=4E11                                             23.2, C
TIME=1900                                            23.3, N
        URP1    - NORMAL POTENTIAL USAGE RATE (CUBIC FEET/
                  YEAR)
        URI     - USAGE RATE INITIAL (CUBIC FEET/YEAR)
        EXP     - EXPONENTIAL FUNCTION
        GC1     - GROWTH CONSTANT ONE (FRACTION)
        TIME    - TIME (YEARS)
```

7. Usage supply multiplier **USM**. The usage supply multiplier reflects the necessity for producers to restrict sales under conditions of limited supply in periods when the price is regulated.[34] The *Wall Street Journal* (April 12, 1971) reported a waiting list of 17,000 residents of Chicago who had ordered gas but were unable to obtain it. Producers are reluctant to take on new customers when the reserve-production ratio RPR is low and will not sell additional gas to existing customers. The multiplier (Figure 8-15) is a function of the relative coverage of reserves, or the reserve-production ratio RPR divided by the desired reserve-production ratio DRPR. It is assumed that when the reserve-production ratio RPR is near the desired ratio producers will restrict supply very little, selling almost as much as is demanded at the current price. But as the reserve-production ratio RPR drops, suppliers restrict the amount of gas they will sell at the regulated price, for the reasons outlined earlier. E. W. Erickson estimated that the rate of supply in 1967 was 10 to 25 percent below current demand.[35] This would corres-

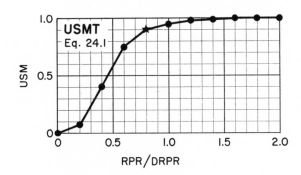

Figure 8-15 Usage supply multiplier

[34] Under normal conditions, producers are free to raise the price when supplies are dwindling, thus restoring market equilibrium. When the price is regulated, however, the only alternative open to producers when supplies of gas decrease is rationing or restriction of sales.

[35] E. W. Erickson, "Supply Response in a Regulated Industry: The Case of Natural Gas," *Bell Journal of Economics and Management Science,* vol. 2, no. 1 (Spring 1971), p. 120.

```
USM.K=TABHL(USMT,RPR.K/DRPR,0,2,.2)                      24, A
USMT=0/.07/.4/.75/.9/.95/.98/.99/1/1/1                   24.1, T
    USM    - USAGE SUPPLY MULTIPLIER (DIMENSIONLESS)
    TABHL  - TERM DENOTING A TABULAR RELATIONSHIP
    USMT   - USAGE SUPPLY MULTIPLIER TABLE
    RPR    - RESERVE-PRODUCTION RATIO (YEARS)
    DRPR   - DESIRED RESERVE-PRODUCTION RATIO (YEARS)
```

pond to the starred point on Figure 8-15, since the reserve-production ratio RPR in 1967 was 16 years.[36] The desired reserve-production ratio DRPR represents simply the average producer's goal, and it certainly can vary from producer to producer: some are willing to tolerate a ratio of 18 years, while others feel safer operating with a 25-year reserve. But because the standard contract length is 20 years, it is assumed that the desired reserve-production ratio DRPR is 20 years.

8. Usage rate **UR**. The usage rate is controlled by a switch function that permits the analyst to control whether the response of the usage rate UR to supply is through the usage supply multiplier USM (regulated case, SW1 = 1) or through changes in price (unregulated case, SW1 = 0). In both the unregulated and the regulated cases, producers must respond to changes in supply, represented by the reserve-production ratio RPR. When the industry is not regulated, producers raise the price when the ratio is low. When the industry is regulated, producers cannot raise the price, so the amount of gas they offer to the market is restricted through the usage supply multiplier USM. The usage rate UR is controlled by the same regulation switch SW1 as the price function.

```
UR.KL=SWITCH(URU.K,UREG.K,SW1)*(UNM.K)                   25, R
    UR     - USAGE RATE (CUBIC FEET/YEAR)
    SWITCH - FUNCTION WHOSE VALUE IS SET INITIALLY BY
             ANALYST
    URU    - USAGE RATE UNREGULATED (CUBIC FEET/YEAR)
    UREG   - USAGE RATE REGULATED (CUBIC FEET/YEAR)
    SW1    - REGULATION SWITCH
    UNM    - USAGE NOISE MULTIPLIER (DIMENSIONLESS)
```

9. Usage rate unregulated **URU**. The usage rate unregulated URU is equal to the consumer demand for gas at any given price multiplied by an exponentially increasing function (usage rate potential URP) growing at 6.57 percent per year. The demand multiplier DM represents the response of consumers to a change in price, ceteris paribus. It is assumed that this curve is constantly being shifted due to growth in population and in per capita gas consumption. In the unregulated industry, the usage rate unregulated URU is equal to the usage rate UR, and producers respond to changes in the reserve-production ratio RPR through the price multiplier.

[36] American Gas Association, *Gas Facts, 1969*, p. 11.

```
URU.K=(URP.K)(DM.K)                                        26, A
    URU    - USAGE RATE UNREGULATED (CUBIC FEET/YEAR)
    URP    - USAGE RATE POTENTIAL (CUBIC FEET/YEAR)
    DM     - DEMAND MULTIPLIER (DIMENSIONLESS)
```

10. Usage rate regulated **UREG**. When price is regulated, supply and demand are no longer in equilibrium; it is no longer true that consumers can buy as much gas as they would demand at the now regulated price. Instead, when the price is regulated at a level lower than the equilibrium price, producers will satisfy only a fraction of the potential demand, depending on their relative coverage (or RPR/DRPR), through the usage supply multiplier USM. In the case of the natural gas industry, regulation had little effect until 1960. Thus the regulated usage rate UREG is represented by a clip function in the model, whose value is equal to the unregulated usage rate URU before 1960. After 1960 the regulated usage rate UREG equals the unregulated usage rate URU multiplied by the usage supply multiplier USM.

```
UREG.K=CLIP((USM.K)(URU.K),URU.K,TIME.K,1960)      27, A
    UREG   - USAGE RATE REGULATED (CUBIC FEET/YEAR)
    CLIP   - FUNCTION WHOSE VALUE CHANGES DURING RUN
    USM    - USAGE SUPPLY MULTIPLIER (DIMENSIONLESS)
    URU    - USAGE RATE UNREGULATED (CUBIC FEET/YEAR)
    TIME   - TIME (YEARS)
```

Description of Model Behavior and Evaluation of Policies

In general, a system dynamics model is most successfully utilized as a descriptor of overall system behavior modes and as an evaluator of the relative effects of alternative policies on system behavior. Short-term events such as wars or economic depressions generally do not change either the longer-term behavior modes of the system or the effects of policies on model behavior. They do, however, render the model unusable for the exact reproduction of historical data. It should be noted then that these runs are not predictive. The absolute values of parameter outputs are not significant, but their direction of change and the possible change in behavior modes are important.

General Model Behavior: The Unregulated Industry. Figure 8-16 shows the behavior of the model of the U.S. natural gas industry under conditions of no regulation. Discovery rate DR and usage rate UR rise exponentially until 1969, for exploration costs are low and rising only very gradually, and proven reserves PR are initially high with respect to the usage rate UR. When the fraction of unproven reserves remaining drops to about 0.4 of its initial value, costs begin to rise more quickly (Figure 8-4), causing the price to rise. The delay in the response of price to total cost TC causes the cost of additional discoveries to rise faster than price. The rise in cost of exploration COE forces the discovery rate DR to drop in 1973.

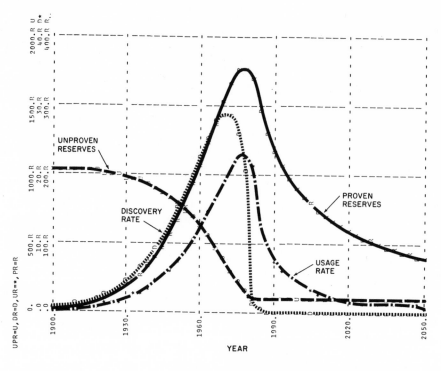

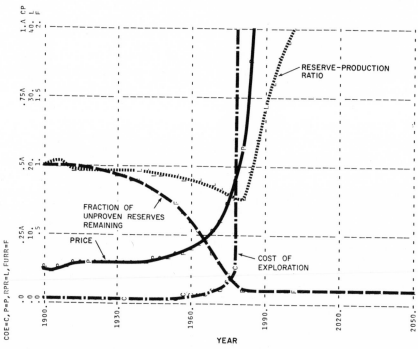

Figure 8-16   Unregulated baseline run
Note: Both plots are from the same run. They are presented sepa-
rately to permit the reader to follow the 8 parameters more easily.

The rising price slows the exponentially rising usage rate UR through reduced demand (demand multiplier DM—Figure 8-14) and eventually causes it to drop in 1978. Proven reserves PR reach a peak of about 350 trillion cubic feet in 1978 and then begin to decrease as the discovery rate DR falls below the usage rate UR. As the fraction of unproven reserves remaining FURR drops to about 0.3, costs are rising so rapidly that the return on investment for new discoveries becomes unattractive; the return on investment multiplier ROIM then forces the percentage invested in exploration PIIE to drop close to zero in 1985. Discoveries thus also drop to almost zero, causing about one-tenth of the initial unproven reserves URPI to remain undiscovered, for the cost of discovering this remnant is so high that it is not worth finding. Concurrently, the reserve-production ratio RPR has begun to rise again due to high proven reserves PR and a low usage rate UR. The total cost smoothing delay TCSD increases, slowing the rise in price (which reflects the smoothed total cost of proven reserves PR). This causes the usage rate UR to decay more slowly from 1985 on, and the accumulated proven reserves PR decline gradually over time. By 2050, almost one-tenth of the total initial U.S. supply of gas remains in proven reserves, for its high price has discouraged demand.

Figure 8-17 shows the same run as Figure 8-16, the unregulated case, but with noise inputs to discovery and usage rates.[37] The discovery and usage data seem to reflect a normalized noise standard deviation of approximately 0.1 and 0.01, respectively.[38] An examination of Figure 8-17 shows that although the noise inputs are in evidence, the overall behavior is hardly affected. In fact, the level of proven reserves PR acts as a buffer, filtering out the short-term variations in discovery and usage. The behavior over time of unproven and proven reserves is almost identical in the two runs.

System Behavior under Regulation. Figure 8-18 shows the effect of the ceiling price regulation based on cost plus a margin that took effect in 1960. The behavior of the model is identical to the unregulated case up to 1960, with both the discovery rate and the usage rate exhibiting an exponential growth rate of about 7 percent per year, keeping up with potential demand. In 1960, however, the FPC established a ceiling on price. Although the ceiling price was above costs plus a 12 percent return on investment, that price was still lower than the gas companies would charge in the unregulated case. In the model run, the price regulation policy depresses investment in exploration almost immediately through the return on investment multiplier. The discovery rate slows its growth and finally peaks in 1969 at a level below that reached in the unregulated case. The low price has encouraged the usage rate to grow faster than it did in the the unregulated case, through stimulated demand, and thus the reserve-production ratio RPR falls dramatically during the 1960s.

---

[37]The inputs in DYNAMO notation take the form DR.KL=DNM.K*(EIIE.K/COE.K); DNM.K= SAMPLE(NORMRN(1,.1),1,1)

[38]Data obtained from *Gas Facts, 1969,* pp. 11, 30.

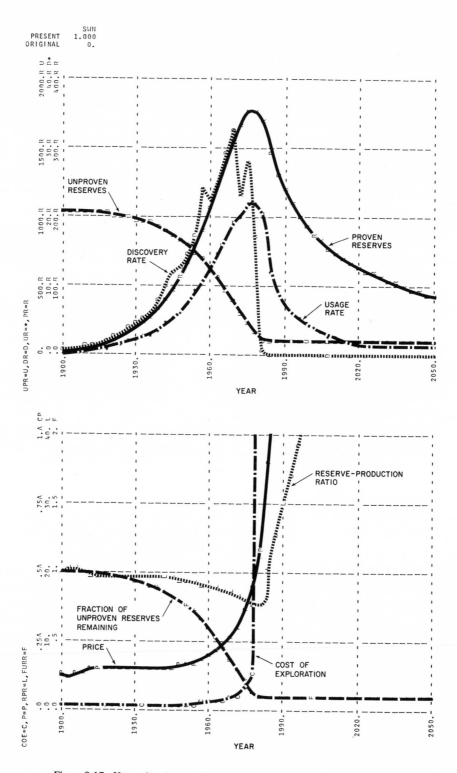

Figure 8-17 Unregulated run with noise inputs to discovery and usage rates

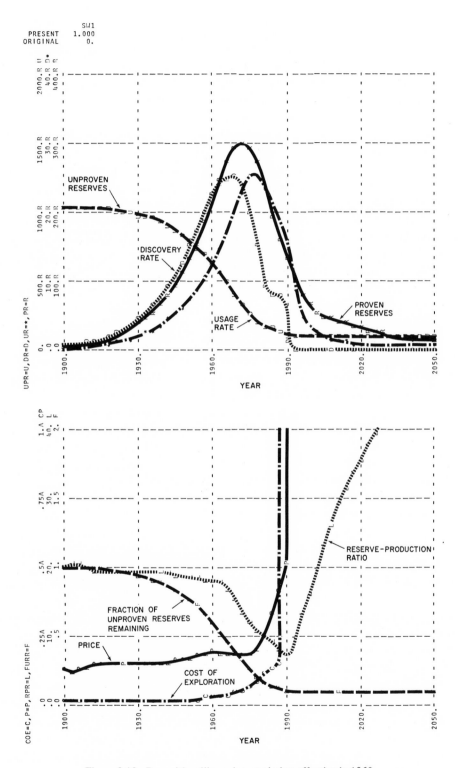

Figure 8-18   Run with ceiling-price regulation effective in 1960

Because of strong industry pressure due to clearly rising costs of exploration, the ceiling price rises in the mid-1970s, but not to the price level of the unregulated run. The higher price stimulates some additional discovery through 1990, due to the higher return on investment. But the added discoveries are insufficient to stop the decline in the reserve-production ratio RPR, which continues to fall because of higher usage rates. Proven reserves, meanwhile, have peaked in 1972 at a lower level than that reached in the unregulated case (about 300 trillion cubic feet, compared with 360 trillion cubic feet). Proven reserves also drop faster than in the unregulated case, for the lower price has increased the usage rate. Thus by 2050 proven reserves have fallen to one-fifth of their value in the unregulated run, or about 15 trillion cubic feet.

The overall effect of regulation on the behavior of the model is to transfer usage away from the future and toward satisfying present needs. Under regulation, the industry is left in the year 2000 with few reserves left to discover and few reserves left to use; the domestic supply of gas has essentially been depleted. In the unregulated case, although the discovery activity is completed earlier (stimulated by higher prices), proven reserves remain high, allowing the usage rate to continue higher after the year 2000.

Effects of Other Policies on System Behavior.   Perhaps the simplest response to the present energy problem in the United States is to say that there is no crisis in supply. It is often suggested that the estimate of initial unproven reserves is wrong and that there are considerably more reserves to be found than the current estimates indicate. Figure 8-19 shows the behavior of the model under price regulation when the estimate of initial unproven reserves UPRI is almost doubled, to 2,000 trillion cubic feet of gas, corresponding to an estimate based on the Zapp hypothesis. Note that the level and rate scales in Figure 8-19 have changed by a factor of two. The principal effect of doubling the initial reserve is to allow the exponential growth of the discovery and usage rates to continue for an additional ten years. During this time, the discovery rate, proven reserves, and the usage rate reach twice the values they attained in Figure 8-18, where the value of initial unproven reserves URPI is only 1,040 trillion cubic feet. This run exhibits an important aspect of the behavior of exponential growth: the general model behavior is relatively insensitive to changes in the initial values of parameters. Because of the rapid exponential growth in the demand for natural gas in this country, doubling the estimate of reserves would allow only a ten-year postponement of the time when usage is forced to decline.

This run also represents the behavior of the system in response to a large increase in future imports of natural gas, for large-scale imports have the effect of increasing the initial value of unproven reserves and of expanding the system boundaries to include other countries. The actual value of unproven reserves when potential imports are included would be determined by the world estimates of reserves and the total amount that each country is willing to export. A likely future influence on the system is a large discovery of natural gas in Alaska in

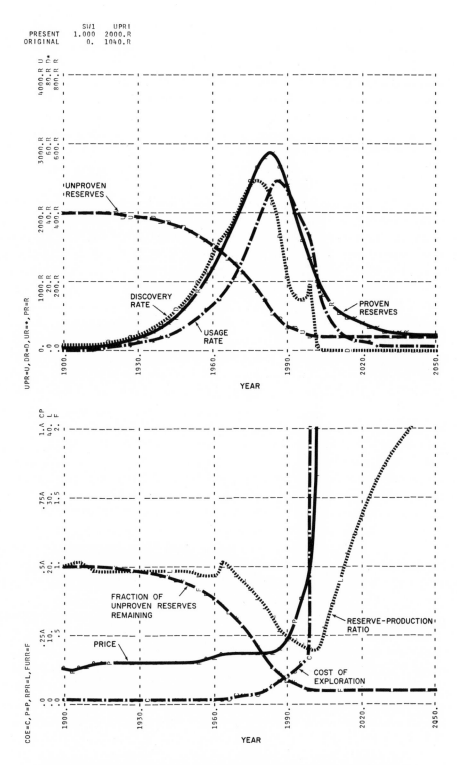

Figure 8-19   Regulated run with 2,000 trillion cubic feet estimated initial reserves

conjunction with the oil strikes already made there. Figure 8-20 shows the effects on the behavior of the regulated run if an estimated 150 trillion cubic feet of natural gas were discovered in Alaska around 1975.[39] This can be simulated both by changing the cost of exploration curve to reflect a period of lower costs after 1975 and by increasing the initial value of unproven reserves to 1,190 trillion cubic feet. The result, as shown in Figure 8-20, is a dramatic increase in discoveries up until 1978, allowing the usage rate to continue climbing three years longer than it would have if the discovery had not been made. Thus the usage rate and the discovery rate peak at higher values (Figure 8-18), but the net result is a postponement of the limitations on growth for only a few years.

Suppose that through a large campaign to conserve resources it were possible to slow the growth rate of potential demand to only 2 percent from 1970 onward, instead of the previous 7 percent. Would this change significantly extend the supply of natural gas? Figure 8-21 shows the effects of this policy on the regulated case (Figure 8-18). The discovery rate is virtually unaffected immediately after 1970, for there is already much need for new reserves because of the low reserve-production ratio RPR. The usage rate slows after 1970 and peaks at a level below that of the normal case (Figure 8-18). As the price begins to rise due to the pressure of rising costs, additional discovery is stimulated. The usage rate falls, but not as quickly as it did in the 7 percent growth case, for the higher reserve-production ratio RPR puts fewer restrictions on usage through the usage supply multiplier. The net result is a lower peak in the usage rate but a slower decline, causing proven reserves to be depleted to about the same level as in Figure 8-18 by the year 2020.

Suppose that in 1971 the U.S. gas industry stepped up its research effort and greatly advanced the technology of exploration and extraction by developing, for instance, increased efficiency of extraction by underground nuclear explosion. This policy can be simulated by holding the cost of exploration down near the 1971 level until almost all the unproven reserves have been discovered. Figure 8-22 shows the behavior of the regulated case when an increase in technology holds down costs beyond 1971. The lower costs allow discoveries to increase about ten years longer than in Figure 8-19—or until 1975. The usage rate continues to grow until 1980; it then falls abruptly as the price rises steeply in response to cost when the fraction of unproven reserves remaining approaches zero. The overall effect of a large increase in technology is to increase the severity of the eventual shortage. Usage and discovery rates rise longer with improved technology but then fall very steeply as unproven reserves are almost depleted.

One of the policies suggested to alleviate the crisis in declining discoveries has been government subsidization of the industry's exploration costs. Figure 8-23 shows the effects on the regulated run of a 25 percent government subsidy of exploration enacted in 1972. It can be seen that the subsidy increases gas reserves, but only in the short run. Discoveries increase until 1975, and then fall, for rising

[39] Hubbert, in *Resources and Man,* p. 193.

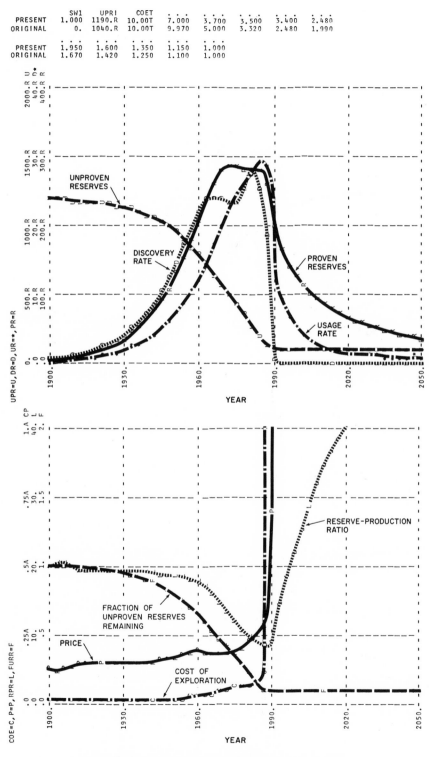

	SW1	UPRI	COET					
PRESENT	1.000	1190.R	10.00T	7.000	3.700	3.500	3.400	2.480
ORIGINAL	0.	1040.R	10.00T	9.970	5.000	3.320	2.480	1.990
PRESENT	1.950	1.600	1.350	1.150	1.000			
ORIGINAL	1.670	1.420	1.250	1.100	1.000			

Figure 8-20   Regulated run with Alaska discovery in 1975

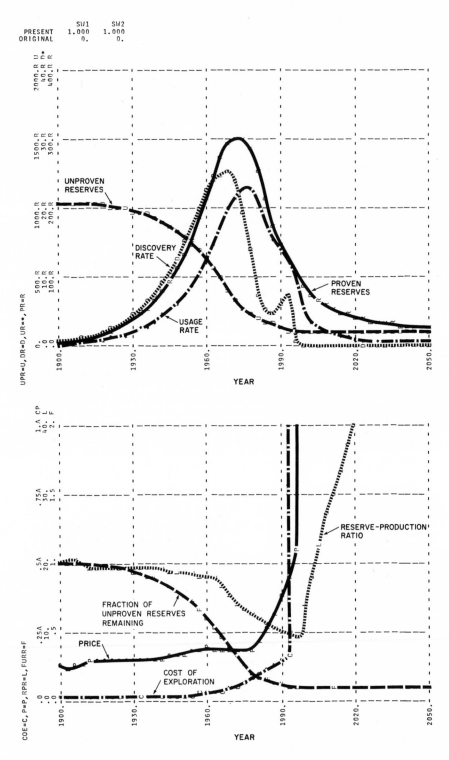

Figure 8-21 Effects on the regulated run of a change in growth in potential demand to 2 percent in 1970

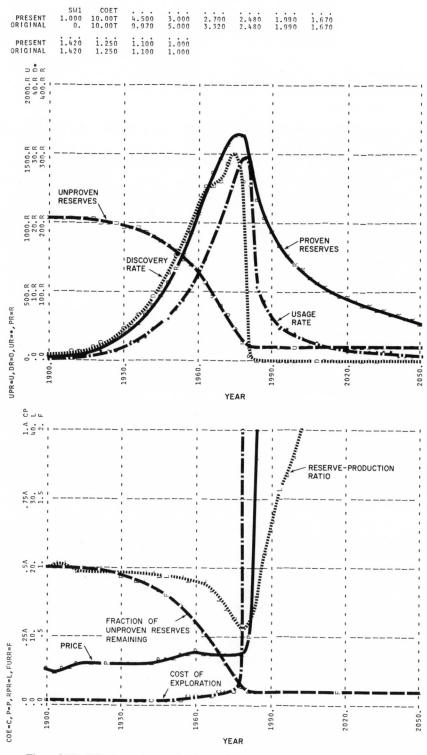

	SW1	COET						
PRESENT	1.000	10.00T	4.500	3.000	2.700	2.480	1.990	1.670
ORIGINAL	0.	10.00T	9.970	5.000	3.320	2.480	1.990	1.670
PRESENT	1.420	1.250	1.100	1.000				
ORIGINAL	1.420	1.250	1.100	1.000				

Figure 8-22 Effects on the regulated run of an improvement in exploration technology beginning in 1971

costs of exploration again discourage investment in discovery. The usage rate rises for a few years more than it did without a subsidy (Figure 8-18), but again falls due to producer restrictions on supply caused by the low reserve-production ratio RPR. The net result of a subsidy on exploration is therefore only a short-run solution to the supply problem, leaving the long-term level of proven reserves virtually unchanged over time.

Figure 8-24 shows the behavior of the model if the gas price regulations were removed in 1975. The price rises immediately in 1975 to its unregulated level, depressing the usage rate and stimulating discoveries. Discoveries stay high until the rapidly rising cost of exploration again discourages investment in discovery almost completely, with about one-tenth of the initial unproven reserves left to be discovered in 1990. The usage rate falls more quickly than it did in the regulated case (Figure 8-18), causing proven reserves to remain high, though lower than in Figure 8-16, where no regulation has taken place. Thus deregulation of the industry is consistent with long-term supply goals, sacrificing immediate usage for possible future usage.

Conclusion

The most fundamental conclusion to be drawn from the behavior of the model is that in the case of finite, nonrenewable resources such as the fossil fuels the normal behavior mode is an initial period of unrestricted growth in supply, a transition period when growth is slowed, and finally a decline in supply. This is a natural result of the assumption of a finite amount of initial unproven reserves—at some point in time, growth will be limited by rising costs due to scarcity of the resource. This conclusion has been drawn by others.[40] However, this type of model does offer a useful experimental tool for determining how various technological, physical, economic, and political factors might alter the pattern of growth and decline.

The exact time of occurrence of the transition that marks the beginning of limitations of growth is determined by many factors, including, for instance, the growth rate of potential usage, the initial level of unproven reserves, and the shape of the cost of exploration curve. However, once the values of these parameters have been approximated, the behavior of the model and the time of transition are remarkably insensitive to changes in these values. For example, an increase by a factor of two in the actual quantity of initial unproven reserves results in postponing the transition in supply for only ten years. A 25 percent subsidy for exploration postpones the transition for only three years.

If a decline in supply is unavoidable, it is imperative that society think about how its available nonrenewable resources should be allocated. Should precautions be taken so that some modest but useful amount of the scarce resource will be available over the long term? Should the immediate use of the resource be encouraged to postpone the decline in usage? It appears from the runs made here

[40] Ibid., p. 167.

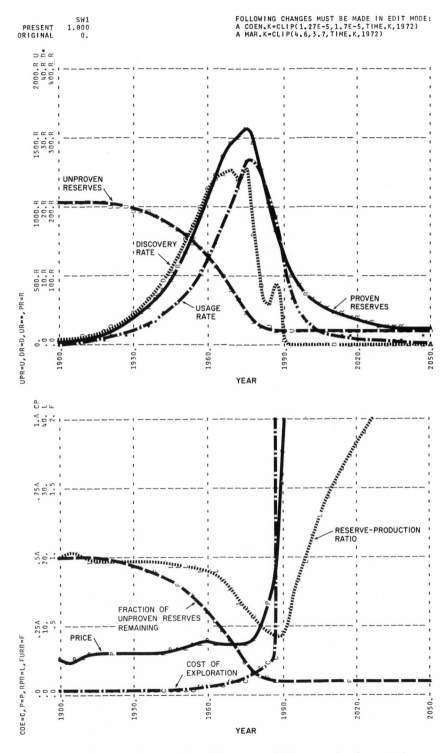

Figure 8-23 Regulated run with a 25 percent subsidy on exploration costs in 1972

250   *Roger F. Naill*

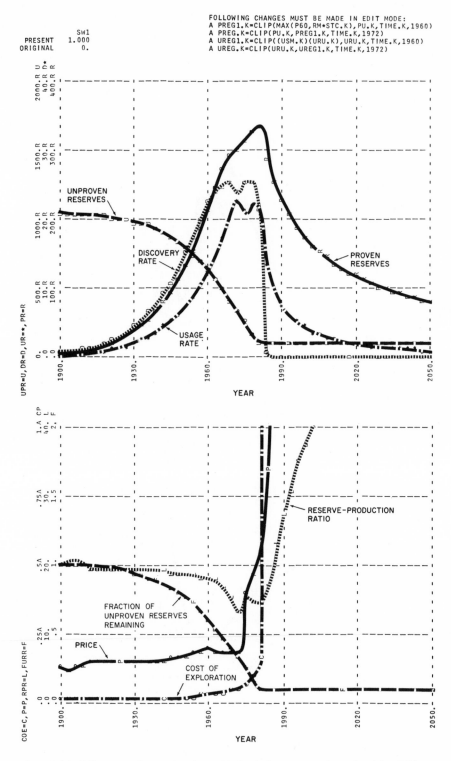

Figure 8-24 Effects on the regulated run if the industry were deregulated in 1972

that the short-term advantages of policies such as regulation and subsidies directed to postponing the decline in usage are minimal. It is clear that the depressed price through regulation has discouraged discoveries in the short run, but it is also apparent that the industry was nearing a period of limitations in supply regardless of regulation. In addition, price regulation carries a large penalty in terms of long-term supply: a low price encourages demand and thus usage, greatly reducing the long-term level of proven reserves.

The particular schedule of natural gas consumption most consistent with national goals depends on many factors outside the gas industry. Probably the most important is the achievement of an orderly transition over the next century from primary dependence on fossil fuels to reliance on some renewable or essentially infinite resource (for example, solar or fusion power). The model described here is not designed to determine how quickly gas reserves should be used, but it does permit one to compare the relative effectiveness of alternative policies in achieving the usage rate that will best fit within a long-term national energy policy.

Appendix A: Derivation of Cost of Exploration Data

The cost of exploration of gas in any given year is difficult to determine because of the joint nature of expenditures for gas and oil. For the purposes of this study, however, an estimate of the cost of exploration for gas alone is needed. This cost has been derived from total exploration cost by allocating gas exploration cost according to the number of gas wells drilled as a percentage of total oil and gas wells drilled. This value is then weighted by the cost per well of gas wells relative to the cost per well of all wells drilled. The resulting product is the year's investment in exploration. The discoveries resulting from this investment are taken from data five years later because of the approximate five-year lag in the effects of investment. The investment in exploration divided by the resulting discoveries gives an estimate of the year's cost of exploration.

Year	1 Cost of Exploration Gas & Oil (billions 1958 $)	2 Gas Wells Gas & Oil Wells	3 Cost/Well, Gas Cost/Well, Total (*estimated)	4 Investment in Exploration 1 x 2 x 3 (billions $ 1958)	5 Discoveries Year + 5 (trillion ft^3)	6 Cost of Gas Exploration 4/5 (¢/Mcf)
1944	1.05	.191	1.80*	.36	12.7	2.84
1948	1.25	.115	1.80*	.26	20.5	1.27
1951	1.77	.114	1.80*	.36	24.7	1.46
1953	2.10	.128	1.80*	.48	18.9	2.54
1955	2.13	.103	1.80*	.39	13.9	2.81
1956	2.24	.124	1.80*	.50	17.2	2.91
1959	1.98	.165	1.88	.61	20.3	3.01
1960	1.99	.197	1.87	.73	21.3	3.44
1961	1.78	.210	1.74	.65	20.2	3.22
1962	2.21	.215	1.66	.75	21.8	3.44
1963	1.73	.187	1.68	.54	13.7	3.94

Cost of exploration

Sources: American Petroleum Institute et al., Joint Association Survey of Industry Drilling Costs, *and American Gas Association,* Gas Facts.

Appendix B: Computer Program for the Gas Model

```
UPR.K=UPR.J+(DT)(-DR.JK)                              1, L
UPR=UPRI                                              1.1, N
UPRI=1.04E15                                          1.2, C
     UPR    - UNPROVEN RESERVES (CUBIC FEET)
     DT     - TIME INCREMENT BETWEEN CALCULATIONS (YEARS)
     DR     - DISCOVERY RATE (CUBIC FEET/YEAR)
     UPRI   - UNPROVEN RESERVES INITIAL (CUBIC FEET)


FURR.K=UPR.K/UPRI                                     2, A
     FURR   - FRACTION OF UNPROVEN RESERVES REMAINING
                 (DIMENSIONLESS)
     UPR    - UNPROVEN RESERVES (CUBIC FEET)
     UPRI   - UNPROVEN RESERVES INITIAL (CUBIC FEET)


COE.K=TABHL(COET,FURR.K,0,1,.1)*COEN                  3, A
COET=1E4/9.97/5/3.32/2.48/1.99/1.67/1.42/1.25/1.1/1   3.1, T
COEN=1.7E-5                                           3.2, C
     COE    - COST OF EXPLORATION (DOLLARS/CUBIC FOOT)
     TABHL  - TERM DENOTING A TABULAR RELATIONSHIP
     COET   - COST OF EXPLORATION TABLE
     FURR   - FRACTION OF UNPROVEN RESERVES REMAINING
                 (DIMENSIONLESS)
     COEN   - COST OF EXPLORATION NORMAL (DOLLARS/CUBIC
                 FOOT)


TC.K=(MAR)(COE.K)                                     4, A
MAR=3.7                                               4.1, C
     TC     - TOTAL COST (DOLLARS/CUBIC FOOT)
     MAR    - COST MARGIN (DIMENSIONLESS)
     COE    - COST OF EXPLORATION (DOLLARS/CUBIC FOOT)


STC.K=DELAY3(TC.K,TCSD.K)                             5, A
     STC    - SMOOTHED TOTAL COST (DOLLARS/CUBIC FOOT)
     DELAY3 - TERM DENOTING A LAGGED RELATIONSHIP
     TC     - TOTAL COST (DOLLARS/CUBIC FOOT)
     TCSD   - TOTAL COST SMOOTHING DELAY (YEARS)


TCSD.K=RPR.K                                          6, A
     TCSD   - TOTAL COST SMOOTHING DELAY (YEARS)
     RPR    - RESERVE-PRODUCTION RATIO (YEARS)


P.K=SWITCH(PU.K,PREG.K,SW1)                           7, A
SW1=0                                                 7.1, C
     P      - PRICE (DOLLARS/CUBIC FOOT)
     SWITCH - FUNCTION WHOSE VALUE IS SET INITIALLY BY
                 ANALYST
     PU     - PRICE UNREGULATED (DOLLARS/CUBIC FOOT)
     PREG   - PRICE REGULATED (DOLLARS/CUBIC FOOT)
     SW1    - REGULATION SWITCH


PU.K=(STC.K)(PM.K)                                    8, A
     PU     - PRICE UNREGULATED (DOLLARS/CUBIC FOOT)
     STC    - SMOOTHED TOTAL COST (DOLLARS/CUBIC FOOT)
     PM     - PRICE MULTIPLIER (DIMENSIONLESS)


PREG.K=CLIP(MAX(P60,RM*STC.K),PU.K,TIME.K,1960)       9, A
P60=1.85E-4                                           9.1, C
RM=1                                                  9.2, C
     PREG   - PRICE REGULATED (DOLLARS/CUBIC FOOT)
     CLIP   - FUNCTION WHOSE VALUE CHANGES DURING RUN
     MAX    - FUNCTION WHICH CHOOSES THE MAXIMUM OF TWO
                 ARGUMENTS
     P60    - CEILING PRICE SET IN 1960 (DOLLARS/CUBIC
                 FOOT)
     RM     - COST-PLUS-MARGIN CONSTANT (DIMENSIONLESS)
     STC    - SMOOTHED TOTAL COST (DOLLARS/CUBIC FOOT)
     PU     - PRICE UNREGULATED (DOLLARS/CUBIC FOOT)
     TIME   - TIME (YEARS)
```

```
SR.K=(UR.JK)(P.K)                                    10, A
     SR     - SALES REVENUE (DOLLARS/YEAR)
     UR     - USAGE RATE (CUBIC FEET/YEAR)
     P      - PRICE (DOLLARS/CUBIC FOOT)


IIE.K=(PIIE.K)(SR.K)                                 11, A
     IIE    - INVESTMENT IN EXPLORATION (DOLLARS/YEAR)
     PIIE   - PERCENT INVESTED IN EXPLORATION (FRACTION)
     SR     - SALES REVENUE (DOLLARS/YEAR)


PIIE.K=TABHL(PIIET,RPR.K/DRPR,.2,2.0,.2)*(ROIM.K)    12, A
PIIET=.43/.43/.42/.38/.35/.26/.16/.05/.01/0          12.1, T
     PIIE   - PERCENT INVESTED IN EXPLORATION (FRACTION)
     TABHL  - TERM DENOTING A TABULAR RELATIONSHIP
     PIIET  - PERCENT INVESTED IN EXPLORATION TABLE
     RPR    - RESERVE-PRODUCTION RATIO (YEARS)
     DRPR   - DESIRED RESERVE-PRODUCTION RATIO (YEARS)
     ROIM   - RETURN ON INVESTMENT MULTIPLIER
                (DIMENSIONLESS)


ROIM.K=TABHL(ROIMT,P.K/TC.K,0,1.8,.2)                13, A
ROIMT=0/0/.07/.3/.75/.9/.97/1/1/1                    13.1, T
     ROIM   - RETURN ON INVESTMENT MULTIPLIER
                (DIMENSIONLESS)
     TABHL  - TERM DENOTING A TABULAR RELATIONSHIP
     ROIMT  - RETURN ON INVESTMENT MULTIPLIER TABLE
     P      - PRICE (DOLLARS/CUBIC FOOT)
     TC     - TOTAL COST (DOLLARS/CUBIC FOOT)


EIIE.K=DELAY3(IIE.K,DD)                              14, A
DD=4.5                                               14.1, C
     EIIE   - EFFECTIVE INVESTMENT IN EXPLORATION
                (DOLLARS/YEAR)
     DELAY3 - TERM DENOTING A LAGGED RELATIONSHIP
     IIE    - INVESTMENT IN EXPLORATION (DOLLARS/YEAR)
     DD     - DISCOVERY DELAY (YEARS)


DR.KL=(EIIE.K/COE.K)*(DNM.K)                         15, R
     DR     - DISCOVERY RATE (CUBIC FEET/YEAR)
     EIIE   - EFFECTIVE INVESTMENT IN EXPLORATION
                (DOLLARS)
     COE    - COST OF EXPLORATION (DOLLARS/CUBIC FOOT)
     DNM    - DEMAND NOISE MULTIPLIER (DIMENSIONLESS)


PR.K=PR.J+(DT)(DR.JK-UR.JK)                           16, L
PR=PRI                                               16.1, N
PRI=5.8E12                                           16.2, C
     PR     - PROVEN RESERVES (CUBIC FEET)
     DT     - TIME INCREMENT BETWEEN CALCULATIONS (YEARS)
     DR     - DISCOVERY RATE (CUBIC FEET/YEAR)
     UR     - USAGE RATE (CUBIC FEET/YEAR)
     PRI    - PROVEN RESERVES INITIAL (CUBIC FEET)


AUR.K=SMOOTH(UR.JK,AURAD)                            17, A
AUR=AURI                                             17.1, N
AURI=2.9E11                                          17.2, C
AURAD=1                                              17.3, C
     AUR    - AVERAGE USAGE RATE (CUBIC FEET/YEAR)
     SMOOTH - FIRST-ORDER EXPONENTIAL SMOOTHING FUNCTION
     UR     - USAGE RATE (CUBIC FEET/YEAR)
     AURAD  - AVERAGE USAGE RATE ADJUSTMENT DELAY (YEARS)
     AURI   - AVERAGE USAGE RATE INITIAL (CUBIC FEET/
                YEAR)


RPR.K=PR.K/AUR.K                                     18, A
DRPR=20                                              18.1, C
     RPR    - RESERVE-PRODUCTION RATIO (YEARS)
     PR     - PROVEN RESERVES (CUBIC FEET)
     AUR    - AVERAGE USAGE RATE (CUBIC FEET/YEAR)
     DRPR   - DESIRED RESERVE-PRODUCTION RATIO (YEARS)
```

```
PM.K=TABHL(PMT,RPR.K/DRPR,0,1.8,.3)                    19, A
PMT=8/5.5/3.75/2.5/1.5/1/.9                            19.1, T
     PM       - PRICE MULTIPLIER (DIMENSIONLESS)
     TABHL    - TERM DENOTING A TABULAR RELATIONSHIP
     PMT      - PRICE MULTIPLIER TABLE
     RPR      - RESERVE-PRODUCTION RATIO (YEARS)
     DRPR     - DESIRED RESERVE-PRODUCTION RATIO (YEARS)


DM.K=CLIP(DM2.K,DM1.K,P.K,1E-3)                        20, A
     DM       - DEMAND MULTIPLIER (DIMENSIONLESS)
     CLIP     - FUNCTION WHOSE VALUE CHANGES DURING RUN
     DM2      - DEMAND MULTIPLIER TWO (DIMENSIONLESS)
     DM1      - DEMAND MULTIPLIER ONE (DIMENSIONLESS)
     P        - PRICE (DOLLARS/CUBIC FOOT)


DM1.K=TABHL(DM1T,P.K,0,1E-3,1E-4)                      21, A
DM1T=6.5/.8/.6/.45/.38/.3/.25/.2/.15/.12/.1            21.1, T
     DM1      - DEMAND MULTIPLIER ONE (DIMENSIONLESS)
     TABHL    - TERM DENOTING A TABULAR RELATIONSHIP
     DM1T     - DEMAND MULTIPLIER TABLE ONE
     P        - PRICE (DOLLARS/CUBIC FOOT)


DM2.K=TABHL(DM2T,P.K,1E-3,1.1E-2,1E-3)                 22, A
DM2T=.1/.05/.025/.018/8.8E-3/4.4E-3/2.2E-3/1.1E-3/     22.1, T
  5.5E-4/2.8E-4/0
     DM2      - DEMAND MULTIPLIER TWO (DIMENSIONLESS)
     TABHL    - TERM DENOTING A TABULAR RELATIONSHIP
     DM2T     - DEMAND MULTIPLIER TABLE TWO
     P        - PRICE (DOLLARS/CUBIC FOOT)


URP1.K=URI*EXP(GC1*(TIME.K-1900))                      23, A
GC1=.0657                                              23.1, C
URI=4E11                                               23.2, C
TIME=1900                                              23.3, N
     URP1     - NORMAL POTENTIAL USAGE RATE (CUBIC FEET/
                  YEAR)
     URI      - USAGE RATE INITIAL (CUBIC FEET/YEAR)
     EXP      - EXPONENTIAL FUNCTION
     GC1      - GROWTH CONSTANT ONE (FRACTION)
     TIME     - TIME (YEARS)


USM.K=TABHL(USMT,RPR.K/DRPR,0,2,.2)                    24, A
USMT=0/.07/.4/.75/.9/.95/.98/.99/1/1/1                 24.1, T
     USM      - USAGE SUPPLY MULTIPLIER (DIMENSIONLESS)
     TABHL    - TERM DENOTING A TABULAR RELATIONSHIP
     USMT     - USAGE SUPPLY MULTIPLIER TABLE
     RPR      - RESERVE-PRODUCTION RATIO (YEARS)
     DRPR     - DESIRED RESERVE-PRODUCTION RATIO (YEARS)


UR.KL=SWITCH(URU.K,UREG.K,SW1)*(UNM.K)                 25, R
     UR       - USAGE RATE (CUBIC FEET/YEAR)
     SWITCH   - FUNCTION WHOSE VALUE IS SET INITIALLY BY
                  ANALYST
     URU      - USAGE RATE UNREGULATED (CUBIC FEET/YEAR)
     UREG     - USAGE RATE REGULATED (CUBIC FEET/YEAR)
     SW1      - REGULATION SWITCH
     UNM      - USAGE NOISE MULTIPLIER (DIMENSIONLESS)


URU.K=(URP.K)(DM.K)                                    26, A
     URU      - USAGE RATE UNREGULATED (CUBIC FEET/YEAR)
     URP      - USAGE RATE POTENTIAL (CUBIC FEET/YEAR)
     DM       - DEMAND MULTIPLIER (DIMENSIONLESS)


UREG.K=CLIP((USM.K)(URU.K),URU.K,TIME.K,1960)          27, A
     UREG     - USAGE RATE REGULATED (CUBIC FEET/YEAR)
     CLIP     - FUNCTION WHOSE VALUE CHANGES DURING RUN
     USM      - USAGE SUPPLY MULTIPLIER (DIMENSIONLESS)
     URU      - USAGE RATE UNREGULATED (CUBIC FEET/YEAR)
     TIME     - TIME (YEARS)
```

```
DNM.K=SWITCH(1,DNVAL.K,SWN)                           29, A
SWN=0                                                 29.1, C
     DNM    - DEMAND NOISE MULTIPLIER (DIMENSIONLESS)
     SWITCH - FUNCTION WHOSE VALUE IS SET INITIALLY BY
              ANALYST
     DNVAL  - DISCOVERY NOISE VALUE (DIMENSIONLESS)
     SWN    - NOISE SWITCH

DNVAL.K=SAMPLE(NORMRN(1,.1),1,1)                      30, A
     DNVAL  - DISCOVERY NOISE VALUE (DIMENSIONLESS)
     SAMPLE - SAMPLE AND HOLD FUNCTION
     NORMRN - RANDOM NOISE FUNCTION

UNM.K=SWITCH(1,UNVAL.K,SWN)                           31, A
     UNM    - USAGE NOISE MULTIPLIER (DIMENSIONLESS)
     SWITCH - FUNCTION WHOSE VALUE IS SET INITIALLY BY
              ANALYST
     UNVAL  - USAGE NOISE VALUE (DIMENSIONLESS)
     SWN    - NOISE SWITCH

UNVAL.K=SAMPLE(NORMRN(1,.01),1,1)                     32, A
     UNVAL  - USAGE NOISE VALUE (DIMENSIONLESS)
     SAMPLE - SAMPLE AND HOLD FUNCTION
     NORMRN - RANDOM NOISE FUNCTION

URP2.K=UR2I*EXP(GC2*(TIME.K-1970))                    33, A
UR2I=3.979E13                                         33.1, C
     URP2   - POTENTIAL USAGE RATE AFTER CHANGE IN GROWTH
              RATE (CUBIC FEET/YEA
     UR2I   - VALUE OF POTENTIAL USAGE RATE IN 1970
              (CUBIC FEET/YEAR)
     EXP    - EXPONENTIAL FUNCTION
     GC2    - NEW GROWTH RATE EFFECTIVE IN 1970
              (FRACTION)
     TIME   - TIME (YEARS)

URP3.K=CLIP(URP2.K,URP1.K,TIME.K,1970)                34, A
     URP3   - POTENTIAL USAGE RATE WITH CHANGE IN GC IN
              1970 (CUBIC FEET/YEAR)
     CLIP   - FUNCTION WHOSE VALUE CHANGES DURING RUN
     URP2   - POTENTIAL USAGE RATE AFTER CHANGE IN GROWTH
              RATE (CUBIC FEET/YEA
     URP1   - NORMAL POTENTIAL USAGE RATE (CUBIC FEET/
              YEAR)
     TIME   - TIME (YEARS)

A   URP.K=SWITCH(URP1.K,URP3.K,SW2)
C   GC2=.02
C   SW2=0
*
* POLICY RUN CONTROL CARDS
*
RUN UNREGULATED
C SWN=1
RUN NOISE INPUTS
C SW1=1
RUN REGULATION
C SW1=1
C UPRI=2E15
RUN DOUBLE UNPROVEN RESERVES
C SW1=1
C UPRI=1.19E15
T COET=1E4/7/3.7/3.5/3.4/2.48/1.95/1.6/1.35/1.15/1
RUN ALASKA DISCOVERY
C SW1=1
C SW2=1
RUN TWO PERCENT GROWTH RATE IN 1970
C SW1=1
T COET=1E4/4.5/3/2.7/2.48/1.99/1.69/1.42/1.25/1.1/1
RUN TECHNOLOGY
```

```
C  SW1=1
*  FOLLOWING CHANGES MUST BE MADE IN EDIT MODE:
*  A COEN.K=CLIP(1.27E-5,1.7E-5,TIME.K,1972)
*  A MAR.K=CLIP(4.6,3.7,TIME.K,1972)
RUN TWENTY-FIVE PERCENT SUBSIDY
C  SW1=1
*  FOLLOWING CHANGES MUST BE MADE IN EDIT MODE:
*  A PREG1.K=CLIP(MAX(PGO,RM*STC.K),PU.K,TIME.K,1960)
*  A PREG.K=CLIP(PU.K,PREG1.K,TIME.K,1972)
*  A UREG1.K=CLIP((USM.K)(URU.K),URU.K,TIME.K,1960)
*  A UREG.K=CLIP(URU.K,UREG1.K,TIME.K,1972)
RUN REGULATED,UNREGULATED
SPEC   DT=.1/LENGTH=2050/PLTPER=3
PLOT COE=C,P=P(0,1E-3)/RPR=L(0,40)/FURR=F
PLOT UPR=U/DR=D,UR=*/PR=R
*
```

Population Control Mechanisms in a Primitive Agricultural Society

Steven B. Shantzis and William W. Behrens III

An important criticism of the global model is that it conceals a wide variety of conditions in its use of global averages. The population-resource ratio varies tremendously from one point to another in the globe, ranging from modern industrialized nations to primitive societies dependent primarily on agricultural production.

To provide the greatest possible contrast with the industrialized West, we chose to model a primitive slash-and-burn agricultural society, one that, fortunately, has been well documented in its natural state by anthropologist Roy A. Rappaport. In this society the technology and the natural resource base are highly simplified. Land is the primary renewable resource. Slash-and-burn agriculture and the husbandry of pigs constitute the primary modes of resource use. The model illustrates how this simple society has managed to establish a form of long-term equilibrium with its resource base; it also shows how easily that equilibrium might be disturbed by well-intended "modernization" policies which eliminate the system's inherent limits to population growth.

9
Population Control Mechanisms in a Primitive Agricultural Society

Introduction

In this paper we show how system dynamics can be used for making explicit a verbal description of a social or anthropological system. We describe an application to the analysis of empirical data provided by the classic anthropological study, Roy A. Rappaport's *Pigs for the Ancestors*.[1] Using the careful account given by Rappaport of the society of Tsembaga tribesmen, we derive a formal, graphical, and mathematical model of this human ecological system in the New Guinea highlands. Transforming such a verbal description into a mathematical model serves four distinct purposes:

1. The theory of complex feedback loop systems can aid in understanding and organizing the important causal relationships in the observed system.

2. Analysis of the model's sensitivity to changes in its parameters can indicate where precise observations or measurements are important and where large observational errors are relatively unimportant in understanding overall societal functions.

3. The model provides a framework within which one can raise new questions and perceive missing information to design further studies more efficiently.

4. Analysis of the model can provide information on the behavioral implications of observed relationships outside the range of parameter values historically observed. Thus it is useful for testing the probable effects on the society of new technologies or social policies.

The focus of this paper is on the natural and sociological population controls that the Tsembaga people practice in order to limit their population to levels below the long-term carrying capacity of the land. The analysis technique employed is system dynamics, a body of concepts and a set of tools specifically designed to translate system descriptions into formal models. The resulting models can be explored through computer simulation to determine the probable behavior of the social system under a variety of conditions.

Computer simulation of cultural systems is certainly no substitute for careful empirical research. A computer model is only a theory. Deriving and testing that theory can only be done with information about the real-world system. In this specific application, Rappaport's study provides a strong, data-rich basis for the modeling process. In other, less intensively studied systems, initial, subjective impressions can be quantified and tested through computer simulation to determine whether they begin to explain the phenomena under consideration. Where they fail to do so, an important area of empirical research has been identified. That research may be used to test and extend the preliminary model until it again fails for lack of data. The process is an iterative and reinforcing one, which ideally uses both theory and data with maximal efficiency to increase understanding of social systems.

---

[1] Roy A. Rappaport, *Pigs for the Ancestors* (New Haven: Yale University Press, 1968).

A System Description of the Tsembaga

Rappaport studied the Tsembaga tribes of eastern New Guinea. They are a subset of a group of clans that speaks one particular dialect, called Maring.

The Maring-speaking peoples number about 7,000. They are aggregated into approximately twenty clans, each within its own subterritory of the region.[2] Because the New Guinea highland region is a very rough country, there is a fair degree of isolation between the Maring speaking peoples and other people of New Guinea, including the Australian government. The Maring practice a primitive form of slash-and-burn agriculture for subsistence. Only a portion of their total acreage is used for cultivation at any given time. This area is cleared of forest and burned over. Burning clears away the underbrush for planting, produces a nutrient ash residue, and improves the soil fertility, probably by catalyzing certain chemical reactions in the upper inches of topsoil. The land is planted with root crops for one or two years until the nutrient store in the soil begins to be depleted and the land's fertility decreases, as indicated by decreasing yields. The people then move on to a new area of land and repeat the procedure, leaving the old land to fallow. The fallowed land is quickly covered by secondary tropical rain forest. In fifteen to twenty years the forest is sufficiently regenerated that the procedure can be repeated.

It should be obvious that this process requires either a very large amount of land or, given limited total available land, a controlled population. The latter is the case for most slash-and-burn agricultural societies. The particular subclan of the Maring under study, the Tsembaga, possesses about 1,350 acres of available land, with about 350 acres in virgin forest and the rest under secondary forest. They are surrounded by dense forest and mountainous terrain, making further expansion opportunities highly limited. Under these circumstances, it is critical to the survival of the population that its natural tendency toward growth be controlled. The Tsembaga accomplish this control through an elaborate automatic societal mechanism that triggers intermittent wars with neighboring populations at intervals of twelve to fifteen years. The triggering device, which sends them to war frequently enough to contain their population, is controlled by a very complex ecological symbiosis between the Tsembaga and their domesticated pig herd. The Maring peoples herd pigs, but not solely for their nutritional value. Although pigs are occasionally eaten, they represent a net energy loss (or at least a comparatively unfavorable return). As will be demonstrated here, the Tsembaga unconsciously use the pig herd as both an information monitor and a homeostat in a complex, automatic population control system.

A Model of a Land-Constrained Population

The Tsembaga and Their Land.   To create a formal model from the descriptive statements of the previous section, we need a general means of representing

---

[2] Ibid., p. 12. The vast majority of information used was acquired from Rappaport's book. Specific pages and chapters are footnoted where additional information from the original source may be of interest to the reader.

Rappaport's statements of system relationships. In system dynamics studies we place descriptive statements into a feedback loop structure. A feedback loop is any closed chain of relationships such that a change in one variable is propagated around the loop to produce a further change in the original variable. As an example, part of the basic feedback loop structure in the Tsembaga system is that relating births, deaths, and level of population (Figure 9-1).

Two feedback loops are involved in this simple population system. If the population were to rise and the fertility (births per thousand) remained constant, then the number of births would also increase, further increasing the population. Because this loop produces a reinforcing change, it constitutes a positive feedback loop. The loop relating human population and human deaths is a negative feedback loop, since an initial rise in population (with constant average life expectancy) would cause a rise in deaths, ultimately decreasing the population. The size of the human population through time will be determined by the relationship between the birth rate and the death rate. If the net growth rate (birth rate minus death rate) is positive, the population will grow; if the net rate is negative, the population will decline.

We have, of course, simplified the system by ignoring the age structure of the population. This is a useful approximation for any study of very long-term population trends. Where shorter-term population levels are of interest, age categories must be distinguished.[3]

For a simple introductory model, let us also temporarily assume that:

1. The Tsembaga keep no pig herd.
2. There are no festivals or wars.
3. The Tsembaga attempt to support their entire population, implying that there is no introduction of population controls such as contraception or infanticide.
4. There is no out-migration or in-migration.

These assumptions allow us to examine only the relationships between the Tsembaga population and its land. We may thus focus on those population constraints derived from the limits to food production. A causal-loop diagram, indi-

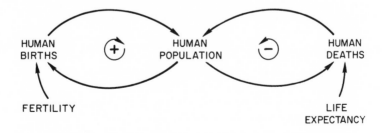

Figure 9-1 Simple feedback loops controlling human population

[3] For an example of a system dynamics study in which age structure is explicitly modeled, see D. H. Meadows, "Dynamics of Population Growth in a Traditional Agricultural Village," unpublished working paper, Dartmouth College, 1972.

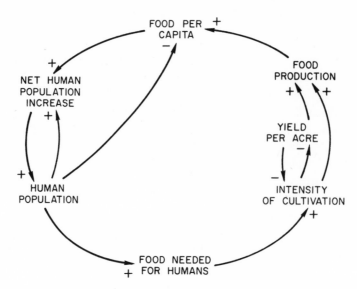

Figure 9-2 Causal-loop diagram of a land-constrained human population

cating the feedback loops of this simplified system, is shown in Figure 9-2. After this simple model is described, the first two of the four assumptions will be eliminated to gain a realistic picture of the complete Tsembaga system.

The large feedback loop of Figure 9-2, relating intensity of cultivation directly to food production, is a positive feedback loop that explains the natural growth tendencies of the population. The smaller loop, relating intensity to food production through yield per acre, is a negative feedback loop that controls the population through the yield of the land, or the land's ability to produce food. We shall examine each loop separately to explain how it was derived from Rappaport's study and then analyze the total interaction of both loops.

Human-Food Feedback Loop. This loop (Figure 9-3) dominates the behavior of the model during the exponential growth phase of the Tsembaga population dynamics. The population is characterized by a moderate infant mortality rate and few taboos concerning sexual intercourse. The result is a population that grows at a small, but steady, rate. Actual data on births and deaths are sparse in Rappaport's study. The fertility and average life expectancy used in the model were taken from U.N. statistics for people of similar stature, nutrition, and technological advancement.[4]

An increase in the human population HP* on Tsembaga land leads to increased food production F through the following mechanism. As the population grows,

---

[4] U.N. Statistical Office, *Demographic Yearbook,* (New York, 1969). Fertility and average life expectancy are two parameters identified in this study as highly critical determinants of long-term system behavior.

*Eds. note—Whenever we use a term that corresponds to a variable in the simulation model, the variable name (as it appears in the model equations in the appendix to this chapter) is printed immediately following that term.

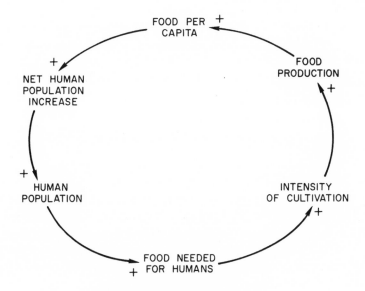

Figure 9-3   Human-food feedback loop

the larger landholdings are parceled out through family ties.[5] The net effect is to
raise the labor input per total available land unit (but not per unit of cultivated
land) and to increase total output. That is, the Tsembaga put more of their total
acreage under cultivation at one time so that the population density on the land
under cultivation does not increase. This practice increases the total food production F, and it keeps the food per capita FPC constant, allowing the population to
grow, unrestricted by lack of food.

The Tsembaga environment of tropical rain forest is remarkably free of other
external input factors bearing on food output. The weather is fairly constant,
domestic animals are (for the most part) controlled, and predators are not a major
problem.[6] A food production function would be a very simple one of only two
variable inputs—labor and land. For normal ranges of the population this dependence can be further reduced to one variable, since land is linearly dependent on
labor. Thus population pressure increases the need for food, which under most
normal circumstances is met by expanding the land under cultivation. It is only as
fallow land decreases under pressure of a growing population that deleterious
effects begin to occur.

Food-Yield Feedback Loop. The Tsembaga possess over 1,000 acres of arable
land in the heart of a virgin forest. For use in the food-yield loop, (Figure 9-4),
the available land resources have been translated into standard acre equivalents,
one standard acre producing 4.4×10^6 calories per year. Each standard acre
requires a fifteen-year fallow period for one year of use.[7] Due to the fixed nature

[5] Rappaport, *Pigs,* p. 22.
[6] Ibid., chap. 3.
[7] Ibid., p. 287.

of the total land, there is a direct relationship between the percentage of land used in any period and the fraction of the cultivation-fallow cycle for which the land is in use. For example, if the Tsembaga leave each acre fallow for fifteen years after one year of cultivation, the intensity of cultivation I is defined as 1/16.

$$I = \frac{\text{years cultivated}}{\text{years cultivated} + \text{years fallow}}$$

The yield of each acre of land YPA is unimpaired as long as the intensity of cultivation I is less than 1/16. However, under unchecked population growth it soon becomes impossible to support the entire population on the sixty-one standard acres that 1/16 intensity I implies. To produce more food the intensity I must rise. As it does so, the fallow period is simultaneously decreased. For example, to put 1/10 of the land into production suddenly, following an interval that has had a 1/16 intensity, requires that 1/10 − 1/16 = 3/80 of the land must be brought into production after only ten years of fallow.

This shortened fallow period prevents the land from regenerating its full potential yield per acre YPA. It consequently produces less food per acre than it would under ideal conditions. Even if the population were to stop growing at this point, more land would have to be brought under cultivation in the next period to produce the same quantity of food F because of the decreasing yield per acre YPA. If the population continues to grow (since sufficient food still is available), the decline in yield YPA is accelerated, and within a matter of a few years the land is of such poor quality and the population so great that even complete and continuous cultivation (I = 1) cannot produce enough food to meet the popula-

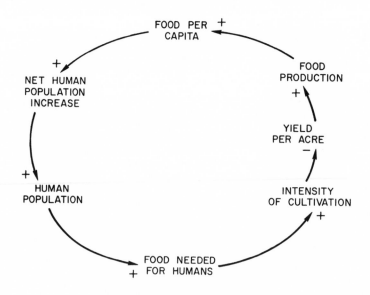

Figure 9-4 Food-yield feedback loop

tion's needs. This lack of food is followed immediately by an increased death rate and a rapid decline of the human population level under the pressure of famine. The system, dominated by the negative food yield feedback loop, would find equilibrium at zero population.

Analysing the Land-Constrained System. The preceding description of population growth and decline is an intuitive analysis of the system relationships. A more

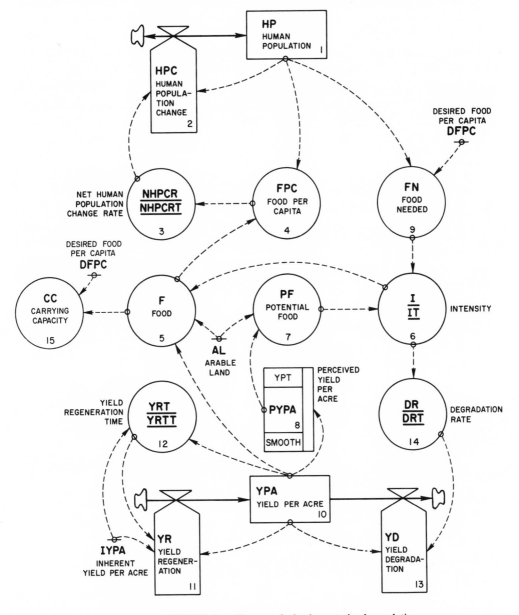

Figure 9-5 DYNAMO flow diagram of a land-constrained population

accurate representation of the model relationships is shown in the DYNAMO flow diagram (Figure 9-5) and in the equations in Appendix A to this chapter.[8] In this simplified Tsembaga model there are two levels, the level of human population HP and the level of sustainable yield YPA. Those levels are changed through time by the action of three rates: the rate at which the human population changes HPC, and rates at which the yield per acre YPA of the land either degenerates or regenerates.

Several of the functional relationships determining these rates are nonlinear and imprecisely known. Thus their specification is often difficult. For example, the degradation rate DR, or the fraction of the land's sustainable yield that degenerates each year, is postulated to be a function of intensity I in Figure 9-6. When the intensity of land use I is less than one-sixteenth, the sustainable yield of the land YPA does not degenerate. When the land intensity I is greater than 1/16, the land yield YPA degenerates faster as intensity increases. At very high intensities the land loses half its potential yield per acre YPA each year. The general direction of this relationship is known, but its precise values have only been estimated for the purpose of this study.

Computer simulation of this simplified model of the Tsembaga system yields the results portrayed in Figure 9-7. The horizontal axis represents time in years. The vertical axis includes the several scales of the variables plotted. In the absence of controlling factors, the carrying capacity of the land CC is exceeded by the growth in human population HP in less than sixty years. The now dominant food-yield feedback loop attempts to stabilize the population HP through decreased food

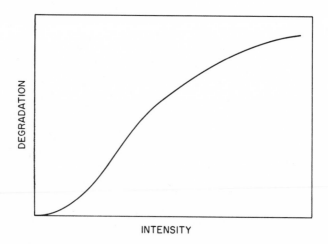

Figure 9-6   Degradation rate as a function of intensity

[8] The system dynamics flow diagram symbols are described in Chapter 2 and summarized in Figure 2-2.

production F. Under continued pressure from a growing population, however, food consumption (and production) is driven higher, depressing the land's potential yield YPA through overintensive cultivation. By the time the food level peaks, the population is still growing, and the yield per acre YPA has been falling for some time. Only then does the negative effect of declining yield per acre YPA make itself felt in the form of famine. Food shortages can no longer be met by increasing intensity I since the land is already being used at a level close to its limit. The population collapses as famine drastically decreases the average life expectancy. Even so, the land fertility YPA continues to fall until it is virtually zero and subsistence is impossible for more than a few tribesmen.

Two aspects of these results are important. First, under conditions of famine, variables exogenous to this model may become important. For the Maring, other natural forces would probably prevent the population from declining to zero. For example, labor shortages could prevent the entire land area from being used at any one time, so that intensity I would never rise to one. Alternatively, a neighboring tribe could take advantage of the starving clan's weakness to invade and absorb their population. In either case the results are essentially the same. The Tsembaga would not persist as a tribal entity, and the land would be substandard (possibly even useless) for as many years as it takes the natural cycle of forest regeneration to restore it.

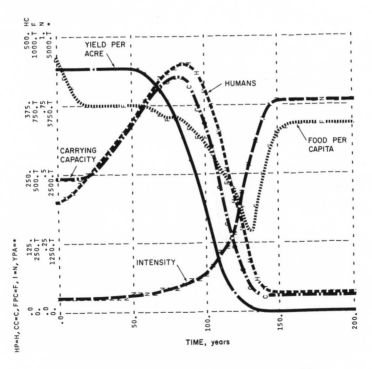

Figure 9-7 Computer simulation of a land-constrained human population

Second, the environmental crisis is not necessarily precipitated by ignorance. Although exceeding the carrying capacity does not influence important model variables immediately, there is no reason to believe that the negative effects of overuse are not immediately perceived by the Tsembaga gardener. Manifestations in terms of decreasing yields and increasing labor requirements would be readily apparent after two or three years. Even before that, the Tsembaga clansmen, having close contact with their land through hand planting, would probably realize the decreasing quality of the soil. Nevertheless, no positive action can be taken to regenerate the soil fertility unless the people are willing to self-impose population controls before the crisis arises. The barriers to the establishment of such controls are attitudinal rather than perceptual in nature. Nor is it only pure ignorance that would lead the tribe to sustain itself in the short run through policies promising the long-term extinction of the entire society. It is necessary only to have a set of values that place primary emphasis on the short-term outcome.

To represent the real Tsembaga system, which is characterized not by growth and decline but, rather, by a fairly stable population, we must explicitly include the population control mechanisms of the pig festival and human warfare.

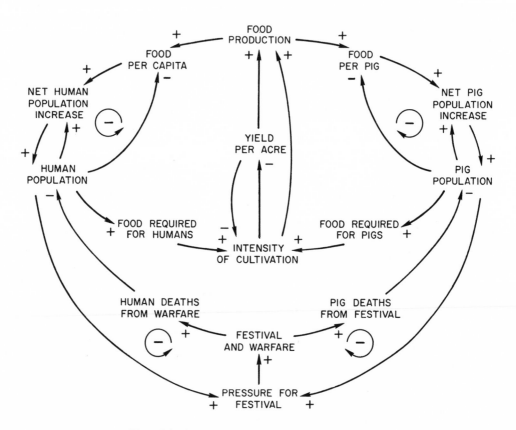

Figure 9-8 Causal-loop diagram of the Tsembaga system

A Model of the Complete Tsembaga System

Tsembaga Population Controls. The Tsembaga tribes have evolved an effective control process that avoids the deterioration of their land and the subsequent population decline portrayed in the previous section. The process involves the pig herd, whose natural increase periodically signals the beginning of the Tsembaga festivals. The pig herd has two basic impacts on the system: it increases pressure on the land, and it acts in conjunction with the human population level as an indicator, signaling the time for the festival. This behavior is modeled by the introduction of four additional feedback loops: pig-food, pig-yield, pig-festival, and human-festival (see Figure 9-8).

Pig-Food Feedback Loop. The mechanisms behind the pig-food loop (Figure 9-9) are similar in nature to those of the human-food loop. Pig ownership provides status to a Tsembaga. An owner of many pigs is accorded both respect and material reward. He is usually more successful with women and enjoys the admiration of colleagues. Therefore, pigs are not usually killed except in times of necessity. In this society, necessity usually is religious in origin. When a Tsembaga becomes sick and dies, it is a religious obligation for his family to sacrifice a pig on his behalf. Friends and neighbors are usually invited, and a banquet is held.

Pigs are fed whatever food is in excess of that demanded by the population. However, the existence of the pig herd is specifically taken into account when land is cleared for planting. Thus a portion of the land under cultivation can be regarded as food production solely for the support of pigs, while the labor involved in cultivating this land can be viewed as the labor required to support the pig herd.

The three factors controlling the pig herd—the status value of pigs, the religious sacrifice of pigs for deaths and illness, and the labor and land requirements

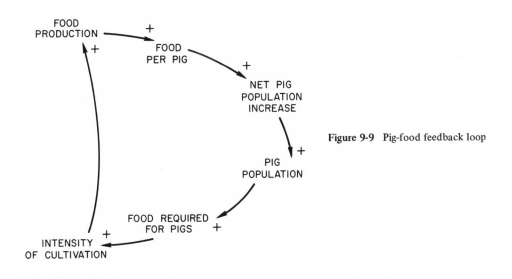

Figure 9-9 Pig-food feedback loop

for supporting pig herds—ensure that the size of the pig herd is a direct indication of the well-being of the Tsembaga population. There will, in general, be a correlation between the population level and the size of the pig herd.

The normal pig rate of increase is not stated explicitly in Rappaport's analysis. However, the description of the causes of pig births and deaths allows one to write an approximate functional form for the pig herd change rate. This function, together with data points provided on the size of the pig herd at several points in time and statistics on the number of pigs lost or shot, allows the calculation of an approximate change rate of the pig herd under normal conditions.[9] The death rate for pigs under famine conditions is inferred from this normal rate. We find, however, that the final mathematical model exhibits little sensitivity to changes in this parameter over a reasonable range.

Pig-Yield Feedback Loop.   The action of the pig-yield loop (Figure 9-10) is similar to that of the human-yield loop discussed previously. It is a natural environmental control that decreases food production because of falling land fertility as the pig population increases. The human-yield and pig-yield feedback loops act in conjunction to put pressure on the land. The driving pressure is the exponential growth of the two population levels. When the pressure created by this growth exceeds the land's carrying capacity, this loop becomes active and exerts a counter pressure on the population through food shortage. The control does not effectively limit population until the land's limit is reached, at which time it acts through a famine crisis.

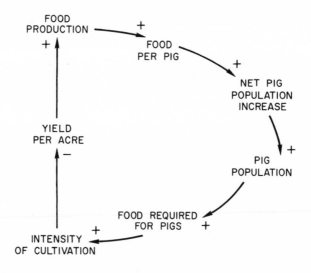

Figure 9-10 Pig-yield feedback loop

[9] A detailed system dynamics model of the factors controlling pig reproduction in western societies is presented in Dennis L. Meadows, *Dynamics of Commodity Production Cycles* (Cambridge, Mass.: Wright-Allen Press, 1971).

The Human-Festival and Pig-Festival Feedback Controls.   The Tsembaga pig festival and subsequent tribal warfare form a complex ecological control mechanism. The one ritual simultaneously promotes trade, provides animal protein for the Tsembaga diet, provides for the next generation of marital ties, and protects the land by keeping both the pig and the human population below the carrying capacity of the land.[10] It is this last function that is of concern here.

The pig festival is an elaborate ritual for slaughtering the pig herd. People from neighboring tribes are invited to the feast, and great ceremony is made of the presentation of pigs to ritual friends and relatives. The precursor of the festival is the uprooting of the *rumbim,* a special garden of tubers planted ten to fifteen years earlier at the close of the previous warfare. While the *rumbim* are in the ground, war is prohibited. Once they are uprooted, the taboo is lifted and the tribe is free to engage in conflicts. War breaks out almost immediately.[11]

Tsembaga Warfare.   The festival-war controls are activated by a trigger representing the culmination of the ritual cycle. The war and festivals involve elaborate rituals and religious taboos but ultimately have two results:

1. The pig festival causes the slaughter of about 85 percent (by live weight) of the pig herd. This prevents the land and population from being completely overrun by pigs.
2. The *rumbim* are uprooted, rescinding the ritual taboo on war. The war acts to reduce the population, mitigating the effects of population growth during the previous part of the ritual cycle.[12]

Although the data regarding the number of human deaths in such a war are incomplete, the nature of the warfare and of the Tsembaga culture indicates that it is not very great. Casualties probably average around five to ten, but could reach as many as thirty, or about 10 percent of the population, in a series of severe conflicts.[13]

Tsembaga warfare is conducted over a period of a few weeks or months in the form of intermittent battles. A battle is a confrontation that lasts about a day until one or both sides get tired or thirsty. During war periods the two groups of warriors, with their allies from neighboring tribes, face off across a clearing and yell, shake spears, and occasionally shoot arrows at one another. The arrows do not usually kill, and it requires a charge to finish off the wounded tribesman. This charge does not occur, however, when the warring parties are of equal strength. To instigate a charge, one side must find itself with a clear majority. This imbalance will usually occur in a matter of a couple of weeks as the less closely bound allies begin to lose interest. That is, after several days of light casualties the war usually culminates in a hand-to-hand battle for a few short moments. Then the two parties carry off their dead and wounded and hold highly ritualized funerals.

---

[10] Rappaport, *Pigs,* chap. 6.
[11] Ibid., p. 165.
[12] Ibid., chap. 5.
[13] Ibid., pp. 142-146.

When this sequence has repeated itself often enough for a consensus to be reached on the undesirability of more fighting (during wars gardens are not worked and sexual intercourse is taboo), an attempt is made to negotiate a truce. A Tsembaga *truce* is not the same as a Tsembaga *peace*. A peace can occur only if the body count on both sides is the same, that is, if each party has suffered the same number of losses. This situation rarely occurs. In its absence, a truce is accepted, which prevents war between the parties for the duration of the next ritual cycle. However, at the end of the cycle, the still uneven score provides a ready-made excuse to reinitiate war.[14] This aspect of war supports the conclusion that warfare evolved not as a way of attaining material or psychological goals (for example, land, booty, or victory) but rather as an institutionalized mechanism for controlling population.

The pressure for the festival and thus the warfare arises through the competition for resources created by growing human and pig populations. As the pig population grows, more labor is required to support it through food production, fence construction, and other activities. Because the pig population grows faster than the human population, each person needs to care for more and more pigs, until the pressure becomes sufficient to initiate the festival. Alternatively, the pressure for a festival can come purely from the combined densities of humans and pigs. Rappaport suggests that at high human population levels the number of pigs needed to induce a festival is reduced. There are thus two parallel mechanisms that can trigger a festival, each of which must be represented in the formal model.

The Population Control Thresholds. The causal-loop diagram of Figure 9-8 shows the influence of the festival and warfare in terms of the feedback loops but does not give their explicit numerical representation. In particular, we need to specify the human and the pig population levels that will trigger a festival, and to determine the exact impact of the festival on the two populations. The festival may be initiated in two ways: through pig-labor demands or through competition of the pigs for needed food.

It is estimated that a Tsembaga woman can take care of three or four pigs.[15] A critical point is reached when the pigs require more effort than the people are willing to expend. An upper bound can be placed on this threshold by the maximum ratio at which it is possible to support the pigs. That is, if all the Tsembaga women expend all their energy above basal metabolism to support the pigs, what is the highest pig-human ratio that could be sustained? On the basis of Rappaport's calculations, this upper bound is about two pigs per person. In practice, however, the decision for the festival is reached when enough people complain

[14] Ibid., p. 163.
[15] Ibid., p. 163.

about the pigs. The value used in the model for the critical festival threshold is one pig per person.[16]

It is also possible to trigger the festival at pig/human ratios well below the critical one determined by the labor problem, as Rappaport suggests. It is thus necessary to postulate an additional trigger mechanism based on a parameter that is a function of (pigs) X (people). The rationale for this formulation involves the motivation for the festival as a remedy for pig competition for food with the human population, a density-dependent phenomenon. The threshold level used in the model is 6 pigs per year.[17]

The model triggers the festival when either threshold is crossed. It is important to note that both thresholds are significantly below the carrying capacity of the land for the range of most reasonable pig-to-human ratios. The immediate effect of the festival on the pig population is to decrease the herd by about 85 percent, the exact amount depending on the pig-to-person ratio. The effect of the subsequent war is to increase the human death rate to 12 percent of the population per year in the first year following the festival, and to about 5 percent the second year. In the third and following years the death rate falls to normal. This formulation was found to correspond most closely to the death rate observed by Rappaport.

The addition of these mechanisms to the previous simplified structure yields the DYNAMO flow diagram for the complete Tsembaga system as illustrated in Figure 9-11. The level of the pig population PP is the only level added to the

---

[16] Calculation of critical level of labor CLL: The pig problem can become acute due to a shortage of available labor for pig care. The basal metabolism of Maring women is given at 950 calories per day, while intake is estimated at 2,150 calories per day. Rappaport also estimates that it requires 100 calories per day to care for a pig. If 50 percent of all energy is used on pig care, then an average woman can care for 6 pigs. At the time of the study, there were 66 Tsembaga women, constituting $66/204 = 0.32$ of the population. These figures yield a critical pig-to-human ratio of

$$\frac{\text{pig}}{\text{human}} = \frac{6 \text{ pigs}}{\text{women}} \qquad \frac{1 \text{ woman}}{3 \text{ persons}} = 2 \text{ pigs per person}$$

This figure represents an upper limit. Actually, all that is needed to trigger a festival is a consensus, which occurs at something less than the maximum tolerable level of the ratio. In the model, the value used was:

$$\text{CLL} = \left[\frac{\text{PIG}}{\text{HUMAN}}\right] = 1$$

[17] Calculation of critical level of competition CLC: An alternative cause for a festival can be related to the number of disputes arising from the pig density. As the numbers of pigs and people increase, the opportunity for conflict between the two also increases. When the number of conflicts actually realized is above a critical level, it can serve to trigger a festival. The number of such incidents realized is proportional to the number of opportunities:

$$\text{incidents} = R \times \text{Pigs} \times \text{People}$$

For the purposes of this formulation, R was taken at C, where C is the constant of proportionality to determine the number of pigs shot by hunters (calculated from Rappaport's data). Then the critical level from competition CLC is in terms of pigs per year:

$$\text{CLC} = [1.8 \times 0.10^{-4} \times \text{pigs} \times \text{persons}] = 6 \text{ pigs per year}$$

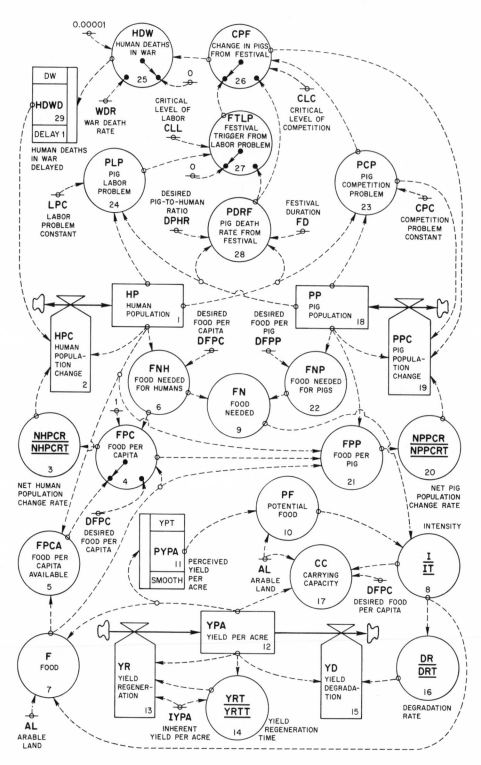

Figure 9-11   DYNAMO flow diagram of the Tsembaga model

model; because no substantial delays are involved in the Tsembaga's reaction to pig crises, the festivals and wars are modeled simply as auxiliary variables. The averaging variable in the war death rate HDWD is introduced to incorporate the previously stated assumptions about human deaths.

When this complete system is simulated, its behavior, exhibited in Figure 9-12, is close to that described in Rappaport's study. The pig and population levels grow quasi-exponentially until they exceed one of the festival thresholds—in this case the competition limit. The results are a pig festival, which drops the pig population level PP drastically, and a war, with more negative effects on the human population level HP. The land intensity I that had been growing as a result of population pressures reaches a maximum value of about 1/18, well below the 1/16 value that causes land degradation.

Analyzing the Complete Tsembaga System.   The Tsembaga system is a delicate one, and the variables are finely tuned. The initial values used in the model are based on the Rappaport studies, which, though fairly accurate, are not precise. Due to this imprecision, the model exhibits transient behavior during the first five or six cycles. After the transients die out, its behavior settles down into an equilibrium cycle that continues indefinitely, as shown in Figure 9-12. We have a high degree of confidence that the behavior of this model, while perhaps not precisely replicating the Tsembaga system, arises from the same mechanisms at work in the real

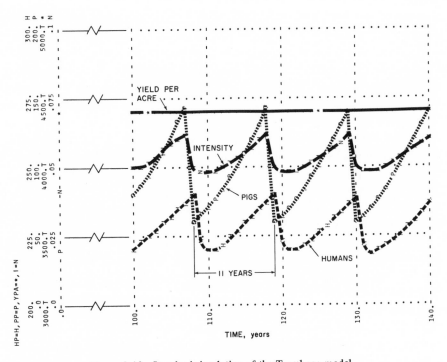

Figure 9-12 Standard simulation of the Tsembaga model

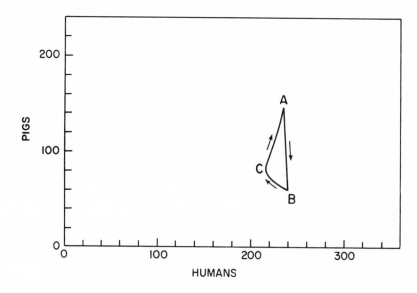

Figure 9-13   A ritual cycle plotted as pigs versus people

society. It is therefore possible to examine this model to aid our understanding of how population controls operate in the actual system and to discover what the reaction of these controls might be to a number of changes that one might consider.

A way of viewing the behavior of systems is to plot the values of important variables at different points in time. Such plots are the primary output form of a system dynamics model. It is also useful in this system to use an alternate method of plotting the system behavior. In Figure 9-12 we observe that, after the first few years, the long-run behavior of the Tsembaga system is a repeated cycle of growth in both human and pig populations, followed by a festival and associated warfare, which cause a decline in both populations. These cycles are regular in that the levels of the two populations are nearly exactly repeated in equal amounts of time. We can thus plot the system's behavior as a point moving in a closed path in a graph of pig population and human population, as in Figure 9-13.

The nearly vertical portion of the path, A ⇒ B, corresponds to the period when the pig festival is being enacted and the number of pigs is drastically reduced. That is followed by the warfare, B ⇒ C, in which the human population falls while the pig population is slowly increasing. Then both populations grow for a number of years, C ⇒ A, until a festival begins the cycle again.

We can add to this graph a set of lines corresponding to the two critical levels of the pig and human populations that will induce a festival, and a line corresponding to the carrying capacity of the land. These lines will define three regions in which the system can operate, as in Figure 9-14. As long as the system remains in the *safe region,* there is generally no inducement to have pig festivals, and the land is able to produce sufficient food to support both the humans and the

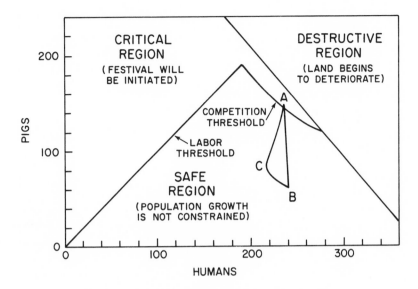

Figure 9-14   A ritual cycle with behavior regions indicated

pigs. If the system enters the *critical region,* the combination of people and pigs has reached a critical level at which a festival is initiated, either through labor problems or through competition. If the system enters the *destructive region,* the combined populations have exceeded the carrying capacity of the land; the natural environment is being destroyed through overintensive cultivation. This state will actually cause the carrying capacity line to move toward the origin (no people and no pigs) for as long as the combined populations exceed the carrying capacity. This behavior is analogous to that illustrated in Figure 9-10, where we assumed no festivals.

In Figure 9-14, the ritual cycle of the Tsembaga is plotted as it appears to be in operation today. The cycle is a relatively stable one, in that the society never comes close to exceeding the carrying capacity of the land. The festival controls act to keep the populations from reaching a level that would begin to destroy the environment. However, if a contemplated change in the society, for example, an improvement in medical care, shifted the cycle toward the maximum carrying capacity, the consequences would be quite dangerous to the population in the long run. A postulated change can thus be mapped into its effect on the ritual cycle, and we can learn what its probable consequences will be.

Suppose we contemplate introducing one change into the Tsembaga system—an improvement in the health of the population so that the normal human population growth rate is 1.5 percent per year rather than 1.3 percent per year. Looking at Figure 9-14, we would expect this change to emphasize the growth in the human population. In time we would expect the human-to-pig ratio of the system to be higher than in our original case. This would mean that the ritual cycle would shift to the right, coming closer to the destructive region and in-

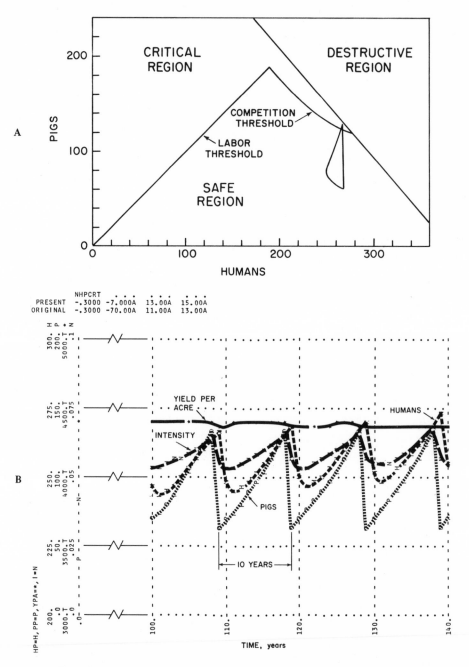

Figure 9-15 Model simulation of improved health (normal growth rate = 1.5 percent)

creasing the probability of damaging the carrying capacity of the land. A policy of improving the population's health, which would seem at first glance to be desirable, might in fact endanger the total population's long-term chances of survival.

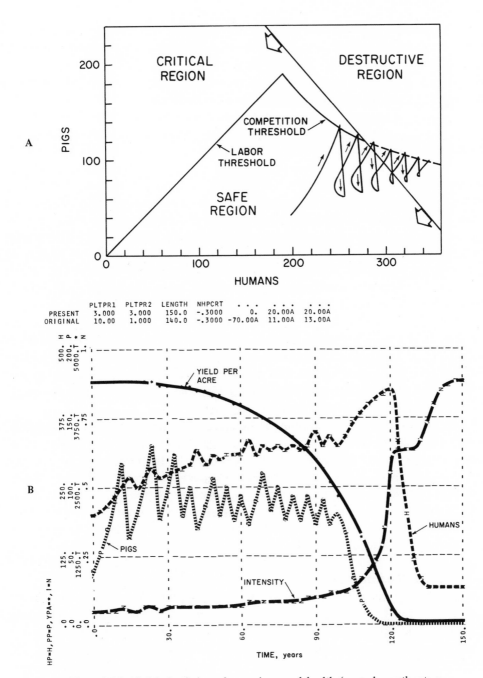

Figure 9-16 Model simulation of more improved health (normal growth rate = 2.0 percent)

When this policy is simulated in the model, the result is as shown in Figure 9-15. The ritual cycle in 9-15A is shifted significantly to the right, coming much closer to exceeding the land's carrying capacity. The time plot of Figure 9-15B indicates that the festivals are now closer together, yet they are still able to control the population without endangering the land's carrying capacity. The two graphs demonstrate that the population growth resulting from this increase in health is very near the maximum growth rate that the system can sustain without surpassing the built-in control mechanisms of the festivals.

If the normal growth rate of the population increases to 2.0 percent per year, corresponding to a public health program with increased effectiveness over the last example, the population soon outstrips the control mechanisms of the pig herd and exceeds the carrying capacity of the land, as shown in Figure 9-16. The first symptom evident in Figure 9-16B is an increase in the frequency of festivals, as festivals are being initiated at succeedingly lower and lower levels of pigs (due to the increase in the human population). By the year 100 the tribes can no longer afford to support the pig herd, so the herd declines to zero. The human population grows for twenty years, unchecked by wars, until the land can no longer support such large numbers of people. Between years 120 and 135, about 80 percent of the population starves. A new population equilibrium is established with few people, a barely subsistence-level food supply, and highly intensive cultivation of very poor land.

Figure 9-16A represents this behavior in the plot of humans versus pigs. Each successive cycle is triggered at increasing levels of human population. Excursions into the *destructive region,* while still part of the ritual cycle, cause the diagonal line that represents the carrying capacity of the land to move toward the origin until only very few people and no pigs can be supported on the land.

In Figure 9-17 we have simulated the effect of convincing the Tsembaga to abandon the warfare usually associated with each festival. Thus each festival cycle brings a decline in the pig herd but no decline in the human population. In the absence of the ritualistic warfare, previously an accepted part of Maring affairs, the human population outgrows the carrying capacity of the land and is forced to a low population level under conditions very similar to the previous simulation. Again, a policy that saved lives in the short run serves only to decrease the population size drastically through starvation in the long run.

Implications of the Study

It has already been noted that pig herding imposes a net energy loss on the Tsembaga people. Even if the added infusion of protein is taken into account, the time, effort, and opportunity costs (the Tsembaga could be gardening instead of pig herding) are large compared to the return. This analysis has documented the utility of the pig herd as a pivotal part of a dynamic information-control system. The pig festival and subsequent warfare are automatic control devices that simultaneously curtail dangerous population growth and reset the monitoring system.

It is interesting that a control mechanism evolved that is discontinuous but, at the same time, nondisruptive. After a short period of war the Tsembaga clans seem to have little trouble returning to the routinized life of subsistence agriculture. Long-term population control is accomplished without large losses in the

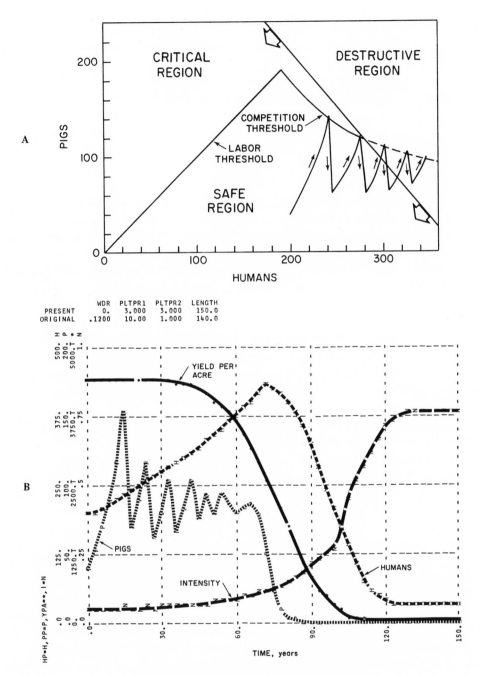

Figure 9-17   Model simulation of no human wars

wars. War kills perhaps ten to twenty people on one side. If the population growth rate rises, equilibrium is reestablished by increasing the frequency rather than the severity of the warfare. This system is in marked contrast to others in which control has been less frequent but much more catastrophic. For example, in the early 1800s the population of Ireland decreased 50 percent within twenty years, partly through famine and partly through emigration, when it had grown past the current carrying capacity of the soil.[18]

In the Tsembaga system several parameters are of major importance: the human population change rate NHPCR, pig population change rate NPPCR, human deaths from war HDW, pig deaths in festivals PDRF, and the levels of both trigger thresholds (CLC and CLL). A more exact representation of the Tsembaga system would require more precise data on these parameters. Even this approximate representation of the whole system, however, leads to a basic appreciation of the essentials of the Maring ritual and religion. For example, a crucial element of the Tsembaga culture is the status value attached to the pigs. Without this or some similar motivation, the pig herd would not receive the continued attention essential to its function as an information indicator. Similarly, the model underscores the utility of specific rituals and religious practices. Rituals classified as nonutilitarian, as not important to the functioning of the system, could possibly provide clues to the evolution of a particular culture. Perhaps they are vestiges of once important utilitarian rituals, or they may represent influences of other cultures absorbed through contact.

On another level, system dynamics can be used to analyze the effects of policy inputs and to predict subsequent system responses. For example, the Tsembaga system is extremely rigid, inflexible, and consequently sensitive to exogenous inputs. It is self-corrective only within a small range of changes in variables. A system so tightly controlled is easily shattered if pushed past this small range to which it can adapt. The delicacy of the system should be kept in mind during any attempt to implement policy. As a specific example, introducing modern medicine, preventing wars, or raising nutritional standards without careful regard to the intrinsic systems controlled could well destroy the population by disrupting the dynamic balance among the variables that influence the ritual cycle.

It may seem to the traditional analyst that the use of formal, mathematical tools in a sociological application is imposing a rigidity uncharacteristic of the real-world system. This argument would indeed be true if one were completely to supplant field analysis with mathematics. Our purpose in this paper has been to demonstrate how the two can be used together. The system dynamics model can aid the analyst in structuring the information he gathers in the field; it can point out to him those elements of the society that may deserve the most attention. We found that both the human and the pig population growth rates were especially crucial to the long-term stability of the Maring system, yet neither of these rates was very well documented in Rappaport's study. The model can assist the analyst in relating the insights of traditional societies to those concerned with more complex societies. The simulation runs of the model point clearly to the need for any society, be it traditional or modern, to evaluate both the long- and the

---

[18] Philip M. Hauser, *The Population Dilemma* (Englewood Cliffs, N.J.: Prentice-Hall, 1969), p. 174.

short-term impacts of any proposed policy change before proceeding to implementation. Finally, the model can provide the context within which responsible
policy design can and should be carried out. A model is simply an analytical tool,
one that can usefully extend the power and richness of anthropological research.

Appendix A: Computer Program for Land-Constrained System

```
HP.K=HP.J+(DT)(HPC.JK)                                    1, L
HP=HPI                                                    1.1, N
HPI=196                                                   1.2, C
    HP     - HUMAN POPULATION (HUMANS)
    DT     - COMPUTATION INTERVAL (YEARS)
    HPC    - HUMAN POPULATION CHANGE (HUMANS PER YEAR)
    HPI    - HUMAN POPULATION INITIAL (HUMANS)

HPC.KL=NHPCR.K*HP.K                                       2, R
    HPC    - HUMAN POPULATION CHANGE (HUMANS PER YEAR)
    NHPCR  - NET HUMAN POPULATION CHANGE RATE (FRACTION
               PER YEAR)
    HP     - HUMAN POPULATION (HUMANS)

NHPCR.K=TABHL(NHPCRT,FPC.K,0,1113E3,371E3)                3, A
NHPCRT=-.3/-.07/.011/.013                                 3.1, T
    NHPCR  - NET HUMAN POPULATION CHANGE RATE (FRACTION
               PER YEAR)
    NHPCRT - TABLE FOR NHPCR
    FPC    - FOOD PER CAPITA (CALORIES PER PERSON PER
               YEAR)

FPC.K=F.K/HP.K                                            4, A
    FPC    - FOOD PER CAPITA (CALORIES PER PERSON PER
               YEAR)
    F      - FOOD (CALORIES PER YEAR)
    HP     - HUMAN POPULATION (HUMANS)

F.K=AL*YPA.K*I.K                                          5, A
AL=972                                                    5.1, C
    F      - FOOD (CALORIES PER YEAR)
    AL     - ARABLE LAND (ACRES)
    YPA    - YIELD PER ACRE (CALORIES PER ACRE PER YEAR)
    I      - INTENSITY (DIMENSIONLESS)

I.K=TABHL(IT,PF.K/FN.K,0,24,4)                            6, A
IT=1/.25/.125/.0834/.0625/.05/.0417                       6.1, T
    I      - INTENSITY (DIMENSIONLESS)
    IT     - TABLE FOR I
    PF     - POTENTIAL FOOD (CALORIES PER YEAR)
    FN     - FOOD NEEDED (CALORIES PER YEAR)

PF.K=PYPA.K*AL                                            7, A
    PF     - POTENTIAL FOOD (CALORIES PER YEAR)
    PYPA   - PERCEIVED YIELD PER ACRE (CALORIES PER ACRE
               PER YEAR)
    AL     - ARABLE LAND (ACRES)

PYPA.K=SMOOTH(YPA.K,YPT)                                  8, A
YPT=5                                                     8.1, C
    PYPA   - PERCEIVED YIELD PER ACRE (CALORIES PER ACRE
               PER YEAR)
    YPA    - YIELD PER ACRE (CALORIES PER ACRE PER YEAR)
    YPT    - YIELD PERCEPTION TIME (YEARS)

FN.K=HP.K*DFPC                                            9, A
DFPC=742E3                                                9.1, C
    FN     - FOOD NEEDED (CALORIES PER YEAR)
    HP     - HUMAN POPULATION (HUMANS)
    DFPC   - DESIRED FOOD PER CAPITA (CALORIES PER
               PERSON PER YEAR)
```

```
YPA.K=YPA.J+(DT)(YR.JK-YD.JK)                        10, L
YPA=YPAI                                             10.1, N
YPAI=4.4E6                                           10.2, C
     YPA    - YIELD PER ACRE (CALORIES PER ACRE PER YEAR)
     DT     - COMPUTATION INTERVAL (YEARS)
     YR     - YIELD REGENERATION (CALORIES PER ACRE PER
                 YEAR PER YEAR)
     YD     - YIELD DEGRADATION (CALORIES PER ACRE PER
                 YEAR PER YEAR)
     YPAI   - YIELD PER ACRE INITIAL (CALORIES PER ACRE
                 PER YEAR)


YR.KL=(IYPA-YPA.K)/YRT.K                             11, R
IYPA=4.4E6                                           11.1, C
     YR     - YIELD REGENERATION (CALORIES PER ACRE PER
                 YEAR PER YEAR)
     IYPA   - INHERENT YIELD PER ACRE (CALORIES PER ACRE
                 PER YEAR)
     YPA    - YIELD PER ACRE (CALORIES PER ACRE PER YEAR)
     YRT    - YIELD REGENERATION TIME (YEARS)


YRT.K=TABHL(YRTT,YPA.K/IYPA,0,1,.1)                  12, A
YRTT=400/140/105/80/60/45/34/25/20/17/16             12.1, T
     YRT    - YIELD REGENERATION TIME (YEARS)
     YRTT   - TABLE FOR YRT
     YPA    - YIELD PER ACRE (CALORIES PER ACRE PER YEAR)
     IYPA   - INHERENT YIELD PER ACRE (CALORIES PER ACRE
                 PER YEAR)


YD.KL=DR.K*YPA.K                                     13, R
     YD     - YIELD DEGRADATION (CALORIES PER ACRE PER
                 YEAR PER YEAR)
     DR     - DEGRADATION RATE (FRACTION PER YEAR)
     YPA    - YIELD PER ACRE (CALORIES PER ACRE PER YEAR)


DR.K=TABHL(DRT,1.0/I.K,0,24,4)                       14, A
DRT=.5/.15/.06/.02/0/0/0                             14.1, T
     DR     - DEGRADATION RATE (FRACTION PER YEAR)
     DRT    - TABLE FOR DR
     I      - INTENSITY (DIMENSIONLESS)


CC.K=AL*I.K*YPA.K/DFPC                               15, S
DT=.5                                                15.1, C
LENGTH=200                                           15.2, C
PLTPER=5                                             15.3, C
PRTPER=0                                             15.4, C
     CC     - CARRYING CAPACITY (HUMANS)
     AL     - ARABLE LAND (ACRES)
     I      - INTENSITY (DIMENSIONLESS)
     YPA    - YIELD PER ACRE (CALORIES PER ACRE PER YEAR)
     DFPC   - DESIRED FOOD PER CAPITA (CALORIES PER
                 PERSON PER YEAR)
     DT     - COMPUTATION INTERVAL (YEARS)


PLOT   HP=H,CC=C(0,500)/FPC=F(0,1E6)/I=N(0,1)/YPA=*(0,5E6)
RUN
```

Appendix B: Computer Program for Complete Tsembaga System

```
     HUMAN POPULATION SECTOR

HP.K=HP.J+(DT)(HPC.JK)                               1, L
HP=HPI                                               1.1, N
HPI=196                                              1.2, C
     HP     - HUMAN POPULATION (HUMANS)
     DT     - COMPUTATION INTERVAL (YEARS)
     HPC    - HUMAN POPULATION CHANGE (HUMANS PER YEAR)
     HPI    - HUMAN POPULATION INITIAL (HUMANS)
```

```
HPC.KL=(NHPCR.K)(HP.K)-(HDWD.K)(HP.K)                2, R
     HPC    - HUMAN POPULATION CHANGE (HUMANS PER YEAR)
     NHPCR  - NET HUMAN POPULATION CHANGE RATE (FRACTION
                 PER YEAR)
     HP     - HUMAN POPULATION (HUMANS)
     HDWD   - HUMAN DEATHS FROM WAR DELAYED (FRACTION PER
                 YEAR)

NHPCR.K=TABHL(NHPCRT,FPC.K,0,1113E3,371E3)           3, A
NHPCRT=-.3/-.07/.011/.013                            3.1, T
     NHPCR  - NET HUMAN POPULATION CHANGE RATE (FRACTION
                 PER YEAR)
     NHPCRT - TABLE FOR NHPCR
     FPC    - FOOD PER CAPITA (CALORIES PER PERSON PER
                 YEAR)

FPC.K=CLIP(DFPC,FPCA.K,F.K/FNH.K,1)                  4, A
DFPC=742E3                                           4.1, C
FPC=FPCI                                             4.2, N
FPCI=742E3                                           4.3, C
     FPC    - FOOD PER CAPITA (CALORIES PER PERSON PER
                 YEAR)
     DFPC   - DESIRED FOOD PER CAPITA (CALORIES PER
                 PERSON PER YEAR)
     FPCA   - FOOD PER CAPITA AVAILABLE (CALORIES PER
                 PERSON PER YEAR)
     F      - FOOD (CALORIES PER YEAR)
     FNH    - FOOD NEEDED FOR HUMANS (CALORIES PER YEAR)

FPCA.K=F.K/HP.K                                      5, A
     FPCA   - FOOD PER CAPITA AVAILABLE (CALORIES PER
                 PERSON PER YEAR)
     F      - FOOD (CALORIES PER YEAR)
     HP     - HUMAN POPULATION (HUMANS)

FNH.K=DFPC*HP.K                                      6, A
     FNH    - FOOD NEEDED FOR HUMANS (CALORIES PER YEAR)
     DFPC   - DESIRED FOOD PER CAPITA (CALORIES PER
                 PERSON PER YEAR)
     HP     - HUMAN POPULATION (HUMANS)


 LAND SUSTAINABLE YIELD SECTOR

F.K=AL*YPA.K*I.K                                     7, A
AL=972                                               7.1, C
     F      - FOOD (CALORIES PER YEAR)
     AL     - ARABLE LAND (ACRES)
     YPA    - YIELD PER ACRE (CALORIES PER ACRE PER YEAR)
     I      - INTENSITY (DIMENSIONLESS)

I.K=TABHL(IT,PF.K/FN.K,0,24,4)                       8, A
IT=1/.25/.125/.0834/.0625/.05/.0417                  8.1, T
     I      - INTENSITY (DIMENSIONLESS)
     IT     - TABLE FOR I
     PF     - POTENTIAL FOOD (CALORIES PER YEAR)
     FN     - FOOD NEEDED (CALORIES PER YEAR)

FN.K=FNH.K+FNP.K                                     9, A
     FN     - FOOD NEEDED (CALORIES PER YEAR)
     FNH    - FOOD NEEDED FOR HUMANS (CALORIES PER YEAR)
     FNP    - FOOD NEEDED FOR PIGS (CALORIES PER YEAR)

PF.K=AL*PYPA.K                                       10, A
     PF     - POTENTIAL FOOD (CALORIES PER YEAR)
     AL     - ARABLE LAND (ACRES)
     PYPA   - PERCEIVED YIELD PER ACRE (CALORIES PER ACRE
                 PER YEAR)

PYPA.K=SMOOTH(YPA.K,YPT)                             11, A
YPT=5                                                11.1, C
     PYPA   - PERCEIVED YIELD PER ACRE (CALORIES PER ACRE
                 PER YEAR)
     YPA    - YIELD PER ACRE (CALORIES PER ACRE PER YEAR)
     YPT    - YIELD PERCEPTION TIME (YEARS)
```

```
YPA.K=YPA.J+(DT)(YR.JK-YD.JK)                      12, L
YPA=YPAI                                           12.1, N
YPAI=4.4E6                                         12.2, C
    YPA    - YIELD PER ACRE (CALORIES PER ACRE PER YEAR)
    DT     - COMPUTATION INTERVAL (YEARS)
    YR     - YIELD REGENERATION (CALORIES PER ACRE PER
                YEAR PER YEAR)
    YD     - YIELD DEGRADATION (CALORIES PER ACRE PER
                YEAR PER YEAR)
    YPAI   - YIELD PER ACRE INITIAL (CALORIES PER ACRE
                PER YEAR)


YR.KL=(IYPA-YPA.K)/YRT.K                           13, R
IYPA=4.4E6                                         13.1, C
    YR     - YIELD REGENERATION (CALORIES PER ACRE PER
                YEAR PER YEAR)
    IYPA   - INHERENT YIELD PER ACRE (CALORIES PER ACRE
                PER YEAR)
    YPA    - YIELD PER ACRE (CALORIES PER ACRE PER YEAR)
    YRT    - YIELD REGENERATION TIME (YEARS)


YRT.K=TABHL(YRTT,YPA.K/IYPA,0,1,.1)                14, A
YRTT=400/140/105/80/60/45/34/25/20/17/16           14.1, T
    YRT    - YIELD REGENERATION TIME (YEARS)
    YRTT   - TABLE FOR YRT
    YPA    - YIELD PER ACRE (CALORIES PER ACRE PER YEAR)
    IYPA   - INHERENT YIELD PER ACRE (CALORIES PER ACRE
                PER YEAR)


YD.KL=DR.K*YPA.K                                   15, R
    YD     - YIELD DEGRADATION (CALORIES PER ACRE PER
                YEAR PER YEAR)
    DR     - DEGRADATION RATE (FRACTION PER YEAR)
    YPA    - YIELD PER ACRE (CALORIES PER ACRE PER YEAR)


DR.K=TABHL(DRT,1.0/I.K,0,24,4)                     16, A
DRT=.5/.15/.06/.02/0/0/0                            16.1, T
    DR     - DEGRADATION RATE (FRACTION PER YEAR)
    DRT    - TABLE FOR DR
    I      - INTENSITY (DIMENSIONLESS)


CC.K=AL*YPA.K*I.K/DFPC                              17, S
    CC     - CARRYING CAPACITY (HUMANS)
    AL     - ARABLE LAND (ACRES)
    YPA    - YIELD PER ACRE (CALORIES PER ACRE PER YEAR)
    I      - INTENSITY (DIMENSIONLESS)
    DFPC   - DESIRED FOOD PER CAPITA (CALORIES PER
                PERSON PER YEAR)


  PIG SECTOR

PP.K=PP.J+(DT)(PPC.JK)                              18, L
PP=PPI                                             18.1, N
PPI=40                                             18.2, C
    PP     - PIG POPULATION (PIGS)
    DT     - COMPUTATION INTERVAL (YEARS)
    PPC    - PIG POPULATION CHANGE (PIGS PER YEAR)
    PPI    - PIG POPULATION INITIAL (PIGS)


PPC.KL=(PP.K*NPPCR.K-CPC*HP.K*PP.K-CPF.K*PP.K)     19, R
    PPC    - PIG POPULATION CHANGE (PIGS PER YEAR)
    PP     - PIG POPULATION (PIGS)
    NPPCR  - NET PIG POPULATION CHANGE RATE (FRACTION
                PER YEAR)
    CPC    - COMPETITION PROBLEM CONSTANT (1/(HUMANS-
                YEAR))
    HP     - HUMAN POPULATION (HUMANS)
    CPF    - CHANGE IN PIGS FROM FESTIVAL (FRACTION PER
                YEAR)
```

```
NPPCR.K=TABHL(NPPCRT,FPP.K,0,885E3,295E3)          20, A
NPPCRT=-.15/.11/.13/.14                            20.1, T
     NPPCR   - NET PIG POPULATION CHANGE RATE (FRACTION
                  PER YEAR)
     NPPCRT - TABLE FOR NPPCR
     FPP     - FOOD PER PIG (CALORIES PER PIG PER YEAR)


FPP.K=(F.K-FPC.K*HP.K)/PP.K                         21, A
     FPP     - FOOD PER PIG (CALORIES PER PIG PER YEAR)
     F       - FOOD)(CALORIES PER YEAR)
     FPC     - FOOD PER CAPITA (CALORIES PER PERSON PER
                  YEAR)
     HP      - HUMAN POPULATION (HUMANS)
     PP      - PIG POPULATION (PIGS)


FNP.K=DFPP*PP.K                                     22, A
DFPP=590E3                                          22.1, C
     FNP     - FOOD NEEDED FOR PIGS (CALORIES PER YEAR)
     DFPP    - DESIRED FOOD PER PIG (CALORIES PER PIG PER
                  YEAR)
     PP      - PIG POPULATION (PIGS)


  FESTIVAL SECTOR

PCP.K=CPC*PP.K*HP.K                                 23, A
CPC=1.8E-4                                          23.1, C
CLC=6                                               23.2, C
     PCP     - PIG COMPETITION PROBLEM (PIGS/YEAR)
     CPC     - COMPETITION PROBLEM CONSTANT (1/(HUMANS-
                  YEAR))
     PP      - PIG POPULATION (PIGS)
     HP      - HUMAN POPULATION (HUMANS)
     CLC     - CRITICAL LEVEL OF COMPETITION (PIGS/YEAR)


PLP.K=LPC*PP.K/HP.K                                 24, A
LPC=1                                               24.1, C
CLL=1                                               24.2, C
     PLP     - PIG LABOR PROBLEM (DIMENSIONLESS)
     LPC     - LABOR PROBLEM CONSTANT (HUMANS PER PIG)
     PP      - PIG POPULATION (PIGS)
     HP      - HUMAN POPULATION (HUMANS)
     CLL     - CRITICAL LEVEL OF LABOR (DIMENSIONLESS)


HDW.K=CLIP(WDR,0,CPF.K,.00001)                      25, A
WDR=.12                                             25.1, C
     HDW     - HUMAN DEATHS IN WAR (FRACTION PER YEAR)
     WDR     - WAR DEATH RATE (FRACTION PER YEAR)
     CPF     - CHANGE IN PIGS FROM FESTIVAL (FRACTION PER
                  YEAR)


CPF.K=CLIP(PDRF.K,FTLP.K,PCP.K,CLC)                 26, A
     CPF     - CHANGE IN PIGS FROM FESTIVAL (FRACTION PER
                  YEAR)
     PDRF    - PIG DEATH RATE FROM FESTIVAL (FRACTION PER
                  YEAR)
     FTLP    - FESTIVAL TRIGGER FROM LABOR PROBLEM
                  (FRACTION PER YEAR)
     PCP     - PIG COMPETITION PROBLEM (PIGS/YEAR)
     CLC     - CRITICAL LEVEL OF COMPETITION (PIGS/YEAR)


FTLP.K=CLIP(PDRF.K,0,PLP.K,CLL)                     27, A
     FTLP    - FESTIVAL TRIGGER FROM LABOR PROBLEM
                  (FRACTION PER YEAR)
     PDRF    - PIG DEATH RATE FROM FESTIVAL (FRACTION PER
                  YEAR)
     PLP     - PIG LABOR PROBLEM (DIMENSIONLESS)
     CLL     - CRITICAL LEVEL OF LABOR (DIMENSIONLESS)
```

```
PDRF.K=1-DPHR*HP.K/(FD*PP.K)                         28, A
FD=1                                                 28.1, C
DPHR=0.2                                             28.2, C
    PDRF    - PIG DEATH RATE FROM FESTIVAL (FRACTION PER
                YEAR)
    DPHR    - DESIRED PIG TO HUMAN RATIO (PIGS PER HUMAN)
    HP      - HUMAN POPULATION (HUMANS)
    FD      - FESTIVAL DURATION (YEARS)
    PP      - PIG POPULATION (PIGS)

HDWD.K=DELAY1(HDW.K,DW)                              29, A
DW=1.5                                              29.1, C
    HDWD    - HUMAN DEATHS FROM WAR DELAYED (FRACTION PER
                YEAR)
    HDW     - HUMAN DEATHS IN WAR (FRACTION PER YEAR)
    DW      - DELAY FROM WAR (YEARS)

   CONTROL CARDS

DT=1                                                29.5, C
LENGTH=140                                           29.6, C
PRTPER=0                                             29.7, C
    DT      - COMPUTATION INTERVAL (YEARS)

PLTPER.K=CLIP(PLTPR2,PLTPR1,TIME.K,SWT)              30, A
PLTPR1=10                                            30.1, C
PLTPR2=1                                             30.2, C
SWT=100                                              30.3, C


A       FTLP.K=CLIP(PDRF.K,0,PLP.K,CLL)
NOTE    NOTE RE: LAST TWO CLIPS
NOTE    TEST FOR FEST. TRIGGER FROM COMPETITION
NOTE    IF NOT, TEST FOR TRIGGER FROM LABOR
NOTE
A       PDRF.K=1-DPHR*HP.K/(FD*PP.K)
C       FD=1
C       DPHR=0.2
A       HDWD.K=DELAY1(HDW.K,DW)
C       DW=1.5
NOTE
NOTE    CONTROL CARDS
NOTE
C       DT=1
C       LENGTH=140
C       PRTPER=0
A       PLTPER.K=CLIP(PLTPR2,PLTPR1,TIME.K,SWT)
C       PLTPR1=10
C       PLTPR2=1
C       SWT=100
PLOT    HP=H(200,300)/PP=P(0,200)/YPA=*(3E6,5E6)/I=N(0,.1)
PRINT   HP/PP/PCP/PLP/CLL/CC
RUN     STANDARD
C       NHPCRT=-.3/-.007/.013/.015
RUN     HEALTH1
C       PLTPR1=3
C       PLTPR2=3
C       LENGTH=150
C       NHPCRT=-.3/0/.02/.02
PLOT    HP=H(0,500)/PP=P(0,200)/YPA=*(0,5E6)/I=N(0,1)
RUN     HEALTH2
C       WDR=0
C       PLTPR1=3
C       PLTPR2=3
C       LENGTH=150
RUN     NO WARFARE
```

Part Three
Interpretive Papers

During the course of this project, members of the M.I.T. team met with many scientific, legislative, religious, and civic groups to discuss the progress of the research and to explore its potential implications. The following four papers were prepared at various times for use in these discussions. Each paper is based on one or more of the substudies described in Part Two or on the world model. Each is an attempt to abstract from the specific models those general conclusions that may serve as guidelines in the design of future policies.

10
Determinants of Long-Term Resource Availability

William W. Behrens III and Dennis L. Meadows

The depletion of domestic resource supplies is forcing many industrial nations to become increasingly dependent on overseas sources of raw materials. This trend presents industrialized nations with a difficult dilemma. Relatively inexpensive resources may be imported in greater quantities from other nations, but at a cost of increasing strategic vulnerability. If increasing dependence on imports is not permitted, the policies and technical changes needed to maintain relative resource self-sufficiency can be expected to increase resource prices. Other costs, in the form of greater personnel hazards, environmental deterioration, and loss of competitive advantage in international markets, will also interfere with the maintenance of an adequate domestic resource supply.

New approaches for managing the flow of material goods through an economy will be needed to resolve this dilemma. To provide a framework for the conduct of studies to assess and manage long-term resource availability, William Behrens and Dennis Meadows prepared the following paper. It summarizes the issues explored in the papers on resource discovery, resource technology, and recycling included in Part Two of this book. It also discusses the literature on the dynamics of resource depletion and indicates some of the more long-term approaches that must be incorporated in the perspectives of a resource management policy.

10
Determinants of Long-Term Resource Availability

Introduction

Two types of information are relevant for analyzing resource availability over the long term. The first, which we shall call *geological assessment,* includes figures on locations and grades of deposits, size of reserves, and projections of growth in resource usage. The second type of information, loosely termed *conceptual assessment,* characterizes the overall role of resources in economic activity. Here we review the primary issues in each area.

Geological Assessment

Of the many publications providing assessments of resource reserves, the most complete and therefore most useful are *Resources in America's Future,* by Resources for the Future, Inc., and *Mineral Facts and Problems,* issued by the U.S. Department of the Interior.[1] Both volumes discuss each raw material separately, presenting reserve estimates, analyses of supply (new discoveries, imports) and demand (substitutes, demand growth). These analyses have been developed to a fairly sophisticated level. For example, in the 1970 volume of *Mineral Facts and Problems,* the demand for coal is projected to grow at a rate as high as 4.1 percent per year, in large part because of expected shortages in petroleum and natural gas.[2]

Figure 10-1 is a compilation of statistics from various sources for nineteen virgin nonrenewable resources. Column 2 gives the currently known global reserves for each resource, and column 4 gives the Bureau of Mines' projections of growth in world demand. Columns 3, 5, and 6 exhibit various derived reserve life indices. A reserve life index is a measure of the long-term availability implied by the known reserve stock and the consumption rate of each resource. It gives the number of years the reserves of a material would last according to a variety of assumptions regarding usage rate. The static reserve life index SRLI, column 3 of Figure 10-1, is the number of years the current supply would last, assuming no change in the current usage. If, for example, the annual usage of aluminum remained constant at its 1970 value, the known global reserves of aluminum would last 100 years.

The use of virgin resources, however, is currently expected to grow exponentially. The exponential reserve life index ERLI, column 5 of Figure 10-1, assumes that the rate of growth in usage is the average Bureau of Mines projection from column 4. Thus, if we assume that the usage rate of aluminum will grow at 6.4 percent per year, known reserves can be expected to last only 31 years instead of 100 years.

Figure 10-2 is a more complex graph relating the static index, which is linearly proportional to absolute reserves, to the exponential index. When annual demand is constant, the static and the exponential indices are equal. When demand is

---

[1] H. Lansberg, et al., *Resources in America's Future* (Baltimore: Johns Hopkins Press, 1963), and U.S. Bureau of Mines, *Mineral Facts and Problems, 1970,* U.S. Department of the Interior, Bureau of Mines, Bulletin 650 (Washington, D.C., 1970).

[2] U.S. Bureau of Mines, *Mineral Facts and Problems, 1970,* pp. 51-52.

1	2	3	4			5	6
Resource	Known Reserves[a]	Static Index (years)[b]	Projected Rate of Growth (% per year)[c]			Exponential Index (years)[d]	Exponential Index Calculated Using 5 x Known Reserves (years)[e]
			HIGH	AV.	LOW		
Aluminum	1.17×10^9 tons[j]	100	7.7	6.4	5.1	31	55
Chromium	7.75×10^8 tons	420	3.3	2.6	2.0	95	154
Coal	5×10^{12} tons	2,300	5.3	4.1	3.0^k	111	150
Cobalt	4.8×10^9 lbs	110	2.0	1.5	1.0	60	148
Copper	308×10^6 tons	36	5.8	4.6	3.4	21	48
Gold	353×10^6 troy oz	11	4.8	4.1	3.4^1	9	29
Iron	1×10^{11} tons	240	2.3	1.8	1.3	93	173
Lead	91×10^6 tons	26	2.4	2.0	1.7	21	64
Manganese	8×10^8 tons	97	3.5	2.9	2.4	46	94
Mercury	3.34×10^6 flasks	13	3.1	2.6	2.2	12	41
Molybdenum	10.8×10^9 lbs	79	5.0	4.5	4.0	34	65
Natural gas	1.14×10^{15} cu ft	38	5.5	4.7	3.9	22	49

Figure 10-1   Nonrenewable natural resources

7 Countries with Highest Reserves (% of world total)[f]		8 Prime Producers (% of world total)[g]		9 Prime Consumers (% of world total)[h]		10 US Consumption as % of World Total[i]
Australia	(33)	Jamaica	(19)	USA	(42)	42
Guinea	(20)	Surinam	(12)	USSR	(12)	
Jamaica	(10)					
Rep. of S. Africa	(75)	USSR	(30)			19
		Turkey	(10)			
USA	(32)	USSR	(20)			44
USSR-China	(53)	USA	(13)			
Rep. of Congo	(31)	Rep. of				32
Zambia	(16)	Congo	(51)			
USA	(28)	USA	(20)	USA	(33)	33
Chile	(19)	USSR	(15)	USSR	(13)	
		Zambia	(13)	Japan	(11)	
Rep. of S. Africa	(40)	Rep. of				26
		S. Africa	(77)			
		Canada	(6)			
USSR	(33)	USSR	(25)	USA	(28)	28
S. Am.	(18)	USA	(14)	USSR	(24)	
Canada	(14)			W. Germany	(7)	
USA	(39)	USSR	(13)	USA	(25)	25
		Australia	(13)	USSR	(13)	
		Canada	(11)	W. Germany	(11)	
Rep. of S. Africa	(38)	USSR	(34)			14
USSR	(25)	Brazil	(13)			
		Rep. of				
		S. Africa	(13)			
Spain	(30)	Spain	(22)			24
Italy	(21)	Italy	(21)			
		USSR	(18)			
USA	(58)	USA	(64)			40
USSR	(20)	Canada	(14)			
USA	(25)	USA	(58)			63
USSR	(13)	USSR	(18)			

1 Resource	2 Known Reserves[a]	3 Static Index (years)[b]	4 Projected Rate of Growth (% per year)[c] HIGH AV. LOW	5 Exponential Index (years)[d]	6 Exponential Index Calcu- lated Using 5 x Known Reserves (years)[e]
Nickel	147×10^9 lbs	150	4.0 3.4 2.8	53	96
Petroleum	455×10^9 bbls	31	4.9 3.9 2.9	20	50
Platinum group[m]	429×10^6 troy oz	130	4.5 3.8 3.1	47	85
Silver	5.5×10^9 troy oz	16	4.0 2.7 1.5	13	42
Tin	4.3×10^6 long tons	17	2.3 1.1 0	15	61
Tungsten	2.9×10^9 lbs.	40	2.9 2.5 2.1	28	72
Zinc	123×10^6 tons	23	3.3 2.9 2.5	18	50

[a]Source: U.S. Bureau of Mines, *Mineral Facts and Problems, 1970,* U.S. Department of the Interior, Bureau of Mines, Bulletin 650 (Washington, D.C., 1970).

[b]The number of years known global reserves will last at current global consumption. Calculated by dividing known reserves (col. 1) by the current annual consumption (from U.S. Bureau of Mines, *Mineral Facts and Problems, 1970*).

[c]Source: U.S. Bureau of Mines, *Mineral Facts and Problems, 1970.*

[d]The number of years known global reserves will last with consumption growing exponentially at the average annual rate of growth. Calculated by the formula

$$\text{exponential index} = \frac{\ln\left((r \cdot s) + 1\right)}{r}$$

where r = average rate of growth from col. 4
s = static index from col. 3

[e]The number of years that five times known global reserves will last with consumption growing exponentially at the average annual rate of growth. Calculated from the above formula with 5s in place of s.

Figure 10-1 *continued*

7 Countries with Highest Reserves (% of world total)[f]		8 Prime Producers (% of world total)[g]		9 Prime Consumers (% of world total)[h]		10 US Consumption as % of World Total[i]
Cuba	(25)	Canada	(42)			38
New Caledonia	(22)	New Cale-				
USSR	(14)	donia	(28)			
Canada	(14)	USSR	(16)			
Saudi Arabia	(17)	USA	(23)	USA	(33)	33
Kuwait	(15)	USSR	(16)	USSR	(12)	
				Japan	(6)	
Rep. of S. Africa	(47)	USSR	(59)			31
USSR	(47)					
Communist		Canada	(20)	USA	(26)	26
countries	(36)	Mexico	(17)	W.Germany	(11)	
USA	(24)	Peru	(16)			
Thailand	(33)	Malaysia	(41)	USA	(24)	24
Malaysia	(14)	Bolivia	(16)	Japan	(14)	
		Thailand	(13)			
China	(73)	China	(25)			22
		USSR	(19)			
		USA	(14)			
USA	(27)	Canada	(23)	USA	(26)	26
Canada	(20)	USSR	(11)	Japan	(13)	
		USA	(8)	USSR	(11)	

[f]Source: U.S. Bureau of Mines, *Mineral Facts and Problems, 1970.*

[g]U.N. Department of Economic and Social Affairs, *Statistical Yearbook, 1969* (New York, 1970).

[h]Sources: *Yearbook of the American Bureau of Metal Statistics 1970* (York, Pa.: Maple Press, 1970); *World Petroleum Report* (New York: Mona Palmer Publishing, 1968); U.N. Economic Commission for Europe, *The World Market for Iron Ore* (New York, 1968); and U.S. Bureau of Mines, *Mineral Facts and Problems, 1970.*

[i]Source: U.S. Bureau of Mines, *Mineral Facts and Problems, 1970.*

[j]Bauxite expressed in aluminum equivalent.

[k]U.S. Bureau of Mines contingency forecasts, based on assumptions that coal will be used to synthesize gas and liquid fuels.

[l]Includes U.S. Bureau of Mines estimates of gold demand for hoarding.

[m]The platinum group metals are platinum, palladium, iridium, osmium, rhodium, and ruthenium.

Additional sources: P. T. Flawn, *Mineral Resources* (Skokie, Ill.: Rand McNally, 1966); American Metal Market Company, *Metal Statistics* (Somerset, N.J., 1970); and U.S. Bureau of Mines, *Commodity Data Summary* (Washington, D.C.: Government Printing Office, 1971).

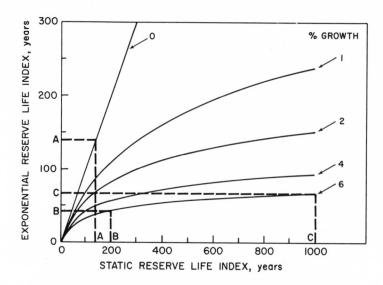

Figure 10-2   Exponential versus static reserve life indices for various
yearly growth rates in nonrenewable resource demand

increasing exponentially, ERLI is less than SRLI. The magnitude of the difference
depends on the rate of growth in demand. The curves in Figure 10-2 indicate the
relationship when the rate of growth is 0, 1, 2, 4, and 6 percent per year. Three
examples will illustrate the relationship. If demand remains constant, that is the
growth rate is zero percent per year, the values of the static and exponential
indices are the same. Line A in Figure 10-2 indicates the case in which both
indices equal 140 years. If demand increases at 6 percent per year until all reserves
are exhausted, resources will last a much shorter time than indicated by the static
index. Line B presents an example in which the static index equals 200 years
while the exponential index for the material, with usage increasing 6 percent per
year, is only 42 years. Suppose technological advance and new discoveries made
available effectively five times as much material as assumed in case B. Then the
static index would increase to 1,000 years. At a steady 6 percent annual growth in
demand, however, the resource would still be depleted in only 70 years, line C.

Of course, no resource is ever fully depleted. As reserves decline, price inevitably rises and forces consumption slowly to zero. However, adding this refinement
to the analysis means that consumption will begin to decline even earlier than
indicated in the simplified illustrations.

The absolute resource supply is only one part of total resource availability.
Equally important is the geographic distribution of those supplies. Columns 7, 8,
9, and 10 of Figure 10-1 point to the discrepancies between the location of
resource reserves and the places where those reserves are consumed. For example,
the countries with the highest known aluminum reserves are Australia, Guinea,
and Jamaica, among them totaling 63 percent of the 1.17×10^9 tons of known
reserves. The countries currently producing the largest fractions of the world's

refined aluminum are Jamaica (19 percent) and Surinam (12 percent). Yet the United States and the USSR are the prime consumers of that refined aluminum. Clearly, long-term resource availability in the United States will depend on the stability of international trade arrangements that govern resource flows, a stability that may be threatened by increasing resource demand in both producer and consumer countries.

The resource data summarized in Figure 10-1 raise several issues that remain unanswered by direct reserve and usage measurements. How can changes in resource availability be predicted and managed? More precisely:

1. Can knowledge about past discoveries be used to project future discoveries that will add to the resource base?
2. How will changing industrialization, population growth, import restrictions, and other determinants of resource usage affect long-term sufficiency?
3. How can the effects of variations in grades, depth of deposit, and geographic location be evaluated?
4. How will new technological developments in extraction, transportation, processing, substitution, and recycling influence overall resource scarcity or abundance?

Better answers to each of these questions are necessary for improved assessment of long-term resource availability. The answers will require not only improved reserve estimates but also a more complete understanding of the role played by resources in the complete socioeconomic system.

Conceptual Assessment

One significant step in understanding the concepts underlying resource usage appeared in 1963 with the publication of *Scarcity and Growth* by H. J. Barnett and C. F. Morse.[3] In an attempt to assess the degree of resource scarcity in the United States, Barnett and Morse examined several classical scarcity models, including those by Malthus, Ricardo, and Mills. Barnett and Morse argued that if any of those models are applicable to resources in the United States, then the economy should be exhibiting decreasing returns to scale in the extractive industries. Their analysis of data over the past one hundred years, however, showed increasing or at least constant returns. From this analysis they concluded that the progress of technological advance in a growing economy has negated the applicability of scarcity models.

While *Scarcity and Growth* was conceptually a step in the right direction, there ⁓ limitations in the analysis presented. For example, it is true that there is no apparent resource scarcity so long as technological and capital improvements sufficiently counteract the forces that tend to raise costs as resource grade declines and new substitutes need to be developed. These improvements have indeed been made in the United States throughout its industrial history. *Yet the absence*

---

[3] H. J. Barnett and C. F. Morse, *Scarcity and Growth* (Baltimore: Johns Hopkins Press, 1963).

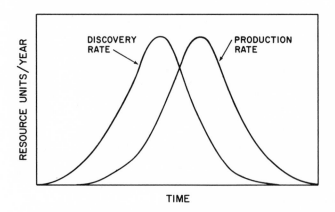

Figure 10-3 Life cycle of a nonrenewable resource

of resource scarcity in the past does not conclusively prove there will be an abundance of inexpensive resources in the future. The issues raised by *Scarcity and Growth* are so critical to a long-term assessment of resource policies that we shall return to them in the next section of this paper.

A second publication that contained significant conceptual analysis of the role of resources in an economy was published in 1969 by the National Research Council of the National Academy of Sciences. Entitled *Resources and Man,* this volume drew on recognized resource experts to assess man's relations with his resources.[4] Of particular interest are the chapters "Mineral Resources from the Land," by Thomas S. Lovering, and "Energy Resources," by M. King Hubbert. The authors describe the role of resource reserves, technological advance, and substitution in determining resource availability. They also discuss the possibility of an economy which is stable in the future so that resource consumption is no longer growing, but is constant through time. Lovering directly refutes the findings of *Scarcity and Growth* with his own analysis of domestic copper.[5]

In his chapter on "Energy Resources," M. King Hubbert develops a preliminary yet useful model of resource supply. Noting in the case of fossil fuels (and minerals as well) that the initial supply in the ground is finite, Hubbert postulates that the behavior of the production and discovery rates through time will be as shown in Figure 10-3. The total area under each curve is equal to the total initial reserves in the geographic area of interest. This concept of resource availability, which takes into account some of the dynamic behavior of resource supplies, is an advance over both the static and the exponential reserve life index analyses discussed earlier.

Resources and Man and *Scarcity and Growth* represent the two conceptual approaches that have been developed in assessing resource availability. A large

---

[4] National Academy of Sciences, National Research Council, *Resources and Man: A Study and Recommendations by the Committee on Resources and Man* (San Francisco: W. H. Freeman and Company, 1970).

[5] Thomas S. Lovering, "Mineral Resources from the Land," in ibid., p. 125.

number of mineral economists feel that adequate resource supplies will be assured by improving technologies and flexible market operations. Another group feels that, because most resources will eventually be depleted, we should be designing policies now that will bring about a controlled adaptation to inevitable depletion. There is a great need to resolve the differences between these two groups by combining the best information available on technology, economics, and geology into a suitable analytic framework to understand better the long-term effects of current resource policies.

Technology and Scarcity

Depletion forces the utilization of increasingly diffuse (high entropy) raw materials in production processes. Although there are short-term effects of small, high-grade discoveries, the overall trend is toward utilizing lower-grade and more remote resources. In the United States the average grade of copper has been steadily declining (Figure 10-4), and the cost of discovering each additional cubic foot of natural gas is also rising steadily (Figure 10-5). Both trends are characteristic of most nonrenewable resources. There is little dispute that the trend toward declining quality in each virgin resource will continue. As that trend proceeds, the process of mineral extraction will:

1. employ more and more energy to concentrate and transport each material so that it is a useful input to the various production processes;
2. produce increasing quantities of mine wastes for each unit of raw material; and
3. increase the potential for monopoly control of the resources if depletion causes the remaining material sources to become more concentrated geographically.

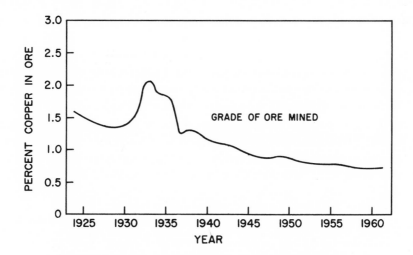

Figure 10-4 Average grade of copper ore mined in the United States
After: Thomas S. Lovering, Resources and Man; *op. cit.*

Counteracting these trends that portend higher costs is the process of technological advance, which:

1. makes it less expensive to apply more energy to the extraction and concentration of a material;
2. decreases the potential environmental impact of a given amount of mine waste;
3. shifts the composition of demand so that more reliance is placed on new and relatively more abundant materials;
4. decreases the amount of material required to provide a given level of services; and
5. decreases the number of functions dependent on one specific material.

Barnett and Morse in their analysis indicate that new discoveries and technological advances have at least counterbalanced the costs engendered by the increasing depletion of the global resource base. It should be noted, however, that the period they analyzed was one in which much land was still unsurveyed, energy costs were low and even declining in some areas, and little cost was imputed to environmental degradation. Many of the cost decreases they noted doubtless came from the substitution of mechanical energy for relatively expensive manual labor inputs. Now the scope for new discoveries, while still large, is less; energy costs are likely to increase substantially; resource users must bear the cost of the associated environmental damage; and mechanization is in most areas essentially complete.[6] The claim that past price trends will continue has no objective basis. It is based only on faith in the power of technology to overcome ever-increasing obstacles and on an unwarranted extrapolation of historical trends.

A related claim is that the economic system will function to allocate resources efficiently even with great increases in price: "As resources become scarce their price goes up and people are motivated to find substitutes or do without."[7] While this statement may be true, it says nothing about the average level of satisfaction afforded by the resources that may be available for allocation in the future. At the limit, the final pound of copper will provide little comfort to society even if the short-term price system does function to allocate it optimally among competing needs. Whether or not adequate substitutes will be available in sufficient quantity to perform the role of a depleted resource is again a matter of faith.

The alternate claim that resource costs will soar in the near future also has no objective basis. The interaction of the geological, technological, and social determinants of resource availability is simply not sufficiently understood to make a well-founded long-term forecast. Case studies of materials like natural gas and

---

[6] Ayres and Kneese provide a list of five reasons to suspect that the price trends revealed by Barnett and Morse may not continue. In addition to those mentioned here, they note that economies of scale, prevalent in the past, may become diminishing returns in the future. See Robert U. Ayres and Allen V. Kneese, "Economic and Ecological Effects of a Stationary Economy," Resources for the Future Reprint no. 99 (December, 1971).

[7] *Wall Street Journal,* March 17, 1972.

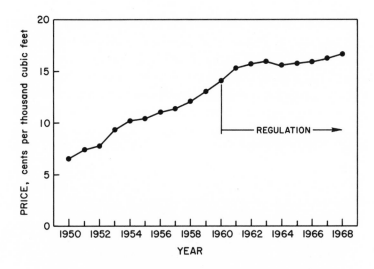

Figure 10-5 Average wellhead price of natural gas in the United
States
Source: American Gas Association, Gas Facts, 1969
(New York, 1969), p. 32.

mercury, which are reaching the end of their depletion life cycles would be very
helpful. The price of mercury has doubled over the past decade.[8] Did this increase
result from the failure of technological advance or from increasing monopolistic
profits taken by the producers? The answer would be an important input to
projections of future prices in other materials nearing depletion.

Four Concerns in Developing a Long-Term Perspective

Complexity of Resource Interactions.   Resource consumption, and thus future
resource availability, is determined by a complex of interactions involving geologic, economic, and sociopolitical relationships. In the real world the resource
usage rate, for example, is dependent on a price that reflects in large part the cost
of obtaining the resource. This cost is currently determined by the technologies of
extraction, by the cost of transportation, by the grade of the resource, and by
public policies to effect tax incentives or to regulate by adjusting prices or stock-
piles. Many of these influences arise from short-term pressures internal to the
resource system. The development of a new extraction technology, for example,
is often a direct response to the pressure to maintain a price competitive with
substitutes. The grade of reserves is a direct function of the deposits currently
being utilized, which is in turn dependent on the deposits exploited in the past.
Current public policies are more often than not a response to shortages or to
pricing activity in the past.

[8] U.S. Bureau of Mines, *Mineral Yearbook, 1967* (Washington, D.C.: Government Printing Office, 1968),
p. 724, and idem, *Commodity Data Summary*, January 1971, p. 90.

Geographic Location.   Availability depends not only on the total supply but on the geographic location of resources. Resource analysts must become increasingly concerned with policies on the national and local level, where trade-offs between local and foreign supplies must be made. Resources have often had the characteristics of common property, modified by location within political boundaries. Resource problems in the future may increasingly be characterized by considerations of political sovereignty over supplies.

Three basic modes of potential resource competition are possible. Conflict may arise between

1. an industrialized, resource-importing nation and a less industrialized resource-exporting nation over price and ownership (for example, the United States and Chile);
2. two industrialized resource-importing nations over control of a resource located in a third country (for example, the United States and Japan); and
3. an industrialized, resource-sufficient nation and an industrialized resource-importing nation over control of a third country's resources or of trade routes vital to the resource-importing nation (for example the United States and the USSR).

Each of these conflict patterns could play a significant role in the availability of resources to a specific country. It is particularly important to understand this aspect of availability, for, unlike the gradual depletion of reserves, it introduces the possibility of a decrease in supplies sudden enough to disrupt an economy seriously.

The Time Horizon for Analysis.   The effectiveness of resource policy design can be greatly improved by an explicit statement of the time horizon for analysis. This statement will, to a large degree, determine the proper relative emphasis on different relationships. If the formulation of policies over a five-year time horizon is the goal, radical changes in technology would not be a concern, as technology will probably remain relatively constant over five years. If, however, a time horizon of fifty years is the concern, then technology becomes extremely important. It is clear that most current resource policies are based on a relatively short (less than twenty years) time horizon.

The planning time horizon might more appropriately be fifty years. The implicit and explicit policies governing resource use today have a significant impact on the resource position fifty years from now. These long-term prospects should thus have some influence on resource policy designs over the intervening years.

Causal and Correlative Relationships.   In long-term policy assessment one must be concerned with the factors that actually *cause* resource consumption, not merely correlate with it. For short-term prediction, over periods of time in which major influencing factors do not change, correlative relationships are useful for analysis. But, to design policies for the long term, one must have a fundamental understanding of the causal relationships in the system. This emphasis on causality implies a highly sophisticated use of statistics in the design of an analytic framework, placing the burden on strong, causative theories that can be substantiated or disproved by the use of statistical inference techniques on real-world data.

The four concepts discussed here, though clearly not an exhaustive list, should provide a rough sketch of the characteristics that must underlie a long-term analytic framework. Resources must be viewed in their totality as part of a complex system. Analysts must understand their own and society's planning time horizon. They must look for causal relationships. Finally, the geographic distribution of resources with respect to political boundaries must be recognized as central to the long-term assessment of any one country's resource policies.

Models of Resource Availability

Each of the three resource studies included in Part Two of this collection is a preliminary attempt to explore the influence of various factors on resource availability.[9] While the preliminary models presented raise a large number of issues which will only be clarified by more extensive efforts to understand long-term resource relationships, the knowledge afforded by these simple studies is nonetheless significant even at this stage. They greatly extend the meaning of the reserve life indices given in Figure 10-1, and they suggest several general conclusions that appear to be relevant to most nonrenewable resources:

1. The length of the period of abundant resource supply is more sensitive to changes in the growth of demand than to changes in supply through new discoveries. Postponing the onset of substantial price increases can thus be achieved more effectively through efforts to reduce the growth of demand than through efforts to increase reserves by exploration.

2. The short-term policy of price regulation, as it has been practiced in the natural gas market, has the dual effect of stimulating current usage through lower than free market prices and of restricting current discoveries through reduced return on investment to the industry. These two impacts are effectively at cross-purposes in the long run. Requisite in this area of policy design is some more explicit statement of both long- and short-run policy goals, with an understanding of the trade-offs that must be made between the two.

3. The advancement of extraction and processing technologies can delay the time when costs rise due to total resource shortage, yet accentuate that cost increase when it does come. The net effect may be to reduce the total time of resource availability.

4. The response of substitution technologies and techniques to rising material costs cannot indefinitely avert declines in the supply of a given material. Constant, low resource prices discourage efforts to devise substitutes and serve

---

[9]Chapters 6, 7, and 8.

only to accentuate difficulties, especially if several resources are nearing depletion simultaneously.

5. Resource recycling is a potentially effective method to counteract resource depletion. However, in addition to new technologies, recycling will require significant social, economic, and institutional changes that can only be partially implemented at present.

6. Problems of distribution may cause difficulty before physical depletion limits supply. Of great importance is the fact that political problems have a potential for discontinuity. Physical depletion is a continuous process taking place over a comparatively long time, giving at least some signals, through rising price, of impending shortage. Politically related interruptions may not provide that warning.

7. Every society must make a choice, either explicitly or implicitly, concerning the future role of nonrenewable resources in its and the world's economy. If the goal is only to satisfy current needs at low cost, resource depletion promises to become a problem of major proportions within thirty to fifty years. If, however, resource costs are allowed to rise relative to current costs, serving as a regulating mechanism to induce substitutes, recycling, and more judicious use of materials, relatively greater supplies of resources will be available for a longer period into the future.

11
Adding the Time Dimension to Environmental Policy

Dennis L. Meadows

A basic dilemma confronting society as it attempts to address environmental problems is that political institutions and other social organizations are specifically adapted to develop and implement solutions to short-term problems only. However, many basic environmental problems must be foreseen far in advance and approached in a consistent fashion over a period of fifty years or more if they are to be solved. It is important to obtain additional data on the causes and consequences of environmental deterioration, but it is also necessary to impart longer time horizons to the institutions involved in environmental policy formulation.

To address this issue Dennis Meadows prepared a paper for inclusion in a special issue of International Organization* *for distribution at the 1972 United Nations Stockholm Conference on the Human Environment. The version included here has been substantially shortened by excluding the original version's summary of the DDT and solid waste studies (Papers 3 and 7). In this paper are listed those aspects of present social and political systems that lead to short-term perspectives in the development of current policy. The paper concludes with a summary of some attributes that should characterize any policy that may be developed to combat the long-term deterioration of the environment.*

This chapter has also appeared in World Eco-Crisis *by David A. Kay and Eugene Skolnikoff (Madison, Wis.: University of Wisconsin Press, 1972) pp. 47-66.*

*David A. Kay and E. B. Skolnikoff, eds., *International Organization*, Spring 1972.

11
Adding the Time Dimension
to Environmental Policy

Introduction

The vast majority of the institutional and individual decisions made in the world are responses to problems in which cause and effect are closely related in time and in space. When such a problem becomes apparent, its source is usually obvious, and an appropriate solution can be found and implemented in time to eliminate the difficulty. For this class of problems it is satisfactory to react after the trouble is widely perceived by all members of the society. Thus the institutions involved need only monitor the current status of the system; they need not look into the future to anticipate problems that are just beginning to evolve. It is important to realize that many environmental problems do not fit into this category. The long delays associated with environmental processes require that institutions designed to deal with them must add an explicit consideration of the time dimension in formulating environmental policy.

Dynamic Characteristics of Environmental Systems

Four attributes of environmental systems introduce significant time delays into the process of environmental management. First, the fundamental source of deterioration is the complex socioeconomic system causing population and economic growth in a finite world. This system has tremendous inertia, and its action tends to undermine simple pollution abatement measures.[1] Second, the physical, chemical, and biological processes governing pollutant flows through the environment introduce significant time lags between the generation of a material and its appearance in some distant part of the ecosystem. Third, the time elapsing between exposure to a pollutant and the first appearance of adverse symptoms in man or other species may often approximate the lifetime of the affected individual. Fourth, the response to environmental pollution generally involves not only new technology but also changes in social values and institutions. Although technology may adapt quickly, the social structure typically does not. Thus environmental pollution is not a momentary problem with an instantaneous solution.

Many characteristics of public and private institutions impart to them a planning horizon far shorter than that required to deal effectively with environmental pollution. Industrial organizations severely discount the future costs and benefits of current actions, assigning little importance to implications more than ten years in the future. Decision makers, overloaded with work, tend to respond to those problems with the closest deadlines. Corporate and public decision makers, seeking rapid promotion or reelection, implement first the policies that promise the most immediate results. Finally, even in democratic elections no vote is given to most of those who will bear, for the next fifty years or more, the future costs of current actions.

---

[1] An excellent example is provided by the attempts to alleviate air pollution in the United States. Although new technologies have been developed and new laws have been enacted to reduce drastically the amount of pollution emitted by many sources, population and production are growing so rapidly that total air pollution continues to worsen. See Council on Environmental Quality *Environmental Quality: Second Annual Report* (Washington, D.C.: Government Printing Office), pp. 212-217.

It is not surprising that this mismatch exists between the time span of development of environmental problems and the time horizons of institutions designed to deal with those problems. Mankind has never had an effective way of understanding, much less controlling, complex processes whose outcomes are revealed decades after they have been set in motion. The future, beyond a few years from now, has been considered unknown and has therefore been left out of policy considerations. Human society has begun in this century to design institutions and laws to deal with problems that span several national boundaries, but it has not yet learned to deal effectively with problems that extend over several decades.

Tools for Environmental Management

Engineers wishing to change the behavior of mechanical or electrical systems have long recognized that they must first understand the time-variant characteristics of a process before they can design appropriate mechanisms to control it. For example, an effective heating and cooling system can be designed only after one has a clear understanding of the laws of thermodynamics, the range of temperatures to which the system is likely to be exposed, the delay between the detection of a temperature discrepancy and the activation of the heating or cooling mechanism, and the rate at which the mechanism can heat or cool the area.

Similarly, to design environmental controls, one must understand the time-variant, or dynamic, characteristics of those processes that generate pollution and control its passage through the physical and biological systems of the globe. If methods that explicitly consider the time dimension in the analysis of environmental problems are not developed and used, new organizations with the long-term planning horizons that are urgently needed cannot possibly be developed.

Does the necessary dynamic information on the time behavior of environmental systems exist for such long-term analysis? The information available today on environmental processes is typically incomplete and inaccurate. The tools necessary for the analysis of complex socioeconomic systems are still undergoing refinement. Nevertheless, it is necessary to use the tools available now to gain as much understanding as possible from the body of information that does exist, since environmental degradation is already taking place and since the policies that will determine future rates of degradation are currently being formulated.

The tools of systems analysis are sufficiently well developed to be useful in bringing together the pieces of information that do exist about environmental processes and to assess the dynamic implications of that information. The conclusions in this paper are based on four such information-ordering studies of environmental deterioration. These four studies—of DDT, mercury contamination, eutrophication, and solid waste flows—are part of a continuing program to understand the dynamics of environmental deterioration.[2] They provide information on environmental time delays and at the same time illustrate the use of

---

[2] See papers 3, 4, 5, and 7, respectively.

system dynamics as a general approach for analyzing the consequences of environmental control policies over time.

Although the studies do not offer detailed specifications for the new institutions that may be needed, they suggest several requirements that must be met by any successful policy to halt or reverse environmental deterioration. These requirements are summarized at the end of this paper.

The Use of System Dynamics in Environmental Policy Design

It is clear that numerous social, economic, political, and biological factors are all involved in the processes that govern man's impact on his natural surroundings. While one can perceive the individual elements of this complex system, the analysis of the total complex of their interactions over time is beyond the capabilities of man's unaided mind. Formal systems analysis tools are required to trace the long-term implications of all the factors involved in pollution and to evaluate alternative control programs.

System dynamics is a theory of system structure that permits an analyst to represent, graphically and mathematically, the interactions governing the long-term behavior of complex socioeconomic systems. As a simulation method, system dynamics is useful both in understanding the causes of present problems and in testing the effectiveness of alternative policies.

No systems analysis tool can provide new empirical data on individual components of the system. The amount of mercury released into the environment for each ton of oil burned, the precise magnitude of the various coefficients that determine the movement of polychlorinated biphenyls (PCBs) through the ecosystem, and the biological implications of various pesticide concentrations in plant or animal species are all examples of information that must be obtained through direct observation of the system. Systems analysis tools first become useful in integrating these diverse data to obtain a comprehensive picture of the system and then in understanding the probable response of the system to alternative policies. In many cases, there is already enough empirical information to formulate improved policies.

However, the information that is available about the determinants of environmental deterioration varies greatly in its comprehension and accuracy. The spectrum of information quality is shown diagramatically in Figure 11-1. Some environmental questions can be answered at present only by the intuitive judgment of experts. In other cases there exist fairly complete physical measurements made under carefully controlled conditions. Often many scattered measurements, gathered under a wide variety of conditions, can be used to infer the underlying relationships through formal statistical techniques.

The language employed by system dynamics to express system relationships can incorporate any level of information from this quality spectrum. Of course, the lower the quality of the inputs the less will be the reliance that can be placed on the results. However, the absence of uniformly good data need not deter any attempt at analysis. When new policies are needed, it is important to base them on

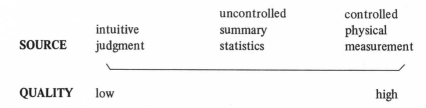

Figure 11-1   The quality spectrum of information

the best information available, even if that information is imperfect. Even intuitive judgments or summary statistics are better inputs to urgent decisions than no information at all.

Improved long-term policies can often be designed in the absence of precise data as long as the underlying structure of the environmental system is understood. It is the basic structure of causal relationships that determines a system's possible behavior modes, not the exact numerical values of its components. While individual coefficients will change over time, the underlying structure typically does not. Effective environmental policies are those that produce the desired behavior mode in the system. Thus policy design can proceed, on the basis of an understanding of system structure, to identify those policies that are robust under a variety of parameter values. Policies of the above nature have been explored in the four pollution studies in this collection.

Time Delays and Pollution Control

The DDT, solid waste, mercury, and eutrophication studies illustrate two common dynamic characteristics of environmental systems:

1. The costs of pollution must be borne for periods much longer than the period of benefit derived from the polluting activity;
2. There may be a delay of ten years or more between the implementation of a control policy and its first obvious benefits. If corrective action is postponed until the actual costs of pollution are unacceptable, there may no longer be an opportunity to avoid those costs for a sustained period.

The DDT study illustrates both of these aspects very clearly. Even when DDT usage is reduced from its 1971 level to zero by the year 2000, DDT levels in fish remain above 1971 levels beyond the year 1995. Two other system studies of DDT flows have found delays of approximately the same magnitude as those shown in this study.[3] DDT plays a useful role in the environment only when present on the surfaces of plants or buildings that may harbor insect pests. Its value is zero or negative at all other points in the environment. Since DDT evaporates quickly, effective pest control requires reapplication as often as every

---

[3] H. L. Harrison et al., "Systems Studies of DDT Transport," *Science,* vol. 170 (1970), p. 503; and G.M. Woodwell et al., "DDT in the Biosphere: Where Does It Go?", *Science,* vol. 174 (1971), p. 1101.

six months. In contrast, after it has evaporated from its original application site, DDT may be found for up to fifty years in the tissues of fish.

The two characteristics cited result from long delays in the processes that govern the transfer of materials through the environment. Delays of the magnitude found in the studies in Part Two are inherent in the transfer and impact of many long-lived materials causing environmental deterioration.

What are the implications of these two dynamic characteristics for the institutions that might be formed to control the deterioration of the natural environment? They mean very simply that long-term improvements in the environment will seldom result from a comparison of short-term costs and short-term benefits of polluting activity. The total costs of that activity may not be realized until long after the immediate benefits. Society must seek in its new environmental institutions a measure of foresight and resolve not often visible in current national and international institutions. At the very least, control decisions must be based on the anticipated consequences of current actions rather than on the perceived costs of past actions.

Basing control decisions on anticipation rather than reaction implies new technical capabilities and new institutional values. The technical implications are clear. Institutions must develop the capabilities to:

1. monitor pollution release rates at the source as well as absolute levels in the environment,
2. develop and employ models that can relate current pollutant release rates and alternative future abatement policies to the levels of environmental pollution these rates and policies will produce in the future, and
3. devise biological testing procedures and ecological experiments *well in advance* of commercial application to provide the factual basis for relating projected pollution levels to the future biological damage they may produce.

The need for better ecological models has been recognized, and useful work is under way to develop them. However, even very sophisticated forecasting capabilities will be of little use until political change is also achieved. In the introduction to this paper we briefly mentioned some attributes of current organizations that lead them to utilize a short planning time horizon. If environmental protection institutions are structured so that they are subject to the same short-term pressures as most current institutions, they cannot be expected to succeed in stopping environmental deterioration.

The long time delays observed in each pollution study force immediate consideration of a fundamental issue. What obligation is owed by the people who currently inhabit the globe to those who will live on it twenty or one hundred years from now? Over the past century the damage done to natural systems was rationalized by the belief that technological and economic progress more than compensated the next generation for the degraded environment and the diminished natural resource base left to them. Today many people question that belief. No formal modeling study can resolve this issue; it is a matter of ethics and the value system on which social organizations are based.

The recent concern over environmental deterioration is a necessary precedent to establishing effective international institutions of the sort sought in the 1972 Stockholm conference. However, intense interest is not alone sufficient. The total nature of the pollution problem must be realistically assessed, and the most effective forms for the organizations and programs that will deal with it must be determined. Implicit in many current environmental programs are the assumptions that pollution control requires only slight extensions in technical capabilities and minor shifts in the magnitude and area of capital investment. Probably neither assumption is correct for most pollutants. The inherent dynamics of ecological processes demand a planning horizon of fifty years or more. Institutions or international agreements based on short-term considerations are likely to fall far short of their goals.

12
The Carrying Capacity of Our Global Environment: A Look at the Ethical Alternatives

Jørgen Randers and Donella H. Meadows

Chapter 11, "Adding the Time Dimension to Environmental Policy," indicated that several aspects of current political and economic institutions lead them to overemphasize the short-term implications of long-term decisions. Western man's personal and social values evolved in the context of an apparently infinite world where attaining more of everything today was not inconsistent with having more tomorrow as well. Thus his ethical system is poorly suited for guiding him in a period when short-term gains often entail long-term sacrifices and vice versa. If a global material and population equilibrium is to be sought, it will be necessary to develop new ethical principles, a goal that will inevitably involve religious institutions. To explore that role with church leaders, the following paper was presented in Italy before a committee of the World Council of Churches.

A version of this chapter has appeared as "The Carrying Capacity of the Globe" in Sloan Management Review, *Vol. 15, No. 2, Winter 1972 (Cambridge, Mass.: Massachusetts Institute of Technology) pp. 11-27.*

12
The Carrying Capacity
of Our Global Environment:
A Look at the Ethical Alternatives

> *For which of you, intending to build a tower, sitteth not down first, and counteth the cost, whether he have sufficient to finish it?*
>
> Luke 14:28

The main thesis of this paper is very simple: because the human environment—the earth—is finite, the growth of human population and industrialization cannot continue indefinitely. This is a simple and obvious fact, but its consequences pose an unprecedented challenge to mankind. The challenge lies in finding an ethical basis for making the trade-offs that will confront human society in the near future, trade-offs that arise because in a limited world everything cannot be maximized for everyone.

The Environment Is Finite

It should be quite unnecessary to point out that the environment is finite. However, many popular beliefs about the world's future tend to be inconsistent with this fact. Thus it will be worthwhile to spend some time discussing a few examples of the physical limitations of the earth, especially because it is not generally recognized that human activities are already approaching several of the physical limitations that define the carrying capacity of the globe.

Agricultural Land.   The quantity that is most obviously in limited supply on the earth is arable land. There are about 3.2 billion hectares of land suitable for agriculture on the earth. Approximately half of that land is under cultivation today. The remaining half will require immense capital costs to settle, clear, irrigate, or fertilize before it can produce food. The costs will be so high that the U.N. Food and Agriculture Organization, which is seeking desperately to stimulate greater food production, has decided that to expand food output it must rely on more intensive use of currently cultivated land, not on new land development.

If, however, society does decide to incur the costs of cultivating all possible arable land and producing as much food as possible, how many people could be fed? The lower curve in Figure 12-1 shows the amount of land needed to feed the growing world population, assuming that the present world average of 0.4 hectares per person is sufficient. (If everyone were to be fed at U.S. standards, 0.9 hectares per person would be required.) The actual growth in population, and thus in land needed, from 1650 to 1970 is depicted with a heavy line; the projected growth of 2.1 percent per year after 1970 by a lighter line. The upper curve indicates the actual amount of arable land available. This line slopes downward because each additional person requires a certain amount of land (0.08 hectares assumed here) for housing, roads, waste disposal, power lines, and other uses that essentially "pave" land and make it unusable for farming.

The graph in Figure 12-1 illustrates that, even with the optimistic assumption that all possible land will be utilized, the world will still face a serious land shortage before the year 2000.

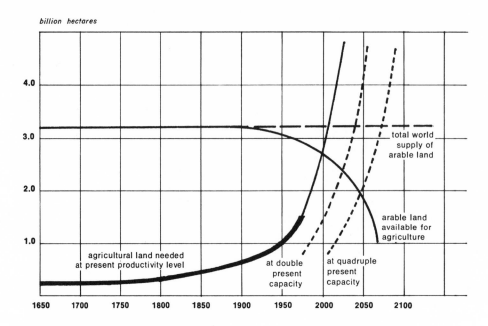

Figure 12-1 Available and needed land area
Figures 12-1,4,5, and 12 reprinted from Meadows et al., Limits to Growth *(New York: Universe Books, 1972).*

The graph also illustrates some important facts about exponential growth within a limited space. First, it shows how a situation of great abundance can change within a few years to one of great scarcity. The human race has had an overwhelming excess of arable land during all its history; now, within thirty years, or one population doubling time, it will be forced to deal with a sudden and serious shortage of land.

A second lesson to be learned from Figure 12-1 is that the exact numerical assumptions made about the limits of the earth are essentially unimportant in the face of the inexorable progress of exponential growth. For example, we might assume that no arable land is taken for cities, roads, or other nonagricultural uses. In that case, the land available is constant, as shown by the horizontal dashed line, and the point at which the two curves cross is delayed by only about ten years. Or we can suppose that the productivity of the land will double, or even quadruple, through advances in agricultural technology. The effect of increasing productivity is shown by the dotted lines in Figure 12-1. Each doubling of productivity postpones the land shortage by just one population doubling time, or about thirty years.

Some people look to the sea to provide the extra food that will be needed as the world's population grows. But the total world fish catch in 1969 represented only a small percentage of the world's caloric requirements, and the total catch in 1970 decreased from 1969. That was the first decrease since World War II, and it occurred in spite of increasing investment and technological developments in the fishing industry. It is conceivable that the world's fish banks have been over-exploited and that prospects are for further decline, not advances, in output from the sea. The seas thus cannot eliminate the constraints imposed on growth by limited land.

Heat Release. Further constraints will have to be faced in connection with natural resources such as fresh water, metals, and fuels. Indications are that several of these resources will be in short supply, even at higher prices, within the next forty years if present growth continues. However, it is argued that mining low-grade ores and desalting the sea's water can alleviate these problems, assuming that the enormous demands for energy required for these operations can be met.

A consideration of the energy that will be necessary to meet man's growing needs leads us to a more subtle and much more fundamental limitation to physical growth on this planet. Even if we assume that the means are found to generate the energy needed—for instance, through controlled fusion—there remains the fundamental thermodynamic fact that virtually all energy generated finally ends up as heat. An everyday example is the energy originally stored in the gasoline in a car. A significant part of this energy is immediately released as heat as it warms the engine and the radiator, because the engine is necessarily inefficient in converting the energy in the gasoline to useful motion of the wheels. But even the useful part of the energy finally is transferred to heat in the tires, the road, the brakes, and ultimately the surrounding air. On a larger scale enormous quantities of heat are released from the condensation of distilled water in a desalination plant.

The final fate of the energy expended by man's activities should not be confused with what is commonly called thermal pollution, namely, the waste heat produced locally at power plants in the generation of electric energy. This localized waste heat is due to inevitable inefficiencies in the generating process. The consequent thermal pollution heats the environment, but the point here is that even the useful energy output from the power plant finally ends up as heat. This is so regardless of whether the energy was generated by burning coal or oil or by nuclear reactions—and regardless of what the energy is being used for. It is theoretically impossible to avoid heat release if energy is consumed. No technical gadgetry or scientific breakthrough will circumvent it.

The heat released from all of mankind's energy-using activities will begin to have worldwide climatic effects when the released amount reaches some appreciable fraction of the energy normally absorbed from the sun. Experts disagree on exactly what the fraction is. They do agree, however, that if major unpredictable changes in the climate are to be avoided there is a fundamental limit to the amount of energy that can be consumed on earth.

If worldwide consumption of energy increases at 4 percent per year for another 130 years, at that time the heat released will amount to 1 percent of the incoming solar radiation—enough to increase the temperature of the atmosphere by an estimated $3/4°C$. That may sound like an unimpressive figure, but on a worldwide basis it may amount to climatic upheavals such as increased melting of the polar ice caps. Local weather perturbations may come much sooner. It is estimated that in just thirty years the heat released through energy consumption in the Los Angeles basin will be 18 percent of the normal incident solar energy of that area.

Pollution Absorption.   A third limitation to population and industrial growth is the globe's finite absorptive capacity for pollution. Until quite recently the environment was considered essentially infinite. It seemed impossible that the use of soap for laundry or pesticides for roses could affect the workings of the world ecosystem. But after the massive eutrophication of Lake Erie, the global increase in atmospheric carbon dioxide, and the prohibition of swordfish in the United States because of mercury content, it is becoming abundantly clear that the environment is able to absorb and degrade only a limited amount of emissions and waste every year. Exceeding this absorptive capacity not only causes pollutants to accumulate in nature but also may tend to destroy the natural degradation processes themselves, thus decreasing the future absorptive capacity. This general principle can be described in more practical terms. The discharge of a small amount of waste into a pond will lower the water quality only slightly, because the pond's microorganisms manage to degrade the pollution as it occurs. A higher, constant discharge rate will result in a lower but constant water quality. The absorptive capacity of the pond is exceeded, however, if the discharge rate increases to the point where the absorbing microorganisms die because of oxygen depletion or the accumulation of toxic wastes. When that happens, continued constant discharge to the pond will simply build up, continuously lowering the quality of the water.

Thus we realize that absorptive capacity—far from being a resource in unlimited supply—is an extremely valuable, scarce resource, which in fact limits the total possible emissions from human activity.

The Present Global Trend: Growth

Growth in a Finite World.   Having established the existence of the purely physical limitations of the earth (and we have described here only a few of the many biological, physical, and social limits that exist), we now ask whether mankind's present behavior takes into account the existence of these limitations.

On a global scale the world is experiencing an exponential growth in population and in productive capital—buildings, roads, trucks, power plants, machinery, ships, and so on. Some inevitable consequences of this growth are the exponentially increasing demands for food and energy and the exponentially increasing emissions of pollution to the environment.

Since there are upper limits both to the supply of food and energy and to the amount of pollution that can be absorbed by the environment, it seems obvious that the present exponential material growth cannot continue indefinitely. More important, it seems that several of the natural constraints to growth will be surpassed within the next few generations.

Do mechanisms exist in the world system as it is currently organized that will bring about a smooth shift from present growth trends to some other kind of acceptable behavior consistent with the world's finite capabilities? Or will the transition be relatively sudden and stressful?

These are the questions our group set out to answer when we embarked on an effort to make a mathematical simulation model of population and capital growth in the world system.

The World Model.   Our model is a set of assumptions relating world population, industry, pollution, agriculture, and nonrenewable resources. The model explicitly represents the growth of population and industry as a function of many biological, political, economic, physical, and social factors. It also recognizes that population growth and industrial growth in turn feed back to alter each of those biological, political, economic, physical, and social factors.

The exponential growth of population and capital is inextricably linked with all global problems—unemployment, starvation, disease, pollution, the threat of warfare, and resource shortages. No attempt to understand the long-term options of human society can succeed unless it is firmly based on an understanding of the complicated relationships connecting these two growing forces and the ultimate limits to their growth.

Figure 12-2 illustrates the two basic circular relationships that result in the exponential growth observed in the world today. Population and births constitute a positive feedback loop. If there are more people, there will be more births each year, and more births result in more people. In any system containing a dominant positive feedback loop of this form, exponential growth will be possible. Capital and investment constitute another positive feedback loop. Capital produces an output of goods and services. Greater output, all else being equal, results in a larger investment and thus in more capital.

The many interactions between population and capital determine the rate at which each grows. The interaction takes many forms (Figure 12-3). As a greater fraction of output is diverted from investment to other needs of society, the growth rate of capital decreases. Output may be diverted to consumption, to

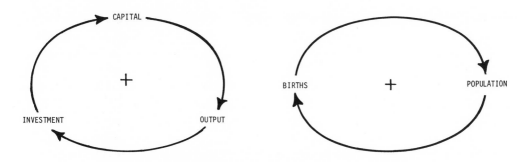

Figure 12-2 The positive feedback loops governing the growth in
population and capital

services, or to agricultural capital such as fertilizer, tractors, or irrigation ditches. As services increase, health and education improve, average life expectancy rises, deaths decrease, and population grows faster. Similarly, output diverted into agricultural capital results ultimately in more food and a higher average life expectancy. The primary determinant of the fraction of output reinvested is the output per capita. If production per capita is low, most of the output must be diverted to consumption, services, and food, just to produce the basic subsistence needs of the population. Those allocations reduce the rate of accumulation of the capital base and, at the same time, stimulate the growth of population. Population can increase much more easily than capital in traditional societies. Hence output per capita remains low in these areas, and they find it very difficult to achieve economic growth.

Industrial output also leads to the depletion of nonrenewable resources. As the stock of nonrenewable resources declines, lower-grade ores must be mined, and raw materials must be transported longer distances. Since more capital must be allocated to obtaining resources, the overall production efficiency of capital decreases, and the capital-output ratio goes up.

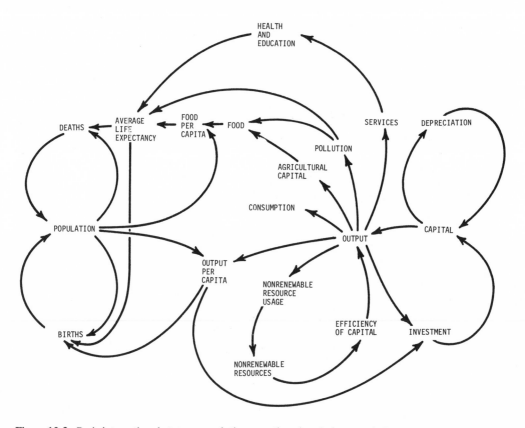

Figure 12-3 Basic interactions between population growth and capital accumulation
Visual materials for Figures 12-3,6,7,8,9,10 and 11 provided by Peter N. Hartberg, Vermont Educational Television Network.

Output per capita is the single force acting in this system to slow the population explosion by reducing the birth rate. As output per capita increases, the desired family size declines and birth control efficiency increases. The birth rate goes down (see Figure 12-4) and the population growth rate typically decreases. The influence of this relationship, which is often called the demographic transition, is accelerated somewhat by the fact that as the death rate declines there is a further decrease in desired family size. A large portion of the world's parents need children as their only possible source of support in their old age. If the mortality rate is high, parents must bear three or four sons to ensure that one will live. Thus, as the perceived death rate decreases, birth rates also decline, since there is a higher probability that children will survive.

Economic output has one additional impact. It leads to the generation of pollution, which can result from industrial or agricultural activities. Pollution may decrease food production and also decrease the average life expectancy.

Most global problems have important roots in this simple set of interactions. There are four advantages in collecting such assumptions about the world into a formal model such as that shown in Figure 12-5, which is an expansion of the simpler model of Figure 12-3. First, listing the assumed interrelations explicitly

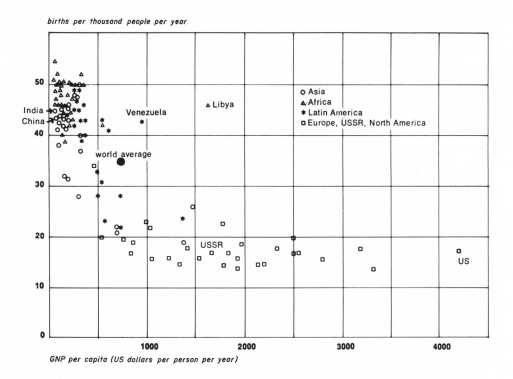

Figure 12-4 The relationship between birth rate and GNP per capita
Source: *U.S. Agency for International Development, Bureau for Technical Assistance, Office of Population,* Population Program Assistance *(Washington, D.C.: Government Printing Office, 1970).*

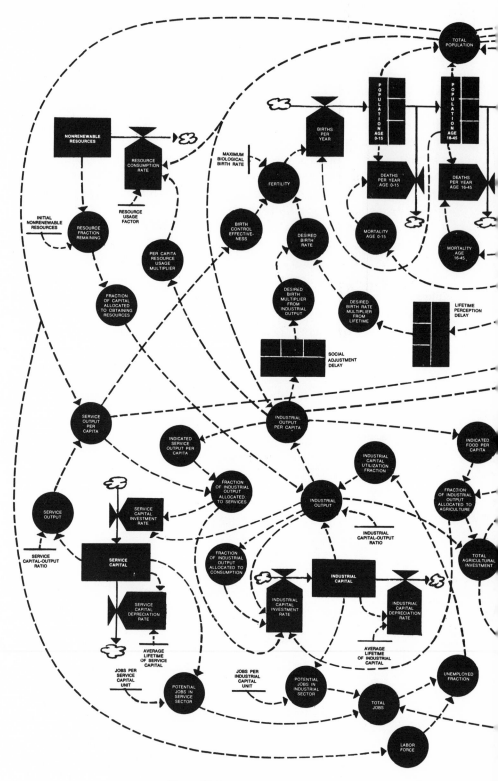

Figure 12-5 The world model

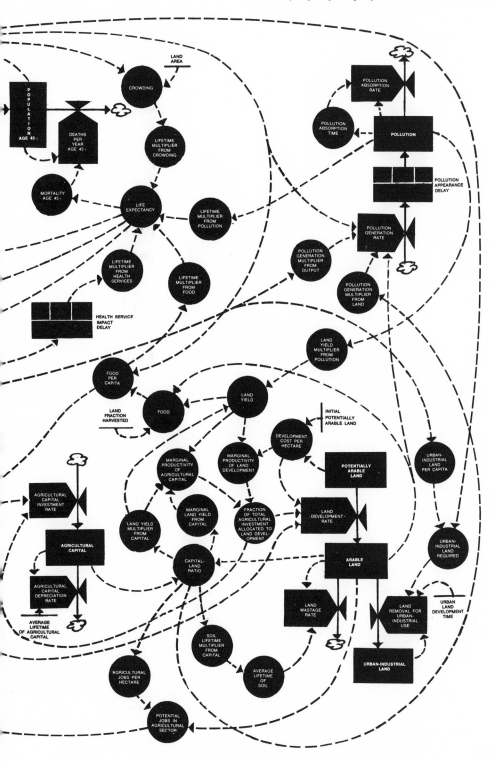

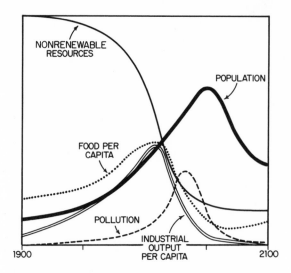

Figure 12-6
The basic world model behavior, showing the tendency
of population and industrialization to rise above the
ultimate carrying capacity of the earth and then to
collapse. This behavior mode is caused by the many
time delays in the natural feedback processes that
oppose population and industrial growth. In this figure, growth is suppressed by the depletion of nonrenewable resources
*Note: These computer simulations (Figures 12-6
through 12-11) are not exact numerical predictions of
the future. Rather, they provide* qualitative *projections
of possible future trends. The precise timing of events
is thus less significant than the* changes *in behavior
among simulations. The years are given only as approximate reference points.*

makes them readily available for criticism and improvement by those with knowledge in each specific problem area. Second, with the aid of a computer it is
possible to follow the implications of this set of assumptions about the world
system as they develop as a function of time. Third, it is also possible through
such simulation to test the effect of some change in the basic assumptions; hence
one may investigate which interrelations are critical to the system's behavior (and
thus deserve close study) and which are not. And fourth, the model permits one
to study the effects of policies believed to improve the behavior of the system.

Figures 12-6 through 12-10 show the behavior of this model of the world
resulting from different policies with respect to nonrenewable resource usage,
pollution control, allocation of capital investment and population control.

Continued Growth Leads to Collapse.   Simulation runs like these have led us to
conclude that no currently operating mechanisms will bring the present population and industrial growth to a smooth stop when the maximum level consistent
with the finite environment is reached.

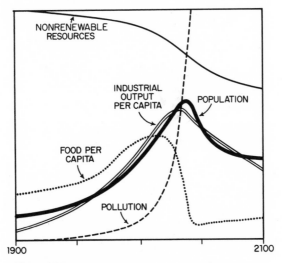

Figure 12-7

It is possible that technological advances, such as recycling and new seabed discoveries, can avert the resource crisis shown in Figure 12-6. Figure 12-7 simulates that possibility by doubling the amount of available resource reserves and reducing the nonrenewable
resource consumption rate by 75 percent in 1975. The
result is another collapse of population and industry,
caused this time by a breakdown in pollution absorption.

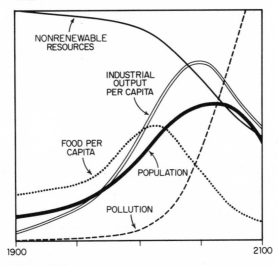

Figure 12-8

In an attempt to avoid a pollution crisis, the normal
rate of pollution generation is reduced by 50 percent
in 1975. The 5 percent increase in capital investment
needed for the pollution control is financed by a reduction in private and public consumption, and resource usage is as in Figure 12-7. As a result of the
pollution control, the population growth rate is reduced somewhat by lack of food before the pollution
crisis occurs again, somewhat later than in Figure 12-7.

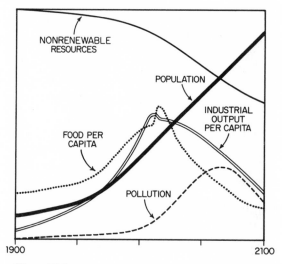

Figure 12-9
Maintaining resource and pollution policies as in Figure 12-8, an attempt is made at the point where food per capita starts to fall to avoid this decline by doubling the resources allocated to food production (at the expense of industrial production). The short-term effect is to increase per capita food availability significantly for a 20-year period. The long-term result of this policy is a population that is much larger (due to more food and less industrial pollution) and materially much poorer than in Figure 12-8, but at the same subsistence food level.

Of course this does not mean that growth will not stop. It only means that, instead of an orderly transition to some feasible final state, the present socioeconomic system is most likely to overshoot the physical limitations of the earth and be forced into a traumatic decline to some level of population and industrialization that can be supported by the physical environment—which by then will be sorely depleted. For once any natural constraint is exceeded, tremendous pressures will develop to halt growth. If it so happens that the first constraint the world system meets is the absorptive capacity for pollution, the pressures will take the form of increases in the death rate due to impurities in food, water, and air; decreases in crop production and fish catches due to similar reductions in plant and animal life; and a significant reduction in the effectiveness of investment, due to the high costs of controlling pollution in all input factors. These pressures will mount until population and industrialization finally start to decline involuntarily. The pressures will cease only when the levels of population and capital reached are consistent with the supporting capacity of the physical environment.

If society attempts to continue growth by removing one set of pressures—for instance, by controlling pollution emissions per unit of industrial output—the situation is alleviated only until the next constraint is encountered. If that constraint is removed, the growing material system will soon reach another one. The

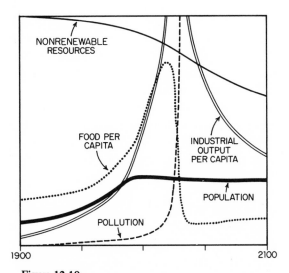

Figure 12-10
Maintaining the same resource and pollution policies
as in Figure 12-8, the population is assumed to be
stabilized in 1990. The short-term result is a significant increase in per capita material wealth and food.
The rate of industrialization is high because of the
low need for additional food, however, and results in
a pollution crisis after a short period of time.

situation is somewhat like growing taller in a room with infinitely many ceilings:
one does not solve the problem by removing the first ceiling upon contact, nor by
removing the second, third, and so on. The only solution to growth in a finite
space is an end to growth. The end to growth can be deliberate and controlled, or
it can be involuntary and uncontrolled.

The Ethical Basis for Action

The Short-Term Objective Function. It seems that the continuation of current
practices concerning material growth in the world system is likely to lead to some
sort of material and population collapse, with a subsequent decrease in the cultural and economic options of the human race. Is this outcome inevitable? Should
society change its current practices?

It is important to realize that an answer to this question is completely dependent on the choice of criteria for what is "good". If society does not know what
it wishes to obtain, if it does not know its "objective function," it is meaningless
to try to decide what to do in a given situation. If the objective is to maximize the
benefits of the people alive today, the course of action will be quite different than
if the goal is to maximize the benefits of all people who are going to live on this
planet over the next two hundred years.

At least in principle (and it is clear that this is far from being a realized
principle), present human behavior is guided by the general idea that all people
alive today are equally important and that the objective function is to maximize

the total current benefits for all these people. The Western democracies have decided that this objective is best served by letting each individual be free to pursue his own interest. It is very simply assumed that if every citizen and institution in society acts to maximize his own position in the short term, the society as a whole will benefit.

This acceptance of "the invisible hand" has, however, introduced a strong emphasis on short-term benefits. When an action will bring both benefits and costs over time, individuals use the concept of net present value and discount the future implications so that they can determine whether an action is profitable— and hence should be taken. The result of this procedure is that an essentially zero value is assigned to anything happening more than twenty years from now. In other words, actions will be taken although their cost to society twenty years hence is going to be enormous, just because the benefits are larger than the costs in the short run (for example, over the next decade).

If one chooses to adhere strictly to the objective of maximizing the short-term rewards of the present generation, there are in fact no long-term trade-offs to be made. Continued pursuit of this objective would involve no major change in the present practice of maximizing current benefits and neglecting any future costs. This is the value system that leads in our world model to eventual overshoot and collapse.

The question about use or nonuse of DDT, for example, is easily resolved, given this short-term value system. The fact that 1.3 billion people today can live in safety from malaria because of DDT, strongly outweighs the costs (such as disruption of bird and fish populations and perhaps the elimination of species of edible fish) inflicted upon future generations through continued use of the chemical.

Only this short-term objective function can lead to the currently accepted conclusion that the value of an additional human being is infinite. The severe restrictions that the existence of every human being will impose on the choices and perhaps even the lives of future generations—because of his consumption of nonrenewable resources and his contribution to the destruction of the life support system of the globe—are completely neglected.

Adherence to the short-term objective function resolves very simply all such trade-offs between current benefits and future cost. Of course there will still remain difficult trade-offs among people alive today; for instance, the choice between giving a factory upstream the freedom to dump waste in the river and giving those who live downstream pure drinking water. But these short-term conflicts are not our concern here, because there are mechanisms in the present society to resolve conflicts between two people alive today.

However, there are not yet any mechanisms or even moral guidelines for resolving conflicts between the current population and the people of the future. This clearly is far from an ideal situation, since our simulation model suggests that the present preoccupation with what seems pleasant or profitable in the short run will fuel the growth that in the long run is going to make the world overshoot some physical constraint, forcing some future population into a period of abrupt, involuntary, and significant changes.

The Long-Term Objective Function.   It is, however, possible to change the objective function—in the same way that Christianity changed the objective of man from selfish gratification to consideration for the welfare of all people living at the same point in time.

Human society could, for example, adopt as its cardinal philosophy the rule that no man or institution in the society may take any action that decreases the economic and social options of those who will live on the planet over the next one hundred years. Perhaps only organized religion has the moral force to bring such a change, or perhaps it could come from an enlightened and widespread change in public education.

Should the current actions of mankind be guided by the short-term objective function, or should there be a longer-term perspective? What time horizon should be used when the costs and benefits of current actions are compared? We feel that the moral and ethical leaders of today's societies should adopt the goal of increasing the time horizon implicit in mankind's activities, that is, introducing the longer-term objective function that will maximize the benefits of those living today, subject to the constraint that it will not decrease the economic and social options of those who will inherit this globe.

This goal is not completely foreign to contemporary society. Individual people usually feel some responsibility for the lives of their own children, and the long-term objective function seems to be the value implicit in the actions of conservationists. However, ultimately this long-term perspective must be present in all human activities—as it is said to have been in the native tribes of Sierra Leone, where nothing could be done to the jungle that would leave it unfit for the use of *any* future generation.

Global Equilibrium: A Desirable Possibility

A Lasting Solution.   Assuming that the long-term objective function is accepted as the guideline for human actions, what should be done about the approaching collision between population and material growth and the physical limits of the earth?

Once society has committed itself to the creation of a long-term, viable world system, one in which the rights and opportunities of future generations are protected, the most important task will be to avoid the trauma connected with actually exceeding any of the globe's limitations on food production capability, pollution absorption capacity, or resource supply. This task can be successfully accomplished because the overshoot and collapse outcome can be avoided by a deliberate decision to stop physical growth. A smooth transition can be managed to a nongrowth situation—a "global equilibrium," a steady state—that is in accordance with the globe's physical limits. Growth can be controlled and halted by developing and employing legal, economic, or religious pressures as substitutes for the more disruptive pressures that would otherwise be exerted by nature to halt physical growth after some limit is exceeded.

There is still time for human society to choose the set of pressures it prefers to employ in stopping population and capital growth. It is not possible to avoid pressures entirely. Nature will supply them if society does not. However, a deliberate choice of the least objectionable counterforces is likely to leave intact many more fundamental, long-term human objectives than would the blind and random action of natural forces such as starvation or social breakdown.

The first requirement for a viable steady state is a constant level of population and capital; that is, the number of people and physical objects must change only very slowly, if at all. A second requirement is equally important. Since the objective is to create a system capable of existing for a long time, the state of global equilibrium must be characterized by minimal consumption of nonrenewable materials and by minimal emissions of nondegradable waste. In this way the time before resources are depleted can be extended, and a critical load of pollutants in the environment can be avoided.

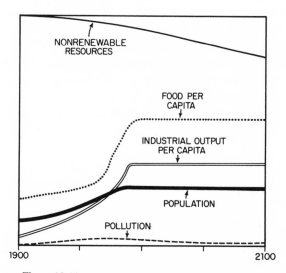

Figure 12-11

Global equilibrium is established by stabilizing population in 1980 and industrial capital in 1990. In addition, a societal value change allocates more industrial output to services and food and slightly less to material goods. Material goods reach a relatively high level, however, by better product design, which allows a longer useful lifetime for each product. Resource and pollution policies are as in Figure 12-8. Equilibrium population is 4 billion and GNP per capita is about twice the present world average. This is only one of several possible global equilibria in which the relative levels of population, food, pollution, and industrialization can be set to reflect different social objectives.

One possible way of achieving such an equilibrium society is depicted in Figure 12-11. Many different possible paths to global equilibrium exist, however, and the one to choose depends on the entire set of social objectives. For instance, should there be many people at a low material standard of living or few people at a higher level of material consumption? Should there be fancy food or just the minimum daily ration of calories, protein, and vitamins?

In this equilibrium mode of human civilization, science and technology could be busily developing ways of constructing products that last very long, do not emit pollution, and can be easily recycled. Competition among individual firms might very well continue, the only difference being that the total market for material goods would no longer expand. The emphasis would be on repair and maintenance rather than on new production.

Although global equilibrium implies nongrowth of all physical activities, this need not be the case for cultural activities. Freed from preoccupation with material goods, people might throw their energy into the development of the arts and sciences, into the enjoyment of unspoiled nature, and into meaningful interactions with their fellow man. The production of services could flourish.

The Distribution of Wealth and Responsibility.   Stopping the population explosion is becoming increasingly more accepted as an important task to be accomplished as fast as possible, but what about stopping capital growth? Would not restrictions on material production permanently condemn the world's poor to their present state of misery?

Striving toward global equilibrium does not imply "freezing" the world in its present configuration of rich and poor nations and peoples. It is overall growth that must finally stop, but that does not preclude redistribution of the world's existing material wealth. One possibility is that the industrialized parts of the world deliberately stop their industrial growth and possibly even "shrink" somewhat, while the nonindustrialized world is allowed (and maybe helped) to grow economically to an acceptable, but not infinitely high, level. Thus initially it would be the developed world that has to take the lead in the path toward global equilibrium; however, the developing world would have serious responsibilities in attempting to stop its rapidly growing populations.

Many people believe that the world must cling to the goal of maximizing material growth, simply because it is still so very far from being a utopia where everything is plentiful for everyone. However, a continued reliance on short-term objectives and continued physical growth only makes it certain that there will be no acceptable future—for any country or people. In other words, such a utopia does not exist, and striving towards it is futile.

It should also be made quite clear that the type of growth the world has experienced over the last century has in no way resulted in increased equality among the world's people. To the contrary, growth in its present form simply widens the gap between the rich and poor, as can be seen from Figure 12-12.

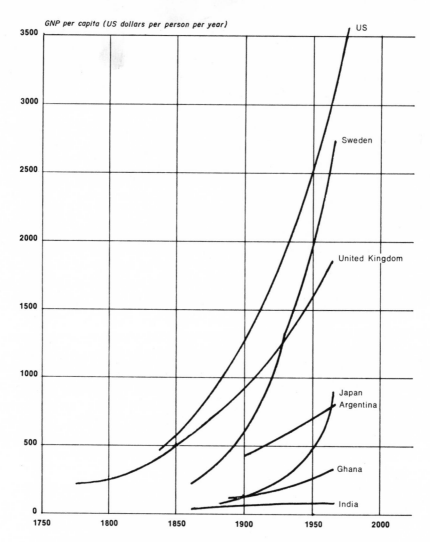

Figure 12-12   The economic growth of several countries
Source: Simon Kuznets, Economic Growth of Nations *(Cambridge, Mass.: Harvard University Press,
1971).*

An end to overall physical growth, however, might very well ultimately lead
to a more equitable distribution of wealth throughout the world, because no one
would accept material inequalities in the present under the (false) pretense that
they would be removed through future growth. Of course the state of global
equilibrium will also have its problems, mainly political and ethical. In the words
of H. E. Daly, the American economist:

For several reasons the important issue of the stationary state will be distribution, not
production. The problem of relative shares can no longer be avoided by appeals to
growth. The argument that everyone should be happy as long as his absolute share of

the wealth increases, regardless of his relative share, will no longer be available. . . . The stationary state would make fewer demands on our environmental resources, but much greater demands on our moral resources.[1]

But these political problems have solutions, and those solutions may be more likely to arise in an equilibrium state than in a collapsing one.

Stopping the overall physical growth on the earth is not an attempt by the rich countries to divert attention from economic development to the protection of "their" environment. Rather, global equilibrium is a necessity if mankind wants to have an equitable future on his small, fragile planet.

The Golden Age. The presence of global equilibrium could permit the development of an unprecedented golden age for humanity. Freedom from the pressures of providing for ever-increasing numbers of people would make it possible to put substantial effort into the self-realization and development of the individual. Instead of struggling merely to keep people alive, human energy could be employed in developing human culture, that is, in increasing the quality of life for the individual to a level far above the present subsistence. The few periods of equilibrium in the past—for example, the three hundred years of Japan's classical period—often witnessed a profound flowering of the arts.

The freedom from ever-increasing capital, that is, from more concrete, cars, dams, and skyscrapers, would make it possible for our great-grandchildren to enjoy solitude and silence. The desirable aspects of the steady state were realized long ago. John Stuart Mill wrote in 1857:

> It is scarcely necessary to remark that a stationary condition of capital and population implies no stationary state of human improvement. There would be as much scope as ever for all kinds of mental culture, and moral and social progress; as much room for improving the Art of Living and much more likelihood of its being improved, when minds cease to be engrossed by the art of getting on. Even the industrial arts might be as earnestly and as successfully cultivated, with this sole difference, that instead of serving no purpose but the increase of wealth, industrial improvements would produce their legitimate effect, that of abridging labor.[2]

This, then, is the state of global equilibrium, which seems to be the logical consequence of the adoption of the long-term objective function.

The changes needed during the transition from growth to global equilibrium are tremendous, and the time is very short. The first step must be to increase the time horizon of individual people and of social institutions. Strong leadership from those institutions already dedicated to ethical and moral concerns—the churches—may be the most effective way to initiate that first and most important step toward a sustainable equilibrium society.

[1] Herman E. Daly, in *The Patient Earth,* ed. John Harte and Robert Socolow (New York: Holt, Rinehart, and Winston, 1971).

[2] J. S. Mill, *Principles of Political Economy,* vol. 2 (London: John W. Parker and Son, 1857).

13
Churches at the Transition Between Growth and World Equilibrium

Jay W. Forrester

The interest elicited by the previous paper led to several invitations to present additional information about the world project before various church bodies. At a meeting in New York City, Jay W. Forrester and Jørgen Randers met with the Division of Overseas Ministries of the National Council of Churches to discuss the role of religious institutions in a society that must make the difficult transition from population and material growth to equilibrium. The following paper was prepared for that meeting.

13
Churches at the Transition Between Growth and World Equilibrium

In recent studies of the dynamic behavior of corporations, cities, and world-wide forces, many general and fundamental characteristics of social systems have been identified. I was invited in this paper to interpret the earlier work for its meaning to the churches, now that population and industrial growth appear to be rapidly overtaking the natural capacity of the earth.

Civilization is in a transition zone between past exponential growth and some future form of equilibrium. The nature of that future equilibrium will depend on present actions. Present actions are determined by the interplay between social forces and the value system that governs our responses. If the churches are to be influential, they will operate through the value system that conditions our responses to the rising worldwide pressures. In studies of other social systems, it has often been found that intended policies lead to unintended consequences.

1. Are the Christian churches propagating an ethical value structure that is incompatible with a desirable future condition of the world?
2. Are the churches today acting in a way that will improve or worsen the future of mankind?
3. What is the primary responsibility of churches in modern society?
4. Because the short-term and long-term objectives are usually contradictory, how is the balance to be struck?
5. Should the churches be responsive to short-term pressures, or should they be custodians of the long-term values of a society?
6. How are churches to resolve the conflicting goals that are always to be found in a social system?

Transition to World Equilibrium

A vast new set of ethical and moral dilemmas now faces man as human society begins to encroach on the physical limits of the world. If the exponential growth of population and industrialization were to continue at the present rate, the entire globe would be inundated in a few decades. Such growth is becoming progressively harder to sustain. Many of the political and economic stresses now occurring can be traced to material growth colliding with a fixed natural environment.

In all the social systems we have examined, from the simplest corporate subsystem to the most complex of world interactions, the great stresses and the great changes in social pressure come at the point where growth begins to slow down and equilibrium begins to be approached. It is during the transition period that turmoil is greatest. Humanity is now approaching the transition from worldwide growth to equilibrium. By equilibrium we mean a condition of constant population, constant use of resources, and constant generation of pollution, all limited so that the equilibrium condition can be sustained indefinitely into the future. Equilibrium does not preclude a shifting composition within the constant level of world industrialization; equilibrium still allows changing cultural and ethical development in all dimensions that do not overload the natural environment.

As the world moves during the next several decades from exponential growth of population and industrialization into some form of equilibrium, we can expect rapidly growing social stresses of a magnitude, distribution, and diversity that have never before been encountered. As all world subsystems begin to reach their collective limits, they become much more highly interdependent. Internal mechanisms that have tended to equalize and redistribute individual stresses can no longer function as all parts of the system simultaneously encounter impenetrable limits. For example, international trade has redistributed resources and products so that the excesses at one point have been used to fill shortages at another. But as growth continues beyond the equilibrium point no excesses will remain anywhere in the world. In retrospect, international trade may at some time in the future be recognized as an inadvertant process for having promoted a nonsustainable world growth up to a time when all countries run out of all reserves at approximately the same time. International trade will have obscured the impending end of the growth phase until everyone faces the transition simultaneously in every facet of existence. The tendency is to relieve all pressures until none can be suppressed. As a result, there may not be a long period of partial shortages to slow growth gradually. Thus mankind will not have the opportunity to learn on a small scale how to navigate the transition from growth to equilibrium. All will face the transition at about the same time and without benefit of a guiding precedent.

The change from the growth mode to the equilibrium mode is a major change in system behavior. During growth, pressures are relieved by expansion. The focus is on change. Problems are not solved but are overlooked in the excitement of conquest. In equilibrium, however, the new no longer dominates the old. Self-renewal must occur within a fixed size. The rules of thumb that served as policy in the growth mode no longer apply.

Figure 13-1 shows a set of feedback loops that produce growth, cause growth to impinge on a fixed space limit, and then shift dominant control to an equilibrium-seeking set of relationships. The figure is simple and illustrative and does not include the multiplicity of factors operating in an actual social system. But the missing factors also contain ultimate limits so that the transition from exponential growth must always eventually occur. In the figure, the upper loops produce growth. In an area with some fertile land, the population rises, people till the land and their labor increases the agricultural capability, the food per person increases, and the rising food supply supports a further increase in population. This growth in population continues until the fertile land has been fully employed and the marginal productivity of an additional agricultural worker does not produce enough food to support the worker. Beyond that point the food per person falls until the population is held in equilibrium and stops growing. But the falling food per person produces distress and may trigger additional investment and more technology in agriculture. The investment and technology may come from within the system or they may come in foreign aid from the outside. In either case, agricultural capability is pushed up further, food per person is again lifted above

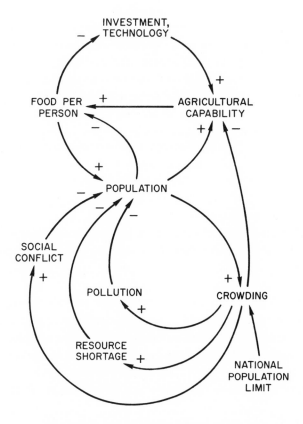

Figure 13-1 Growth and equilibrium pressures

the subsistence level, and the population continues upward, assuming that non-agricultural aspects of crowding are still well below the national population limit set by other factors that will eventually restrain population. If food production continues to support a growing population, the population approaches the national population limit, crowding rises, other uses occupy the best agricultural land, and agricultural capability declines faster than it can be restored by investment and technology. At the same time, crowding leads to forces that limit population—pollution, resource shortage, and social conflict, as well as disease and others. The upper loops have only a limited potential for generating growth. The consequence of growth is to induce ever-rising, growth-restraining forces in the lower loops. In time, the forces of growth and restraint come into balance and growth gives way to equilibrium. During the transition, the suppressive forces must and will rise as far as necessary to produce an ultimate equilibrium. The greater the growth forces that society sustains in the upper loops, the greater must and will become the restraining forces that develop in the lower loops.

Multiple pressures arise as the world reaches the limits of resource usage, agricultural production, pollution dissipation, and living space. As man attempts to alleviate these pressures by intensifying agriculture, seeking resources on the ocean floor, constructing skyscrapers, and building pollution-control equipment, he permits growth to continue. But growth rapidly consumes the gains from these efforts; the task of outrunning growth becomes harder and harder; and eventually the social-economic structure will become nonsustainable. The forces of nature will become as high as necessary to overwhelm efforts to exceed the capacity of the environment. As long as human society succeeds in driving forward along the historical growth path, counterpressures will become stronger and will appear in ever-proliferating aspects of existence. By our efforts we are increasing the forces we fight.

Characteristics of Social Systems

Several generalizations from the dynamic examination of social systems will serve here as a background for discussing ethical concepts as part of the policy structure of society.

Structure and Policies Cause the Problems. One should address problems in a social system by first identifying the fundamental causes and then moving on to design revised policies for alleviating the problems. One should never attempt to find a solution without first establishing the dynamic causes. Such a results-directed beginning is likely to lead to the treatment of symptoms without benefit. For example, the nation has acted on its urban crisis during the last several decades without focusing on the causes of urban stagnation and decay. Government has sequentially attempted to relieve symptoms as they arose. Congested traffic led to more highways, the central city became more crowded, parking garages were built, more people entered the city, buildings became taller, traffic continued to increase, and crowding and social dislocation worsened. All these actions were taken without facing the questions of proper city size, desirable population density, and how to control both so that the other symptoms of overloading would not arise. Instead of first trying to relieve immediate social system pressures, an analysis should begin by establishing a model of the structure and relationships that interact to produce the problems. That is, one should start by replicating the system that generates the symptoms. Only then can one be confident that he is beginning to understand the underlying causes.

Surprising as it seems, the difficulties in most social systems are caused by the interplay of elements that individually are well known and highly visible. Social troubles do not come from hidden causes or capricious behavior. Rather, they come from evident policies that are not recognized for either their true importance or the dynamics of their interaction.

In urban decay the interaction of social, economic, and physical factors can form a destructive spiral. The poor do not have jobs and income to afford adequate housing. So low-cost housing is built. The housing occupies land that should have been allocated to job-creating activities, and, as a consequence, jobs become scarcer. But the new housing attracts more of the poor and unskilled. The unemployed population rises, jobs decline, income per capita remains low, and destitution continues.

In our study of world interactions, it appears that hunger and poverty trigger efforts toward industrial production and more efficient agriculture. But more food, better sanitation, technology, and public health measures allow the population to rise. The circular process of people increasing production and production increasing population is responsible for the overwhelming rise in population that is creating a new set of global stresses.

Could it be that some of the actions being taken by religious institutions in the belief that they will alleviate human suffering may actually be a part of the processes that produce that suffering?

Goal Conflict. A social system, if it is to fulfill human needs, must meet a multiplicity of goals. These goals can conflict with one another in several dimensions—in current trade-offs, in time, and in hierarchy. Furthermore, the nature of the most important goal conflicts can change, depending on the mode in which the system is operating.

1. Goals can conflict in current trade-offs. That is, many goals exist simultaneously in different parts of a system. Efforts to reach one goal may mean that another is put further beyond reach. These are simultaneous goals for food, clean air, material goods, peace, sense of mission, elimination of current stresses, and confidence in the future. These objectives are coupled in various ways. Actions toward one goal may produce quite unexpected responses and deterioration in other system objectives. For example, efforts to improve the economic and technological aspects of cities attract population. Population densities rise until the economic and technological improvements are compensated by rising psychological tensions, crime, drug addiction, despair, and social disorganization. Society knows how to work toward economic and technical goals. But such effort shifts the system pressures into the more intangible sectors with which present social institutions cannot cope.

2. A second goal conflict exists in time—between the present and the future. Actions to enhance the present generally deteriorate the future. For example, if one has an urgent report to finish, he can accomplish the most in the next twenty-four hours by working through the night, but the price is paid in lower effectiveness during the next two days. Or, if one wishes to improve his material living in the short run, he has only to borrow money, use his credit cards, and live beyond his means. But in the long run, the price must be paid. If the debts are to be met, the standard of living must fall below one's average income. Likewise, the corporation can improve short-term profitability by postponing expenditures on new product research and on the repair of equipment. But in time the quality of products suffers, the efficiency of production declines, and profits drop lower than they were at the start. On a larger scale, hunger can be reduced for a time by a rapid increase in agricultural produc-

tion. But in the long run, more food permits more population. Food per capita falls back and, in addition, the greater population density generates new stresses and complications.

3. A third goal conflict exists in hierarchy—between the goals of subsystems and the goals appropriate to the total system. For example, maximum wages to individual workers is in conflict with the profitability of the business. Or, the minimum-cost goal of the business leads to excessive generation of pollution with the price paid by the larger public in a poorer environment.

   Attempting to enhance each subgoal of a social system does not assure the best possible outcome for the system as a whole. In fact, efforts to improve each component of a system can lead to far less than the best possible total results.

   Churches, like other institutions, can fall into the trap of believing that the pursuit of subgoals is the equivalent of maximizing the quality of life in the total social system. Pursuing separate subgoals in education, medicine, agriculture, and disaster relief contributes to the population explosion, shifts people from agriculture to the cities, and sets the stage for greater social conflict.

4. The patterns of goal conflict can change. The most likely kind of goal conflict depends on the mode in which the social system is operating. Two behavior modes of the world social system are of immediate interest: growth and equilibrium. During growth it is easy to enhance immediate objectives by actions that defer the unpleasant consequences to the future—goal conflict is in the time dimension. On the other hand, a system in equilibrium seems more apt to shift pressures quickly between coexisting goals—the goal conflict is between current trade-offs.

   One can illustrate these shifting patterns of goal conflict by the changes that are likely to occur as growth gives way to equilibrium. For the last several hundred years the world has been in a period of sustained growth of population, geographic occupancy, and production of food and goods. During that time, production in many areas of the globe has been able to outrun the growing population and thereby produce a rising standard of living. Likewise, public health measures, modern medicine, antibiotics, and insecticides have been able to improve the health of many populations. But all these measures are now seen as merely postponing the day of reckoning. The very actions that yielded the short-term improvements are the ones that are producing overpopulation, depletion of resources, crowding, and the reemerging threat of food shortage.

   Now as the world system moves toward an equilibrium state, it becomes less possible to push problems into the future. More often now the goal conflicts will be between coexisting goals in the present rather than between the present and the future. For example, imagine a population being held constant by two pressures. One pressure arises from a degree of malnutrition and the other pressure from a certain incidence of epidemics and poor health arising from crowding. Now suppose that the food supply is increased to remove the pressure from hunger. The population rises, the crowding becomes worse, and the pressure from disease increases. In other words, the pressure shifts relatively rapidly, within a few decades, to a new point in the system. The consequences of current actions can no longer be deferred, as was once possible, for centuries into the future.

Collapse of Goals and Values.   Social systems tend to decay if a collapse in their long-term goal structures occurs. As the enduring values erode, emphasis shifts to short-term objectives. As the present is emphasized over the future, the result is long-term deterioration and further emphasis on the short run. As the goals decline, the decision processes change, and a downward spiral begins. For example, the collapse of values is often seen in a young corporation whose founders start a business dedicated to high product quality. Under the inevitable business pressures, quality may fall short of the goal. If the leaders are not firm in their convictions about quality, they become accustomed to and accept the lower quality. Because of the lower quality, prices must be reduced. Revenues are then so low that even the existing quality cannot be sustained. A new lower quality is accepted as inevitable, and the spiral of collapse continues from the initial high standards. Unless some effective institutional mechanism exists for sustaining a vision of the future and subordinating short-term conflicting goals, all social systems are subject to the erosion of long-term goals.

Any operating goal of a social system can be thought of as depending on three components: long-term value, the traditional past accomplishment, and the weighting influence that determines the relative force of long-term value versus traditional accomplishment.

The long-term value component in an operating goal is an enduring standard that transcends adversity and short-term pressures. It is deeply embedded in the collective character of the system. If the long-term values are to be sustained, there must be social processes for propagating and perpetuating them.

The second component of an operating goal is the perception of actual past performance. A social system that operates on past accomplishment as its only goal is merely striving to do as well as it did in the past.

The third component of an operating goal determines where the operating goal lies between the long-term goal and the past accomplishment. If the long-term values are persuasive and if there is an institutional structure to project them into day-by-day decision-making, then the long-term values are influential. If the long-term values are weak, poorly perceived, irrelevant, inappropriate, or not sufficiently timeless in concept, then they fail to be influential and the past performance becomes the only effective goal.

If one is only striving to equal his past accomplishment, adversity will probably cause him to fall somewhat short of that goal. As time progresses, the new lower performance becomes the historical tradition and performance continues to decline. It is the role of the enduring long-term components of the goal structure to prevent this downward spiral. In the corporation the long-term, enduring goals are usually set and perpetuated by the founder-manager type of strong leader. In nations the goal structure is cast into the constitutions and the laws. But where is the even longer-term goal structure to be found that can guide people in setting national goals?

There is no custodian of the long-term goals unless it be the religious institutions. On religion rests the responsibility for maintaining long-term values and preventing the collapse of operating goals. But a religion and its teaching cannot make its long-term values influential if those values are contradictory, self-defeating, inapplicable, or inappropriate to a new dynamic mode into which the social system may have moved.

Churches in the Dynamics of Social Values

The "policies" of a social system describe the manner in which decisions are made. A policy states the process by which the existing circumstances are interpreted into a course of action. In the broadest sense, policies include folklore, emotional reactions, self-interest, humanitarianism, and all the influences that govern action. Ethical structure is part of the governing policies of a society. To the extent that religious teachings have influence and carry weight in social decision making, those religious beliefs must be included in a model that explains the dynamics of a society. Religious beliefs interact with other decision-making influences in a social system and are a part of the total policy structure that may produce either good or evil. Ethical principles interact with the principles of economics, technology, sociology, agriculture, and medicine to create today's pressures and social stresses.

From a system dynamics viewpoint, religious teachings are a part of the policy structure of a society. The religious attitudes, traditions, and morality influence day-by-day decisions. Historically, religious values have probably developed in response to long-term social needs. To survive, a society must have a long-term value structure to counteract the short-term pressures. Without the long-term values, "living for the present," if carried to an extreme, makes the future impossible. The societies that have grown and prevailed are those with a viable concept of the future. Without such an enduring value set, the society fails to develop, decays from the inside, or is replaced by a more future-oriented social system.

As enduring values are gradually perceived by a society, those values are cast into religious codes. The religious codes serve to freeze and to propagate the long-term values. The enduring values take the form of religious documents, rituals, taboos, and doctrine. Added force and influence are often imparted by the belief that the values have been handed down from a deity above and outside the human system.

But the long-term value structure of a society can be too permanently frozen. The value structures of our great religions developed at a time when social systems were beginning to evolve. The values were suitable to the conditions of the times and to the particular mode in which the social system was then functioning. But the values were products of the early times. Values were developed by trial and error. Societies with value structures that served poorly did not survive. The values that survived were suitable to the conditions under which they evolved. But if the fundamental dynamic mode of a social system changes, there is little reason to believe that the earlier long-term values will have been so timeless that they will still apply equally well to the new mode.

Christianity developed in the context of one particular dynamic mode of our social system. It developed when man was sparsely settled on the earth, when geographic expansion was still possible, when man was puny compared to the forces of nature, and when science was yet to be exploited. The Christian values were effective for social survival and expansion. In fact, Christianity is a value code that enhances growth. It is a code that gives man the obligation to develop missionary zeal. It gives man the right to mastery over nature. The values were interpreted as imposing a duty to extend God's chosen people and religion across the face of the earth. Christianity has made its believers responsible for the welfare of others, and that becomes an obligation to protect others from themselves, from the restrictions of more equilibrium-oriented religions, and from the vicissitudes of man's interaction with nature. In short, Christianity is a religion of exponential growth.

But exponential growth cannot continue forever. Tremendous internal pressures must be generated to suppress growth. During growth, the promise of new expansion shifts attention from old failures. During growth, the onward-and-outward orientation diverts a society from introspection and self-doubt. But as growth becomes less possible, long-term values directed at growth become less useful. Then the very institutions and psychological processes that perpetuated the old values become a liability. The institutions, processes, folklore, and traditions were designed to keep the old values from being diluted and changed. But if the values are not sufficiently fundamental to span both the old and the new dynamic modes of the system—if the ethical principles are not sufficiently timeless to serve equally in growth and in equilibrium—then the institutions that once were the necessary protectors of effective values become the perpetuators of obsolete values.

Because the fundamental modes of social systems can and do change, the long-term values must either be so basic that they span all modes, or the long-term values must themselves be subject to gradual change. If the values can be changed too rapidly, they fail to serve their purpose in protecting the system against short-term expediency. But if they are too inflexible, they are unresponsive to essential change.

The importance of having a correct blend of ease and difficulty in changing a set of social values is illustrated by the U.S. Constitution. Perhaps the great strength of that document lies in its mechanisms for amendment. The means for change seem to be neither too rapid nor too slow. Change is sufficiently difficult that the Constitution cannot be altered in response to fleeting pressures that lack enduring value. On the other hand, the Constitution is not so inflexible and frozen that people despair of change and therefore react by abandoning its guiding values.

Is there the correct degree of responsiveness for modifying and interpreting Christian principles? Is there a suitable way to redefine and extend religious principles in response to pressures that arise when the principles are no longer suitable? Is there any procedure for anticipating social changes so that modification can begin before the discrepancies between old values and new realities have become so great that society rejects the principles? Unlike the national Constitution, the Bible contains no explicit process for revision and updating, no way to introduce new insights that recognize newly emerging modes of behavior in our social systems. Without a means of revision, the escape from discrepancy between old doctrine and modern conditions has been by reinterpreting the meaning of the old principles. By reinterpretation, society moves away from the literal words to figurative symbolism. Symbolism is more flexible and is subject to wider interpretation. But in the face of discrepancies between the stated long-term values and the actual social necessities, the reinterpretation is apt to allow the long-term principles to drift into short-term expediencies. Secular forces supercede the long-term values, and the goal structure of the society is swayed by immediate pressures.

Much of the "credibility gap" currently experienced by organized religion arises from the dynamic failures to fulfill the goal-setting need of society. Long-term values that served well during the centuries of growth are found wanting as the world is faced with the pressures of moving into equilibrium. Processes do not exist for revising those long-term values that should be more fundamental and enduring than even national constitutions. Without change, the discrepancies between the values and social relevance widen. To some extent the old values are rejected. But partly they are reinterpreted and are alleged to coincide with the short-term expediencies. Without an appropriate long-term value structure, the society begins to falter.

Predicament of the Churches

The changes in our social systems have shifted the ground on which religious principles were established. The new system modes are dynamically quite different from those that prevailed when the principles evolved. The churches, without adequate processes for changing the value structure they propagate, are now in several predicaments.

Shortened Time Horizon. Churches should be custodians of the longest term values in a society. Those values should look beyond civilian laws and national constitutions. As custodians of the future, churches should understand that long-term values will conflict with the short-term values and goals of man and society. Churches must have effective ways to project long-term goals into the current processes of everyday decision-making.

But what do the churches today say about the ethical questions that arise during the transition from growth to equilibrium? What do they say about individual and national responsibility for the future? Are not the churches partners with secular society in maximizing present human welfare at the expense of future societies? Are not the churches an active force dedicated to social changes that can be realized only if growth is to be sustained beyond the likely limits?

Churches will not be effective if they have lost their distant time horizon. If their values are the same as those of the secular society, churches need not exist. If church values are inappropriate to a newly emerging mode in the surrounding social system, the values will not be persuasive and cannot be projected.

But many of the old values of humanitarianism and the unique rights of man in preference to other living things have contributed to an exponential growth in human population and man's technology, which brings man face to face with the ultimate global limit. What was once a long-term ethical structure that succeeded by deferring difficulties into the distant future has become a set of reactions that shifts stresses quickly from point to point. The value structure of the churches is caught in the fundamental dynamic changes that occur when growth comes under pressure and the transition to the equilibrium mode begins.

Obsolescence of the Growth Ethic.   Now that growth in population, growth by geographic expansion, and growth in the conquest of nature can no longer serve as a unifying focus for the future, the churches must seek a new set of values to hold before mankind. A new ethical structure with long-term values suitable for a future of world equilibrium is needed.

How is responsibility for the future to be imposed? How are the economic and psychological costs of the transition to equilibrium to be assessed? What degree of coercion and restriction on individual freedom is necessary? What is the ethical foundation for penalties against the transgressors who overemphasize the present at the expense of the future?

Compartmentalism.   Religion, like other aspects of living, has established itself in a compartment that is nearly cut off from other aspects of human existence. It shares this fault with most other kinds of human activity. Science, law, economics, and psychology are also in compartments as if each could exist in its own subworld. But our studies of systems show that the important modes of behavior and the serious troubles arise because of interaction between the subsystems. Human existence will not be understood or safely managed if each compartment is treated separately.

But who will assume responsibility for understanding the interactions? Corporations are compartmentalized into production, sales, research, and other functions; but the intuitive processes of management give no adequate capability for understanding the interactions of those functions. Medicine studies organs and diseases, but has no specialty dealing with the dynamics of medical systems. Nations have departments of state, agriculture, defense, commerce, and health but have little capability for understanding the interactions of the many national efforts. A governmental research program would not address itself to social values of the time horizon that should interest churches because such an effort would clearly lie outside the responsibility, wisdom, or political feasibility of any government agency.

The institution with the longest time horizon is in the best tactical position to lead in exploring the nature of the social system; the churches should establish that distant horizon. Long-term values are closely tied to what society is to be one hundred, two hundred, or one thousand years hence. If not the churches, who is to look that far ahead? But the churches are in the predicament of undergoing a shortening time horizon when they should be leaving the near-term to other institutions and should be turning their attention to a horizon beyond that of any other unit in the society.

Egocentricity.   Man through his religious concepts has established for himself, in his own mind, a unique position at the center of the universe. At one time this meant literally the physical center with the sun and stars revolving around the earth. Much more recently it has meant man as a uniquely chosen creature in nature with special rights and privileges over the natural surroundings. But that egocentric view of man at the center, with nature at his disposal, is becoming as untenable as the geocentric theory of the world at the center of the universe. When man made graven images to worship, those images were usually in the form of man. As religion became more spiritual, physical images were discarded but the mental images of God remained in the pattern of man both in form and in emotion.

Man's view of his world and his place in it has gradually broadened. The change is illustrated by the expanding concept of selfishness. When man was being admonished to be literally his brother's keeper, selfishness was an act against one's family; but generosity was not expected to extend to other family tribes who were one's enemies. Later, the boundary within which generosity was expected was expanded. First, the city became each person's responsibility; then nations became the boundary of one's obligations. Much more recently, the contention has grown that all humanity falls within the boundary; but it has remained permissible to be selfish toward anything outside of mankind, that is, toward the natural surroundings. This latest view drives churches to help men everywhere, but with what consequence? By helping the human population grow and by protecting man from the retaliation of nature, mankind is showing the height of social selfishness toward the environment. One must ask when generosity is a virtue and when it is a sin against the world? When is generosity a duty and when is it only a means of self-satisfaction? Is selfishness any less sinful when exercised in favor of mankind as a whole rather than oneself? Such questions must be explored anew now that the alleviation of one pressure can actively increase some other pressure in the present or the near future. What are the proper trade-offs? Our ethical and religious beliefs are in disarray because they contain contradictions and conflicting goals.

Fallacy of Human Equality. The collapse of the religious time horizon has had a curious effect on our attitudes toward human equality and responsibility. When the focus of attention has shrunk to only the immediate present, then responsibility for one's actions is irrelevant because responsibility implies consequences in the future, and the future no longer weighs heavily in decisions. All people are then considered equal at any moment in time and should be treated alike because they bear no responsibility for their past or toward their future. But consider what this viewpoint does for the goals of a civilization confined in a fixed environment.

Imagine two countries side by side, each with a population and an industrial capability that can sustain them indefinitely at a high standard of living. Assume that Country L has a long time horizon, realizes that it cannot allow population and industry to grow without exceeding the natural capacity and thereby lowering the standard of living, and accepts the self-restraints and the short-term penalties necessary to come into equilibrium with nature at a high quality of life. On the other hand, assume that Country S has a short time horizon, lives for the present only, does not plan for the future, avoids traumatic self-discipline, allows population and industry to grow, exhausts the capability of the environment, and after 50 years falls to a miserable human condition. After the 50 years, what is to be the responsibility of Country L toward Country S? If Country L must in the future share with Country S, then Country L suffers in both the short run and the long run. Country L accepted the strain of establishing a national equilibrium at an early date and then is to be denied the fruits of that action by also suffering the misery that must come from sharing equally with Country S when S has overcommitted its resources. If the ethical principles teach that Country L and Country S are to share equally in the future, there are no incentives for anyone to manage for the future.

If all men are not to be equal at every point in time, then some boundary must be established around the concept that one is to be his brother's keeper. Furthermore, with the very long time delays that are inherent in our social systems, responsibility to the future must extend well beyond a person's own lifetime. In Country S the penalties of living for the present will not mature until two more human generations have moved onto the scene.

If one has a responsibility for the future, an inescapable symmetry commits him to a legacy from the past. There is no basis for world equilibrium unless the sins of the fathers are to be visited on the sons. One can have no right to equality in the present, but only to an accumulated equality that reflects the actions of his heritage and the long-term goals of his ancestors. The ethical and religious issues need to be reexamined and made consistent with the dynamic realities of our social systems.

Potential Evil in Humanitarianism. Humanitarian concern means help for one's less fortunate fellowman. At times such help is based on a much too simplistic view of the situation. It is usually aimed at immediate goals. Long-term and short-term goals may be in conflict. When does help in the present lead to increased distress in the future? What concepts of right should govern?

Consider an overpopulated country. Its standard of living is low, food is insufficient, health is poor, and misery abounds. Such a country is especially vulnerable to any natural adversity. There are no stores of food. Medical facilities are always overloaded. Floods make many homeless; but is that because of the flood or because overpopulation forced people to live in the flood region? Droughts bring starvation; but is that due to weather or to the overpopulation that made sufficient food stocks impossible? The country is operating in the overextended mode where all adversities are resolved by a rise in the death rate. The process is part of a natural mechanism for limiting further growth in population. But suppose that humanitarian impulses lead to massive relief efforts from the outside for each natural disaster. What is the long-term result? The people who are saved raise the population still higher. With more population, the vulnerability of the country is increased. Epidemics become more likely, and internal social strife is more probable. A smaller adverse event can now trigger a crisis. Disasters occur oftener and relief is required more frequently. But relief leads to a net increase in the population, to more people in crisis, to a still greater need for relief, and eventually to a situation that even relief cannot handle.

A point is reached where humanitarian action generates the demand for still more humanitarian intervention until the entire socioeconomic system falters. Churches should begin to examine the limits and consequences of humanitarianism. They should bring humanitarian concepts into a consistent relationship with the pressures accompanying the transition to global equilibrium.

"Right" Is Not Absolute.   Human concepts of "right" are system policies. The concepts of right and wrong are guides to action. But do they refer to action that is right for the immediate future or for the distant future?

In the teaching of the church is often the implication that right is absolute, that it knows no compromise, that it is independent of the future time toward which one looks. This is a fallacy. Generally a system policy that is desirable in the short run is detrimental in the long run and vice versa. An action that seems right in the present may prove to be wrong in its ultimate consequences. Churches have taken an overly simplistic view of right and ethics. As a consequence, they contribute to the goal conflicts between present and future.

The world's churches should take the leadership in reexamining right and wrong in the context of the time horizon. The time conflict should be recognized. If the churches are to be the custodians of long-term values, they must define right in terms of the enduring and future welfare of mankind. Other institutions will adequately defend the short run.

Action

This paper has described part of the predicament of churches as seen from a system dynamics viewpoint. I have not attempted to answer the questions that have been raised. Generating these answers is a major task for the future.

The issues raised here are amenable to treatment by a properly planned research program. The process calls for integrating the long-term dynamics of the ethical value structure into the social-economic-technical models that are coming into existence. Some of the best minds from theology, law, philosophy, economics, and science should convene, along with professionals in system dynamics to interrelate the various social subsystems, including the dynamics of goal and value creation. By using dynamic system models to organize thought and to determine the consequences of assumptions, there should emerge a sharper image of the future role of the churches in society's impending transition from growth to world equilibrium.

The Authors

Dr. Alison H. Anderson is a Research Associate, Bryn Mawr College, Bryn Mawr, Pennsylvania.

Dr. Jay M. Anderson is an Associate Professor of Chemistry, Bryn Mawr College, Bryn Mawr, Pennsylvania.

William W. Behrens III is a Research Associate, System Dynamics Group, M.I.T. Alfred P. Sloan School of Management, Cambridge, Massachusetts.

Dr. Jay W. Forrester is a Professor of Management and Director of the System Dynamics Group, M.I.T. Alfred P. Sloan School of Management, Cambridge, Massachusetts.

Dr. Dennis L. Meadows is an Associate Professor of Engineering and of Business, Dartmouth College, Hanover, New Hampshire.

Dr. Donella H. Meadows is an Assistant Professor of Environmental Studies, Dartmouth College, Hanover, New Hampshire.

Roger F. Naill is a Research Associate in the Thayer School of Engineering, Dartmouth College, Hanover, New Hampshire.

Jørgen Randers is a doctoral candidate and member of the System Dynamics Group, M.I.T. Alfred P. Sloan School of Management, Cambridge, Massachusetts.

Steven B. Shantzis is a B.S. candidate in the departments of physics and operations research, Massachusetts Institute of Technology, Cambridge, Massachusetts.

Related Books

Forrester, Jay W. *Industrial Dynamics.* Cambridge, Mass.: The M.I.T. Press, 1961.
The first book on system dynamics. The text provides a detailed description of the philosophy and tools developed by Professor Forrester and his associates to study the dynamic behavior of complex systems. Use of the methodology is illustrated through the analysis of problems in an industrial firm. The text also deals with many difficult modeling issues such as the uses of empirical data in model construction and the tests of model validity appropriate for determining the confidence one may have in the results of a modeling effort.

_____. *Principles of Systems.* Cambridge, Mass.: Wright-Allen Press, 1968.
The basic introductory text to the philosophy and tools of system dynamics. This book includes an extensive student workbook section which tests the student's ability to describe simple feedback-loop structures and to represent those structures in DYNAMO flow diagram and DYNAMO equation form. The dynamic responses of simple first- and second-order nonlinear feedback-loop structures are described and used to explain the behavior of several real-world systems.

_____. *Urban Dynamics.* Cambridge, Mass.: The M.I.T. Press, 1969.
An application of system dynamics modeling techniques to urban problems. This text presents a theory of the way in which land constraints, human goals, and the aging of structures interact to stop urban growth and bring about a stagnation characterized by unemployment, deteriorating housing, and high taxes. One chapter describes the dynamic attributes, characteristic of most social systems, that make them resistant to understanding and control by policy makers.

_____. *World Dynamics.* Cambridge, Mass.: Wright-Allen Press, 1971.
A presentation of Professor Forrester's preliminary global model, World2. World2 is a theory of the long-term causes and consequences of population

growth and material progress. The model is presented in detail and used to discuss the dynamic implications of various physical, biological, and social constraints on growth of the globe's population and material output.

Meadows, Dennis L. *The Dynamics of Commodity Production Cycles.* Cambridge, Mass.: Wright-Allen Press, 1970.
A summary of the economic literature on static theories of commodity price cycles and a description of a general dynamic model of long-term commodity price and production fluctuations. The U.S. hog industry is described in detail and used as a test of the model's ability to explain empirical data.

Meadows, D. L., W. W. Behrens III, D. H. Meadows, R. F. Naill, J. Randers, *The Dynamics of Growth in a Finite World.* Cambridge, Mass.: Wright-Allen Press, Forthcoming 1973.
The technical report of The Club of Rome project. The book describes the purpose and methodology of the global modeling effort and presents the World3 model, equation by equation. All the data underlying the model are included, as are simulations of the model illustrating its response to a variety of technical and social policies. The relative strengths and weaknesses of the model are described, along with suggestions for future extensions of the research. This manuscript will be published in 1973.

Meadows, Donella H., Dennis L. Meadows, Jorgen Randers, and William W. Behrens III. *The Limits to Growth.* New York: Universe Books for Potomac Associates, 1972.
The general report of the Club of Rome project. The book discusses the exponential growth trends that currently dominate global society. The World3 computer model of those relationships which cause and ultimately limit growth is described. Simulations of the model illustrate the implications of current policies. The concept of a global equilibrium in population growth and material wealth is presented as an attractive and feasible alternative to current trends. The report is nontechnical and does not list the equations constituting the World3 model.

Pugh, A. L., III. *DYNAMO II User's Manual.* Cambridge, Mass.: The M.I.T. Press, 1970.
A computer manual providing all the information necessary to represent system relationships in the format of DYNAMO equations and to simulate the resulting models. It is of interest to those who want to formulate computer models of continuous, dynamic, nonlinear feedback-loop systems.

To obtain information on the various DYNAMO compilers and software maintenance options currently available, write Pugh-Roberts Associates, Inc., 65 Rogers Street, Cambridge, Mass., 02142.